ANGLO-SAXON EMOTIONS

Studies in Early Medieval Britain and Ireland

Series editors:

Joanna E. Story, University of Leicester, UK,
Roy Flechner, University College Dublin, Ireland

Studies in Early Medieval Britain and Ireland illuminates the history of Britain and Ireland from the start of the fifth century to the establishment of French-speaking aristocracies in the eleventh and twelfth centuries, for historians, archaeologists, philologists and literary and cultural scholars. It explores the origins of British society, of communities, and political, administrative and ecclesiastical institutions. It was in the early middle ages that the English, Welsh, Scots and Irish defined and distinguished themselves in language, customs and territory and the successive conquests and settlements lent distinctive Anglo-Saxon, Scandinavian and Norman elements to the British ethnic mix. Royal dynasties were established and the landscape took a form that can still be recognised today; it was then too that Christian churches were established with lasting results for our cultural, moral, legal and intellectual horizons.

Studies in Early Medieval Britain and Ireland reveals these roots and makes them accessible to a wide readership of scholars, students and lay people.

Other titles in the series

Bede and the Future
Edited by Peter Darby and Faith Wallis

Heaven and Earth in Anglo-Saxon England
Theology and Society in an Age of Faith
Helen Foxhall Forbes

Bede and the End of Time
Peter Darby

Women's Names in Old English
Elisabeth Okasha

Anglo-Saxon Emotions
Reading the Heart in Old English Language,
Literature and Culture

Edited by

ALICE JORGENSEN
Trinity College Dublin, Ireland

FRANCES MCCORMACK
National University of Ireland, Galway

JONATHAN WILCOX
University of Iowa, USA

LONDON AND NEW YORK

First published 2015 by Ashgate Publishing

2 Park Square, Milton Park, Abingdon, Oxfordshire OX14 4RN
52 Vanderbilt Avenue, New York, NY 10017

Routledge is an imprint of the Taylor & Francis Group, an informa business

First issued in paperback 2019

Copyright © 2015 Alice Jorgensen, Frances McCormack and Jonathan Wilcox

Alice Jorgensen, Frances McCormack and Jonathan Wilcox have asserted their right under the Copyright, Designs and Patents Act, 1988, to be identified as the editors of this work.

All rights reserved. No part of this book may be reprinted or reproduced or utilised in any form or by any electronic, mechanical, or other means, now known or hereafter invented, including photocopying and recording, or in any information storage or retrieval system, without permission in writing from the publishers.

Notices:
Product or corporate names may be trademarks or registered trademarks, and are used only for identification and explanation without intent to infringe.

British Library Cataloguing in Publication Data
A catalogue record for this book is available from the British Library

The Library of Congress has cataloged the printed edition as follows:
Anglo-Saxon Emotions : Reading the Heart in Old English Language, Literature and Culture / edited by Alice Jorgensen, Frances McCormack and Jonathan Wilcox.
　　pages cm. – (Studies in Early Medieval Britain and Ireland)
　Includes bibliographical references and index.
　ISBN 978-1-4724-2169-2 (hardcover)
1. English literature–Old English, ca. 450–1100
–History and criticism. 2. English language–Old English, ca. 450–1100–History.
3. Civilization, Anglo-Saxon. 4. Emotions in literature. 5. Literature and society–Great Britain–History–To 1500. 6. Great Britain–History–Anglo-Saxon period, 449–1066.
I. Jorgensen, Alice, editor. II. McCormack, Frances (Frances Mary) editor. III. Wilcox, Jonathan, 1960– editor.
　PR173.A57 2015
　829'.09–dc23
　　　　　　　　　　　　　　　　　　　　　　　　　　　　　　　　　　　　　2014026193

ISBN 978-1-4724-2169-2 (hbk)
ISBN 978-0-367-87922-8 (pbk)

Contents

Foreword   *vii*
Acknowledgements   *ix*

1   Introduction   1
       Alice Jorgensen

2   Affective Poetics: The Cognitive Basis of Emotion in
       Old English Poetry   19
       Antonina Harbus

3   The Limited Role of the Brain in Mental and Emotional
       Activity According to Anglo-Saxon Medical Learning   35
       Leslie Lockett

4   The Curious Case of *TORN*: The Importance of
       Lexical–Semantic Approaches to the Study of Emotions
       in Old English   53
       Daria Izdebska

5   'So what did the Danes feel?' Emotion and Litotes in
       Old English Poetry   75
       Stephen Graham

6   An Embarrassment of Clues: Interpreting Anglo-Saxon Blushes   91
       Jonathan Wilcox

7   Naming Shame: Translating Emotion in the Old English
       Psalter Glosses   109
       Tahlia Birnbaum

8   Learning about Emotion from the Old English Prose Psalms
       of the Paris Psalter   127
       Alice Jorgensen

9   Those Bloody Trees: The Affectivity of *Christ*   143
       Frances McCormack

10	Emotion and Gesture in Hroðgar's Farewell to Beowulf *Kristen Mills*	163
11	*Ne Sorga*: Grief and Revenge in *Beowulf* *Erin Sebo*	177
12	*Maxims I*: In the 'Mod' for Life *Judith Kaup*	193
13	The Neurological and Physiological Effects of Emotional Duress on Memory in Two Old English Elegies *Ronald Ganze*	211
14	Early Medieval Experiences of Grief and Separation through the Eyes of Alcuin and Others: The Grief and Gratitude of the Oblate *Mary Garrison*	227

Bibliography   *263*
Index   *299*

Foreword

This book is a welcome addition to the series *Studies in Early Medieval Britain and Ireland (SEMBI)*. Our title reflects an early medieval reality, since the cultural, intellectual, and political histories of the islands of Britain and Ireland between the fifth and twelfth centuries were closely linked. It also reflects the vibrance of contemporary, twenty first-century scholarship on the early middle ages, and the series offers a publishing opportunity for academic books that focus on early medieval Ireland as well as those that explore the lives and ideas of the peoples who lived in the island of Britain in the medieval centuries before AD 1100, and the connections of all these people and places with the wider world. The move to include Ireland into the long-running series *Studies in Early Medieval Britain* was enthusiastically welcomed by Professor Nicholas Brooks, the founding editor, who had always intended it to be a vehicle for the publication of ground-breaking scholarship – both monographs and edited collections – by new scholars as well as those with established academic reputations. He was keen for it to embrace all disciplines (including history, archaeology, numismatics, language, literature) that contribute to our knowledge of Britain in the long period between the collapse of Roman imperial authority and the establishment of French-speaking aristocracies in different areas in the eleventh and twelfth centuries, and for the focal length of published studies to extend beyond the boundaries of Anglo-Saxon England. The expanded series title gives the current editors an opportunity to extend his vision and to welcome proposals from scholars, old and new, for *Studies in Early Medieval Britain and Ireland*.

The book that follows exemplifies these goals as a collection of essays from established and emerging scholars that use primarily Old English prose and poetic literature to examine *Anglo-Saxon Emotions*. The essays are deeply informed by the theory and practice of other sociological and scientific disciplines which examine the causes, contexts, and consequences of human emotions. As such, the collection demonstrates profound knowledge of the literary corpus underpinned by an interdisciplinary intellectual approach; it is both reflexive and closely analytical. Its approach and its content offers much that is new for scholars of Anglo-Saxon England, and provides an insight for those working on other periods and places, or who study human emotions from different perspectives, into the richness and diversity of the earliest evidence written in English for the human experience of emotions.

JOANNA STORY
The University of Leicester

ROY FLECHNER
University College, Dublin

November 2014

Acknowledgements

The editors would like to express their thanks to all who have supported, assisted, contributed to and, not least, financed this project in its various stages: all the speakers, assistants and delegates at the Anglo-Saxon Emotions workshop held at Trinity College, Dublin, in July 2012; the Arts and Social Sciences Benefactions Fund, the School of English, and the Long Room Hub at Trinity College, Dublin, for funding the event; the School of Languages, Literatures and Cultural Studies at Trinity College, for a research grant that was used to support the preparation of the book; Stephen Graham for his careful help with the style edit; Gerard Hynes for compiling the index; Jo Story, series editor, for taking us on and for her acute comments and advice; and Tom Gray and all at Ashgate for their efficiency and friendliness. We gratefully acknowledge permission granted by the British Library to reproduce BL MS Harley 2904, f. 3v, as our cover image. Finally, the editors would like to thank the contributors, for making the emotional side of editing so unusually serene.

Note on Referencing

All quotations from Old English poetry are from the Anglo-Saxon Poetic Records edition, ed. George Philip Krapp and Elliott Van Kirk Dobbie, unless otherwise stated.

Chapter 1
Introduction

Alice Jorgensen

Hwæðre ic þurh þæt gold   ongytan meahte
earmra ærgewin,   þæt hit ærest ongan
swætan on þa swiðran healfe.   Eall ic wæs mid sorgum gedrefed.
Forht ic wæs for þære fægran gesyhðe.
(The Dream of the Rood, ll. 18–21a)

[Yet through the gold I was able to perceive the ancient strife of wretched ones – that it first began to bleed on the right-hand side. I was completely troubled with sorrows. I was afraid on account of the beautiful sight.][1]

Repeatedly in the most familiar Old English texts we find references to inner life and to the emotions. In this example from *The Dream of the Rood*, the vision of the cross is focalised through the experience of the dreamer, and that experience is not only sensory – he sees the gold and blood – but involves both interpretation (recognising the signs of ancient strife) and a powerful, complex emotional reaction. The emotion is simultaneously part of the meaning-making of the poem, conveying the mystery and the overwhelming personal importance of the crucifixion in a way that sheer statement could not, and part of the persuasive armoury of a text that models the devotion it exhorts its audience to practice. The figure of the dreamer forms a point of access to the formidable theological claims at the poem's heart, a space of subjectivity into which the audience can enter. The subjective and affective dimension – brilliantly handled in this case – is a factor that makes the poem attractive to modern audiences, despite its great antiquity. At the same time, the evocation of interiority and psychological processes is something *The Dream of the Rood* shares with much of Old English literature, especially Old English poetry. As Antonina Harbus puts it, with specific reference to the poetry,

> the mind was an idea of particular importance in Anglo-Saxon society. Not only is the mind privileged over other aspects of the human person in this culture,

---

[1] Translation my own.

but also the mental world is of far more interest than other possible narrative concerns, such as material culture or social institutions.[2]

For Britt Mize, attention to mentality is a feature of the traditionality of Old English poetry; when poets are working from non-poetic or non-English source material, amplifying or importing references to the inner life is part of what they do to give their texts the character of *echt* Old English verse:

> Subjectivizing moments ... are so rooted in Old English compositional priorities and methods as to be part and parcel of making poems in the traditional register.[3]

In fact, Mize argues that there is a danger of misinterpreting the presence of the 'poetics of mentality' in texts such as *Beowulf*; the fact that the *Beowulf*-poet pays attention to the interiority of Grendel is not an unusual feature, for Old English poets do not restrict focalisation to protagonists.[4] The prominence of the mind and emotions in Old English poetry thus, on the one hand, makes thousand-year-old texts seem immediate and accessible and, on the other hand, remains in need of careful scrutiny and contextualisation; we must not forget that that our own assumptions may lead us wrong.

The present collection, which focuses specifically on the emotions, thus addresses a rich but also challenging field. It appears at a time of unprecedented interdisciplinary interest in emotions, a topic that has achieved a major place in psychology, anthropology, neurology and philosophy over the last thirty years but has only recently begun to be investigated historically.[5] The collection provides a snapshot of the study of Anglo-Saxon emotions at an exciting moment of emergence. It showcases scholars who have made important pioneering contributions (such as Leslie Lockett and Antonina Harbus) alongside newer voices, providing a foretaste of research currently under way. The stress is predominantly on literary and linguistic evidence and on Old English, areas that

---

[2] Antonina Harbus, *The Life of the Mind in Old English Poetry* (Amsterdam and New York, 2002), p. 25.

[3] Britt Mize, *Traditional Subjectivities: The Old English Poetics of Mentality* (Toronto, 2013), p. 6; for the point about poets amplifying or inserting references to mentality, see p. 236 and passim.

[4] Ibid., pp. 16 and 237–9.

[5] Some important considerations of how to write the history of emotions are: Peter N. Stearns and Carol Z. Stearns, 'Emotionology: Clarifying the History of Emotions and Emotional Standards', *American Historical Review* 90 (1985): 813–36; William Reddy, *The Navigation of Feeling: A Framework for the History of Emotions* (Cambridge, 2001); Barbara H. Rosenwein, 'Worrying About Emotions in History', *American Historical Review* 107 (2002): 821–45; Joanna Bourke, 'Fear and Anxiety: Writing about Emotion in Modern History', *History Workshop Journal* 55 (2003): 111–33.

are especially rich for our purpose but that also raise specific problems; many of the chapters tackle theoretical issues as well as giving readings of particular texts or dimensions of emotion. This introduction contextualises the collection in relation to the wider topic of what emotions are and how we can study them, with an accent less on paradigms that can be directly applied to Anglo-Saxon studies than on distinctions, questions and complexities. It then offers an account of what has been done so far on Anglo-Saxon emotions and what this volume will add.

Emotions: Some Problems and Distinctions

Studies of emotions commonly begin by puzzling over definitions. In modern English, we can distinguish between emotion in general and particular emotions (for example, anger, love, envy), and between emotions, moods and dispositions (where an emotion is generally seen as having a specific occasion and intentional object – for example, grief on hearing of the death of a friend – in a way that feeling generally low or being prone to depression do not).[6] Depending on disciplinary biases, the definitions may indeed be trying to explain rather different things. Evolutionary biologists may want an account of responses to stimuli such as meeting a predator or hearing an infant's cry; neuroscientists look for terms in which to investigate and classify chemical and electrical processes in the brain; philosophers, on the other hand, are likely to want to clarify and test the concepts underlying the term 'emotion' in ordinary language, while sociologists might focus on emotion as a dimension of social interaction and communication. For a long time there has been a basic divide between, on the one hand, hard-science approaches focused on physical processes, somatic gestures (such as facial expressions, weeping and so forth), and other elements of what is seen as a biologically founded, evolved, 'hard-wired' and essentially universal set of human emotions,[7] and, on the other hand, anthropological and ethnographical perspectives that insist on the culture-specific nature of emotions and that investigate vocabularies, rules for display and folk psychologies.[8] Some current approaches seek to overcome the dichotomy between biology and

---

[6] For more fine-tuned and technical distinctions along these lines see Aaron Ben Ze'ev, 'The Thing Called Emotion', in Peter Goldie (ed.), *The Oxford Handbook of Philosophy of Emotion* (Oxford, 2010), pp. 41–62, at 54–6.

[7] Key contributions include Charles Darwin, *The Expression of the Emotions in Man and Animals* (London, 1873); William James, 'What is an Emotion?', *Mind* 9 (1884): 188–205 and *The Principles of Psychology*, 2 vols (London, 1890); multiple publications by Paul Ekman, for example *Emotions Revealed: Understanding Faces and Feelings* (London, 2003).

[8] Influential works include Michelle Rosaldo, *Knowledge and Passion: Ilongot Notions of Self and Social Life* (Cambridge, 1980); Lila Abu-Lughod, *Veiled Sentiments: Honor and*

culture, for example by stressing the extent to which the formation of neural pathways in the brain is itself a highly malleable, fluid process, responsive to life experiences and the social contexts that condition them.[9] However, others question the helpfulness of using emotion as an analytical category at all, on the grounds that it is itself culture and language specific, not to mention fuzzy at the edges. Thomas Dixon states this position strongly when he writes that 'the emotions did not exist until just under two hundred years ago'; rather, earlier ages in Western Europe thought in terms of passions, affections and sentiments.[10] For the psychologists James Russell and Ghyslaine Lemay, everyday emotion categories are simply too imprecise for science; we should be using only those concepts necessary to describe what is empirically observed, and looking for elemental units at a more basic level than 'anger' or 'fear'.[11]

It seems that framing a historical or literary investigation in terms of emotions does, after all, need some defending. A short defence would be to say that it is by starting from the concept of emotions that Dixon, Russell and Lemay are able to offer the insights they do. We need not be bound by our everyday, culturally instilled concepts, but it is only by applying them that we can begin to critique them, and get a sense of what our evidence is showing us instead. In addition, we can argue that our category of emotion gets at something extremely important for how humans relate to each other and their world. There are many different definitions of emotion, but most of them associate it closely with people's values, needs and goals. For Martha Nussbaum, a philosopher advancing a cognitivist, neo-Stoic theory, emotions constitute 'eudaimonistic' judgements that 'view the world from the point of view of [one's] own scheme of goals and projects, the things to which [one] attach[es] value in a conception of what it is for [one] to live well'.[12] Antonio Damasio, from the very different vantage-point of neuroscience, distinguishes 'emotions', in his account automatic, bodily responses, from 'feeling', which is the conscious perception of such responses; however, he sees both as adaptive behaviours that allow the organism to detect and evaluate

---

Poetry in a Bedouin Society (Berkeley, 1986); Catherine Lutz, *Unnatural Emotions: Everyday Sentiments on a Micronesian Atoll and their Challenge to Western Theory* (Chicago, 1988).

[9] Margaret Wetherell, *Affect and Emotion: A New Social Science Understanding* (London, 2012), pp. 44–6.

[10] Thomas Dixon, *From Passions to Emotions: The Creation of a Secular Psychological Category* (Cambridge, 2003), pp. 1 (quotation) and 11–12.

[11] James A. Russell and Ghyslaine Lemay, 'Emotion Concepts', in Michael Lewis and Jeannette M. Haviland-Jones (eds), *Handbook of Emotions. Second Edition* (London, 2000), pp. 491–503, at 499–500.

[12] Martha C. Nussbaum, *Upheavals of Thought: The Intelligence of Emotions* (Cambridge, 2001), p. 49.

changes in its environment and react to them.[13] In a textbook aimed primarily at psychology students, Keith Oatley and his co-authors offer the following as an uncontroversial starting definition of emotions: '*multi-component responses to challenges or opportunities that are important to the individual's goals, particularly social ones*' (italicisation original).[14] Thus, with respect to the present volume, we can suggest that the study of emotions offers a way to ask questions about how Anglo-Saxons encountered their personal goals, values and needs within a specific cultural setting.

Further, it is useful to expand on Oatley's description of emotions as 'multi-component responses'. Emotions involve multiple levels or systems, which are not simply hierarchically dependent on each other but interact in a series of feedback loops. The philosopher Jenefer Robinson argues we should see emotions as processes. Rejecting the idea that emotions are or always involve cognitive judgements, she views them as based on 'affective appraisals', which bypass higher cognitive processing and cause physiological reactions and action tendencies; but these initial reactions are followed by 'cognitive monitoring', which can include reassessment of circumstances and reflection on or labelling of the emotional state, and these in turn modify the somatic reaction. Moreover, the character of emotion episodes is strongly affected by background moods and also by personal dispositions, bringing them too into the feedback loop.[15] Klaus Scherer's 'component process model' identifies the following elements: appraisals, motivational changes and action tendencies, 'somatovisceral changes' (for example, changes to heart and breathing rates) and 'motor expressions' (such as cries, running away), a 'central representation' that may be partially conscious and represents the raw experiential side of the emotion, and conscious categorisation and labelling. All these elements continuously modify each other in a 'dynamic, recursive' fashion, while the appraisals themselves are repeated and operate at multiple levels including those of biologically primed reflexes, socially learned schemata and cultural concepts.[16] Approaches like these give us a sense that the phenomena as well as the concepts of emotion are messy and plural. 'Emotion' can be a way of talking about the fluid interactions between multiple factors, rather than just a way of 'carving up human mental life'.[17] When

---

[13] Antonio Damasio, *Looking for Spinoza: Joy, Sorrow and the Feeling Brain* (London, 2004), pp. 27–35 (emotions vs. feelings) and 54–5 (emotions and evaluation).

[14] Keith Oatley, Dacher Keltner and Jennifer M. Jenkins, *Understanding Emotions*, 2nd edn (Oxford and Malden, 2006), p. 29.

[15] Jenefer Robinson, *Deeper Than Reason: Emotion and its Role in Literature, Music, and Art* (Oxford, 2005), pp. 57–99.

[16] Klaus Scherer, 'The Dynamic Architecture of Emotion: Evidence for the Component Process Model', *Cognition and Emotion* 23 (2009): 1307–51, at 1307–14.

[17] Dixon, p. 6. Wetherell writes of 'the ongoing flow of affective activity .... Affective practices unfurl, become organised, and effloresce with particular rhythms' (p. 12).

studying the emotions of the past, therefore, we are not looking for a single, monolithic entity but trying to trace networks of perceptions, values, gestures and reactions. While Robinson and Scherer both start from biology, psychology and the individual organism, models like theirs also give us ways to think about the interaction of the biological and psychological with the social and cultural, a nexus that can similarly be seen as dynamic and recursive.

Bearing in mind this stress on the dynamic and recursive, therefore, I want to set out some contrasting pairs that may help us puzzle more productively over the distance and the closeness between what we, based on contemporary experience, think of as emotions, and what we might find in Anglo-Saxon sources. We start at the opposite end of the scale from the neuroscientist or the psychologist: not from living experimental subjects, not from flares of neural activity or observable bouts of weeping, but from textual representations, and to a lesser extent visual ones. Questions of semantics, of genre, of models and sources, must all arise (and such questions are variously tackled in this book). The relationship between actual and represented emotion is at issue in several of the chapters collected here, for instance in Harbus's consideration of how readers engage emotionally with poetry, in McCormack's comments on how *Christ* stimulates compunction and in my own discussion of the Old English Prose Psalms as a vehicle for emotional learning. Here let us highlight two distinctions that can be seen as subsets of the problem of represented versus actual emotion: *emotion* versus *emotion concepts*, and *emotion talk* versus *emotional talk*.

The first distinction is made by Russell and Lemay, mentioned earlier, before they go on to argue that our emotion concepts are too fuzzy to form a basis for empirical study.[18] Given the nature of our sources, Anglo-Saxonists can perhaps study emotion concepts more readily than emotion itself.[19] Concepts are highly culturally variable, and folk psychologies, and indeed learned emotional theories, form an important ethnographical focus in their own right.[20] However, as the summary of Scherer's model above indicates, concepts and culture also impinge at various points on emotional processes, at the same time as culture cannot be reified as a free-floating absolute, independent of biology and individual psychology.[21] Emotional concepts are thus not merely a parallel track but essential to investigation of the *qualia*, the 'feeling' of emotional experience, not to mention how emotion episodes issue in action. Both folk psychologies

---

[18] 'Emotion Concepts'.
[19] See below for an account of work so far.
[20] See Richard A. Schweder and Jonathan Haidt, 'The Cultural Psychology of the Emotions', in Lewis and Haviland-Jones (eds), pp. 397–414; Karl G. Heider, *The Cultural Context of Emotion: Folk Psychology in West Sumatra* (New York, 2011).
[21] Nancy Chodorow makes the point about culture from a psychoanalytic perspective, emphasising particularly the role of individual psychological formation: *The Power of Feelings: Personal Meaning in Psychoanalysis, Gender, and Culture* (New Haven, 1999), pp. 143–65.

and more learned theories (such as the medical learning discussed by Leslie Lockett in her chapter here) are responses to lived emotion that in turn shape how experience is perceived, comprehended and recalled.

The distinction between *emotion talk* and *emotional talk* comes from linguistics. *Emotion talk* is language that denotes emotion, such as *love, joyful, dislike, a broken heart*. *Emotional talk* signals or expresses emotions, for example through interjections, expletives, metaphors, intonation and the like.[22] Some of the chapters in this volume (for example, Izdebska and Birnbaum) are more obviously directed to emotion talk, some (for example, Ganze) to emotional talk, but again we need to recognise how they impinge on each other. Relevant here is William Reddy's concept of 'emotives'. These are explicit declarations about emotion (for example, 'I love you') that, like Austin's performatives, have relational intent (telling you I love you affects our relationship) and can alter what they appear to describe (having declared love, my love may seem realer and more important to me).[23] Reddy has been criticised for his emphasis on emotives, given that this kind of explicit emotion claim may be rather rare in practice,[24] but he usefully draws attention to the ways description and expression, naming and performance of emotions can interpenetrate. At the same time, the distinction between emotion talk and emotional talk remains important. The choice to name emotions explicitly can be a highly charged one: emotions are linked to values and goals, and naming emotions can involve making ethical claims. For example, asserting that someone is ashamed can amount to accusing them of having a reason to be ashamed, while saying that one acted out of sadness rather than anger can be a way to claim the moral high ground of a patient victim.[25] We need to ask questions of our sources not just about how they conceptualise emotion and how they express emotion, but how they use emotion talk to take up rhetorical positions, establish ethical orientations, or assert authority.

In relation to the notion of performance, and of emotion talk having a performative dimension, it is appropriate to turn to the topic of the body and gesture. David McNeill makes a distinction between gesture as 'a "window" into the mind ... part of the individual speaker–gesturer's ongoing mental life' and 'gesture as part of the social interaction' in which it is, among other things, 'a communicative resource'.[26] The body, with its neural circuits and its automatic

---

[22] Monika Bednarek, *Emotion Talk across Corpora* (Basingstoke, 2008), pp. 10–12.
[23] Reddy, pp. 96–111.
[24] Wetherell, pp. 71–3. Wetherell gives an excellent summary and critique of Reddy's rather dense theoretical arguments, of which emotives form only one aspect.
[25] Geoffrey M. White, 'Moral Discourse and the Rhetoric of Emotion', in Robert A. LeVine (ed.), *Psychological Anthropology: A Reader on Self in Culture* (Chichester, 2010), pp. 68–82; originally published in Catherine A. Lutz and Lila Abu-Lughod (eds), *Language and the Politics of Emotion* (Cambridge, 1990), pp. 46–68.
[26] David McNeill (ed.), *Language and Gesture* (Cambridge, 2000), p. 11.

physiological changes, seems to be the obvious site and foundation of precultural, spontaneous, individual emotion, but it is also, of course, a vehicle of display, carefully scrutinised, moved (sometimes) by the will. We can ask how the gestures we encounter operate (or are understood to operate) along a sliding scale from the spontaneous and involuntary to the staged or ritualised. We can also ask about the strategies we can deploy for reading or decoding gestures. Mills and Wilcox in this volume both have interesting points to make on these topics.

Finally, before turning to a review of what has been written so far on Anglo-Saxon emotions, I want to mention some other dimensions of plurality, less easily set out as binary pairs, that we do well to bear in mind. It will have become apparent that the study of emotions is profoundly plural in that it encompasses not only different individual emotions (anger, shame, love) but physiological changes and deliberate gestures, descriptions and expressions, appraisals and reappraisals, communications and social positionings, personal quirks and cultural trends. It also needs to take account of the intersections of different emotional styles and repertoires associated with particular social groups ('emotional communities', as Barbara Rosenwein terms them[27]), particular occasions and settings, and also different languages. The present collection, like most foregoing work on the topic, focuses predominantly on the English literature of England, but many of our authors – including the anonymous poets – must have been bi- or multi-lingual, speaking Old English, Latin and maybe also Old Norse; Old Saxon, Friesian and Old French are also possibilities. Individuals may well have been strongly dominant in one of these languages, but they may have had a sense of 'having somewhat distinct emotional lives in two languages'.[28] Old English, perhaps, might have been associated with a rather different ethic to Latin, maybe the community- and honour-orientated ethic of the heroic poetry with its stress on courage, loyal love and yearning for lord and hall, while Latin might have been linked more to the fear of God, disgust at the world, and the ardour of monastic fraternity.[29] This is a schematisation, of course; monks also read Virgil and there is plenty of religious literature in Old English. My point is, rather, that we should recognise that the culture itself was plural, and that individuals operated with multiple sets of norms, expectations and interpretive possibilities, and thus with scope for creativity and change.[30]

---

[27] Barbara H. Rosenwein, *Emotional Communities in the Early Middle Ages* (Ithaca, NY, 2006).

[28] Aneta Pavlenko, *Emotions and Multilingualism* (Cambridge, 2005), p. 77.

[29] For the hypothesis that cultures can be viewed in terms of three basic moral codes, each associated with characteristic moral emotions, see Paul Rozin, Laura Lowery, Sumio Imada and Jonathan Haidt, 'The CAD Triad Hypothesis: A Mapping Between Three Moral Emotions (Contempt, Anger, Disgust) and Three Moral Codes (Community, Autonomy, Divinity)', *Journal of Personality and Social Psychology* 76 (1999): 575–86.

[30] See Birnbaum, this volume, for an example of linguistic creativity at the intersection of Old English and Latin.

Emotion in Anglo-Saxon Studies

In Anglo-Saxon studies, emotion is simultaneously a new topic and a very old one. In the vernacular poetry, as has already been suggested, emotion plays an obvious part, and criticism has been taking account of it in one way or another for many years. For example, the many students of *The Wanderer* and *The Seafarer* who have examined the structure, coherence and artistic impact of these poems have had much to say about their emotional trajectories, the extent to which they can be seen as representing changes of mood and attitude within individual minds.[31] The emotional effect of texts on readers has long been a concern. This can be illustrated by the many studies that examine the way the *Beowulf*-poet induces fear through the portrayal of Grendel's approach to Heorot and in the description of the mere.[32] The generic categories applied to poetry often have obvious relevance to questions of the expression and management of emotion: *planctus, consolatio*, lament.[33] Investigations of social roles in the heroic world of the poetry also raise issues of emotion. For instance, the bonds of lords and thegns have been widely discussed, sometimes more in terms of moral or legal obligation but sometimes explicitly in terms of love, as for example in Joseph Harris's essay 'Love and Death in the *Männerbund*'.[34]

---

[31] e.g. Peter Orton, 'The Form and Structure of *The Seafarer*', *Studia Neophilologica* 63 (1991): 37–55; Margrét Gunnarsdóttir Champion, 'From Plaint to Praise: Language as Cure in "The Wanderer"', *Studia Neophilologica* 69 (1998): 187–202.

[32] Arthur G. Brodeur, 'Design for Terror in the Purging of Heorot', *JEGP* 53 (1954): 503–13, and *The Art of 'Beowulf'* (Berkeley, 1959), pp. 88–94; Alain Renoir, 'Point of View and Design for Terror in *Beowulf*', *Neuphilologische Mitteilungen* 63 (1962): 154–67; Stanley B. Greenfield, 'Grendel's Approach to Heorot: Syntax and Poetry', in Robert P. Creed (ed.), *Old English Poetry: Fifteen Essays* (Providence, 1967), pp. 275–84; G. Storms, 'Grendel the Terrible', *Neuphilologische Mitteilungen* 73 (1972): 427–36; Richard Butts, 'The Analogical Mere: Landscape and Terror in *Beowulf*', *English Studies* 68 (1987): 113–21; Michael Lapidge, '*Beowulf* and the Psychology of Terror', in Helen Damico and John Leyerle (eds), *Heroic Poetry in the Anglo-Saxon Period* (Kalamazoo, 1993), pp. 373–402.

[33] See, for example, Rosemary Woolf, '*The Wanderer, The Seafarer*, and the Genre of *Planctus*', in Lewis E. Nicholson and Dolores Warwick Frese (eds), *Anglo-Saxon Poetry: Essays in Appreciation for John C. McGalliard* (Notre Dame, 1975), pp. 192–207; J.E. Cross, 'On the Genre of *The Wanderer*', *Neophilologus* 45 (1961): 63–75 (identifying the poem as *consolatio*); Anne L. Klinck, '*Resignation*: Exile's Lament or Penitent's Prayer?' *Neophilologus* 71 (1987): 423–30, and *The Old English Elegies: A Critical Edition and Genre Study* (Montreal, 1992); Jane Tolmie and M.J. Toswell (eds), *Laments for the Lost in Medieval Literature* (Turnhout, 2010) (essays on lament in Old and Middle English, Old Norse and Latin).

[34] Joseph Harris, 'Love and Death in the *Männerbund*: An Essay with Special Reference to the *Bjarkamál* and *The Battle of Maldon*', in Damico and Leyerle (eds), pp. 77–114. An early, famous and provocative contribution to the issue is C.S. Lewis's contention that, in the literature of the Dark Ages, 'the deepest of worldly emotions ... is the love of man for man,

Yet, until recently, there has been surprisingly little work in our field that focuses directly on emotion. Most of the studies mentioned above are not centrally conceived as studies of emotion, and the majority rest on conceptions of emotion that are not strongly theorised.[35] The pioneers of early medieval emotion have not been Anglo-Saxonists; one thinks in particular of Barbara Rosenwein, William Ian Miller and Gerd Althoff.[36] Moreover, large-scale interdisciplinary and inter-institutional projects on emotion have tended to leave our period out of their remit (for example, the Australian Research Council Centre for Excellence for the History of Emotions – Europe 1100–1800).[37] The publications now available on Anglo-Saxon emotion specifically have almost all appeared since the turn of the century. They can be roughly grouped under four headings: meditations on how to approach the topic; work on Anglo-Saxon conceptions of the mind and folk psychologies; studies of emotion vocabulary; and, overlapping with the previous category, studies of individual emotions or aspects of emotional expression.

Under the first heading, we should mention the brief but stimulating essays collected in a 2001 issue of *Early Medieval Europe* under the topic of 'The History of the Emotions: A Debate'.[38] These are not in fact framed as focusing on Anglo-Saxon England, but they make extensive use of Anglo-Saxon examples. They are notable in that they are mostly written by historians, who have tended to be underrepresented in this area. They focus particularly on the problem of how we might get through to real individuals and their emotional experience: can we do more than identify the conventions of our texts? What is

---

the mutual love of warriors who die together fighting against odds, and the affection between vassal and lord': *The Allegory of Love: A Study in Medieval Tradition* (Oxford, 1936), p. 9.

[35] Lapidge, 'Psychology of Terror' and Champion are notable exceptions, making use (respectively) of psychological and psychoanalytic approaches.

[36] Their most relevant publications for our purpose are: Barbara H. Rosenwein, 'Worrying About Emotions in History' and *Emotional Communities*; Barbara H. Rosenwein (ed.), *Anger's Past: The Social Uses of an Emotion in the Middle Ages* (Ithaca, 1998); William Ian Miller, *Humiliation and Other Essays on Honor, Social Discomfort, and Violence* (Ithaca, 1993), and *The Anatomy of Disgust* (Cambridge, MA, 1997); Gerd Althoff, 'Empörung, Tränen, Zerknirschung. Emotionen in der Öffentlichen Kommunikation des Mittelalters', *Frühmittelalterliche Studien* 30 (1996): 60–79 and 'Freiwilligkeit und Konsensfassaden. Emotionale Ausdrucksformen in der Politik des Mittelalters', in K. Herding and B. Stumpfhaus (eds), *Pathos, Affekt, Gefühl. Die Emotionen in den Künsten* (Berlin, 2004), pp. 145–61.

[37] Starting in January 2011, this is a current project at the time of writing: see http://www.historyofemotions.org.au/ [consulted 29 May 2013]. In fact two contributors to the present volume have links with the Research Centre, suggesting some temporal flexibility in its work.

[38] *Early Medieval Europe* 10 (2001): 225–56, introduced by Catherine Cubitt (225–7), with contributions by Barbara Rosenwein (229–34), Stuart Airlie (235–41), Mary Garrison (243–50) and Caroline Larrington (251–56).

the relationship between representation and reality? The interface of emotions and texts is also interrogated, in very different terms and at much greater length, in Antonina Harbus's important recent monograph *Cognitive Approaches to Old English Poetry*. Harbus's question, which she also addresses in her contribution to the present volume, is how cognitive science can help us to understand the ways both modern and Anglo-Saxon readers make or made sense of Old English poetry, including how they respond(ed) to its emotional content.[39]

Under the heading of concepts of the mind and folk psychologies, Malcolm Godden's essay 'Anglo-Saxons on the Mind' remains foundational. It has important claims to make about Anglo-Saxon concepts of emotion as well as the mind and soul; it also draws extensively on prose sources, not only on poetry, and on Latin as well as OE.[40] In the past decade or so a number of scholars have built on this foundation. Harbus's 2002 book on the mind in Old English poetry has already been cited. She addresses emotion particularly in the chapter on the elegies, complicating the common perception that the self seeks to control the disruptively emotional mind in these texts by observing that the mind, which experiences emotion and thinks, 'constructs the present and future versions of the self'.[41] The boldest and most thorough contribution is Leslie Lockett's 2011 monograph.[42] Lockett refines Godden's distinction between a learned, classicising tradition represented by Alcuin, Alfred and Ælfric and a vernacular tradition reflected in the poetry; she emphasises the plurality of the Christian Latin inheritance, including a distinction between Platonic/Augustinian and Stoic influences, and sees the Augustinian, incorporeal model of the mind as only really entering Old English with Ælfric. Lockett argues that the vernacular tradition offers a cardiocentric and hydraulic model of emotion: emotions such as anger are conceived as swelling or boiling up within the chest cavity. Soon Ai Low, in an earlier examination of the hydraulic model, approached it as a conceptual metaphor, but Lockett argues that it is likely to have been taken literally; the hydraulic model is a *physiological* model that understands emotions as bodily processes.[43] This is a paradigm-shifting view. Others to have worked on conceptions and representations of the mind, though not so specifically on

---

[39] Antonina Harbus, *Cognitive Approaches to Old English Poetry* (Cambridge, 2012), esp. ch. 7, pp. 162–76.

[40] M.R. Godden, 'Anglo-Saxons on the Mind', in Michael Lapidge and Helmut Gneuss (eds), *Learning and Literature in Anglo-Saxon England: Studies Presented to Peter Clemoes on the Occasion of his Sixty-fifth Birthday* (Cambridge, 1985), pp. 271–98.

[41] Harbus, *Life of the Mind*, pp. 127–60, quotation at 156.

[42] *Anglo-Saxon Psychologies in the Vernacular and Latin Traditions* (Toronto, 2011).

[43] Soon Ai Low, *The Anglo-Saxon Mind: Metaphor and Common Sense Psychology in Old English Literature* (PhD thesis, University of Toronto, 1998). See Lockett, *Anglo-Saxon Psychologies*, pp. 7–9.

emotions, include Britt Mize, Eric Jager, Michael Matto and Peter Clemoes.[44] This strand of scholarship has illuminated some important themes that analyses of Anglo-Saxon emotions must take account of: the 'hydraulic model'; the motif of the mind as a container; the relationship of mind and body; and the fact that the concept of the *mod* encompasses both emotion and cognition.

Work on the Old English vocabulary of emotion has been pursued particularly by Japanese and continental European scholars, though one should not ignore the groundwork laid down by the authors of the *Thesaurus of Old English* and the many heroic researchers of the Toronto *Dictionary of Old English*. Michiko Ogura, who ranges between Old and Middle English, has looked at emotion vocabulary in general; individual studies concentrate on selected texts or grammatical categories.[45] Ogura was one contributor to a special issue of the journal *Poetica* devoted to 'The Expression of Emotions in English, with an Emphasis on Old and Middle English', published in Japan.[46] Another contributor, Małgorzata Fabiszak, has published semantic studies of various sets of emotion terms, including joy, fear, grief, anger and shame.[47] Of these individual emotions, anger has perhaps received the most lexical study,

---

[44] Britt Mize, 'The Representation of the Mind as an Enclosure in Old English Poetry', *Anglo-Saxon England* 35 (2006): 57–90, and 'Manipulations of the Mind-as-container Motif in *Beowulf*, *Homiletic Fragment II*, and Alfred's *Metrical Epilogue to the Pastoral Care*', *JEGP* 107 (2008): 25–56; Eric Jager, 'The Word in the "Breost": Interiority and the Fall in *Genesis B*', *Neophilologus* 75 (1991): 279–90; Michael Matto, 'True Confessions: *The Seafarer* and Technologies of the *Sylf*', *JEGP* 103 (2004): 156–79; Peter Clemoes, *Interactions of Thought and Language in Old English Poetry* (Cambridge, 1995).

[45] Michiko Ogura, 'Verbs of Emotion with Reflexive Constructions', in Christian Kay and Louise Sylvester (eds), *Lexis and Texts in Early English: Studies Presented to Jane Roberts* (Amsterdam and Atlanta, 2001), pp. 203–12; 'Words of EMOTION in Old and Middle English', in Javier E. Díaz Vera (ed.), *A Changing World of Words: Studies in English Historical Lexicography, Lexicology and Semantics* (Amsterdam, 2002), pp. 484–99; 'Words of Emotion in Old and Middle English Psalms and Alliterative Poems', *Chiba University Studies in Humanities* 32 (2003): 393–427; 'Words of Emotion in Old and Middle English Translations of Boethius's *De Consolatione Philosophiae*', in Akio Oizumi, Jacek Fisiak and John Scahill (eds), *Text and Language in Medieval English Prose: A Festschrift for Tadao Kubouchi* (Frankfurt am Main, 2005), pp. 183–206. See also next footnote.

[46] Michiko Ogura, 'Old and Middle English Verbs of Emotion', *Poetica* 66 (2006): 53–72. Other contributions to this special issue to deal with OE are Małgorzata Fabiszak and Anna Hebda, 'Emotions of Control in Old English: Shame and Guilt', pp. 1–35 (a corpus-based vocabulary study), and Hans Sauer, 'Ælfric and Emotion', pp. 37–52 (largely concerned with the *Grammar*, in particular its treatment of interjections). Eric Stanley, 'FEAR chiefly in Old and Middle English', pp. 73–114, examines the changing meanings of the word *fær*, which in OE means 'a sudden danger' (p. 76).

[47] 'A Semantic Analysis of Emotion Terms in Old English', *Studia Anglica Posnaniensia* 34 (1999): 133–46; *The Concept of 'Joy' in Old and Middle English: A Semantic Analysis* (Piła,

though there is much scope for further work.[48] Linguistic work such as this has produced many detailed insights. If we are to look for broad lessons, we might highlight the importance but also the difficulty of trying to identify the semantic connections between Old English terms when starting from Modern English ones; the need to consider the text-types (and so the registers and discourse-domains) in which lexical items occur, and the need to consider how linguistic systems themselves – for example, the prevalence of impersonal or reflexive verb constructions – may affect how a language talks about emotions.

Other studies devoted to particular emotions – some making use of lexical evidence but predominantly more literary and/or historical in emphasis – include a scattering of articles on Anglo-Saxon shame and remorse;[49] and a rather larger body of work, unsurprising given the topic's prominence in the poetry, on grief and mourning, particularly from a gender perspective.[50] Scholars have

---

2001); 'A Semantic Analysis of FEAR, GRIEF and ANGER Words in Old English', in Díaz Vera (ed.), pp. 255–74; Fabiszak and Hebda.

[48] Caroline Gevaert, 'The evolution of the lexical and conceptual field of ANGER in Old and Middle English', in Díaz Vera (ed.), pp. 275–99, and *The History of Anger: The Lexical Field of ANGER from Old to Early Modern English* (PhD thesis, Leuven, 2007); Dirk Geeraerts and Caroline Gevaert, 'Hearts and (Angry) Minds in Old English', in Farzad Sharifian, René Dirven, Ning Yu and Susanne Niemeier (eds), *Culture, Body, and Language: Conceptualizations of Internal Body Organs across Cultures and Languages* (Berlin and New York, 2008), pp. 319–47; Manuela Romano Mozo, '*Anger* in Old English', *Selim* 9 (1999): 45–56; Agnieszka Mikolajczuk, 'Anger in Polish and English: A Semantic Comparison with Some Historical Content', in Christian J. Kay and Jeremy J. Smith (eds), *Categorization in the History of English* (Amsterdam, 2004), pp. 159–78. See further Izdebska, this volume.

[49] Jonathan Wilcox, 'Naked in Old English: the Embarrassed and the Shamed', in Benjamin C. Withers and Jonathan Wilcox (eds), *Naked Before God: Uncovering the Body in Anglo-Saxon England* (Morgantown, 2003), pp. 275–309; Alice Cowen, '*Byrstas and bysmeras*: The Wounds of Sin in Wulfstan's *Sermo Lupi ad Anglos*', in Matthew Townend (ed.), *Wulfstan, Archbishop of York* (Turnhout, 2004), pp. 397–411; Catherine Cubitt, 'The Politics of Remorse: Penance and Royal Piety in the Reign of Æthelred the Unready', *Historical Research* 85 (2012): 179–92, at http://onlinelibrary.wiley.com/doi/10.111/j-2281.2011.00571.x, published online 8 June 2011 [consulted 7 November 2011]; Alice Jorgensen, '"It Shames Me to Say It": Ælfric and the Concept and Vocabulary of Shame', *Anglo-Saxon England* 41 (2013 for 2012): 249–76.

[50] e.g. Linda Georgianna, 'King Hrethel's Sorrow and the Limits of Heroic Action in *Beowulf*', *Speculum* 62 (1987): 829–50; Ruth Wehlau, '"Seeds of Sorrow": Landscapes of Despair in *The Wanderer*, *Beowulf*'s Story of Hrethel and *Sonatorrek*', *Parergon* 15 (1998): 1–17; Joyce Hill, '"Þæt wæs geomoru ides!" A Female Stereotype Examined', in Helen Damico and Alexandra Hennessey Olsen (eds), *New Readings on Women in Old English Literature* (Bloomington, 1990), pp. 235–47; J.A. Tasioulas, 'The Mother's Lament: *Wulf and Eadwacer* Reconsidered', *Medium Ævum* 65 (1996): 1–18; Pat Belanoff, '*Ides ... geomrode giddum*: The Old English Female Lament', in Anne L. Klinck and Ann Marie Rasmussen (eds), *Medieval Woman's Song: Cross-cultural Approaches* (Philadelphia, 2002), pp. 29–46;

also begun to re-evaluate the place of affective piety in Anglo-Saxon England.[51] The gestures of laughter and weeping have received some attention;[52] we should additionally mention the little that has been written so far on emotion and gesture in Anglo-Saxon ritual.[53] Studies of ritual and gesture, like studies of individual emotions such as shame, are helpful in illuminating how emotion shades into other issues such as political performance or personal identity.[54]

This brief survey (restricted largely to English-language publications but reasonably thorough within that scope) gives an impression of a rapidly growing but still fragmented body of work. Much remains to be done. One of the purposes of this volume, and one of the advantages of framing inquiry in terms of 'emotion', is to allow studies to be related to each other that may otherwise seem to be ploughing separate furrows – of gender, poetics, lexis, syntax, medical history and so forth. A focus on emotion allows us to revisit and reframe the earlier work on poetry mentioned at the start of this section and apply its findings in new ways, as well as critique them. The chapters in the present collection continue the lines of research outlined above but also ask new questions and expand the range of sources used to talk about emotions. Recognising the plurality and the necessarily fuzzy boundaries of the topic, and

---

Patricia Clare Ingham, 'From Kinship to Kingship: Mourning, Gender, and Anglo-Saxon Community', in Jennifer C. Vaught with Lynne Dickson Bruckner (eds), *Grief and Gender: 700–1700* (New York, 2003), pp. 17–31. See further Mills and Sebo, this volume.

[51]   Allen J. Frantzen, 'Spirituality and Devotion in Anglo-Saxon Penitentials', *Essays in Medieval Studies* 22 (2005): 117–28; Scott DeGregorio, 'Affective Spirituality: Theory and Practice in Bede and Alfred the Great', *Essays in Medieval Studies* 22 (2005): 129–39. See further McCormack, this volume.

[52]   Hugh Magennis, 'Images of Laughter in Old English Poetry, with Particular Reference to the "Hleahtor Wera" of *The Seafarer*', *English Studies* 73 (1992): 193–204; John D. Niles, 'Byrhtnoth's Wordplay and the Poetics of Gesture', in Jonathan Wilcox (ed.), *Humour in Anglo-Saxon Literature* (Cambridge, 2000), pp. 11–32; T.A. Shippey, 'Folly and Wisdom in Anglo-Saxon Humor', in ibid., pp. 33–48 at 35–8; Jonathan Wilcox, 'A Place to Weep: Joseph in the Beer-Room and Anglo-Saxon Gestures of Emotion', in Stuart McWilliams (ed.), *Saints and Scholars: New Perspectives on Anglo-Saxon Literature and Culture in Honour of Hugh Magennis* (Cambridge, 2012), pp. 14–32; and for further bibliography on weeping see Mills, this volume.

[53]   Julia Barrow, 'Demonstrative Behaviour and Political Communication in Anglo-Saxon England', *Anglo-Saxon England* 36 (2007): 127–50; Levi Roach, 'Public Rites and Public Wrongs: Ritual Aspects of Diplomas in Tenth- and Eleventh-century England', *Early Medieval Europe* 19 (2011): 182–203, at 191–2. See also Wilcox, this volume, on somatic gestures.

[54]   A recent study of identity with extremely interesting things to say about how inner motivations and intentions were 'read' within Benedictine monasticism and its texts is Katherine O'Brien O'Keeffe, *Stealing Obedience: Narratives of Agency and Identity in Later Anglo-Saxon England* (Toronto, 2012).

taking advantage of the opportunity for diversity provided by the form of an essay collection, they do not advance a single theory of Anglo-Saxon emotions; rather, they offer a variety of perspectives on the problems of tracing emotions and emotion concepts, and understanding the people of a distant period through their representations and our interpretations.

The Collection

The volume begins with chapters that explicitly address the theoretical foundation for reading Anglo-Saxon emotions, before proceeding to studies of particular emotions and individual texts. The opening chapter, by Antonina Harbus, directly confronts the central questions of what Anglo-Saxonists can gain from and contribute to contemporary developments in the study of emotions, especially in cognitive science, and addresses specifically how modern readers can understand and respond to the emotions encoded in Old English poems. Using recent research on emotional contagion and mirror neurons, she argues that many types of Old English poetic texts can invite intense, involved readings from both Anglo-Saxon and present-day audiences precisely because they produce emotional experiences based on a shared human biology. Next, Leslie Lockett offers an examination of a basic feature of the Anglo-Saxon emotional landscape that is, for modern Western readers, strikingly unfamiliar: the lack of a head/heart binary and the unitary mind–emotion concept expressed by the term *mod*. Adding a new dimension to the argument of her important recent book, Lockett discusses a small number of medical texts that do seem to ascribe some psychological role to the brain, arguing that this role is confined to the processing of sensory data and the emission of phlegm. The brain is the seat neither of rational thought nor of the *mod*. Daria Izdebska, Stephen Graham and Jonathan Wilcox then offer different perspectives on the problems of reading the linguistic and textual evidence. Izdebska, focusing on emotion vocabulary, proposes a methodology that tries to cope with the problems of cultural and linguistic ethnocentrism: a lexical, corpus-based, interdisciplinary approach that integrates findings from cognitive semantics, cultural anthropology and literary theory. The *TORN* word-family is used as a case study. Stephen Graham revisits the question of how to read emotion in poetic litotes – statements that actors do not experience certain emotional states. Such statements illuminate the ways Anglo-Saxons related emotions to each other, but they also highlight the need for audiences to exercise emotional intelligence in their reception of poetry. Jonathan Wilcox moves to another major topic in emotion: the role of the body. How are we to interpret references to somatic gestures? As an example, he looks at blushes, which need to be read carefully in the light of sources and glossary evidence.

Wilcox's focus on blushes leads into the first of the more narrowly focused papers, Tahlia Birnbaum's study of shame in the Old English psalter glosses. The chapter concludes that the shame conveyed in the Psalms had a wide emotional range, incorporating not only humiliation and humility, but also fear, awe and reverence. The present writer also looks at the Psalms, specifically the Old English prose versions of the first fifty psalms in the Paris Psalter. I argue that the Arguments that precede most of these psalms encourage the pious to inhabit them as expressions and templates for their emotional life, but I also ask what we can learn from the ways the translation sometimes impedes identification with the psalmist. Frances McCormack examines the specifically religious emotion of compunction and its manifestation in bloody tears. She shows how compunction operates in the Exeter Book poem *Christ*, offering a rich comparative context to demonstrate the distinctive ways *Christ* meshes shame and sadness to produce devotion. Kristen Mills and Erin Sebo both study emotion in *Beowulf*. Mills continues the theme of gesture with a discussion of Hrothgar's farewell to Beowulf, in which the king embraces the hero and weeps. Mills reviews previous scholarship and advances non-poetic comparanda, including the Old English Heptateuch, the Old English *Life of St Eustace* and the *Encomium Emmae Reginae*, to argue that Hrothgar need not be viewed as weak or unmanly in this scene. Sebo revisits the relationship of vengeance and grief with a subtle review of four great scenes of grieving in the poem, of which two issue in revenge and two do not. Judith Kaup then shows how *Maxims I* needs to be read in terms of an inclusive emotion–mind concept and seeks to educate the individual into both intellectual and emotional strength. Ronald Ganze applies neurological understandings of the relationship between trauma and memory to the Old English elegies. Finally, Mary Garrison's paper moves the discussion towards lived emotional experience, though retaining the collection's concern with textual interpretation. Her study examines the powerful emotionality, especially in relation to grief and loss, in Alcuin's letters, and relates it to the early separation experience of the monastic oblate. This chapter returns us explicitly to questions of the universality of emotion: it provides an opportunity both to use modern parallels and to pay heed to the particular meanings conferred on oblation in the early medieval period and their implications for oblation's emotional impact.

Together, the chapters in this volume trace multiple links in what I have suggested is the network of phenomena we label emotion. Individual contributions bring together questions of poetic convention with folk psychology; spontaneous bodily signals with social meaning; emotion scripts with translation; and the emotions texts describe with the emotions they provoke (for example, compunction). Themes that link chapters to each other include the role of emotion in religious devotion and the influence of religion on emotional experience; various aspects of Anglo-Saxon psychological lore, both popular and learned; emotion concepts at the meeting of Latin and Old English;

and ways of applying new insights from cognitive science and neurology to our texts. While the elegies and *Beowulf* retain their prominent place, rightly given their rich suggestiveness, the Psalms also turn out to be another particularly important focus. Within Anglo-Saxon studies, we hope that this volume will mark the emergence of emotion as a major theme, alongside the closely linked topics of identity, subjectivity and the mind. To the wider interdisciplinary audience we offer the collection as a sample of what scholars of Old English language and literature can offer: an intriguing set of questions about text, language and expressivity that are also tools for exploring the play of the local and the universal in this most familiar, yet most mysterious human experience.

Chapter 2
Affective Poetics: The Cognitive Basis of Emotion in Old English Poetry

Antonina Harbus

The representation of emotions has long been held as a typical feature of literary texts, especially those considered 'elegiac', but the ways in which those texts can also trigger emotional engagement and empathy in their audiences have only recently begun to be investigated technically. Recent cross-disciplinary inquiries are showing new ways of approaching a fuller understanding of these processes, as well as demonstrating the fruitfulness of an exchange between Literary Studies and Cognitive Science.

Scholars of Anglo-Saxon literature, used to crossing disciplinary boundaries, are particularly well poised to participate in the emerging dialogues between Literary Studies and philosophical, psychological, and scientific studies of emotion, in order to explore the capacity of literary texts to represent, simulate, and cause emotions. Like other literary scholars, they would find useful the concepts and methods deployed by Keith Oatley, one of the foremost scholars of the emotions, working in Cognitive Psychology. Oatley deploys pre-modern literary texts in instructive ways when he argues that, in audiences of Shakespeare's plays, emotion is instantiated: 'the words and emotions become the mind of the reader.'[1] More broadly, Oatley asserts as a fundamental truth the interrelationship of emotion and literature.[2] His and others' scientific study of emotion has produced findings of value to Anglo-Saxonists, literary scholars more broadly, as well as to cognitive scientists: most importantly the close interdependence of all cognitive functioning and emotion; and the biological priority of all affective experience (that is, emotions are experienced in the body before they are acknowledged cognitively).

The application of these ideas by textual scholars has permitted a fuller consideration of the literary experience, and has ushered in dynamic, fundamentally cognitive lines of inquiry to literary affect. Like the more linguistically focussed field, Cognitive Poetics, Cognitive Cultural Studies focusses on the mental

---

[1] Keith Oatley, 'Simulation of Substance and Shadow: Inner Emotions and Outer Behavior in Shakespeare's Psychology of Character', *College English* 33 (2006): 15–33 at 30.
[2] Keith Oatley, *Emotions: A Brief History* (Malden, 2004), esp. pp. 6 and 13.

processes at work during meaning-making, including the role of emotion in all aspects of the literary encounter. These and other cognitive approaches deploy Cognitive Science in order to explore the relationship between mind and meaning from the perspective that the mind and human emotion are the result of the close and dynamic interplay of culture and biology.[3] Literary scholars, like their scientific counterparts, are thereby finding new ways of considering the two related dimensions of literature and emotion, both of which are essentially cognitive and can be analysed via specifically cognitive approaches: how emotion is represented in literature, and how literary texts can trigger emotional reactions in readers. In turn, Literary Studies have much to offer the sciences in relation to the study of emotion. As Patrick Colm Hogan points out, 'literature provides a vast and largely unexplored body of data for emotion research [by psychologists and other cognitive scientists].'[4]

This intersection is particularly productive for the consideration of texts created in temporally or geographically remote societies, such as Anglo-Saxon England. From the perspective of the history of emotions, consideration of the affective potential of such texts, written down over 1000 years ago in a language that is the antecedent of our own, allows us to examine the role of culture in the experience of emotions. In turn, we can pursue how that experience and its literary representation might change over time, especially given differing deployments of language, including metaphorical constructions, but also how the emotional trigger works beyond the immediate context, via the consistent biological functioning of mirror neurons and emotional contagion – ideas from Cognitive Science discussed below. This deep historical perspective on the interplay of culture and biology can only advance cognitive studies of culture and literature. Instances from Old English poetry can allow us to ask whether the experience being represented in these medieval texts is the same as similarly named emotions experienced by us today; and more broadly, to what degree emotions are intelligible cross-culturally. We can thereby develop our understanding of the literary and cognitive dynamics of Old English poetry from this approach, as well as contribute to the cultural history of emotions.

---

[3] For a useful overview of this field, see Alan Richardson, 'Studies in Literature and Cognition: A Field Map', in Alan Richardson and Ellen Spolsky (eds), *The Work of Fiction: Cognition, Culture and Complexity* (Aldershot, 2004), pp. 1–29. A lengthy annotated bibliography by Alan Richardson and Mary Crane appears at https://www2.bc.edu/~richarad/lcb/home.html#bib (accessed 16 January 2013). See also Mark Turner, *Reading Minds: The Study of English in the Age of Cognitive Science* (Princeton, 1991); and David Herman (ed.), *Narrative Theory and the Cognitive Sciences* (Stanford, 2003); and issues of journals devoted to the subject: *Poetics Today* 23/1 (2002), and *The European Journal of English Studies* 9/2 (2005).

[4] Patrick Colm Hogan, *What Literature Teaches Us About Emotion* (Cambridge, 2011), p. 2.

Vernacular verse is especially suited to this treatment, given the Anglo-Saxon tendency to refer to the mind rather than to the individual or the body as the site of emotion and the recipient of fate, and taking into account the distinctively emotional quality of much of the extant poetry. Offsetting the distinctiveness of this poetry, and the culturally determined mind schema represented in it, are the evident similarities between early medieval and modern embodied affective experiences, and the consistency of conceptual processing in the brief evolutionary span between the Middle Ages and the present day. It is unsurprising, then, that Old English poetry shares with more recent literary texts a reliance on representations of consciousness, an embodied mind, and a hard-wired predisposition for narrative, as well as an expansive use of conceptual metaphor to communicate abstract ideas. Given the durability and transmission of these literary characteristics, audiences beyond the immediate context of composition are able to recognise and appreciate literary representations of embodied emotions, and to deploy the same combination of cognitive and emotional responses in literary processing. The discussion below combines insights from neuroscientific work on the role of emotion in human mental processes with literary approaches to the role of emotion in the aesthetics of reading, in order to chart a way into these difficult issues with the assistance of new disciplinary perspectives. First, though, these perspectives on the emotions need to be explored in order to clarify what precisely is under discussion, and how the parameters are drawn in different fields.

Cultural history was initially host to the recent interest in the history of emotions, which has focussed on the classical world,[5] but has paid some attention to medieval communities, with a focus on Scholasticism.[6] While this inquiry brings scholars from several fields together, most of them are from disciplinary backgrounds in the humanities, and treat emotion from an historical perspective that draws very little on Cognitive Science. Similarly, the interest paid to the subject of emotions by Cognitive Science is restricted by a lack of interest in the diachronic aspect of the affective life, and a delayed and still only minor interest in affective responses to the arts.[7] Given the distinctly separate nature of these lines of research, a more open consideration of the evidence available in the

---

[5] For example, see Robert A. Kaster, *Emotion, Restraint and Community in Ancient Rome* (Oxford, 2005); and David Konstan, *The Emotion of the Ancient Greeks: Studies in Aristotle and Classical Literature* (Toronto, 2006).

[6] See Barbara H. Rosenwein, *Emotional Communities in the Middle Ages* (Ithaca, 2006); and Peter King, 'Emotions in Medieval Thought', in Peter Goldie (ed.), *The Oxford Handbook of Philosophy of Emotion* (Oxford, 2010), pp. 167–87.

[7] Oatley, *Emotions: A Brief History*; and Jenefer Robinson, *Deeper than Reason: Emotion and its Role in Literature, Music, and Art* (Oxford, 2005). For the comparative linguistic point of view, see Anna Wierzbicka, *Emotions across Language and Cultures: Diversity and Universals* (Cambridge, 1999).

documents of earlier cultures provides a particularly fruitful potential for more actively interdisciplinary inquiry in a history of the emotions, in which ideas and methods from Cognitive Science play a role.

Emotions are attracting a great deal of interest in the many disciplines captured by the phrase 'Cognitive Science' – in Philosophy, Psychology, Anthropology, Sociology, Cognitive Neuroscience, and beyond.[8] In Cognitive Science, an emotion is commonly defined as 'a psychological state or process that functions in the management of goals', a state 'seen to serve important intracognitive and interpersonal functions'.[9] The concept of 'management' in these statements captures the foundational role of emotions in determining the entire quality of lived experience. Many cognitive psychologists, like Keith Oatley, favour this 'appraisal' theory to account for the source of emotions. This essentially functionalist theory holds that emotions are caused not by events, but by 'appraisal of events in relation to goals and plans, an idea that has found its way into cognitive studies of literature.'[10]

Similarly, in neuroscience, emotions are seen as 'brain states and bodily responses'[11] that act as 'managers of mental life, prompting heuristics that relate the flow of daily events to goals and social concerns'.[12] Goldie goes even further, denying that emotions such as grief are mental states, but rather processes that have a particularly narrative character.[13] These conceptions of emotions as essentially narrative managers or regulators whose remit extends beyond the life of mere feelings are especially interesting to the literary or cultural historian, as they underscore the interpenetration of the emotional life with cognitive functions, consciousness, and an enduring sense of the self. Research into the emotions from several fields has shown us that though we might recognise apparently separate emotions, such as happiness or anger, the emotional web is tangled and interconnected with other aspects of being, sensing, and interacting. For example, major streams within Psychology include the study of the way in which

---

[8] The situation has changed since Joseph LeDoux's observation that most cognitive scientists avoid the study of emotions (*The Emotional Brain: The Mysterious Underpinnings of Emotional Life* (London, 1998), pp. 33–5).

[9] Keith Oatley, 'Emotions', in R.A. Wilson and F.C. Keil (eds), *MIT Encyclopedia of the Cognitive Sciences* (Cambridge, MA, 1999), pp. 273–5, at 273.

[10] Lalita Pandit, 'Emotion, Perception and Anagnorisis in *The Comedy of Errors*: A Cognitive Perspective', *College Literature* 33 (2006): 94–126, at 95. For a challenge to the appraisal view, see Patrick Colm Hogan, 'On Being Moved: Cognition and Emotion in Literature and Film', in Lisa Zunshine (ed.), *Introduction to Cognitive Cultural Studies* (Baltimore, 2010), pp. 237–56.

[11] LeDoux, *The Emotional Brain*, p. 302.

[12] Oatley, 'Emotions', p. 275.

[13] Peter Goldie, *The Mess Inside: Narrative, Emotion, and the Mind* (Oxford, 2012), p. 61.

emotions are at the foundation of human motivational systems;[14] the distinction between emotions and feelings;[15] and between an emotional reaction and an empathetic response. Pragmatically, scholars in Psychology recognise seven basic emotions – fear, anger, disgust, sadness, joy, shame, and guilt[16] – though the list and the number of items on it changes depending on who is consulted, and many scholars distinguish primary from secondary or 'social' emotions.[17] Furthermore, cross-cultural studies have shown how difficult the terminology around the emotions is in relation to semantic range and translation across cultures.[18]

Scholars of literature and history can benefit from becoming aware of the emerging orthodoxies from these disciplinary studies of emotion. The prominent neuroscientist Antonio Damasio, for example, has shown convincingly that cognitive functioning and the experience of emotions are fully inter-reliant, and that emotions register in the body before they do in the mind. In a series of books that have had wide public as well as scientific appeal,[19] he has demonstrated that the emotional life is thoroughly embedded

---

[14] Notably, in the work of Silvan Tomkins. See E.V. Demos (ed.), *Exploring Affect: The Selected Writings of Silvan S. Tomkins* (Cambridge, 1995).

[15] Jesse Prinz, 'Are Emotions Feeling?', *Journal of Consciousness Studies* 12 (2005): 9–25.

[16] Morton L. Kringelbach, 'Emotions, Feelings, and Hedonics in the Human Brain', in Helena Wulff (ed.), *The Emotions: A Cultural Reader* (Oxford, 2007), pp. 37–60, at 41.

[17] Antonio Damasio includes on this list, embarrassment, jealousy, guilt, and shame, and lists six primary emotions, with surprise in the place of guilt and shame in the list above. See *The Feeling of What Happens: Body and Emotion in the Making of Consciousness* (New York, San Diego, and London, 1999), p. 51. He also posits the idea of 'background emotions' such as 'well-being or malaise, calm or tension' (p. 52).

[18] The literature is huge, and dominated by studies of particular groups of words and specific cultural contrasts. For the Cognitive Semantics view, see 'Happiness: Cognition, Experience, Language', *Collegium: Studies Across Disciplines in the Humanities and Social Sciences* 3 (2008), eds Heli Tissari, Anne Birgitta Pessi, and Mikko Salmela, at http://www.helsinki.fi/collegium/e-series/volumes/volume_3/index.htm (accessed 16 January 2013); and Zoltán Kövecses, 'Metaphor and Thought', in Raymond W. Gibbs (ed.), *The Cambridge Handbook of Metaphor and Thought* (Cambridge, 2008), pp. 380–96. For an Old English example, see Dirk Geeraerts and Caroline Gevaert, 'Hearts and (Angry) Minds in Old English', in Farzad Sharifian, René Dirven, Ning Yu, and Susanne Niemeier (eds), *Culture, Body, and Language: Conceptualizations of Internal Body Organs across Cultures and Languages* (Berlin and New York, 2008), pp. 319–47. For a broader overview of key concepts and readings in Cultural Studies, see Jennifer Harding and E. Deidre Pribram (eds), *Emotions: A Cultural Studies Reader* (London, 2009).

[19] *Descartes' Error: Emotion, Reason and the Human Brain* (New York, 1994); and *Looking for Spinoza: Joy, Sorrow, and the Feeling Brain* (Orlando, 2003). Damasio's most recent book advances from an evolutionary perspective even more evidence for a biological basis of human consciousness (*Self Comes to Mind: Constructing the Conscious Brain* (New York, 2010)). As with his other studies, he places memory at the centre of consciousness and the self.

in and interacts with cognitive functioning and embodied experience. He thereby confirms what William James postulated in 1884 (that emotions are the perceptions of changes in the body).[20] Furthermore, once it is granted that emotions are determined biologically, the implication follows that the evolved human brain behaves consistently and even automatically when it comes to emotions, notwithstanding some cultural variations: 'the considerable amount of individual variation and the fact that culture plays a role in shaping some inducers do not deny the fundamental stereotypicity, automaticity, and regulatory purpose of the emotions.'[21] This orthodoxy sensibly acknowledges, albeit in a perhaps minimalist way, the constitutive function of cultural context, but lays greatest emphasis on biological consistency. Consequently, many neuroscientists are currently investigating the brain functioning of emotion, and increasingly stress, as Damasio does, the role of memory in the process.[22] In particular, the reliance of consciousness on working memory implicates the role of emotions: 'feelings result when working memory is occupied with the fact that one's brain and body are in a state of emotional arousal.'[23]

As with these ideas, the Anglo-Saxonist, and literary scholars more broadly, can learn about the cross-cultural expression of emotions from other disciplines beyond Cognitive Science. Sociologists, for example, have long argued for the way in which societies condition the way in which emotions are processed,[24] and have settled on the culturally specific experience of emotions, and therefore 'how mistaken it would be to assume that emotions are unproblematically translatable from one culture or historical period to another'.[25] Similarly, cultural anthropologists insist upon the constitutive role of social context in the very experience of emotions, and have increasingly emphasised the discursive resources of a community as a factor: 'the most productive analytical approach to the cross-cultural study of emotion is to examine discourses on emotion and emotional discourses as social practices within diverse ethnographic contexts.'[26]

---

[20] Damasio, *The Feeling of What Happens*, pp. 287–8.

[21] Ibid., p. 51.

[22] 'Emotion has important effects on mental functions that are indisputably cognitive, such as memory, attention, and perception'. See Richard D. Lane et al., 'The Study of Emotion from the Perspective of Cognitive Neuroscience', in Richard D. Lane and Lynn Nadel (eds), *Cognitive Neuroscience of Emotion* (Oxford, 2000), pp. 3–11, at 4.

[23] Joseph LeDoux and Michael Rogan, 'Emotion and the Animal Brain', in Wilson and Keil (eds), *MIT Encyclopedia*, pp. 269–71, at 270.

[24] Cas Wouteres, 'The Civilizing of Emotions: Formalization and Informalization', in Debra Hopkins et al. (eds), *Theorizing Emotions: Sociological Explorations and Applications* (Frankfurt and New York, 2009), pp. 169–93.

[25] Robert A. LeVine, 'Afterword', in Wulff (ed.), *The Emotions: A Cultural Reader*, pp. 397–9, at 398.

[26] Lila Abu-Lughod and Catherine A. Lutz, 'Introduction: Emotion, Discourse, and the Politics of Everyday Life', in Lutz and Abu-Lughod (eds), *Language and the Politics of*

Literary scholars in turn have something valuable to communicate to scientists and social scientists. As Jonah Lehrer says, 'neuroscience is useful for describing the brain; and art is useful for describing our actual experience.'[27] Notwithstanding this interest in culture and emotion, scholars in the social sciences rarely consider literary texts as sources of information on the emotional life, even when considering emotions as 'psychosocial' phenomena in social life and popular culture,[28] though there are some notable exceptions. Keith Oatley and his colleagues, for instance, briefly discuss the ubiquitous textual focus on the emotions: 'written narrative literature, from ancient times to the present, concentrates on our emotional lives ... Publicly available stories give members of society common exemplars of action of emotion and of responsibility.'[29] Similarly, moral philosopher Martha Nussbaum approaches literature as a site in which philosophical and religious views on emotions are represented, in her model in which there is an ethical dimension to appraisal.[30] Other philosophers of emotion, such as Jenefer Robinson and Susan L. Feagin, attempt to describe how emotional reaction operates within the cognitive process of reading narrative fiction (and the appreciation of other art forms). Robinson's work, especially her study, *Deeper than Reason*, asserts that emotions tag highly salient features of narrative that cumulatively influence reader interpretation.[31] Feagin's conclusion, that 'feelings are a way of apprehending a work'[32] and that 'they reveal its complexity',[33] make sense from a literary aesthetic perspective, even though neither she nor Robinson pays any attention to literary criticism, nor to literary commentary on emotional response. On the other hand, there is a lack of cross-disciplinary inquiry from the other direction too: scholars working

---

Emotion (Cambridge, 1990), pp. 1–23, at 1.

[27] Jonah Lehrer, *Proust was a Neuroscientist* (Boston, 2008), p. 192.

[28] See, for example, Shelley Day-Sclater et al. (eds), *Emotion: New Psychosocial Perspectives* (London, 2009), 'Part II: Emotions in the Public Sphere'.

[29] Keith Oatley, Dacher Keltner, and Jennifer M. Jenkins, *Understanding Emotions*, 2nd edn (Oxford and Malden, 2006), p. 401. See also Keith Oatley, 'A Taxonomy of the Emotions of Literary Response and a Theory of Identification in Fictional Narrative', *Poetics* 23 (1994): 53–74.

[30] Martha C. Nussbaum, *Upheavals of Thought: The Intelligence of Emotions* (Cambridge, 2001), esp. pp. 457–613. Nussbaum's work, though influential, has been the subject of serious criticism. See, for example, Dorothy J. Hale, 'Aesthetics and the New Ethics: Theorizing the Novel in the Twenty-First Century', *PMLA* 124/3 (2009): 896–905.

[31] Noted above, n. 7. See chapter 2.

[32] Susan L. Feagin, 'Affects in Appreciation', in Goldie (ed.), *The Oxford Handbook of Philosophy of Emotion*, pp. 617–50, at 648.

[33] Ibid., p. 649.

explicitly on emotional histories often entirely ignore the biology and psychology of emotions, to focus exclusively instead on philosophical or theological ideas.[34]

Approaches to emotion and literature from outside Cognitive Science that are nevertheless avowedly cognitive are seeking to broach this divide between cognition and culture from the other direction. They consider how cognitive functioning shapes culture, and also how cognition is culturally determined, an influence that Damasio acknowledges ('learning and culture alter the expression of emotions and give emotions new meanings'[35]). Further, these humanities scholars consider how cognition and emotion are deeply interrelated, and how literary texts can model that interaction, and indeed embody cognitive structures.[36] More broadly, there is now some consideration of the emotional pull of the literary text, of how 'fiction gives people the chance to practice their emotional connections with other people.'[37] Scholars working at the interdisciplinary nexus of science, social science, and the arts are coming to appreciate the rich potential of considering the complex inter-reliance of culture, cognition, and emotion.

For literary scholars, the fictional, imaginative, and figurative aspects of textual meaning provide further dimensions to the question of whether we engage with representations of emotions in the same way as we do with real-life emotional encounters. The cognitive literary scholar, Patrick Colm Hogan, for instance, argues against the appraisal theory in his discussion of emotions experienced in fictional encounters.[38] Emotional reactions to fiction, Hogan argues, use the same sort of neurologically created 'concrete images' and 'emotional memories'[39] that determine real-life emotional responses. There are implications for genre and story shape too, in that, according to Hogan, human emotional systems determine narrative structures.[40] He recruits ideas from neurobiology to

---

[34] For example, Ramsay MacMullen, *Feelings in History, Ancient and Modern* (Claremont, 2003); and Simo Knuuttila, *Emotions in Ancient and Medieval Philosophy* (Oxford, 2004).

[35] Damasio, *The Feeling of What Happens*, p. 51.

[36] Lalita Pandit and Patrick Colm Hogan, 'Introduction: Morsels and Modules: On Embodying Cognition in Shakespeare's Plays', *College English* 33/1 (2006): 1–13; and Evelyn Tribble, *Cognition in the Globe: Memory and Attention in Shakespeare's Theatre* (London, 2011).

[37] Blakey Vermeule, *Why Do We Care About Literary Characters?* (Baltimore, 2010), p. 165. Vermeule's argument bears some similarity to that of Lisa Zunshine, *Why We Read Fiction: Theory of Mind and the Novel* (Colombus, 2006), p. 164: 'Fiction helps us to pattern in newly nuanced ways our emotions and perceptions', though the latter's main focus is Theory of Mind rather than the emotions.

[38] Hogan, 'On Being Moved'.

[39] Ibid., p. 246.

[40] Patrick Colm Hogan, *Affective Narratology: The Emotional Structure of Stories* (Lincoln and London, 2011), p. 1.

argue this symbiotic relationship. In this schema, imagination, when engaged in reading or viewing a text, creates a distance between the 'emotional object' represented in that text and 'the egocentric space of direct action'[41] – the range of proximity that triggers a direct response. In other words, the reading brain responds to perceived spatial distance, senses a buffer zone that allows us to experience an emotion, but less directly than in real life, and with some degree of cultural variation. More broadly, Hogan has demonstrated that 'literature may play a role in fostering openness to empathetic response',[42] an idea with enormous potential for combination with existing understandings of the social functions and rhetorical mechanics of literature, and one that accommodates the persistent preoccupation of literary texts, including those produced in Anglo-Saxon England, with grief and deeply felt emotions. Gregory Currie, on the other hand, presents a different solution to the problem of how emotions are engaged via fiction, but likewise accounts for the apparent distance between emotional trigger and reaction. He suggests that a virtual reader is created in the mind of the reader, a 'reader of fact', who reacts to the characters and events of the narrative, whose perspective we use as a guide for emotional interaction.[43]

Other scholars who study how emotion can be a product of fictionality focus on popular culture, especially film. Noël Carroll, for instance, explores the 'affective address of popular fiction',[44] and Amy Coplan examines the distinctive capacity of film to trigger genuine emotional reactions.[45] Both scholars emphasise the powerful emotional triggers of audiovisual cues, especially facial expressions, and come up with different explanations for the viewer's emotional response. Carroll denies that, as some scholars argue, consumers of fiction simulate the emotional experience of characters, but rather 'mobilize an affective stance' that is distinctly produced in response to a fiction whose content we imagine rather than believe.[46] Coplan prefers the theory of 'emotional contagion', whereby an automatic affective response is produced when we observe the experience of emotion in others, a phenomenon requiring the sensory input of a visual experience as occurs when viewing a film; literary fictions, on the other hand,

---

[41] Ibid., p. 248.
[42] Hogan, *What Literature Teaches Us*, p. 74.
[43] Gregory Currie, 'The Paradox of Caring: Fiction and the Philosophy of Mind', in Mette Hjort and Sue Laver (eds), *Emotion and the Arts* (Oxford, 1997), pp. 63–77, at 71.
[44] Noël Carroll, 'On the Ties that Bind: Characters, the Emotions, and Popular Fictions', in William Irwin and Jorge J.E. Gracia (eds), *Philosophy and the Interpretation of Pop Culture* (Lanham, 2007), pp. 89–116, at 89.
[45] Amy Coplan, 'Catching Characters' Emotions: Emotional Contagion Responses to Narrative Fiction Film', *Film Studies* 8 (2006): 26–38.
[46] Carroll, 'On the Ties that Bind', p. 91.

can produce reactions that are more cognitive, but less affective because they produce experiences more removed from real-world sensations.[47]

Coplan, like other scholars working in this area, distinguishes emotional contagion from empathy, 'a complex and unique imaginative process involving both cognition and affect',[48] which is why literary narratives can produce empathy.[49] Empathy, or 'a vicarious, spontaneous sharing of affect', can be created through character identification and emotional simulation, primarily via the activation of mirror neurons,[50] which function pragmatically to assist in the understanding of the actions and emotions of others. Mirror neurons allow us to experience the emotional meaning of our interpersonal encounters – and perhaps also experience empathy – by producing 'reflexive processing of the sensory aspects linked to how they appear in the facial expressions or acts of others'.[51] Clearly, imagination can produce images in the brain of facial expressions that in turn trigger the same sort of emotive mirroring response, even in an acknowledged fictional encounter.[52] Fritz Breithaupt, in his fuller treatment of this area, covers four main models of empathy, including one from narratology, concluding that 'narrative fiction can only exist because it invites, triggers, channels, controls, and manages empathy.'[53] Other theories of affective response to literary fictions often rely on one of Breithaupt's models, Simulation Theory. For instance, Meskin and Weinberg cite the orthodoxy that 'engaging with fiction is a matter of "off-line simulation"', before offering their own modification that relies on the idea that fictions trigger the creation of possible worlds in the mind of the recipient.[54]

In order to develop these ideas and this cross-disciplinary potential further, it would be useful to consider how a modern reader can have an emotional

---

[47] Coplan, 'Catching Characters' Emotions', p. 35.
[48] Ibid., p. 31.
[49] For a good overview on philosophical perspectives on readers' empathetic engagement with fictional narratives and characters, see Amy Coplan, 'Empathetic Engagement with Narrative Fictions', *Journal of Aesthetics and Art Criticism* 62 (2004): 141–52. See also Noël Carroll, 'On Some Affective Relations between Audiences and the Characters in Popular Fictions', in Amy Coplan and Peter Goldie (eds), *Empathy: Philosophical and Psychological Perspectives* (Oxford, 2011), pp. 162–84.
[50] Suzanne Keen, 'A Theory of Narrative Empathy', *Narrative* 14 (2006): 207–36, at 208; and Carroll, 'On Some Affective Relations', pp. 177–80.
[51] Giacomo Rizzolatti and Corrado Sinigaglia, *Mirrors in the Brain: How Our Minds Share Actions and Emotions*, trans. Frances Anderson (Oxford, 2008), p. 190.
[52] See Graham McFee, 'Empathy: Interpersonal vs Artistic', in Coplan and Goldie (eds), *Empathy: Philosophical and Psychological Perspectives*, pp. 185–208.
[53] Fritz Breithaupt, 'How is it Possible to Have Empathy? Four Models', in P. Leverage et al. (eds), *Theory of Mind and Literature* (West Lafayette, 2011), pp. 273–88, at 274.
[54] Aaron Meskin and Jonathan M. Weinberg, 'Emotions, Fiction, and Cognitive Architecture', *British Journal of Aesthetics* 43 (2003): 18–34.

reaction to a medieval text, in combination with an intellectual and aesthetic experience produced by that literary encounter. The Anglo-Saxon literary corpus, and in particular its fictional representations of emotional experience, is readable to us, but only via the process of linguistic and cultural relocation that operates through translation into present-day English. Nevertheless, a core degree of intelligibility remains, because we share the human experience of an embodied mind and, apparently, a hard-wired predisposition for narrative, a distinctly 'narrative sense of self', and reliance on narrative structure for memory and imagination.[55] Evolutionary proximity means that the similarity of our embodied emotional experiences with other humans from remote cultures makes cross-cultural intelligibility possible.

The literature of Anglo-Saxon England has been analysed with respect to emotions, but not from a particularly cognitive perspective. Simon Nicholson has studied abstract Old English nouns connoting moods, to conclude that there is evidence in the corpus of both 'psychological and somatic expressions of emotional distress', thereby disputing the idea that such a distinction is relatively recent.[56] Other studies have been similarly mainly lexical.[57] But the archaeology of emotions in Anglo-Saxon England, and the capacity of its literature to produce an emotional engagement, even an empathetic response, is

---

[55] The narrative quality of the sense of self is now a widely held idea in Cognitive Science. See Antonina Harbus, 'Exposure to Life-writing as an Impact on Autobiographical Memory', *Memory Studies* 20 (2011): 1–15, esp. pp. 2–4, and Goldie, *The Mess Inside*.

[56] Simon Nicholson, 'The Expression of Emotional Distress in Old English Prose and Verse', *Culture, Medicine and Psychiatry* 19 (1995): 327–38, at 337.

[57] Edwin N. Gorsuch, 'Emotional Expression in a Manuscript of Bede's *Historia Ecclesiastica*: British Library Cotton Tiberius A XIV', *Semiotic* 83 (1991): 227–49; Edgar C. Polomé, 'Some Comments on the Vocabulary of Emotion in Germanic', in G.F. Carr, W. Harbert, and L. Zhang (eds), *Interdigitations: Essays for Irmengard Rauch* (Bern, 1998), pp. 129–40; Malgorzata Fabiszak, 'A Semantic Analysis of Emotion Terms in Old English', *Studia Anglica Posnaniensia* 34 (1999): 133–46; Michiko Ogura, 'Verbs of Emotion with Reflexive Constructions', in Christian Kay and Louise Sylvester (eds), *Lexis and Texts in Early English: Studies Presented to Jane Roberts* (Amsterdam and Atlanta, 2001), pp. 203–12; Hans-Jürgen Diller, 'The Growth of the English Emotion Lexicon: A First Look at the *Historical Thesaurus of English*', in Katja Lenz and Ruth Möhlig (eds), *Of Dyuersitie & Chaunge of Language: Essays Presented to Manfred Görlach on the Occasion of His 65th Birthday*, Anglistische Forschungen 308, Winter (Heidelberg, 2002), pp. 103–14; Michiko Ogura, 'Words of EMOTION in Old and Middle English', in Javier E. Díaz Vera (ed.), *A Changing World of Words: Studies in English Historical Lexicography, Lexicology and Semantics* (Amsterdam and Atlanta, 2002), pp. 484–99; Michiko Ogura, 'Words of Emotion in Old and Middle English Translations of Boethius's *De Consolatione Philosophiae*', in Akio Oizumi, Jacek Fisiak, and John Scahill (eds), *Text and Language in Medieval English Prose: A Festschrift for Tadao Kubouch* (Frankfurt am Main, 2005), pp. 183–206; Michiko Ogura, 'Old and Middle English Verbs of Emotion', *Poetica* 66 (2006): 53–72; and Hans Sauer, 'Ælfric and Emotion', *Poetica* 66 (2006): 37–52.

as yet little explored. More broadly, the history of emotions can be advanced by a consideration of the emotional content and expression of Old English verse. To indicate how we might undertake such a project, I shall briefly suggest below how these ideas, particularly the shared cognitive basis of meaning and feeling, might be approached in relation to medieval literary texts. I take as my examples extracts from the elegiac texts, *The Wife's Lament* and *The Wanderer*.[58]

The Wife's Lament, one of the so-called elegies of The Exeter Book, is a first-person narration that expresses emotional anguish:

> forþon ic æfre ne mæg
> þære modceare   minre gerestan,
> ne ealles þæs longaþes   þe mec on þissum life begeat.
> (*The Wife's Lament*, ll. 39b–41)

[There I can sit for a summer-long day, there I can weep for my miseries, for many hardships. Therefore I can never rest from my anxieties of mind, nor from all this longing that this life has begotten for me.][59]

This text invites empathetic engagement from its audience through emotional contagion, made possible through the combination of imagery produced in the mind in the process of making sense, and the embodied emotional response produced automatically while entertaining a recognisably affecting scenario created during that act of interpretation. In this brief comment, weeping, anguish, and longing are all foregrounded, and grief is represented as active, encompassing, and time-consuming. The reader is required to call up not only narrative schema, but also emotional schema, created from memories, personal experience, and embodied feeling, to fill out the sketchy scenario, make sense of the sequence of ideas, and account for a potential cause for such extreme abandonment to the emotional life. In doing so, the reader enacts feeling, which is implicated in cognitive processing, and thereby becomes emotionally engaged in the narrative. Because we now know that cognition and affect are mutually reliant, it is possible to see how a reader can respond emotionally to culturally remote, poetically communicated fictional narrative, a process that occurs at both the specific and general levels.

---

[58] For a fuller discussion of what ideas and methods from Cognitive Science can do for Anglo-Saxon studies, see Antonina Harbus, *Cognitive Approaches to Old English Poetry* (Cambridge, 2012).

[59] All line numbers to Old English poems refer to the ASPR (*The Anglo-Saxon Poetic Records: A Collective Edition*, ed. George Philip Krapp and Elliott Van Kirk Dobbie, 6 vols (New York, 1931–53)). All translations are my own.

The poem invites universal recognition and provides an exemplification of affective reaction. The speaker generalises typical emotional reactions to particular situations, which are then specified by attributions made to 'my lord':

> A sceal geong mon   wesan geomormod,
> heard heortan geþoht,   swylce habban sceal
> bliþe gebæro,   eac þon breostceare,
> sinsorgna gedreag,   sy æt him sylfum gelong
> eal his worulde wyn,   sy ful wide fah
> feorres folclondes,   þæt min freond siteð
> under stanhliþe   storme behrimed,
> wine werigmod,   wætre beflowen
> on dreorsele.   Dreogeð se min wine
> micle modceare;   he gemon to oft
> wynlicran wic.   Wa bið þam þe sceal
> of langoþe   leofes abidan.
>
> (*The Wife's Lament*, ll. 42–53)

[Ever must the young man be sorrowful, and the thought of his heart harsh. Likewise, he must have a cheerful demeanour, along with the care of the heart, a constant multitude of sorrows. May all his worldly joy be dependent on him alone, may he be outlawed widely in a distant tribal land, since my friend sits under a stony cliff, covered with hoar-frost by the storm, my heart-weary lord, surrounded by water in a dreary hole. He, my lord, experiences great sorrow of mind; he remembers too often a more joyful dwelling. Woe it is for the one who must await the dear one in longing.]

After the personal expression of feeling in the first quotation, the focus moves to an account of the state of mind imagined in the loved one, then proceeds on to a generalised account of feeling and response. The text thereby demonstrates the progression from the recognition of feeling, to imagination and empathy, to universal emotional response. The line 'Dreogeð se min wine / micle modceare' both represents enacted theory of mind, and requires the reader to attribute empathetic imagining to the narrator who is recounting this process. To keep up with the rapid traversal of this emotional terrain, the reader needs to engage memory, imagination, empathy, and embodied feeling, as well as cognitively processing the shifting focalisation into and beyond the minds of the narrator and the object of her affection.

As these extracts show, a distinction between hidden inner and visible outer lives is conceptualised and represented textually, as is a mind/self division, phenomena familiar in everyday existence, and subject to cognitive theorisation. Moreover, memory can be activated, or managed to create a motivated emotional response, here both negative and positive, producing respectively grief and joy. As Hogan argues, 'grief results from the sharp conflict between reality and spontaneous expectation derived from imagination.'[60] *The Wife's Lament* textually focuses on depicting this disjunction, and typically fits it into a narrative account of the autobiographical self, one that invites an empathetic response. As Goldie argues, grieving is best understood in terms of narrative thinking:

> An emotion ... is a relatively complex state, involving past and present episodes of thoughts, feelings, and bodily changes, dynamically related to a narrative part of a person's life, together with dispositions to experience further emotional episodes, and to act out of the emotion, and to express that emotion.[61]

This narrative constitution of the self is largely informed by a dynamic interplay among emotion, knowledge, and autobiographical memory: 'Our memories are infused with what we now know, and how we now feel about what happened in light of what we now know.'[62] In cases of grieving, this interplay naturally results in a form of communication or expression that enacts the 'special explanatory, revelatory, and expressive powers of narratives, whether just thought through in narrative thinking, or whether publically expressed to others, in writing or in speech.'[63] This spontaneous combination of memory, narrative, and emotion can provide the impetus for the creation of affective poetry, uttered by a speaker who is apparently speaking to himself or to an unidentified audience, as in Old English texts such as *The Wife's Lament*. The reader or hearer of this text, even at a distant cultural remove, is invited to engage in narrative thinking and emotional reaction, and to recruit memory, imagination, and synthetic reasoning, a process made possible by the shared cognitive basis of meaning and feeling.

The Wanderer similarly enacts the process of emotional remembering, and thereby invites affective engagement – the activation of mirror neurons as a result of the cognitive process of interpreting narrative and poetic imagery – and in turn facilitating emotional contagion from that act of imagination. When the speaker's

>   cearo bið geniwad
> þam þe sendan sceal   swiþe geneahhe
> ofer waþema gebind   werigne sefan.
>
>   (*The Wanderer*, ll. 55b–7)

[care is renewed for the one who must very often send his weary mind over the shackle of the waves]

---

[60] Hogan, *What Literature Teaches Us*, p. 123.
[61] Peter Goldie, *The Emotions: A Philosophical Exploration* (Oxford, 2000), p. 144.
[62] Goldie, *The Mess Inside*, p. 54.
[63] Ibid., p. 75.

he is generalising an experience that invites an emotional and potentially an empathetic response, subject to cognitive analysis. Briefly, the combined mental effort of distinguishing and keeping track of the 'one' and the 'mind', and the processing of the metaphor, 'shackle of the waves', recruits emotional investment and embodied feeling, both of which are subject to biological continuity as well as some cultural specificity. The brain attempts to reconcile the information provided according to emotional experience and narrative schema, resolving questions such as why (repetitive, enforced) remembering creates sorrow, and why social isolation has been imposed. This interpretive process requires the inclusion of provisional information, strategically deployed in response to textual cues, to fill the conceptual gaps, but also the recollection of how it feels to be burdened by strong emotion. The motivated selection of information from memory, imagination, and embodied experience is a synthetic process that requires complex cognitive handling. In taking this effort, we read – and feel – across time and location, as a result of the consistency of human emotional arousal, and the reliance on memory and narrative thinking. What is interesting to note here is that the familiar sensation of the self, fragmented by emotional response, is not only captured in poetic language and narrative creation, but is the chief focus of that literary expression, in a text that dramatises cognitive and emotional management in action. As a result, the experience of emotion as the perception of change in the body is evoked through figurative expression and narrative discourse, and the text acquires an emotional pull grounded in recognisable embodied feeling.

Poetic products from remote cultures can, when considered in light of recent findings in Cognitive Science on the sensation and expression of emotions, provide a deeply diachronic viewpoint on pervasive, perpetual, traditional, or biologically determined character of the affective life. These matters can be considered both in terms of the representation of emotional experience in literary texts, but also in capacity of those texts to trigger or invite the recollection of such experiences or sensations: both *The Wife's Lament* and *The Wanderer* appear to rely on the production as well as the representation of emotion.

These examples represent only a small sample; many types of Old English poetic texts, like other medieval and other poems, portray recognisable human emotions, and in turn invite emotional reactions from readers today, as they presumably did their contemporary audiences. We can distinguish the intense and conflicted emotional texture of *The Wife's Lament* and *The Wanderer* precisely because we are familiar with the way in which emotions function in the management of goals and to stimulate action. These texts can arouse intense, involved readings from a modern audience because they model emotional reactions and narratively produce emotional experiences and genuine sensations, notwithstanding their acknowledged cultural remoteness, and even their acknowledged fictionality. This readerly implication, or emotional investment, arises from rich, textured features within discourse that can be analysed in the context of ideas about emotion that are still emerging from the cognitive sciences. Such subjective investment arises from the evocation of recognisable embodied emotions, producing a spontaneous sharing of affect, in which imagination and memory play a role.

As the above examples show, a consideration of the emotional basis of the mental processes activated during textual interpretation provides an explanation for cross-cultural intelligibility, as well as the affective capacity of a fictional narrative. Because cognitive processes grounded in the emotional life determine both individual experience and also literary structure and response, the broad continuities in human emotional experience over time ensure the similarity of the emotional quality of textual creation and reception. Notwithstanding this consistency, emotions are subject at least in part to cultural impact, so can be studied in the context of cultural history. More specifically, the textual capacity both to represent the flux of emotional states and also to trigger an emotional reaction in the reader provides a rich resource for a wide range of studies of the emotional life.

Given this inter-reliance of culture, cognition, and literary expression, scholars of earlier cultures can and should contribute to a fuller diachronic examination of the affective potential of literary texts, as well as the capacity of these texts to represent human emotional experience that is both embodied (and therefore biologically consistent) and also subject to the localised shaping power of a specific cultural context. Scholars open to these cross-disciplinary currents can thereby take part in motivated and productive analyses of both the textual representation and evocation of emotion, and more precisely consider how a text might invite empathy via the shared cognitive/emotional basis of meaning-making in both proximate and distant literary responses.

Chapter 3
The Limited Role of the Brain in Mental and Emotional Activity According to Anglo-Saxon Medical Learning

Leslie Lockett

Among Modern English idioms for narrating emotional experiences, one of the most productive ascribes emotions and passions to the heart or breast, and rational thought to the head or brain, resulting in either a complementary or antagonistic relationship between head and heart. This convention is several centuries old: abundant evidence attests to its currency in the Elizabethan era. In Shakespeare's *Antony and Cleopatra*, for instance, Enobarbus sharply criticizes Antony for allowing his courage to undermine his reason:

> A diminution in our captain's brain
> Restores his heart. When valour preys on reason,
> It eats the sword it fights with.[1]
>
> (III, xiii, 203–5)

The first sonnet of Sidney's *Astrophil and Stella*, likewise, portrays the suppliant lover seeking 'Some fresh and fruitful showers upon my sunburnt brain' as he reads and mimics other poets' verses; when this fails to woo his beloved, the lover's Muse commands him, 'look in thy heart and write', contrasting the creativity and genuine emotion of the heart with the erudite verses begotten by the brain.[2] The Middle English period also provides attestations of the conventional opposition of head and heart. For example, *Piers Plowman* (A-text) localizes Inwit 'intellect' or 'conscience' in the head:

> Inwyt in þe heuid is, and an help to þe soule,
> For þoruȝ his connyng is kept *Caro* and *Anima*
> In rewele and in resoun.
>
> (X.49–51)

---

[1] William Shakespeare, *Antony and Cleopatra*, ed. John Wilders (London, 1995), p. 225.
[2] Sir Philip Sidney, *Astrophil and Stella*, Sonnet 1, lines 8 and 16, in Katherine Duncan-Jones (ed.), *Sir Philip Sidney* (Oxford, 1989), p. 153.

[Intellect is in the head and an aid to the soul, for through its skill Flesh and Soul are kept in proper conduct and in sound judgement.][3]

Opposing the wholesome influence of Inwit is the heart, or in this instance, the heart's blood:

> For whan blood is bremere þanne brayn, þan is Inwit bounde,
> And ek wantoun and wilde, wiþoute any resoun.
>
> (X.56–8)

[For when the blood is more powerful than the brain, then Intellect is hindered, and also reckless and wild, without any sound judgement.]

Numerous additional examples could be adduced to demonstrate that English narratives of emotional experience and internal conflict have relied upon the metonymic mapping of different kinds of thought onto the brain and the heart since at least the fourteenth century.

However, if this line of inquiry is extended further back into the Old English period, evidence for the head–heart opposition dries up entirely. I maintain that that this is because the Anglo-Saxons, especially those of the pre-Conquest period, did not localize the mind (Old English *mod*) in the organ of the brain. Evidence of pre-Conquest understandings of the brain is found in literary, exegetical, and medical texts; the present chapter emphasizes the medical evidence, which attributes to the brain a peripheral role in psychological activity but does not characterize the brain as the seat of the *mod*.[4] Though this is a subtle distinction, it is a meaningful one for historians of emotions and historians of the English language, because as long as English speakers did not localize rational thought in the brain, they could not have developed or adopted the metonymic mapping that pits the rational head against the impassioned heart. Thus the origins of this convention must be sought in later centuries or other languages.

Anglo-Saxon Concepts of Mind

To begin, it is useful to clarify what most Old English authors meant by *mod* and its poetic synonyms *hyge*, *sefa*, and *ferhð*. Modern English speakers

---

[3] A.V.C. Schmidt (ed.), *Piers Plowman: A Parallel-Text Edition of the A, B, C and Z Versions*, vol.1: Text (London, 1995), pp. 376–7. Except where credited otherwise, all translations from Middle English, Old English, and Latin are my own.

[4] I plan, in a separate study, to supplement the findings of this chapter with an analysis of the literary and exegetical evidence for Anglo-Saxon views of the brain.

distinguish between the mental and the emotional according to the degree of rationality attributed to a particular thought or psychological state, and when we conceptualize 'mind' we usually foreground rational faculties and implicitly marginalize emotions. In contrast, the *mod* of Old English narrative encompasses the faculties of reason, memory, imagination, deliberation, will, and governance of the body, along with the whole range of emotions and passions.[5] Old English narrative does not ascribe more rational thoughts to the *mod* and less rational thoughts to some other entity; the conceptual divide between reason and emotion that we rely heavily upon in Modern English was little used by Old English authors and indeed seems to have been limited to the few texts that adhere closely to Latin discourses on the tripartition of the soul into rational, impassioned, and appetitive faculties.[6] Moreover, the *mod* differs significantly from the entity called *mens* or *animus* in Latin, which in the patristic tradition usually acts as the rational faculty of the transcendent soul (*anima*), and accordingly shares in the properties and experiences of the *anima*. In contrast, Old English narratives depict the *mod* tightly bound to its home in the chest cavity except when it is said to depart during episodes of remembering or imagining; it does not share in the afterlife experience of heaven and hell, which belongs to the *sawol* (soul). Conversely, as long as it remains in the living body, the *sawol* of Old English narrative does not participate in the *mod*'s daily activities such as cogitation, perception, emotion, and regulation of the body's actions.[7]

A third crucial distinction pertains to the localization of the *mod*. In the present-day West, even those who believe that human beings possess a non-material component (be it the mind, the soul, the self, etc.) acknowledge that psychological activity largely depends upon the organ of the brain; most would say that thoughts and feelings are localized there. But in Old English texts, the *mod* is routinely localized in the chest cavity, adjacent to or within the heart.[8] A small minority of Anglo-Saxon authors challenged this heart-centred concept of mind, almost exclusively in the context of theological discourse (as opposed

---

[5] Leslie Lockett, *Anglo-Saxon Psychologies in the Vernacular and Latin Traditions* (Toronto, 2011), p. 34 and n. 67; Malcolm Godden, 'Anglo-Saxons on the Mind', in Michael Lapidge and Helmut Gneuss (eds), *Learning and Literature in Anglo-Saxon England: Studies Presented to Peter Clemoes on the Occasion of his Sixty-fifth Birthday* (Cambridge, 1985), pp. 271–98, at 289 and 291.

[6] Lockett, pp. 322, 415; Paul E. Szarmach, 'Alfred, Alcuin, and the Soul', in Robert Boenig and Kathleen Davis (eds), *Manuscript, Narrative, Lexicon: Essays on Literary and Cultural Transmission in Honor of Whitney F. Bolton* (Lewisburg, PA, 2000), pp. 127–48; and Godden, pp. 296–8.

[7] Again, a minority of Old English authors who depended heavily on Latin discursive sources (particularly Ælfric and the author of the *Old English Boethius* and *Soliloquies*) are excepted from this generalization: see Godden, pp. 274–85.

[8] Lockett, pp. 54–87.

to narrative or proverbial contexts), yet the concept of mind that they advanced was not brain-centred, as we might expect, but instead followed the Platonist–Christian principle that the *mens* was part of the incorporeal *anima* and hence not localizable anywhere in the body.[9]

When all these characteristics of the *mod* are accounted for, only one piece of Old English textual evidence unambiguously localizes the *mod* in the head. In the riddle-dialogue *Adrian and Ritheus*, likely composed in the first half of the twelfth century, one interlocutor says, 'Saga me hwær byð mannes mod',[10] and the other replies, 'Ic þe secge, on þam heafde and gæð ut þurh þone muð'.[11] Other texts that seemingly advance a brain-centred concept of mind are, on closer inspection, susceptible to anachronistic misinterpretation. For instance, the poem *Maxims I* advises, 'Hond sceal heofod inwyrcan' (l. 67).[12] To present-day readers, conditioned to expect that the head houses the mind, this sounds like a metonymic way to say that the rational mind (in the head) ought to hold sway over the deeds of the limbs (including the hands).[13] However, some fifty lines later in *Maxims I*, the 'thoughts of the mind' are definitively localized in the breast:

> Hyge sceal gehealden,   hond gewealden,
> seo sceal in eagan,   snyttro in breostum,
> þær bið þæs monnes   modgeþoncas.
> (*Maxims I*, ll. 121–3)

[The mind ought to be restrained, and the hand ought to be governed; seeing must reside in the eye and wisdom in the breast, where a man's mind-thoughts are.]

The speaker not only localizes thought in the breast, but he also clarifies how the head sways the actions of the hand: it receives stimuli through the sense organs. 'The head must influence the hand' because the head can see, not because it can engage in deliberative thought.

The foregoing example illustrates a principle that I would like to apply to the medical texts of Anglo-Saxon England: our own brain-centred concept of mind leads easily to anachronistic assumptions about the role of the head in Old English depictions of psychological states and events. Where an Old

---

[9] Ibid., pp. 179–227 and 440–43.

[10] 'Tell me where a person's mind is.' *Adrian and Ritheus* §23, ed. James E. Cross and Thomas D. Hill, *The Prose* Solomon and Saturn *and* Adrian and Ritheus (Toronto, 1982), p. 38. On the date of composition, see ibid., pp. 15 and 18.

[11] 'I tell you, it is in the head and it goes out through the mouth.'

[12] 'The head must influence the hand.' George Phillip Krapp and Elliot Van Kirk Dobbie (eds), *The Exeter Book*, ASPR 3 (New York, 1936), pp. 156–63.

[13] See, for instance, Antonette diPaolo Healey, 'Old English *hēafod* "head": A Lofty Place?' *Poetica* 75 (2011): 29–48, at 34.

English author may have meant only that the head is where sensory data enters the body, we hastily infer that the *mod* is housed in the head, even though the highly personal and complex *mod* clearly encompasses much more than mere sense perception. With this caution in mind, I turn now to the medical literature copied and composed in Anglo-Saxon England, which implicates the head and the brain in psychological events and states, not as the organic seat of the *mod* but, as I shall show, as the source of harmful humours that emanate from the brain and derange the mind.

Latin Medical Cephalocentrism and its Reception in Early Medieval England

A recent study by James McIlwain demonstrates that many of the ultimate Latin sources of the surviving Old English medical literature localize the soul (*anima*) and certain specific mental functions in the brain.[14] For example, the chapter on epilepsy in the *Practica Alexandri* states, 'Capitis enim est ista passio ubi princeps omnium sensuum est intellectus ... [P]ossideat templum id est cerebrum ubi anima habitat'.[15] According to the pseudo-Galenic *Liber tertius*, the brain (*cerebrum*) is the organ 'in quo principaliter anima habitat'.[16] In his *Epitome altera*, Vindicianus teaches that numerous slender channels run throughout the brain, and we have more of these channels than other animals: 'ideoque omnibus illis sapientiores sumus, fistulas plus habendo unde intellectus nobis aduenit, uisus auditus odoratus et gustus'.[17] More widely circulated in Anglo-Saxon England than any of the aforementioned medical treatises were the selected medical doctrines contained in Isidore of Seville's encyclopedic *Etymologiae*. While discussing the five senses, Isidore describes an extramission theory of vision, which implicates 'a luminous inner spirit that proceeds from

---

[14] James T. McIlwain, 'Brain and Mind in Anglo-Saxon Medicine', *Viator* 37 (2006): 103–12.

[15] 'This is a disorder of the head, where the first apprehension of all the senses exists ... It may besiege the sanctuary where the soul resides, that is, the brain.' *Practica Alexandri yatros greci cum expositione glose interlinearis Jacobi de partibus et Januensis in margine posite* (Lyon 1504), fol. 10v; available online at http://cisne.sim.ucm.es/record=b1784077*spi, and qtd in part by McIlwain, p. 105.

[16] 'in which the soul primarily resides'. I quote the *Liber tertius* as preserved in Cambridge, Peterhouse, MS 251 (s. xi), from the transcription provided by McIlwain, p. 105.

[17] 'and therefore we are more knowledgeable than other animals, by virtue of possessing more channels through which sensory perception reaches us, namely sight, hearing, smell, and taste'. Vindicianus, *Epitome altera*, in V. Rose (ed.), *Theodori Prisciani Euporiston libri III cum physicorum fragmento et additamentis pseudo-Theodoreis* (Leipzig, 1894), pp. 467–83, at 467–8; qtd in McIlwain, p. 106, n. 18.

the brain through thin passages' and out into the air where it apprehends visible objects; he also, rather opaquely, states that the brain is the organ 'from which everything emanates.'[18] In another work moderately well known to the Anglo-Saxons, the *Differentiae uerborum*, Isidore localizes sensory processing, memory, and motor control in the front, middle, and rear lobes of the brain respectively, and he states that 'in capitis arce mens collocata est'.[19]

On the basis of such evidence, McIlwain rightly concludes that the ultimate Latin source materials underlying Old English medical texts 'explicitly link mental functions, and even the soul [i.e. the rational mind] to the head or brain.'[20] However, it does not necessarily follow that these cephalocentric doctrines were accessible throughout the Anglo-Saxon period; nor that they were assimilated into Anglo-Saxon thought even if they were accessible; nor that the localization of the *anima* or of a few specific mental faculties in the brain was tantamount to the localization of the *mod* in the brain. It is worth examining the reception of McIlwain's representatives of cephalocentric psychology in order to assess how great an impression they left on Anglo-Saxon readers.

Discerning Isidore's influence on Anglo-Saxon concepts of mind is challenging, not because of the transmission history of his works – the *Etymologiae* was ubiquitous and the *Differentiae uerborum* fairly well attested – but because of their internal contradictions. As encyclopedic works, their purpose was rather to amass information than to promote consistent and correct doctrine; accordingly, both the *Etymologiae* and the *Differentiae uerborum* juxtapose cephalocentric doctrines with a wide array of cardiocentric teachings.[21] It is difficult to discern how Anglo-Saxon readers may have reacted to Isidore's conflicting depictions of the mind, but most likely, neither the *Etymologiae* nor the *Differentiae uerborum* was capable of converting Anglo-Saxon readers from a heart-centred to a brain-centred view of the *mod*.

---

[18] Isidore, *Etymologiae*, XI.1.20–21, in Stephen A. Barney et al. (trans.), *The Etymologies of Isidore of Seville* (Cambridge, 2006), p. 232. For the Latin text, see *Etymologiarum sive Originum libri XX*, ed. W.M. Lindsay, 2 vols (Oxford, 1911), II, XI.1.20–21.

[19] 'The mind is concentrated in the citadel of the head.' Isidore, *Liber differentiarum* [*II*], II.17 and II.28, ed. María Adelaida Andrés Sanz, CCSL 111A (Turnhout, 2006), pp. 35–6 and 65–6; cf. Augustine, *De Genesi ad litteram* VII.18, and see Christopher D. Green, 'Where Did the Ventricular Localization of Mental Faculties Come From?' *Journal of the History of the Behavioral Sciences* 39 (2003): 131–42.

[20] McIlwain, p. 105.

[21] Lockett, pp. 205–12. The same difficulty attends Vindicianus' *Epitome altera*: though McIlwain classifies it as a text promoting cephalocentric psychology, Vindicianus also teaches, 'Our heart ... has two lobes, where the *mens* and *animus* of humans dwells. Therefore whatever capacity for judgement (*quicquid iudicii*) we have comes through those lobes of the heart' (ch. 18, ed. Rose, p. 474).

As for the Latin medical treatises, scholars are divided between optimistic and conservative assessments of their transmission histories in Anglo-Saxon England. On the optimistic side, a small number of isolated references and quotations in Anglo-Latin works of the seventh and eighth centuries suggests 'a long tradition of study and translation of classical [medical] literature, which may have originated with Archbishop Theodore',[22] and the Latin works identified as ultimate sources of the surviving Old English compilations are presumed to have been consistently available at multiple centres of learning, in their integral forms rather than solely in epitomes and digests.[23] M.L. Cameron adopts a more circumspect approach in his study of *Bald's Leechbook*, in which he proposes concrete criteria for distinguishing between Latin sources that were known directly to the *Leechbook* compiler from those that were known through intermediaries.[24] Nevertheless, though rigorous, Cameron's method cannot determine at what stage recipes were selected, and he credits the Anglo-Saxon compiler with decisions that may have been made by earlier generations who digested and epitomised the Latin materials. Perhaps the most cautious assessment is that of Debby Banham, whose research foregrounds surviving manuscripts and establishes that the content of ninth- through early-eleventh-century Old English medicine differs significantly from that of the Latin medical treatises that arrived in England during and after the reign of Edward the Confessor.[25] The earliest complete English copies of the *Practica Petrocelli*, the *Liber tertius*, and other treatises belonging to the Galenic tradition date to the second half of the eleventh century or later, and Banham sees 'very little connection between these [Latin] texts and the Old English medicine that was already in circulation in England; the *Practica Petrocelli* is the only one that shares any material with the Old English texts, most notably with *Bald's Leechbook*.'[26] Banham's research is at odds with McIlwain's conclusion that the Anglo-Saxons of the tenth century and earlier assimilated from the medical literature a brain-centred theory of mind; however, it must also be said that Banham's studies do

---

[22] Stephanie Hollis, 'Scientific and Medical Writings', in Phillip Pulsiano and Elaine Treharne (eds), *A Companion to Anglo-Saxon Literature* (Oxford, 2001), pp. 188–208, at 194.

[23] McIlwain's argument relies implicitly on this line of reasoning: 'a key assumption' of his argument is 'that ideas articulated in identified sources, especially ideas found in more than one text, formed part of the collective, medical knowledge base of the Anglo-Saxons' (p. 105).

[24] M.L. Cameron, 'Bald's *Leechbook*: Its Sources and their Use in its Compilation', *Anglo-Saxon England* 12 (1983): 153–82.

[25] Debby Banham, 'England Joins the Medical Mainstream: New Texts in Eleventh-century Manuscripts', in Hans Sauer and Joanna Story (eds) with Gaby Waxenberger, *Anglo-Saxon England and the Continent* (Tempe, 2011), pp. 341–52.

[26] Ibid., p. 344; for corroboration see also Cameron, 'Bald's *Leechbook*', p. 161: 'Using the criteria concerning borrowing given above, much of the material in the *Leechbook* could not be said to derive directly from primary sources.'

not address the question of how and in what form the authors of ninth- and tenth-century Old English medicine gained what indirect access they must have had to classical medical literature, as attested by Cameron's source studies.

Despite the obstacles that obscure our understanding of the transmission of Latin medical literature in pre-Conquest England, it is nonetheless clear that, among the cephalocentric doctrines quoted above from the *Practica Alexandri*, the *Liber tertius*, and Vindicianus' *Epitome altera*, not a single one has been assimilated into any Old English medical text. Such an absence implies that, even if these texts were available in their integral forms before the mid-eleventh century, their cephalocentric doctrines were actively rejected by compilers who made use of other teachings within these same texts. Likewise, although Isidore's encyclopedic works were familiar to the Anglo-Saxons, only one faint echo of his functional tripartition of the brain survives in a medical context, namely in the Hiberno-Latin poem *Lorica* that appears, with an Old English gloss, among the healing charms of *Lacnunga*. *Lorica* catalogues the members of the body for which the supplicant seeks God's protection, including the 'threefold brain' (Latin *cerebro triforme*; Old English *exon þære ðryfealdan*).[27] Without further contextual clues, however, the word 'threefold' would not have communicated the tripartition of mental functions to any reader not already acquainted with this idea as found in Augustine or Isidore; instead, it likely suggested a purely structural tripartition, much like the phrase 'three-forked liver' (Latin *trifidum iacor*, Old English *þriofealdan libre*), which appears later in the poem.[28]

Active rejection of cephalocentric doctrines is more firmly attested by late Anglo-Saxon treatments of the Latin *Practica Petrocelli*. This text usually circulated with a prefatory *Epistola peri hereseon* (*Letter on the sects*), derived chiefly from explications of Galen's *De sectis* by Agnellus of Ravenna.[29] The version of the *Epistola* preserved in continental manuscripts localizes three mental faculties in the brain: 'Animales [*scil.* uirtutes] sunt IIIes: mobilis, sensibilis et rationalis. ... Rationabilis [*sic*] sunt III: fantastica, logysmus et [mnemi]. Fantastica est in [anteriori] parte cerebri; logysmus est in medio cerebro, quo discernitur bonum et malum; [mnemi] est in posteriori parte cerebri, ubi est memoria'.[30]

---

[27] *Lorica* (=*Lacnunga*, ch. 65), line 39, in Edward Pettit (ed.), *Anglo-Saxon Remedies, Charms, and Prayers from British Library MS Harley 585: The Lacnunga*, 2 vols (Lewiston, 2001), I, p. 46. Earlier editions of *Lacnunga* employ different chapter numbers; for a concordance, see ibid., I, pp. lv–lviii.

[28] *Lorica*, line 71, ed. Pettit, I, p. 52.

[29] Florence Eliza Glaze, 'Master–Student Medical Dialogues: The Evidence of London, British Library, Sloane 2839', in Patrizia Lendinara et al. (eds), *Form and Content of Instruction in Anglo-Saxon England in the Light of Contemporary Manuscript Evidence* (Turnhout, 2007), pp. 467–94, at 477–85.

[30] 'Three faculties are characteristic of animate beings: the mobile, the sensory, and the rational. There are three rational faculties: imagination, reasoning, and recall. Imagination is

Our earliest record of the Latin *Practica Petrocelli* in England survives in a series of brief excerpts in Cambridge, University Library, Gg. 5. 35, fols 427v–431v and 444v–446v (after 1039, probably before 1066); another group of extracts survives in London, British Library, Sloane 475, fols 224–227v (s. xi ex. or xii in.).[31] Neither manuscript includes the section of the *Epistola peri hereseon* concerning the tripartition of the brain, but both groups of excerpts are brief and highly selective, so it would be unfair to draw from these manuscript witnesses any stronger conclusion than that cephalocentric doctrines were likely to be among many items passed over when Anglo-Saxon compilers copied selections from the *Practica Petrocelli*.

On the other hand, the copyist of the *Practica Petrocelli* in London, British Library, Sloane 2839, fols 7r–110v (s. xi ex. or xii in.) – or the copyist of an earlier manuscript from which Sloane 2839 descends – appears to have expressly rejected the functional tripartition of the brain.[32] Danielle Maion identifies 13 sections in the composite *Practica Petrocelli*, among which Sloane 2839 omits the brief incipit and the table of contents, but includes the rest, from the *Epistola peri hereseon* through the four theoretical tracts.[33] The Sloane 2839 copy of the *Epistola*, however, omits the passage on the tripartition of the brain and replaces it with a pastiche of teachings on the four humours, drawn from Isidore's *Etymologiae* and Bede's *De tempore rationum*.[34]

---

in the front part of the brain; reasoning is in the middle of the brain, where good and evil are distinguished; recall is in the rear part of the brain, where memory resides.' *Practica Petrocelli*, in S. de Renzi (ed.), *Collectio Salernitana ossia documenti inediti e trattati di medicina appartanenti alla scuola medica salernitana*, 5 vols (Naples, 1852–66), IV, pp. 185–291, at 189. Where de Renzi prints *anima* (twice) and *interiori*, I prefer the readings *mnemi* and *anteriori*, supported by the antecedent version of this material in Agnellus of Ravenna, *Lectures on Galen's De sectis*, ed. and trans. Leendert G. Westerinck et al. (Buffalo, 1981), p. 26. On the flaws in de Renzi's edition, and on the relationship between the *Epistola peri hereseon* and Agnellus, see Glaze; and on the sections of the *Practica* that de Renzi does not print, see Danielle Maion, 'The Fortune of the So-called *Practica Petrocelli Salernitani* in England: New Evidence and some Considerations', in Lendinara et al., pp. 495–512, at 497.

[31] Banham, p. 343; Maion, 'Fortune', pp. 504–7. The Cambridge manuscript may be consulted in microfiche facsimile in *Deluxe and Illustrated Manuscripts Containing Literary and Technical Texts*, ed. A.N. Doane and Tiffany J. Grade, Anglo-Saxon Manuscripts in Microfiche Facsimile 9 (Tempe, 2001), no. 96.

[32] On this manuscript see Banham, p. 343; Glaze, p. 478.

[33] Two additional sections (Remedies and Book III) belong only to a later tradition and are not part of the original *Practica Petrocelli*: see Maion, 'Fortune', pp. 499–500.

[34] In Sloane 2839, the *Epistola* roughly follows (with some brief omissions) de Renzi's text up to 7v line 22. From 7v line 22 ('Equidem sanguis') through 8r line 17 ('blandi sunt'), the manuscript text blends quotations and paraphrases of Bede, *De temporum ratione*, ch. 35; Isidore, *Etymologiae* V.35.8 (or Bede, *De temporum ratione*, ch. 8); and Isidore, *Etymologiae*

Equally striking is the evidence of *Peri Didaxeon*, which Maion characterizes as 'the translation into Old English of *Epistola* [*peri hereseon*] and part of the collection of remedies of *Book I* of *Practica Petrocelli*.[35] Surviving only in a late-twelfth-century copy (London, British Library, Harley 6258B, fols 51v–66v), it may have been translated as early as the late eleventh century.[36] Even at this late date, when texts representing the Galenic tradition had been circulating in England for several decades, the translator chose to omit the tripartition of the brain from his adaptation of the *Epistola peri hereseon*.[37] The translator omitted other sections of the *Epistola* as well, but those omissions primarily affect the 'most authority-dense sections' including the 'doxography and scholastic *diareseis*', which – being highly theoretical and historical – were scarcely useful to the practising Anglo-Saxon physician.[38] The omission of the tripartition of the brain, and indeed of all the material on the *uirtutes animales*, cannot be explained by the same reasoning. In place of the *uirtutes animales* material, *Peri Didaxeon* provides a few sentences about the organic origins of each of the four humours (which I shall return to below), the times of year when each humour dominates the body, and the *dies caniculares*, all drawn from the *Disputatio Platonis et Aristotelis*, which circulated as part of the composite *Practica Petrocelli*.[39] Taken together, these three Latin witnesses of *Practica Petrocelli*, combined with *Peri Didaxeon*, vividly demonstrate why the mere availability of a cephalocentric doctrine in a Latin medical text did not guarantee that its Anglo-Saxon readers would copy or translate it, much less that they would grant it a formative influence over their concept of the *mod*.

Organic Influences on Mental States and Events

In the Old English medical texts themselves, several passages unequivocally implicate the head or brain in a mental state or event. (1) The Old English

---

IV.5.1–6. I owe my awareness of this interpolation to McIlwain, p. 106, and I have consulted microfilm images of the manuscript in order to confirm and source the interpolation.

[35] Maion, 'Fortune', p. 500.

[36] Danielle Maion, 'Il lessico tecnico *Peri Didaxeon*. Elementi di datazione', *Il Bianco e il Nero* 6 (2003): 179–86; see also Banham, pp. 344–5.

[37] *Peri Didaxeon. Eine Sammlung von Rezepten in Englischer Sprache aus dem 11./12. Jahrhundert*, ed. Max Löweneck (Erlangen, 1896), p. 2; the Old English of lines 1–15 adheres to the *Epistola peri hereseon*. Maion ('Fortune', p. 503) has determined that *Peri Didaxeon* is not directly related to the Sloane 2839 copy of *Practica Petrocelli*, so the rejection of the brain's tripartition in the former cannot be attributed to the absence of the brain's tripartition in the latter.

[38] Glaze, pp. 484–5 n. 56.

[39] László Sándor Chardonnens, *Anglo-Saxon Prognostics, 900–1100: Study and Texts* (Leiden, 2007), p. 42; Maion, 'Fortune', pp. 497–9.

Herbarium offers a remedy 'Wið þa adle þe Grecas frenesis nemnað, þæt is on ure geþeode gewitlest þæs modes, þæt byþ ðonne þæt heafod aweallen byþ'.[40] (2) In *Bald's Leechbook* we read, 'Sio wamb sio ðe bið cealdre oððe wætre gecyndo oððe misbyrdo, him cymð brægenes adl & ungewitfæstnes him bið'.[41] (3) *Leechbook III* prescribes a salve of pennyroyal in oil or butter to be placed on the temples, eyes, and crown of the chronic headache sufferer; the recipe concludes with the unnerving provision, 'þeah him sie gemynd oncyrred he biþ hal'.[42]

If we read the foregoing passages through the lens of our brain-centred concept of the mind, they intuitively confirm that the Anglo-Saxons, too, localized the mind in the head. However, it is problematic to reason that every organ that influences mental states is necessarily the seat of the mind. If the *mod* is to be localized wherever it is affected by organic diseases, then the bulk of the evidence shows the *mod* to be affected by the organs in the midsection of the body. For instance, *Lacnunga* advises: 'Wið innoðes hefignese: syle etan rædic mid sealte, ⁊ eced supan; sona bið þæt mod leohtre'.[43] *Leechbook III* prescribes a 'leoht drenc wiþ weden heorte',[44] employing the expression *weden heorte* that appears regularly in non-medical prose, where it refers literally to the organ most affected by madness.[45] *Bald's Leechbook* lists 'geswogunga & modes geswæþrunga' among the signs of downward progress of liver disease,[46] and it additionally numbers 'modes elhygd' among the complications that can follow upon a non-specific 'æghwæþerre sidan sare'.[47] The *capitula* preceding Book II of *Bald's Leechbook* describe how 'se hata omihta maga ungemet þurst & swol

---

[40] 'For the illness that the Greeks call *frenesis*, which in our language is stupidity of mind that occurs when the head is (?)swollen up.' *The Old English Herbarium*, ch. 96.2, in Hubert Jan de Vriend (ed.), *The Old English Herbarium and Medicina de Quadrupedibus*, EETS o.s. 286 (London, 1984), pp. 1–233, at 142. The precise meaning of *aweallen* is unclear; I revisit this remedy below.

[41] 'The gut that is of a cold or wet or flawed nature: upon this person comes disease of the brain, and he will not be of sound mind.' *Bald's Leechbook*, ch. 27, in Thomas Oswald Cockayne (ed.), *Leechdoms, Wortcunning and Starcraft of Early England*, Rolls Series 35, 3 vols (London, 1864–66; repr. Millwood, 1965), II, pp. 2–298, at 222.

[42] 'Although his memory may be disrupted, he will be healthy.' *Leechbook III*, ch. 1; ed. Cockayne, II, pp. 300–360, at 306.

[43] 'Against a sensation of heaviness in the bowels: give (the patient) radish to eat with salt, and vinegar to drink; soon his mind will be lighter.' *Lacnunga*, ch. 125, ed. Pettit, I, p. 88.

[44] 'a light drink to treat the insane heart'. *Leechbook III*, ch. 68, ed. Cockayne, II, p. 356.

[45] A search of the Old English Corpus reveals ten occurrences of *wedenheortnes* and seven of *wedenheo(r)t* or *weden heorte*; see Antonette diPaolo Healey et al., *The Dictionary of Old English Corpus on the World Wide Web* (Toronto, 2009).

[46] 'fainting spells and deficiencies of the mind'. *Bald's Leechbook*, II.21, ed. Cockayne, II, p. 206.

[47] 'delirium or abstraction of the mind'; 'pain in either side'. *Bald's Leechbook*, II.46, ibid., II, pp. 256–8.

þrowað & nearonesse & geswogunga & gemodes tweonunge'.[48] Most notable of all is the opening of Book II in *Bald's Leechbook*, where there appears a catalogue of mental problems caused by an unhealthy stomach: 'Eac of þæs magan adle cumað monige & missenlica adla geborstena wunda & hramma & fyllewærc & fienda adl & micla murnunga & unrotnessa butan þearfe ... & on unmode & on ungemet wæccum & ungewitlico word'.[49]

I adduce these passages not to support the localization of the mind in the body's midsection, but rather to show that the seat of the *mod* cannot be determined by individual organic influences on mental disturbances.[50] Unless we are prepared to conclude that the *mod* was localized in many different bodily organs – a proposition that would find absolutely no corroboration in other genres of Anglo-Saxon writing – then we must consider what other role an organ might play in psychological events and disorders.

Mental Disturbances, Phlegm, and the Brain

To refine our understanding of the brain's precise role in mental activity, let us turn again to *Bald's Leechbook*. After the catalogue of complications accompanying stomach illness (quoted above), the text continues: 'se maga biþ neah þære heortan & þære gelodr & geadortenge þam brægene of þam cumað þa adla swiþost of þæs magan intingan & on yflum seawum wætan atterberendum'.[51] If we may posit some consistency of doctrine between *Bald's Leechbook* and *Peri Didaxeon*, the latter text clarifies that the malign liquid emanating from the brain is phlegm (*wæta*): 'feower wætun syndon on þan manniscen lichama ... þat ys þa wæte on þan heafode and þæt blod on þara breosta, and se ruwa gealla on þan innoþe, and

---

[48] 'The heated and irretentive stomach suffers excessive thirst and swelling and constriction (or anxiety) and fainting and vacillation of the mind.' *Bald's Leechbook*, Book II *capitula*, ibid., II, p. 160.

[49] 'Also from disease of the stomach arise many and various illnesses of erupting wounds and cramps, and falling-sickness (*i.e.*, epilepsy) and devil-sickness, and great anxiety and gloominess without cause ... and dejection and immoderate wakefulness (*i.e.*, insomnia) and nonsensical speech.' *Bald's Leechbook*, II.1, ibid., II, pp. 174–6.

[50] Based on such evidence, I cannot concur with McIlwain when he states, 'What the various [mental] disorders have in common is that, when an organ is identified as ultimately responsible for the manifestation, that organ is the brain' (p. 111).

[51] 'The stomach is near the heart and the spine and in contact with the brain, from which come the strongest diseases caused by the stomach and harmful liquids, poison-bearing humours.' *Bald's Leechbook*, II.1, ed. Cockayne, II, p. 176; where this edition prints *brægene* the manuscript reads *bræge*.

se swerta gealle innan ðare blædran'.[52] Similar allocations of the four humours to these organs could be found throughout the standard Latin medical treatises of the Hippocratic and Galenic traditions – although the finer points of the humoral system seem not to have been assimilated by the Anglo-Saxons.[53] Moreover, the identification of the skull cavity or the brain as the origin of phlegm was more than a theoretical dogma mechanically transmitted from ancient authorities; it was reinforced empirically by the observation that the nasal sinuses drain phlegm or mucus downward from the region of the brain. A remedy for headache due to sinus congestion communicates an awareness of this connection:

> Wið heafodwærce: betan wyrtruman; cnuca mid hunige; awring; do þæt seaw on þæt neb; gelicge upweard wið hatre sunnan, ⁊ ahoh þæt heafod nyþerweard oððæt seo ex sy gesoht; hæbbe him ær on muðe buteran oððe ele; asitte þonne uplang; hnige þonne forð; læte flowan of þæn nebbe þa gilstre; do þæt gelome oððæt hyt clæne sy.

> [For headache: pound root of beet with honey; strain; put the juice into the nose; lay him face upward toward the hot sun, and hang the head downward until the brain is reached; before that let him have butter or oil in his mouth; then set him upright; then let him bend forward; let the mucus flow from the nose; do that often until it is clean.][54]

Despite their rather superficial assimilation of humoral theory, the Anglo-Saxons seem to have approved of the notion that phlegm – that is, the humour as well as the substance emitted by coughing and sneezing – emanated from the brain. But what does this have to do with mental states and events?

According to the *Thesaurus of Old English*, the Anglo-Saxons employed a wide range of nouns and adjectives to denote mental illness and its sufferers. Some terms carry no etiological connotations (*ungewitfulnes*, *wodscipe*), while others pin the cause of madness on demons (*deofolseocnes, feonda adl*), elves (*ylfig*), the phases of the moon (*monseoc*), the brain (*brægenseoc*), and the flow of phlegm, signified by the adjective (*ge*)*bræcseoc*.[55] The first element of this word,

---

[52] 'There are four humours in the human body ... that is, phlegm in the head and blood in the breast and yellow bile in the gut and black bile in the bladder.' *Peri Didaxeon*, ch. 1, ed. Löweneck, p. 1.

[53] Lois Ayoub, 'Old English *wæta* and the Medical Theory of the Humours', *JEGP* 94 (1995): 332–46; see esp. pp. 338 and 343–4, on the conflation of humoral phlegm with secreted mucus, and on the contextual clues that indicate whether *wæta* means 'humour' or 'phlegm'.

[54] *Lacnunga*, ch. 3, ed. Pettit, I, p. 4; I print Pettit's translation with slight modifications. Another version of this recipe appears in *Bald's Leechbook*, I.3, ed. Cockayne, II, p.18.

[55] Jane Roberts and Christian Kay with Lynne Grundy, *A Thesaurus of Old English in Two Volumes*, 2nd edn (Amsterdam, 2000), I, pp. 128–9.

(*ge*)*bræc*, occurs as a simplex, meaning 'phlegm' or 'catarrh' (rendering Latin *rheuma*); it also forms other compounds, including *nebgebræc* 'nasal mucus, sneezing' and *bræccoþu* 'epilepsy, demonic possession'.[56]

Although lunacy, demonic possession, epilepsy, and undifferentiated madness may represent distinct illness categories for the present-day reader, the lumping of these disorders together in the *Thesaurus* parallels the conflation of these disorders in Anglo-Saxon literature and some of its Late Latin antecedents.[57] Isidore's *Etymologiae*, for example, observes that 'common people' call the epileptic *lunaticus* 'moon-sick' and *laruaticus* 'possessed by spirits'.[58] Such conflation is particularly striking in Anglo-Saxon exegesis and glosses on Matthew 17:14, in which a father pleads with Jesus: 'Lord, have pity on my son, for he is a lunatic [*lunaticus*], and suffereth much: for he falleth often into the fire, and often into the water.'[59] Commentaries emanating from the seventh-century Canterbury school of Theodore and Hadrian propose two explanations for the boy's lunacy: '*Lunaticus* est cuius minuente luna minuatur uel mutatur cerebrum et, intrante daemone per narum, dementem facit. Aliter lunatici dicuntur qui incipiente luna uel in medio siue in fine cadunt et prosternuntur'.[60] The complex etiology of the boy's illness is evident in the first explanation: the brain, which is reached by way of the nasal passages, is influenced by both the moon and a demon. The conflation of moon-sickness and devil-sickness with epilepsy is reinforced by the second explanation, in which lunacy leads to uncontrolled prostration. Subsequent Old English glosses on Mt 17:14 support a similarly complex etiology for the boy's disorder: although the evangelist states plainly that Jesus heals the child by driving out a demon (Mt 17:17), glosses render

---

[56] Angus Cameron, Ashley Crandell Amos, Antonette diPaolo Healey et al., *Dictionary of Old English: A to G Online* (Toronto, 2007) [hereafter called *DOE*], s.v. (*ge*)*bræc*.

[57] On the conflation of epilepsy with *phrenesis*, lunacy, and possession (both divine and demonic) from antiquity into the Middle Ages, see Owsei Temkin, *The Falling Sickness: A History of Epilepsy from the Greeks to the Beginnings of Modern Neurology*, 2nd edn (Baltimore, 1971), pp. 85–102 and 118–21.

[58] Isidore, *Etymologiae*, IV.7.6, trans. Barney et al., p. 111; for Latin text, see Lindsay, II, IV.7.6.

[59] *The Holy Bible: Douay Rheims Version* (Baltimore, 1899; repr. Rockford, IL, 2000); for Latin text, see *Biblia Sacra iuxta vulgatam versionem*, ed. Robert Weber et al., 4th edn (Stuttgart, 1994).

[60] 'A lunatic is someone whose brain diminishes or changes as the moon wanes and makes him demented when a demon enters through his nostrils. Alternatively, they are called lunatics who fall down and prostrate themselves when the moon is waxing, full, or waning.' *The Canterbury Biblical Commentaries of Theodore and Hadrian*, ed. Bernhard Bischoff and Michael Lapidge (Cambridge, 1994), p. 404; see also pp. 249–55 on Theodore's medical education.

lunaticus variously as *monsek* (moon-sick), *fylle-seoc* (falling-sick, epileptic), and *bræc-cec* (phlegm-sick).[61]

Literary and medical texts further solidify the connection among mental illness, the brain, and phlegm. *Brægenseoc* occurs only four times in the Old English corpus, glossing Latin *freneticus* 'delirious, raving' in Aldhelm's prose *De uirginitate*.[62] Somewhat more common is *(ge)bræcseoc*, which occurs 15 times, typically translating *freneticus, lunaticus, demoniacus* 'possessed by a demon', *caducus* 'falling-sick', and *comitialis* 'epileptic'.[63] In *Bald's Leechbook*, a single chapter combines remedies 'wiþ feondseocum men', 'wiþ bræcseocum men', and 'wið weden heorte':[64] each cure similarly requires prayers and potions of herbs including lupine, which may have been efficacious against seizures.[65] The conflation of these classes of mental disturbance, the association of each of them with *(ge)bræc*, and the observation that harmful phlegm originates in the brain all lead to the conclusion that the brain was ascribed a prominent role in epilepsy and mental illness not because the brain housed the mind but rather because the brain gave rise to the phlegm that disturbed the mind.

This etiology of epilepsy was widespread, though not uncontested, in classical medicine going back to the Hippocratic corpus. *On the Sacred Disease*, dating from ca. 400 BC, argues that epilepsy is not a form of divine possession but 'its cause lies in the brain, a brain overflowing with a superfluity of phlegm'.[66] Over the next six centuries, some physicians attributed partial or full responsibility for epilepsy to a superfluity of black bile rather than phlegm, but the association between epilepsy and phlegm always had its defenders, and even Galen (fl. ca. 200 AD) maintained that most cases of epilepsy resulted from 'a cold and moist dyscrasia of the brain leading to the collection of a thick phlegm in its ventricles'.[67] While many works of the Hippocratic and Galenic traditions localize the soul or its rational faculty in the brain, the brain's chief role in epilepsy was not to

---

[61] *The Holy Gospels in Anglo-Saxon, Northumbrian, and Old Mercian Versions*, ed. Walter W. Skeat (Cambridge, 1871–87; repr. Darmstadt, 1970), pp. 142–3; these glosses come from the Rushworth Gospels; Cambridge, Corpus Christi College 140; and the Lindisfarne Gospels respectively.

[62] *DOE*, s.v. *brægen-sēoc*; the four occurrences come from two copies of similar Aldhelm glosses. A fifth possible occurrence, glossing *freneticus* in the *Colloquia* of Ælfric Bata, is damaged and reads *br*.

[63] *DOE*, s.v. *brǣc-sēoc, ge•brǣc-sēoc*.

[64] 'for a devil-sick man'; 'for a phlegm-sick man'; 'for an insane heart'.

[65] *Bald's Leechbook* I.63, ed. Cockayne, II, pp. 136–8; see also Peter Dendle, 'Lupines, Manganese, and Devil-Sickness: An Anglo-Saxon Medical Response to Epilepsy', *Bulletin of the History of Medicine* 75 (2001): 91–101.

[66] Temkin, p. 4.

[67] Ibid., pp. 51–64 and 70, paraphrasing Galen's commentary on Hippocrates' *Epidemics*.

house the mind but to generate excess phlegm. This etiology, moreover, was entirely compatible with the cardiocentric psychologies of classical physicians such as Diocles and Praxagoras (fl. 4th c. BC), who taught that epileptic seizures occur when phlegm, overflowing the brain, aggregates in the region around the heart, where the mind resides.[68]

We cannot presume that the Anglo-Saxons absorbed all the nuances of their forerunners' views on epilepsy and other mental disturbances; nonetheless, the basic idea that epilepsy, and the other disorders that came to be conflated with it, originates in an excess of phlegm in the brain does appear to have been assimilated by the Anglo-Saxons long before the new influx of Latin medical works in the mid-eleventh century, to judge from the uses of the word (*ge*)*bræcseoc* discussed above. It has been suggested that the morpheme *bræc* does not signify the phlegmatic humour as a substance but refers instead to the liquid's 'breaking' out of the head or throat, as in a coughing fit or a seizure, implying an etymological connection with the verb *brecan*.[69] Emphasizing the action of 'breaking', however, obscures the fact that the substance of phlegm itself, both as a humour and as a secretion, is the common thread tying together Old English words pertaining to sinus and bronchial congestion (including *bræc*, *gebræc/gebræcu*, and *nebgebræc*, as well as *gebræcdrenc* 'medicinal drink for the throat') with the terms pertaining to epilepsy (*bræcoþu* and (*ge*)*bræcseoc*).[70]

Understanding that the brain's chief role in mental disturbances is to generate phlegm can, in turn, illuminate other troublesome passages in the Old English medical texts. Earlier I cited a remedy for 'the illness that the Greeks call *frenesis*, which in our language is stupidity of mind that occurs when the head is *aweallen*'.[71] Though the significance of *aweallen* is not immediately obvious, the fact that *freneticus* is repeatedly glossed *bræcseoc* or *brægenseoc* suggests that the brain is 'overflowing' or discharging with an excess of phlegm. Similarly, *Lacnunga* prescribes a potion to be drunk 'wið heafodecce, ⁊ wið brægenes

---

[68] Ibid., pp. 55–6.

[69] Joseph McGowan, 'Elves, Elf-shot, and Epilepsy: OE *ælfādl*, *ælfsiden*, *ælfsogeþa*, *bræccoþu*, and *bræcsēoc*', *Studia Neophilologica* 81 (2009): 116–20, at 117: 'The forms *bræccoþu* and *bræcseoc* seem not to suggest "falling" or "lunacy" so much as they seem to refer to the physical symptoms of epilepsy: the convulsing, spasmodic bodily contortions ... the frothing, coughing, and respiratory difficulty associated with epileptic seizure.' Although *DOE* deals very little in etymology, entries for *bræc-coþu* and *bræc-sēoc* refer the reader to the verb *brecan*, implying a historical connection.

[70] *DOE*, s.v. *bræc*¹, *ge·bræc*, *ge·bræcu*, *bræc-coþu*, *ge·bræc-drenc*, *bræc-sēoc*, and *ge·bræc-sēoc*; on *nebgebræc*, which glosses *coryza* 'nasal discharge', see also Herbert Dean Meritt, *Some of the Hardest Glosses in Old English* (Stanford, 1968), pp. 9–10.

[71] See above, p. 45.

hwyrfnesse ⁊ weallunge, wið seondre exe' among various other infirmities.⁷²
While one might argue that the potion is meant to heal an external injury that has left the brain swelling and oozing through a wound in the skull, it is worth considering whether the brain is instead 'overflowing' and 'discharging' excess phlegm, an interpretation supported by Latin analogues of this remedy, which indicate its utility 'ad reuma' ('against phlegm or humours') and 'ad reumaticos humores deponendos' ('in suppressing phlegmatic or flowing humours').⁷³

Conclusions

The exercise of setting aside presentist presuppositions about the brain increases our awareness of some intriguing and indeed counterintuitive ways in which premodern concepts of mind differ from ours. In the case of Old English medical texts, the brain's chief role in mental disturbance turns out to be the generation of phlegm. These texts give no indication that their compilers had assimilated Latin cephalocentric doctrines that would place the highly personalized and complex *mod* in the brain, and the role that they do allocate to the brain is wholly compatible with the cardiocentric psychology that pervades all other genres of Old English literature. Distinguishing the true role of the brain in mental activity is important for students of the history of emotions, because as long as the English resisted the notion that the *mod* was localized in the head, they could not have had recourse to the highly productive conceptual system that we employ when we pit the rational head against the emotional heart. This conventional usage could only have gained currency after the localization of rational thought in the brain became widely accepted in England, a development for which the medical evidence suggests a date no earlier than the twelfth century.

---

[72] 'against headache and against dizziness and overflowing of the brain, and against discharging brain'. *Lacnunga*, ch. 170, ed. Pettit, I, p. 118; I've borrowed the useful phrase 'discharging brain' from Pettit's translation.

[73] For the Latin analogues see Pettit, II, p. 342.

Chapter 4

The Curious Case of *TORN*: The Importance of Lexical–Semantic Approaches to the Study of Emotions in Old English

Daria Izdebska

Understanding Emotions

In this chapter I would like to discuss the importance of lexical approaches to the study of emotions in Old English first by outlining the most common linguistic approaches to the study of emotions and then by analysing one of the ANGER word-families using an interdisciplinary methodology based on corpus linguistics, cognitive semantics, etymology, and close reading of relevant passages.

One of the greatest limitations to understanding Anglo-Saxon emotions is that we can only access information about them through a body of fragmentary textual evidence.[1] Often, however, the fact that this is essentially a *cross-linguistic* investigation is not brought to the forefront. On the level of language and discourse, Present-Day English lexis is used to discuss Old English emotions. On a conceptual level, the study of emotions in Old English is potentially directed by implicit and often subconscious understanding of what a particular emotion is and how it is conceptualised and expressed in our own cultures and languages. On the one hand, there is a need to approach any study of emotions in a multidisciplinary fashion, as other disciplines bring valuable insights into understanding primary processes guiding the experience and display of emotions. On the other hand, research into historical emotions cannot be divorced from a careful analysis of the emotional lexicon, and how it represents the underlying conceptual structures specific to that language. Because our material is textual, issues such as genre or

---

[1] I am very grateful to the British Federation of Women Graduates Charitable Foundation, as this chapter has been written whilst I have been in receipt of their Main Foundation Grant from the Funds for Women Graduates. I would also like to take this opportunity to thank Carole Hough and Kathryn Lowe for their very helpful comments on the earlier drafts of this paper.

convention will also have a large role to play. Rather than attempting to make the available data fit with modern categorisations, there is need to develop a methodology that will be sensitive to lexical and semantic nuances.

Despite decades of research, there is no firm consensus on the definition and composition of emotions in general, nor of distinct emotions in particular. Emotions involve both the activation of higher brain functions and the autonomous nervous system: internal experiences, external interactions, and the cognitive or conceptual construction of emotions. Emotions are also 'inherently social in nature',[2] resulting from our interactions with others and regulating society.

The biological nature of emotions in terms of physiology and neurology is indisputable. In the *universalist* perspective, emotions are understood as 'biologically determined processes, depending on innately set brain devices, laid down by a long evolutionary history'.[3] Such research concentrates on the universality of facial expressions[4] and the existence of *basic emotions*,[5] which usually comprise anger, disgust, fear, joy, sadness and surprise.[6]

Cultural and linguistic anthropology proposes an opposite view: *relativist* or *social constructionist*.[7] Emotions are viewed as unique, socio-culturally constructed phenomena, and the emotion concepts are distinct and untranslatable. Whilst some psychologists posit the existence of a universal emotion of 'anger', cultural anthropologists stress that Ifaluk *song*,[8] Ilongot *liget*,[9] or Malay *marah*[10] are all different from one another and from English *anger*, and the rules regarding

---

[2] Antony S.R. Manstead, 'A History of Affect and Emotion Research in Social Psychology', in Arie W. Kurglanski and Wolfgange Stroebe (eds), *Handbook of the History of Social Psychology* (Hove, 2012), pp. 176–98, at 177. The chapter also provides a good overview of the history of emotion research.

[3] Antonio Damasio, *The Feeling of What Happens: Body, Emotion and the Making of Consciousness* (London, 2000), p. 51.

[4] Begun most famously by Charles Darwin, *The Expression of Emotions in Man and Animals* (London, 1872). See also: Paul Ekman, 'Facial Expression and Emotion', *American Psychologist*, 48 (1993): 384–92.

[5] Paul Ekman, 'Basic Emotions', in Tim Dalgleish and Mick Power (eds), *The Handbook of Cognition and Emotion* (Chichester, 1999), pp. 45–60.

[6] David Matsumoto, Seung Hee Yoo and Joanne Chung, 'The Expression of Anger Across Culture', in Michael Potegal et al. (eds), *International Handbook of Anger* (New York, 2010), pp. 125–37, at 126.

[7] Pavlenko provides an apt summary of the two opposing sides and adds the third category of *nativist*. Aneta Pavlenko, *Emotions and Multilingualism* (Cambridge, 2005), pp. 78–81.

[8] Catherine Lutz, *Unnatural Emotions: Everyday Sentiments on a Micronesian Atoll and their Challenge to Western Theory* (Chicago, 1988).

[9] Michelle Rosaldo, *Knowledge and Passion: Ilongot Notions of Self and Social Life* (Cambridge, 1980).

[10] Cliff Goddard, 'The "Social Emotions" of Malay (Bahasa Malayu)', *Ethos* 24 (1996): 426–64, at 437–40.

their display are not identical. Matsumoto suggests that, whilst the framework of basic emotions is supported by research, 'cultures endorse the modification of universal angry expressions',[11] and both the universal and the culture-specific aspects need to be taken into consideration in any study of emotions.

ANGER – Linguistic Methodologies

Any study into emotions can be classified as relativist or universalist, and on the surface both approaches can employ the same tools for analysis, but with a completely different focus. Cognitive linguistics provides several such tools to analyse emotions, primarily metaphor theory and prototype theory.

Metaphor theory has traditionally pointed to the universality of emotion metaphors, which are stable and predictable, both cross-culturally and cross-linguistically.[12] Distant cultures arrive at similar conceptualisations, whether metaphoric or metonymical, for example ANGER IS HEAT, or the MIND IS A CONTAINER.[13] This approach has yielded studies into language and literature that help uncover conceptualisations often going beyond the word-level.[14] Some of these metaphors can be explained by the *embodiment* theory, where particular experiences of the body direct the conceptualisation of an emotion. For instance, anger is accompanied by such physiological reactions as elevated heart-rate, elevated temperature, and a feeling of pressure in the head. This is why the conceptualisation ANGER IS THE HEAT OF A FLUID IN A CONTAINER (as in 'You make my blood boil') is found among so many unrelated cultures.[15]

---

[11] Matsumoto et al., p. 125.

[12] Most importantly, George Lakoff, W*omen, Fire and Dangerous Things: What Categories Reveal about the Mind* (Chicago, 1987) and also George Lakoff and Mark Johnson, *Metaphors We Live By* (Chicago, 1980).

[13] For the purposes of this chapter I shall be following several typographic conventions. The words or phrases in small capital letters refer to the conceptual level, so either to a conceptualisation (e.g. ANGER IS HEAT) or a concept (e.g. ANGER). Words in italics refer to specific lexical items in a given language (e.g. PDE *anger*, OE *torn* or OE *tornlice*). If the word does not have a reflex in Present-Day English, it is translated with the use of single quotation marks (e.g. OE *yrre* 'angry'). Finally, words that are both capitalised and italicised, such as, for instance, *TORN*, refer to an entire word-family, including all its members (with regard to word category, derivation, etc.). In this case, *TORN* encompasses the noun and adjective *torn*, as well as the compound verb *tornwyrdan* or the adverb *tornlice*, and others. I follow Hans-Jürgen Diller in using italicised capital letters. See: '*ANGER* and *TĒNE* in Middle English', in Manfred Markus et al. (eds), *Middle and Modern English Corpus Linguistics: A Multi-dimensional Approach* (Amsterdam, 2012), pp. 109–24.

[14] For instance, Antonina Harbus, *Cognitive Approaches to Old English Poetry* (Cambridge, 2012).

[15] Zoltán Kövecses, 'Cross-cultural Experience of Anger: A Psycholinguistic Analysis', in Potegal et al. (eds), *International Handbook of Anger*, pp. 157–74. For case studies of

However, this approach can also yield examples of conceptualisations and metaphorical expressions that are unique to a given culture. Additionally, whilst cognitive approaches to emotions utilising metaphor theory in a diachronic perspective have been fruitful in recent years, an investigation of historical emotions should not overlook the lexical–semantic features of words and rely simply on lexicographic definitions; such definitions are often insufficient for fine-detailed work, particularly when for a large portion of that lexicon the Toronto *Dictionary of Old English* still possesses no entries.[16]

Prototypicality or prototype theory is yet another crucial set of concepts with several applications.[17] The general understanding is that 'linguistic categories may be fuzzy at the edges but clear in the centre',[18] which means that words belonging to the same category can be more representative of that category (core) or less representative (centre), and in fact belong to some other categories as well. For instance, in Present-Day English, we may think of *anger* as the prototypical representative of the category, whereas *aggravated* might be more peripheral. On the level of the word, it also suggests that a word will have more prototypical usage and meaning, but will also have some unique or unexpected applications.[19]

The concepts of prototypical scenario or cognitive script are based on the assumption that the human brain is highly capable of forming generalised, abstracted frames of events. A cognitive script can be defined as 'a predetermined, stereotyped sequence of actions that defines a well-known situation'[20] and this definition can apply to a prototypical scenario as well. These scripts are abstractions and generalisations of common situations that provide a rough framework of 'how things should generally happen'. Emotions, as internal states and social interactions, follow a scenario that regulates the rules of their expression. The universalist position would suggest that there is one universal prototypical scenario

---

particular languages in this vein, see for instance: John R. Taylor and Thandi G. Mbense, 'Red Dogs and Rotten Mealies: How Zulus Talk about Anger', in Angeliki Athanasiadou and Elżbieta Tabakowska (eds), *Speaking of Emotions: Conceptualisation and Expression* (Berlin, 1998), pp. 191–226.

[16] Angus Cameron, Ashley Crandell Amos, Antonette diPaolo Healey et al. (eds), *Dictionary of Old English: A to G online* (Toronto, 2007), at http://www.doe.utoronto.ca (accessed 18 January 2013), henceforth referred to as DOE.

[17] The prototype theory has been initiated primarily by Eleanor Rosch. See for instance: Eleanor Rosch, 'Human Categorization', in Neil Warren (ed.), *Studies in Cross-cultural Psychology*, 2 vols (London, 1977), I, pp. 1–49.

[18] Dirk Geeraerts, *Theories of Lexical Semantics* (Oxford, 2010), p. 183.

[19] For a good overview of Prototype Theory see: Geeraerts, *Theories*, pp. 183–203. For its application in diachronic semantics, see: Dirk Geeraerts, *Diachronic Prototype Semantics* (Oxford, 1997).

[20] Roger Schank and Robert Abelson, *Scripts, Plans, Goals, and Understanding: An Inquiry Into Human Knowledge Structures* (Hillsdale, NJ, 1977), p. 210.

for an emotion. Kövecses proposes such a prototypical scenario for ANGER. This Cognitive Model of Anger assumes a five-stage process: (1) offending event, (2) anger, (3) attempt at control, (4) loss of control, (5) act of retribution.[21]

On the other hand, we can assume that scenarios found for emotions in different cultures will not be the same. Some scholars go further, combining this understanding with a lexical approach, which is based on the underlying assumption that separate terms suggest separate concepts. Thus, if we can distinguish lexically between certain emotions, the scenarios attached to them will also be different. These scenarios are often delineated with the use of the conceptual framework of the Natural Semantic Metalanguage (NSM).[22] The NSM aspires to be a culture-free meta-tool that eliminates ethnocentric bias by using semantic primes or universals found in any language.[23] It means that, whilst there is a generic similarity between such terms as Ifaluk *song* and English *anger*, they will differ in one or two, often crucial, elements of the scenario. Wierzbicka proposes the following NSM explications for Ifaluk *song* and English *anger*:

> *song*
> 1. X thinks something like this
> 2. this person (Y) did something bad
> 3. people should not do things like this
> 4. this person should know this
> 5. because of this, X feels something bad
> 6. because of this, X wants to do something[24]
>
> *anger*
> 1. X thinks something like this
> 2. this person (Y) did something bad
> 3. I don't want this
> 4. I would want to do something bad to this person
> 5. because of this, X feels something bad toward Y
> 6. because of this, X wants to do something[25]

---

[21] Zoltán Kövecses, *Metaphors of Anger, Pride, and Love: A Lexical Approach to the Study of Emotion Concepts* (Amsterdam, 1986), pp. 28–31.

[22] Most prominently works by Anna Wierzbicka and Cliff Goddard. But see also Uwe Durst, 'Why Germans Don't Feel "Anger"', in Jean Harkins and Anna Wierzbicka (eds), *Emotions in Cross-linguistic Perspective* (Berlin, 2001), pp. 115–48.

[23] For recent overview and development see: Cliff Goddard (ed.), *Cross-linguistic Semantics* (Amsterdam, 2008).

[24] Anna Wierzbicka, *Semantics, Culture and Cognition: Universal Human Concepts in Culture-specific Configurations* (New York, 1992), p. 147.

[25] Ibid., p. 569.

The two emotions are different in that, prototypically, the assessment of the action causing the emotion is different. *Song* is glossed as 'justified anger' and prototypically experienced when 'people should not do things like this'. *Song* 'is considered "good"; ... this "goodness" is of a higher, moral level.'[26] NSM can capture these differences in an objective fashion, since these explications can be translated into any language whilst retaining their meaning with the use of semantic universals.

In Present-Day English, ANGER refers to the entire semantic field, i.e. a group of ANGER-related words, such as *anger, fury, rage, wrath, indignation*, and it may be therefore be treated as a hyperonym. However, the superordinate category ANGER is not equivalent to the usage and range of the English word *anger*. The word has been chosen as representative of the semantic field, because it is the most prototypical of the set, but Wierzbicka argues that, whenever there is a separate term, there *are* different emotions, both within and across languages. It matters in Present-Day English whether we use a phrase *He was angry* or *He was enraged*. The difference is not only in the scale of the emotion (*rage* being of a greater intensity than *anger*), but also in the prototypical scenario, evaluation and consequences (*rage* is more unrestrained and potentially destructive[27] than *anger*).

If such differences occur intra-linguistically, it is no wonder that they would be even more pronounced cross-linguistically. Translation studies and cross-linguistic research show that languages model reality in a different fashion. This is equally true for words having material objects as referents and for words denoting abstract concepts.[28] The vocabulary of a culture reflects its main preoccupations and interests, and the organisation of vocabulary into categories reflects the conceptual structures this culture imposes upon the world. Unfortunately, a common problem for researchers is 'to engage in terminological ethnocentrism ... to impose culturally alien categories as an interpretive grid on other linguistic and conceptual systems. ... Terminological ethnocentrism necessarily introduces distortion and inaccuracy because it imposes the perspective of a cultural and linguistic outsider.' Whilst broad correspondences exist between languages, they are hardly ever one to one. For instance, both Mikołajczuk and Wierzbicka have to resort to several English equivalents when glossing Polish ANGER-words:

---

[26] Catherine Lutz, 'The Domain of Emotion Words on Ifaluk', *American Ethnologist* 9 (1982): 113–28, at 117.

[27] Rage is defined by the OED as 'violent anger, fury, usually manifested in looks, words or action', so in some ways it is an excessive or intensified version of anger. *Oxford English Dictionary Online*, s.v. 'rage, n.' (Oxford University Press, March 2013), at http://www.oed.com (accessed 18 January 2013).

[28] An early observation of this was made by Sapir and Whorf. See, for instance: Edward Sapir, *Selected Writings of Edward Sapir in Language, Culture and Personality* (Berkeley, 1949), p. 27. Whilst the Sapir–Whorf theory is obsolete, it has nonetheless drawn the needed attention to the differences between languages in defining human experience.

złość 'anger'/'exasperation',[29] *Jestem wściekła* 'I am displeased/angry/furious' and *Jestem zła* 'I am displeased/angry/furious.'[30] Similarly, Durst stresses that 'there is no German word that perfectly matches the English word *anger*, and none of the German words ... has a clear counterpart in English.'[31]

Whilst NSM's theoretical base is sound, there are difficulties in applying it to historical semantics. As Biggam points out, the data of a historical semanticist are 'non-representative of the former spoken language' and there are no 'native speakers with whom to conduct a substitutability test',[32] one of the major criteria for verifying an NSM explication. Another drawback of the NSM is that, whilst useful for uncovering prototypical scenarios, it often does not take into consideration literary convention and textual issues.

In historical studies these are of primary concern, since our data are textual, governed by genre and style. Diller points out the need to reconstruct context for our data, and he divides them into *microcontext*, the immediate syntactic environment and behaviour of a lexeme, *mesocontext*, the episodic or situational context and *macrocontext*, the socio-historical context. Whilst *microcontext* is most relevant to corpus linguistics and semantics, a historical semanticist cannot operate without at least a working knowledge of the remaining two.[33] Thus, the textual criterion can be more important than the temporal criterion, as a given text type will utilise certain vocabulary with more stability due to literary convention, as is the case with poetic vocabulary in Old English.

Another distinction that is useful for understanding semantic and lexical studies into emotions is that between onomasiological and semasiological approaches. Geeraerts explains the difference between them:

> Given that a lexical item couples a word form with a semantic content, the distinction between an onomasiological and a semasiological approach is based on the choice of either of the poles in this correlation as the starting-point of the investigation. Thus, the onomasiological approach starts from the content side, typically asking the question 'Given concept *x*, what lexical items can it be

---

[29] Agnieszka Mikołajczuk, 'The Metonymic and Metaphorical Conceptualisation of *Anger* in Polish', in Athanasiadou and Tabakowska (eds), *Speaking of Emotions*, pp. 153–90, at 155.

[30] Anna Wierzbicka, 'Emotion, Language and "Cultural Scripts"', in Shinobu Kitayama and Hazel Rose Markus (eds), *Emotion and Culture: Empirical Studies of Mutual Influence* (Washington, DC, 1994), pp. 130–98, at 135.

[31] Durst, p. 118.

[32] Carole Biggam, *The Semantics of Colour: A Historical Approach* (Cambridge, 2012), p. 98.

[33] Hans-Jürgen Diller, 'Historical Semantics, Corpora, and the Unity of English Studies', in Monika Fludernik and Benjamin Kohlmann (eds), *Anglistentag 2011 Freiburg Proceedings* (Trier, 2012), pp. 321–37, at 323.

expressed with?' Conversely, the semasiological approach starts from the formal side, typically asking the question 'Given lexical item *y*, what meaning does it express?' In other words, the typical subject of semasiology is polysemy and the multiple applicability of a lexical item, whereas onomasiology is concerned with synonymy and near-synonymy, name-giving, and the selection of an expression from among a number of alternative possibilities.[34]

Most studies on metaphoric expression and conceptualisations, as well as lexical field research, are onomasiological, because their focus is extended to various means of expressing the same concept. The studies utilising NSM can be termed semasiological, as they focus on isolated words. However, the semasiological approach is also interested in polysemy and vagueness and how the same word can function differently in a different context. In a diachronic perspective, onomasiology looks at how innovations change the 'lexical inventory of the language',[35] whilst semasiology is more interested in 'changes of denotational, referential meaning and changes of connotational meaning (specifically, of emotive meaning or Gefühlswert)'[36] of a given lexical item. However, what is often neglected is that both approaches should be complementary. A broad analysis of conceptualisations that begins with abstract emotional macrocategories (such as ANGER or SADNESS) and already pre-existing types of metaphors but fails to analyse the specific lexical items runs a higher risk of ethnocentric bias. There is a likelihood for non-prototypical examples (from a Present-Day English perspective) to fall outside the bracket of research or be placed in a different category. On the other hand, lexical studies of isolated words do not show us how those words fit within their own semantic and lexical fields and how they link with other broader concepts in the lexicon.

There is an obvious tension in various approaches between what is universal and what is culture specific, between words as they are used in language and the concepts and cognitions behind them. The methodologies developed are often geared towards showing one or the other in greater relief. The universality of emotional experience resulting from a shared biology is pitted against the complexities of social norms regulating emotional expression and complicated further by cognitive maps and linguistic categorisations. In the case of historical semantics, textual concerns need to be accounted for as well.

---

[34] Geeraerts, *Diachronic*, p. 16.
[35] Geeraerts, *Theories*, p. 26.
[36] Ibid.

ANGER in Old English

There is an ever-growing body of research into emotions and mind in general,[37] and ANGER in particular in Anglo-Saxon studies. There have been several semantic studies of ANGER in Old English, focusing on conceptual metaphors and metonymies, and providing only partially overlapping conceptualisations, which are analysed either on a phrasal level or on a lexical level. Romano traces in Old English the same six metaphorical systems identified by Johnson and Kövecses in American English.[38] Fabiszak proposes metaphors similar to Romano's, such as ANGER IS FIRE/HEAT, ANGER IS AN OPPONENT, ANGER IS A WILD ANIMAL, but they are not identical.[39] These studies analyse phrases into which ANGER-words enter (i.e. 'ANGER IS A LIQUID, which one can *ageōtan* "pour", "shed on somebody"').[40] Conversely, Gevaert's studies are limited to words denoting ANGER and her conceptualisations are mostly based on etymology. She traces the changes in the conceptual and lexical fields,[41] whilst calling for an approach that combines 'historical, cognitive and prototype semantics ... based on quantitative corpus analysis'.[42] A similar approach is also proposed in this chapter, but from a different perspective. Both Romano's and Fabiszak's studies work on a limited set of data, but Gevaert's are more extensive, covering the entire Toronto *Corpus of Old English*,[43] and tracing changes in conceptualisations in Middle and Early Modern English.

One other concern with such studies is that, in order to designate a given conceptualisation as ANGER AS X, first we must define our source domain X

---

[37] Malcolm Godden, 'Anglo-Saxons on the Mind', in Michael Lapidge and Helmut Gneuss (eds), *Learning and Literature in Anglo-Saxon England* (Cambridge, 1985), pp. 271–98; Antonina Harbus, *The Life of the Mind in Old English Poetry* (Amsterdam and New York, 2002); Leslie Lockett, *Anglo-Saxon Psychologies in the Vernacular and Latin Traditions* (Toronto, 2011).

[38] Manuela Romano, '*Anger* in Old English', *Selim* 9 (1999): 45–56.

[39] Małgorzata Fabiszak, 'A Semantic Analysis of Emotion Terms in Old English', *Studia Anglica Posnaniensia* 34 (1999): pp. 133–46; Małgorzata Fabiszak, 'A Semantic Analysis of FEAR, GRIEF and ANGER words in Old English', in Javier E. Díaz Vera (ed.), *A Changing World of Words: Studies in English Historical Lexicography, Lexicology and Semantics* (Amsterdam, 2002), pp. 255–74.

[40] Romano, p. 50.

[41] Caroline Gevaert, 'The evolution of the lexical and conceptual field of ANGER in Old and Middle English', in Díaz Vera (ed.), *A Changing World of Words*, pp. 275–99; *The History of Anger: The Lexical Field of ANGER from Old to Early Modern English* (PhD thesis, Leuven, 2007).

[42] Gevaert, 'Evolution', p. 294.

[43] Toronto *Dictionary of English Web Corpus*, later referred to as *DOE Corpus* (Antonette diPaolo Healey (ed.), with John Price Wilkin and Xin Xiang, *Dictionary of Old English Web Corpus*, http://www.doe.utoronto.ca (accessed 18 January 2013).

with a Present-Day English word carrying its own cultural valence. Whilst this does not pose problems with simpler concepts (i.e. FIRE or HEAT), it becomes an issue when more abstract concepts are the source domain – there are *two* heuristic crutches in the same conceptualisation, which increases the potential for ethnocentric bias twofold.

Anger is often portrayed as insanity throughout European history,[44] and Gevaert identifies the conceptualisation of ANGER AS INSANITY in a single occurrence of *ellenwōd* in *Juliana*.[45] However, using the shorthand INSANITY may obscure semantic and contextual ranges of *wōd*. DOE defines *ellenwōd* as both a 'strong negative emotion' and a 'strong positive emotion', meaning 'furious' and 'zealous'.[46] OE *wōd* 'mad, raging', *wōda* 'a madman, an insane person, one possessed', *wōda* 'epilepticus, demoniaticus', *wōden-dream* 'madness, fury, *furor animi*' are all related to insanity, but not in its modern understanding. Etymologically and conceptually they are linked with the name of Woden, associated with poetic or battle fury. Pokorny gives the definition of the PIE root **uāt* as 'geistig angeregt sein'[47] and provides cognates: Latin *vates* 'prophets' or Proto-Celtic **wātus* 'mantic poetry'.[48] Adam of Bremen's *Gesta Hammaburgensis*, chapter 26, relates: 'Alter Wodan, id est furor, bella gerit, hominique ministrat virtutem contra inimicos.'[49] In the case of the Old English word, that inspiration of warriors with courage is echoed in the second part of the compound, as *ellen* means 'courage, strength'.[50] Madness was also explained as demonic possession (*wōda* glosses *demoniaticus*). Consequently, treating *ellenwōd* as an example of the conceptualisation of ANGER AS INSANITY does not provide this fine-grained view. In fact, the conceptualisation could better be rendered with ANGER AS INSPIRATION BY SUPERNATURAL FORCES or ANGER AS POSSESSION.

Adopting a more semasiological, lexical–semantic approach allows us to first understand the words in their own right, with all the nuances of application and usage, and only then look at links in the entire semantic field and between various word-families. If we want to study the semantic field of ANGER, our approach is initially onomasiological, and we need to select

---

[44] Durst, p. 115.

[45] Gevaert, 'Evolution', p. 286.

[46] Gevaert uses ANGER AS A STRONG EMOTION for some of her conceptualisations, but does not attribute it to *ellenwōd*.

[47] '[being] intellectually [or mentally] animated'.

[48] Julius Pokorny, *Indogermanisches etymologisches Wörterbuch*, 3 vols (Bern, 1959), II, s.v. **uāt*.

[49] 'The other is Wodan, that is fury, he wages war and gives man courage against enemies.' J.M. Lappenberg, *Adami Gesta Hammaburgensis ecclesiae pontificum. Ex recensione Lappenbergii*, ed. G. Waitz and L.C. Weiland, 2nd edn (Hanover, 1876), lib. IV, ch. 26, pp. 174–5.

[50] DOE, s.v. *ellen* 1.

ANGER-words in Old English with the help of *Thesaurus of Old English*[51] or the *Historical Thesaurus of the Oxford English Dictionary*[52] (looking at the section on 'anger, wrath, fury, rage'). But once the choice of material has been made, a semasiological study should analyse the entire range of meaning for a given word-family. This bottom-up approach, which allows categorisations to emerge from the material, minimises the dangers of 'an outsider's perspective'. It means that examples which do not fit the presupposed ANGER-scenario are not disregarded, and it leaves room to deal with ambiguity, context and genre, as well as cultural richness. It is not enough to acknowledge cultural differences; the methodology needs to be aimed at minimising the ethnocentric bias, and there is a need to supplement the cognitive and conceptual studies with a careful lexical–semantic analysis of the key terms.

Methodology

Old English has several word-families to which ANGER is attributed,[53] but they differ in usage, frequency, time frame and distribution among text types. The dictionary definitions provide a range of Present-Day English equivalents, sometimes suggesting separate meanings for a lexeme where Old English might have treated it as a single meaning. The lexicographic data suffice as an introduction, but they can be misleading. As not all Old English ANGER-words are covered by DOE, Bosworth and Toller's *Anglo-Saxon Dictionary* serves as a starting point,[54] but needs to be supplemented with data from several other sources. Initially, as has been proposed by Györi,[55] the etymology of a given word and its cognates in closely related contemporary languages (Old High German, Old Saxon, Old Frisian, Old Norse, Gothic) should be considered, together with other relevant Indo-European cognates. This process allows to determine the meaning of the root of a word-family at the earlier stages of language development. It helps to determine whether the conceptualisation is transparent in Old English, and points to alternative lines of semantic development. A look

---

[51] Jane Roberts, Christian Kay, with Lynne Grundy (eds), *A Thesaurus of Old English*, 2 vols (Amsterdam, 2000).

[52] Christian Kay, Jane Roberts, Micheal Samuels and Irené Wotherspoon (eds), *Historical Thesaurus of the Oxford English Dictionary*, 2 vols (Oxford, 2009).

[53] YRRE, BELGAN, GRAM, HĀTHEORT, WRĀÐ, TORN, WĒAMOD and, arguably, ANDA, WŌD.

[54] John Bosworth and T. Northcote Toller, *An Anglo-Saxon Dictionary* (Oxford, 1898); T. Northcote Toller, *An Anglo-Saxon Dictionary: Supplement* (Oxford, 1921). Henceforth referred to as BT.

[55] Gabor Györi, 'Cultural Variation in the Conceptualisation of Emotions: A Historical Study', in Athanasiadou and Tabakowska (eds), *Speaking of Emotions*, pp. 99–124.

at the diachrony of the word-family and its reflexes in Middle and Early Modern English gives further clues to semantic development and the word-family's survival. Then, a word-family should be analysed by determining the number of distinct types (the existing lexemes, both simplex and compounds, and the grammatical categories), and how those occurrences are distributed in the corpus with regard to text types. Initially, broad categories such as poetry, prose, glosses, are used, and where needed, broken down into particular genres, text types or named authors (e.g. saints' lives, laws, homilies, heroic poetry). The syntactic and conceptual behaviour is analysed by looking for the most frequent patterns of collocations, near-synonymy and co-occurrences, with regard for formulaic phrases and alliteration. At this stage, a comparison with conceptual metaphors and metonymies is appropriate. Finally, the implicit scripts are analysed by identifying common referents and typical scenarios.

TORN – A Case Study

The *TORN* word-family has been chosen to illustrate the proposed approach for a number of reasons. In comparison to other ANGER word-families it is one of the smallest, both in terms of number of occurrences (47 occ.) and the individual lemmas (14), but substantial enough to provide conclusive data. The occurrences are confined almost exclusively to poetry, with one in prose, none in glosses and one in a runic inscription. This word-family belongs to poetic vocabulary, usually more archaic, and does not survive into Middle English. Whilst it is problematic to pinpoint when the family went out of use, the word *torn* appears early in the runic inscription on the Auzon Casket (c. 700).[56] Thus, it is a word-family characterised by a limited use and timeframe, but showing variation.

Lexicographic Evidence

TORN is listed in the *Thesaurus of Old English* under the headings ANGER and GRIEF. The dictionaries attribute a range of meanings to this word-family and do not always agree on the choice of Present-Day English equivalents. This is either because the meaning is not stable in Old English, or because the conceptual system of Present-Day English is ill suited for mirroring that of Old English. Some of the senses are 'anger', 'grief', 'pain' for the simplex noun, and 'bitter' or 'grievous' for the simplex adjective.[57] In addition to simplex forms, there are ten compounds

---

[56] R.I. Page, *An Introduction to English Runes* (Woodbridge, 1999), pp. 25–6.
[57] *torn* (n.) 'violent emotion of anger or grief', *torn* (adj.) 'causing violent emotions of grief or anger, grievous, distressing', *torne* ' in a way that causes grief or distress', *tornlic* 'grievous, bitter' (BT, s.v. *torn*, n., *torn*, adj., *torne*, adv. and *tornlic*, adj.).

employing -*torn*- in their morphology, either as base or modifier.[58] For those using *torn*- as modifier, it is difficult to ascertain whether it is an adjective or a noun, and the different interpretations choose either 'anger' sense of the noun or 'grievous, offensive' sense of the adjective. Three compounds (*torncwide*, *tornwyrdan* and *tornword*) refer to a harmful or offensive acts of speech.[59]

Etymology and Cognates

OE *torn* is descended from the PIE root **der*- 'skin, flay, split'[60] or 'break, burst'.[61] Cognates in Indo-European languages mean physically rending something, or separating it with force, whether it is Tocharian AB *tsär*- 'to be separated, to separate', Sanskrit *dṛṇāti* 'to burst, to tear', or Greek δέρω 'to flay'.[62] Some cognates refer to mental states, such as Lithuanian *durnas* (adj.) 'mad' and *durnûti* (v.) 'to rage'.[63] Figuratively, it means breaking relations between people, as in OIr *drenn* (v.) 'to quarrel'[64] or OHG (v.) *zeran* 'to quarrel'.[65] Cognates of OE *torn* are attested only within the West Germanic branch of Germanic languages, for the adjective: OS *torn* 'bitter, painful', MHG *Zorn(e)* 'angry, furious';[66] for the noun: OHG *Zorn* 'anger, bitterness, wrath, indignation', earliest recorded in the ninth century.[67] Pfeifer suggests the development proceeded from a Proto-Germanic verb **teranan* 'to tear asunder',[68] also responsible for OE *teran* 'to tear'. Old Saxon and Old English have a greater range of meanings in common with each other than Old High German, which narrows *Zorn* to 'anger'. Although the extant Old English and Old High German corpora are different in sizes, *Zorn* seems better rooted in the Old High German lexicon than *torn* is in Old English. The first attestation of OE *torn* appears early (mid-eighth century) and it might have preserved an earlier range of meanings present either in Proto-Germanic or in the Ingvaeonic group. In Old High German, the earliest attestation of *Zorn* is

---

[58] These are: *lygetorn, gārtorn, torncwide, tornwyrdan, tornword, torngemōt, torngenīþla, tornwracu* and *tornsorh*.

[59] BT, s.v. *torncwide, tornwyrdan* and *tornword*.

[60] Winfred Lehmann, *A Gothic Etymological Dictionary* (Leiden, 1986), s.v. D22. **dis-tairan*.

[61] Helmut Rix et al. (eds), *Lexicon Der Indogermanischen Verben. Die Wurzeln und ihre Primärstammbildungen* (Wiesbaden, 2001), s.v. **der*-¹.

[62] Lehmann, *Gothic*, s.v. D22. **dis-tairan*; Vladimir Orel, *A Handbook of Germanic Etymology* (Leiden, 2003), s.v. **turnaz*.

[63] Friedrich Kluge, *Etymological Dictionary of the German Language*, trans. John Francis Davis (London, 1891), s.v. *Zorn*.

[64] Lehmann, *Gothic*, s.v. D22. **dis-tairan*.

[65] Orel, s.v. **turnaz*.

[66] Ibid.

[67] Wolfgang Pfeifer, *Etymologisches Wörterbuch des Deutschen* (Berlin, 1993), s.v. *Zorn*.

[68] Orel, s.v. **turnaz*.

from the ninth century and it means only 'anger, angry'. The word goes on to become one of the central words of the German lexical field of ANGER, which suggests narrowing took place.

Distribution

TORN occurrences are evenly distributed among different poetic texts. The largest number of occurrences is found in *Guthlac* (9 occ.), then in *Beowulf* (7 occ.) and *Genesis* (7 occ.). Texts range from heroic (*Beowulf*) through poetic retellings of Biblical stories (*Genesis, Christ, Judith*), to stories of saints (*Elene, Andreas*) and translations of psalms (*PPs*). In both the Biblical material and in the saints' lives *TORN* is more prominent than in any other type of text. Several of the poems from these two groups can be assigned to or associated with Cynewulf and there are seven occurrences of *TORN* in the signed Cynewulfian poems. Thus the possibility of the poet's preference for this word-family should be considered. The only prose example is in the Old English *Orosius* – a relatively early prose text, dating from the late ninth century.[69]

Referents

TORN may occasionally have animate actors or referents, but it is more often used for abstract ideas or as modifiers of inanimate nouns. It is used to refer to God's anger, but all five occurrences are found in *Genesis* only. Similarly, the only five occurrences referring to devils are found in *Guthlac*. This suggests that in both cases the usage is not typical. Among other referents are Myrmedonians in *Andreas* and Assyrians in *Judith*, as enemies *en masse*. Women are referred to three times, in both positive and negative contexts. Other referents include Cain, Abraham, Hrothgar, Beowulf, and a nameless father from *Precepts*.

Analysis of referents/actors shows that *TORN* does not follow the patterns of other ANGER-words, where God is universally the most common referent. There are several poetic texts that could have well accommodated the usage of *TORN* for God, since those texts employ different ANGER-words in a similar fashion, for instance *Christ and Satan, Christ* and *The Paris Psalter*. The lack of those occurrences may be significant, suggesting that other, more suitable ANGER-words were used in those contexts and that *TORN* might not have been a good word choice for expressing the wrath of God, despite its use in *Genesis*. Later comparative evidence shows that the German cognate *Zorn* is used in Martin Luther's Bible as one of the most frequent equivalents for Latin *ira Dei*,[70] which again stresses the differences between Anglo-Saxon and German developments.

---

[69] Janet Bately, *The Old English Orosius*, EETS s.s. 6 (Oxford, 1980), pp. lxxxvi–xciii.
[70] Durst, p. 136.

Co-occurrences

When analysing collocations and co-occurring words, the main assumption is that, if a given word consistently co-occurs with other groups of words in emphatic constructions, those groups of words are likely to share meaning(s) or be conceptually related.[71] The collocations and co-occurrences of *TORN* fall into categories of anger,[72] sadness/grief,[73] suffering/enduring,[74] harm/torment,[75] tears/weeping,[76] insults/blasphemy,[77] hotness[78] and vengeance.[79]

TORN-words occur with both ANGER- and GRIEF-words in similar proportions, with a slight predominance of the GRIEF group, but it is worth mentioning that differences between grief and anger are 'less fundamental than current taxonomies suggest'.[80] The correlation of *TORN* with ANGER-words is strongest in *Genesis*, and with GRIEF-words in *Guthlac*, although both texts show examples of other usages. *Beowulf* contains examples of both patterns of co-occurrence, with a predominance of GRIEF-words, and ANGER-words attributable to just several occurrences. The only text in which *TORN* occurs alongside ANGER-words, but not GRIEF-words is *The Paris Psalter*. Conversely, there are three texts containing only GRIEF-words, but no ANGER-words – *The Riming Poem*, *Maxims I* and the runic inscription on the Auzon Casket. *Judith* contains GRIEF and INSULTS, but arguably no ANGER. This suggests that the co-occurrences of ANGER-words for *TORN* is unusual, and may constitute non-prototypical usage.

Regardless of whether *TORN* means 'anger', 'grief' or both, the third group of collocations shows it is something harmful, to be endured. The emotion or internal state denoted by *TORN* is accompanied by physical manifestations, such as hotness, tears or weeping, and is of high intensity.

Examples

Some occurrences of *TORN* can be rendered with PDE 'anger', mostly on the basis of co-occurrences with other ANGER-words. The passage below, from

---

[71] This is known as the 'distributional hypothesis', where 'words that occur in the same contexts tend to have similar meanings' (Geeraerts, *Theories*, p. 59).
[72] e.g. *gegremed, gebolgen, yrre*.
[73] e.g. *hygesorg, hrēohmōd, geomormōd*.
[74] e.g. *þolian, druge*.
[75] e.g. *hearm, tēon, tintreg*.
[76] e.g. *tear, wōpes hring*.
[77] *hosp, tēoncwide, tælness*.
[78] *hāt hēafodwylm*.
[79] *wrecan, gyrnwræce*.
[80] Diller, '*ANGER* and *TĒNE*', p. 109.

Genesis A, relates God's anger at Satan. The emotional vocabulary builds up tension and creates an image of God not unlike Beowulf in his grappling match with Grendel:

> Þa he **gebolgen** wearð,
> besloh synsceaþan   sigore and gewealde,
> dome and dugeðe,   and dreame benam
> his feond, friðo   and gefean ealle,
> torhte tire,   and his **torn gewræc**
> on gesacum swiðe   selfes mihtum
> strengum stiepe.   Hæfde styrne mod,
> **gegremed** grymme,   grap on **wraðe**
> faum folmum,   and him on fæðm gebræc
> **yrre** on mode.
>
> (*Genesis*, ll. 54b–63a)[81]

[Then he became <u>enraged</u>, deprived the wicked ones of victory and power, dominion and glory, and took away the happiness from his enemies, all peace and pleasure, shining glory; and by his own power he <u>avenged his injury</u>/<u>wreaked his wrath</u> greatly on his enemies with a forceful overthrowing. He had a <u>stern</u> heart, fiercely <u>angered</u>/<u>provoked</u>; he grasped them in <u>wrath</u> with hostile hands and crushed them in his grip, <u>angry</u> in mind.][82]

But even in this passage, with several ANGER-words, *TORN* is not unambiguous. The phrase *torn gewræc* (l. 58) may refer to an internal emotional state: '[he] wreaked his wrath/anger' or '[he] externalised his negative emotions by performing a violent physical action'. However, it could also be translated as '[he] avenged his injury', where *torn* denotes the offending event. This is not unexpected, as anger is related to the perceived sense of 'being wronged', but this distinction between 'emotion' and the 'event that causes the emotion' might not be as clearly perceived in Old English as it is in Present-Day English.

The main reason for rendering *TORN* as 'anger' is because it collocates with *wrecan*. However, as in the below example of *Judith*, the sole co-occurrence of *wrecan* is not enough to identify this emotion as anger, as *wrecan* itself has a broad range of meanings, e.g. 'drive out, punish, avenge, wreak'.[83]

---

[81] All Old English texts are quoted after the *DOE Web Corpus*. In all the passages I have marked the relevant *TORN*-word as underlined and in bold. The words in bold are those which have impact on the analysis of meaning of *TORN* itself.
[82] All translations are mine, unless otherwise noted.
[83] BT, s.v. *wrecan*.

> **Gewrec** nu, mihtig dryhten,
> torhtmod tires brytta, þæt me ys þus **torne** on mode,
> **hate on hreðre** minum.
>
> *(Judith*, ll. 92b–94a)

[Avenge now, mighty Lord, illustrious Prince of glory, that which is so <u>painful</u> to me in my mind, and so hot in my breast.]

Judith prays to God asking for help in avenging her *torn* and guiding her sword to kill Holofernes. Whilst *gewrecan* could help classify this instance as 'anger' or 'offence', several lines earlier Judith's emotional state is described clearly:

> **þearle** ys me nu ða
> heorte **onhæted** ond hige **geomor**,
> swyðe mid **sorgum** gedrefed.
>
> *(Judith*, ll. 86b–88a)

[The heart is now in me severely heated up and my mind sad, greatly troubled with sorrows.]

The repetition of the state of the heart as heating up under the influence of emotions allows for a link between *torne on mode* and *hige geomor*. Judith does not seem to be experiencing anger – there are no other lexical or contextual clues in the passage to warrant that – but a very painful emotion. She distances herself from the act of punishment by asking God to avenge her sorrows in her stead, as she appears incapable of performing the deed on her own. She cuts off Holofernes' head only after being inspired with courage ('mid elne', l. 95) by God.

In *Beowulf* there are two potential instances of ANGER and/or OFFENCE. Upon hearing of the destruction caused by the dragon, Beowulf wishes to act and engage in a battle with the creature:

> Gewat þa XIIa sum **torne gebolgen**
> dryhten Geata   dracan sceawian.
>
> *(Beowulf,* ll. 2401–2)

[Then he went, one of 12, the Lord of the Geats, <u>swollen with torn</u>/<u>enraged with anger</u> to see the dragon.]

Gebolgen falls into this pattern with another ANGER word, *yrre*, in an emphatic, but possibly redundant construction *yrre gebolgen*, which may suggest *torn* is synonymous with *yrre* or with *gebolgen*.[84] This phrase type occurs six times in the corpus, as *x a/on/gebolgen*, where x is a noun in the dative or an adverb. These are *yrre gebolgen, torne gebolgen, sare gebolgen, facne gebolgen* and *bitere abolgen*. *Yrre* and *facne* are nouns in dat.sg., and *bitere* is clearly an adverb.[85] *Torne* and *sare* can be interpreted as either nouns in dat.sg. or adverbs. If we treat both *torne* and *sare* as adverbs, they would have the intensifying meaning of 'severely, grievously, greatly'; in this case, *ā/gebolgen* is better rendered with PDE 'offended, angered'. If, however, we treat *torne* and *sare* as nouns, *gebolgen* is better rendered with PDE 'swollen up with'. This would account for the wide semantic range of the first element of the phrase: *yrre* 'anger', *facen* 'treachery', *sār* 'pain, suffering' and *torn* 'a painful, violent emotion',[86] thus indicating that different things cause internal swelling of the mind, following Lockett's hydraulic model.[87]

The situation in the passage could call for the reading 'anger', since Beowulf has a reason to be angry. Indeed, 'anger' is a preferred choice for many translators.[88] It is true that Beowulf exhibits anger often when fighting the monsters. Here, however, he learns of the destruction caused by the dragon, a cause for grief or pain.

In contrast to Beowulf, Hrothgar cannot personally defeat Grendel, but is also suffering *torn*:

> Wæs seo hwil micel;
> XII wintra tid **torn geþolode**
> wine Scyldinga, **weana** gehwelcne,
> sidra **sorga**.
>
> (*Beowulf*, ll. 146b–149a)

[This time was long. For the period of twelve winters the lord and friend of the Scyldings suffered/endured the <u>misery/pain</u>, each of the <u>woes/afflictions</u>, the immense <u>miseries</u>.]

---

[84] If *gebolgen* is understood as simply 'swollen', the construction would not be redundant, but would emphasise the physiological feelings accompanying 'anger'. In this case, both *yrre* and *torn* could be treated as different emotions.

[85] DOE, s.v. *bitere*: '1. bitterly; used as an intensifier with a wide range of verbs: 1.a. grievously, cruelly; 1.b. greatly; 1.c. bitterly'.

[86] Gevaerts uses both *TORN* and *SARE* as examples of the conceptualisation ANGER AS AFFLICTION.

[87] Lockett.

[88] For example, Crossley-Holland translates it as 'fury' (Kevin Crossley-Holland (trans.), *Beowulf* (Oxford, 2008), p. 80), Jack glosses it with 'anger' (George Jack (ed.), *Beowulf: A Student Edition* (Oxford, 1997), p. 168), Bradley translates the phrase as 'bursting with anger' (S.A.J. Bradley (ed. and trans.), *Anglo-Saxon Poetry* (London, 1982), p. 474), and Heaney chooses 'rage' (Seamus Heaney, *Beowulf: A New Verse Translation* (London and New York, 2000), p. 163).

Not only does Hrothgar 'suffer' *torn* for a long time, but the meaning 'pain, affliction' is strengthened by *wēa* and *sorh*, both belonging to the category of MENTAL PAIN OR AFFLICTION.[89] Another instance is found in a passage where Beowulf is describing Hrothgar's emotions after the death of Æschere:

> þæt wæs Hroðgare   **hreowa <u>tornost</u>**
> þara þe leodfruman   lange begeate.
>
> (*Beowulf*, ll. 2129–30)

[That was to Hrothgar the most painful/grievous of sorrows that the lord of the people had received for a long time.]

The loss of the most trusted and faithful of advisors is the source of grief (*hreow*), which is described as *tornost* 'the most painful or grievous'. The main difference between these passages is in the action of the two characters – where Beowulf sets off to kill the dragon, Hrothgar cannot inflict physical retribution.

A *TORN* word is found in *Beowulf* with a meaning closer to 'anger' or 'offence':

> Ne bið swylc cwenlic þeaw
> idese to efnanne,   þeah ðe hio ænlicu sy,
> þætte freoðuwebbe   feores onsæce
> æfter **ligetorne**   leofne mannan.
>
> (*Beowulf*, ll. 1940b–1943)

[It is not queenly for a lady to behave like this, even if she be without match, that a peace-weaver deprives of life the beloved man because of <u>a false offence</u>/<u>false cause for anger.</u>]

This compound is variously translated as 'imagined insult'[90] or 'feigned anger or grief'.[91] The queen punishes the man in response to an offence that did not take place. It is probably one of the least ambiguous uses of *TORN* for 'offence', and tentatively 'anger', however, 'injury' is still as likely.

This is mirrored in the *TORN*-compounds that denote blasphemy or insults, as in *Christ*, where Joseph addresses Mary, confronting her about her uncleanliness:

> Ic lungre eam
> deope gedrefed,   dome bereafod,

---

[89] Kay et al. (eds), *Historical Thesaurus*, Section 02.02
[90] Bradley, p. 462; Jack, p. 141.
[91] BT, s.v. *lygetorn*.

> forðon ic worn for þe worde hæbb
> **sidra sorga** ond **sar**cwida,
> **hearmes** gehyred, ond me **hosp** sprecað,
> **tornworda** fela. Ic tearas sceal
> geotan **geomormod**.
>
> (*Christ*, ll. 167b–173a)

[I am suddenly deeply offended, deprived of honour, because I have heard on your account a great many words of countless afflictions and reproach, and harm, and they have told me insults, many painful words/insults. I must shed tears, sad at heart.]

Crucially, this passage emphasises that the insults and reproaches are so painful to Joseph that they cause him to cry, but there is no visible anger or need to avenge his injury.

Similarly to *Judith* above, physical or physiological reactions are often portrayed, as in *Christ*:

> þær wæs **wopes hring**,
> **torne** bitolden; wæs seo treowlufu
> **hat æt heortan**, **hreðer** innan weoll,
> beorn breostsefa.
>
> (*Christ*, ll. 533b–540a)

[There was the sound of weeping, overwhelmed with grief/misery. The true love was hot at/around the heart, the mind welled up within, the mind-in-the-breast of the men.]

The apostles witness Christ's ascension into heaven and are overwhelmed by *torn*. The hydraulic model is at work here, and *torn* wells up in the heart, accompanied by weeping.[92] Bearing in mind Lockett's argument that the hydraulic model as a folk psychology model has a strong presence in Old English, emotions can be treated as a mental and a physical sensation – localised in the breast and evidenced by physiological symptoms. *TORN* can be seen as physical pain or suffering, accompanied by hotness, weeping, and gnashing of the teeth.

An NSM explication

I propose two NSM models, the first one [1] corresponding to the ANGER group, the second [2] to the GRIEF group:

---

[92] Lockett, pp. 61, 64.

1. *torn*
   (a) X thinks something like this
   (b) this person (Y) did something bad
   (c) I don't want this
   (d) I feel bad inside
   (e) I will do something because of it now
   (f) because of this, X feels something very bad
   (g) because of this, X wants to do something bad to Y

2. *torn*
   (a) X thinks something like this
   (b) this person (Y) did something bad
   (c) I don't want this
   (d) I feel bad inside
   (e) I will do something because of it now
   (f) I know that I can't do anything
   (g) because of this, X feels something very bad for some time

The two models differ in what happens after the emotion is felt (in bold). *Torn* is a response to 'something bad' that is a result of someone else's actions. In case [1] God, Beowulf or the queen do something about it, most often violently. In case [2], Hrothgar, Joseph, the Apostles, and even Judith know that they cannot do much about the event that has caused *torn*, apart from expressing it in a physiological manner (e.g. tears). It is altogether too easy to assign all the instances of [1] to PDE *anger* and [2] to PDE *grief*, because [1] follows our expectations of an ANGER-scenario and [2] corresponds more to the GRIEF-scenario.

Conclusions and Relevance to Historical Semantics and the History of Emotions

TORN is unusual in that it is a clearly archaic and poetic word-family that happens to cover the usage of both PDE *anger* and PDE *grief*. Its etymology suggests close links with pain caused by physical destruction through breaking and bursting. Whilst Old High German narrowed the meaning to ANGER, or, as in the case of Lithuanian, to MADNESS, Old English has retained the broadened sense of a negative, strong and painful emotion, which is strengthened by collocating with other PAIN-words. At the same time, it is often used with other Old English words from both ANGER and GRIEF groups and applied to both grief (more common) and anger (less common) scenarios in our Present-Day English understanding. Dictionary definitions propose 'anger' with a high degree of certainty and distinguish it from 'grief', but these clear-cut distinctions are not justified. The least ambiguous instances that warrant the translation 'anger' or 'angry' appear in one text only, *Genesis*, and even there it is unclear whether they refer to ANGER or to an INJURY or OFFENCE. *TORN* might be viewed as a superordinate category that blends anger and grief; however, its kernel meaning is concerned with physical suffering and experience of mental pain caused by external events. These events can range from the departure of a loved lord, through insults, to a dragon ravaging one's kingdom.

Whilst studies into conceptualisations help uncover pervasive metaphors, an onomasiological study into either ANGER or GRIEF, guided by lexicographic data, can often end up treating *TORN* as an example of either of the two, and shoehorning it into the preconceived Present-Day English categories. This is what both Goddard and Wierzbicka warn against. A semasiological, lexical–semantic study, on the other hand, is more likely to treat the term in its own right.

Such lexical studies are relevant outside historical semantics, as translating instances of *TORN* with 'anger' or 'angry' has wide-ranging implications for our interpretation of the motivation of such characters as Judith, Beowulf and Hrothgar. Whether we choose to assign anger or grief on the basis of one word will often determine or change the reading. It is therefore crucial to examine the words in detail and avoid misreading. Lexical approaches underscored by an understanding of cross-cultural and cross-linguistic differences between emotion concepts in different languages, informed by prototype theory, and sensitive to genre and textual concerns are essential as a counterweight to cognitive studies following metaphor theory, and can be useful for all scholars dealing with the history of emotions in Old English.

Chapter 5
'So what did the Danes feel?' Emotion and Litotes in Old English Poetry

Stephen Graham

In *Beowulf*, the defeat of Grendel gives rise to perhaps the most intense example of positive emotion in the entire poem. The morning after the fight at Heorot, the long-suffering Danes gather around the battered hall to inspect physical evidence of the creature's demise. The poet uses litotes to describe what they feel, or rather do not feel, as they realise their tormentor is no more:

> Ða wæs on morgen   mine gefræge
> ymb þa gifheallc   guðrinc monig;
> ferdon folctogan   feorran ond nean
> geond widwegas   wundor sceawian,
> laþes lastas.   No his lifgedal
> sarlic þuhte   secga ænegum
> þara þe tirleases   trode sceawode,
> hu he werigmod   on weg þanon,
> niða ofercumen,   on nicera mere
> fæge ond geflymed   feorhlastas bær.
>
> (*Beowulf*, ll.837–46)[1]

[Then in the morning, as I've heard, there were many warriors around the gift-hall; the folk-leaders journeyed from far and near through distant regions to examine the wonder, the tracks of the enemy. His parting from life in no way seemed sorrowful to any of those men who inspected the glory-less tracks, how he, disheartened, overcome by violence, bore his life-failing steps from there to the water-monsters' mere, fated and put to flight.]

---

[1] All line numbers to Old English poems refer to the ASPR (*The Anglo-Saxon Poetic Records: A Collective Edition*, ed. George Philip Krapp and Elliott Van Kirk Dobbie, 6 vols (New York, 1931–53)) apart from *Beowulf*, which refers to *Klaeber's Beowulf and the Fight at Finnsburg*, 4th edn, ed. R.D. Fulk, Robert E. Bjork and John D. Niles (Toronto, 2008). Unless otherwise indicated, all translations are my own.

The strength of Danish feeling is conveyed here by not being stated. As Lanham notes, litotes is a kind of ironic 'understatement that intensifies', achieved by 'denial of the contrary'.[2] However, while litotes gives a clear sense of how strongly the Danes felt about Grendel's passing, it is purposely unclear about what exactly they did feel. The poet states that, in Grendel's defeat, 'Denum eallum wearð / ... willa gelumpen' (ll. 823b–4);[3] later, he says that the Danes who follow Grendel's tracks to the mere return 'high-spirited' ('modge', l. 855) from their 'cheering journey' ('gomenwaþe', l. 854).[4] Yet their initial reaction is never explicitly recorded. This lack of a definitive statement has led at least one critic to attribute multiple emotions to the Danes at this point. In his 1937 article on understatement in Old English poetry, Frederick Bracher mentions the above passage twice.[5] The first time he does so he says that the *Beowulf*-poet is describing the Danes' joyfulness.[6] Later, speaking about the humorous potential of litotes, he claims the statement may 'have been used as a kind of humorous relief, appropriately expressing the feeling of relaxed tension after danger'.[7] The two feelings he mentions are not the same: joyfulness on the one hand and a feeling of being relieved of a great psychological burden on the other. Both are plausible responses to news of Grendel's defeat. The Danes could have been joyful; they could have been relieved; the two feelings could also be part of a single, complex emotional reaction, with one feeling accompanying or being prompted by the other.

Bracher's response to this passage is not inconsistent, however. Rather, it is a natural consequence of the use of litotes, a device that provides much useful information about how Anglo-Saxons understood emotion. This example of litotes, for instance, indicates that Anglo-Saxons believed emotions to exist in opposition to one another; a negated reference to 'sorrow' only suggests 'joy' if it is accepted that there are certain basic relationships between emotions – that some can be paired with others. Bracher's recognition of multiple emotions further suggests that the use of litotes is based on more than just a knowledge of such pairs. As this example demonstrates, the negation of a single emotion can often evoke several 'opposed' emotional states in those who listen to or read the poem. This ambiguity means that litotes can potentially capture more complex

---

[2] Richard A. Lanham, *A Handlist of Rhetorical Terms*, 2nd edn (Berkeley, 1991), p. 95; similarly, 'a figure of speech by which an affirmation is made indirectly by denying its opposite, usually with the effect of understatement', Chris Baldick, *The Oxford Dictionary of Literary Terms*, 3rd edn (Oxford, 2008), p. 190.

[3] 'The wish of all the Danes was fulfilled.'

[4] This translation of *gomenwaþe* is from the fourth edition of *Klaeber's Beowulf*. Earlier editions have 'joyous journey'.

[5] Frederick Bracher, 'Understatement in Old English Poetry', *PMLA* 52 (1937): 915–34.

[6] Ibid., p. 916.

[7] Ibid., p. 922.

emotional states than a series of oppositions might initially suggest. Litotes is thus based on two very different approaches to emotion, one premised on the broad symmetry of certain emotions, and another that recognises their uniquely complex character. The following discussion explores both these approaches in Old English poetry and examines how they are reconciled in the use of litotes. In doing so, it addresses the question contained in the title of this chapter: what did the Danes really feel about Grendel's death?

Emotional Oppositions in Old English Poetry

To suggest Anglo-Saxons were aware of emotional oppositions is perhaps to state the obvious. Understanding emotions in terms of contrastive pairs has been a cultural commonplace from the Greeks to the present day. In *The Art of Rhetoric*, Aristotle's definition of emotions includes a reference to such pairs: 'emotions are those things by the alteration of which men differ with regard to those judgements which pain and pleasure accompany, such as anger, pity, fear and all other such *and their opposites*.'[8] Models of emotion that are structured around a series of contrastive pairs also occur in the work of several influential contemporary theorists. Robert Plutchik, for example, has graphically represented the structure of human emotion as a kind of circle or wheel, with each individual emotion facing its opposite.[9] Some of his oppositions seem obvious: sadness/joy, anger/fear; others appear less so: surprise/anticipation, disgust/trust.[10]

Unlike Plutchik and other theorists, Anglo-Saxon poets did not see single, unchanging relationships between emotional states. In the case of the Danish-reaction passage, the corpus contains evidence for both contrastive pairs identified by Bracher (sorrow/joy; sorrow/relief). In some instances, the way these pairs are presented suggests that Anglo-Saxon poets were not only aware

---

[8] Aristotle, *The Art of Rhetoric*, trans. H.C. Lawson-Tancred (London, 2004), p. 141. For a discussion of some of the problems associated with understanding emotional oppositions in Aristotle see David Konstan, *The Emotions of the Ancient Greeks: Studies in Aristotle and Classical Literature* (Toronto, 2006), pp. 77–90.

[9] Robert Plutchik, *Emotion: A Psychoevolutionary Synthesis* (New York, 1980), pp. 152–72; see also James A. Russell, 'A Circumplex Model of Affect', *Journal of Personality and Social Psychology* 39 (1980): 1161–78.

[10] Plutchik's oppositions are further sub-categorised according to emotional intensity. 'Joy' is thus accompanied by two other states, a less intense feeling Plutchik calls 'serenity' and the more intense 'ecstasy'. Likewise, sadness is a middle-state separating the more intense feeling of 'grief' and the less intense 'pensiveness' (p. 156); see also Robert Plutchik, 'The Nature of Emotions: Human Emotions Have Deep Evolutionary Roots, a Fact That May Explain Their Complexity and Provide Tools for Clinical Practice', *American Scientist* 89/4 (2001): 344–50, at 349.

of emotional oppositions; they often consciously set out to highlight them. In *The Rune Poem*, for example, the definition of 'joy' *wyn(n)*[11] is presented as the absence of sorrow:

> **w**(wen)ne bruceþ   ðe can weana lyt,
> sares and sorge,   and him sylfa hæfþ
> blæd and blysse   and eac byrga geniht.
>
> (*The Rune Poem*, ll. 22–4)

[He partakes of joy who knows little of miseries, grief and sorrow, and has for himself prosperity and bliss and also the abundance of cities.]

This passage stresses the difference between sorrow and joy by the use of two similarly structured alliterative pairs positioned at the same point on two successive lines. It calls attention to the very different content of those pairs by making everything else about them identical. The poet thus not only recognises an antithetical relationship between joy and sorrow; he uses that contrast to better define one of the emotions involved.

The opposite of sorrow in Old English poetry could also be *sibb* 'peace'. At the end of the third section of *Christ*, for example, Heaven is described in terms of the emotions experienced there.[12] In the following passage, alliteration and rhyme are again used to create two similarly structured phrases that foreground the opposition of *sibb* and *sorh*:

> Ðæt is se eþel   þe no geendad weorþeð,
> ac þær symle forð   synna lease
> dream weardiað,   dryhten lofiað,
> leofne lifes weard,   leohte biwundne,
> sibbum biswedede,   sorgum biwerede.
>
> (*Christ*, ll. 1639–44)

[That is the land which will not be ended, but there the sinless will always from then on have joy, praise the lord, the dear guardian of life, enveloped in light, swathed in peace, protected from sorrows.]

---

[11] Sometimes, as in *The Rune Poem*, spelled with an *e* rather than *y*; not to be confused with *wen* 'hope', with which it sometimes forms an alliterative pair (see below).

[12] Emotional oppositions are particularly evident in descriptions of states like Heaven (see also *Guthlac*, ll. 10–15) that are characterised by extremes of emotion. They also feature in descriptions of Hell (e.g. *Christ and Satan*, ll. 40–48) and Judgement Day (e.g. *The Judgement Day I*, ll. 22–6; *The Judgement Day II*, ll. 43–6; *Soul and Body II*, ll. 97–102).

Sibb was not simply the opposite of sorrow. Significantly for a reading of the Danish-reaction passage, it was also a state that could succeed and be a remedy for emotional suffering. In *Andreas*, for instance, one of the Mermedonians tries to persuade his companions to release Andrew from imprisonment and thus end what the poet elsewhere calls the *meoduscerwan* (l. 1546); this is the feeling of terror caused by the floods and other natural disasters inflicted upon the Mermedonians as a punishment for their treatment of the saint. He tells them:

> Us bið gearu sona
> sybb æfter sorge, gif we secaþ to him.
> (*Andreas*, ll. 1567b–8)

[Peace after sorrow will be prepared for us at once, if we go to him.]

Once again, alliteration is used here to emphasise the contrast between sorrow and the feeling of relief that will follow it.[13] Brooks notes that the term *meoduscerwan* in *Andreas* is unique and appears to be modelled on *ealuscerwan* (l. 769) in *Beowulf*; this feeling is the sense of panic that grips the Danes as they listen to Grendel and Beowulf fighting inside Heorot.[14] If it is the case that the *Andreas*-poet is following the *Beowulf*-poet here, then Bracher's reading of the Danish reaction as a kind of relief is well supported. In the case of the Danes, the death of Grendel can also be said to represent the coming of *sybb æfter sorge*.

Finally, for some poets *sibb* was close enough in meaning to both *wyn* and *wen* 'hope' to be used in apposition to them, suggesting this group of positive emotions could collectively constitute an alternative to a negative emotion like sorrow:

> Bidan we þæs longe,
> setan on sorgum, sibbe oflyste,
> wynnum ond wenum, hwonne we word godes
> þurh his sylfes muð secgan hyrde.
> (*The Descent to Hell*, ll. 80b–84)

[We waited a long time for Him, seated in sorrows, desiring peace, joys and hopes, when we might hear the word of God spoken through His own mouth.]

---

[13] The *Andreas*-poet uses this type of formula – a contrastive pair of alliterating terms separated by *æfter* – elsewhere to similarly suggest another transition between two opposed states: *geoc æfter gyrne* 'help after affliction' (l. 1585).

[14] Both expressions appear to refer ironically to a dispensing of ale/mead as the serving of a bitter drink that must be consumed. The critical discussion of these terms, and their relationship to each other, is reviewed in Fulk, Bjork and Niles, pp. 161–2.

The above passages indicate that highlighting emotional oppositions was a common feature of Old English poetic style. Yet unlike more formal theorised models of emotion, these passages also demonstrate that Anglo-Saxon poets had a fluid understanding of what such oppositions could entail. There were no strict pairings of one emotional state with another and the boundary between states could be more porous: a single feeling could exist in opposition to several others; a number of similar emotions could be grouped together to represent one element in a contrastive pair. In terms of the Danish reaction to Grendel's death, the above passages demonstrate that the emotional pairings identified by Bracher are broadly similar to those that an Anglo-Saxon audience might have recognised. This mutual intelligibility confirms that some emotions are universal. Irrespective of the historical period or circumstances, there are certain 'basic' or 'primary' emotional states and these do not change.[15]

Knowledge that Bracher's oppositions exist in the corpus does not reveal, however, which emotion (or combination of emotions) the Danes experienced when they came across Grendel's tracks. They provide a sense of the range of possible emotions that could have been experienced, but equally significant here is the way the information about emotions is presented. Although the above passages and the Danish-reaction passage both call attention to emotional polarity, they do so very differently. The above passages exploit formal features of Old English poetic style to contrast two opposing emotional states; the Danish-reaction passage, by contrast, describes one emotion, and negates it to infer the presence of another opposed emotion. In the above passages, information about both emotions is provided by the poet; in the Danish-reaction passage, information about one emotion is provided by the poet, and the audience must infer the identity of the other emotion. As Bracher's experience demonstrates, this introduces an element of subjectivity into the process so that the same reader can potentially infer the presence of different emotions at different times. It suggests, therefore, that interpreting a negated reference to emotion in poetry requires more than just a knowledge of contrasting emotional pairs.

Negation and Emotion

The kind of negation that forms the basis of the Danish-reaction passage is one of several types of negation that occur in Old English poetry. The use of *no*, 'not at

---

[15] For a review of the various theories of, and criteria for recognising, 'primary' or 'basic' emotions see Plutchik, *Emotion*, pp. 138–51; Andrew Ortony and Terence J. Turner, 'What's Basic About Basic Emotions?', *Psychological Review* 97 (1990): 315–31; Warren D. TenHouten, *A General Theory of Emotions and Social Life* (Oxford, 2007), pp. 10–24; Jonathan H. Turner and Jan E. Stets, *The Sociology of Emotions* (Cambridge, 2005), pp. 10–21.

all', in the passage is both syntactic and a form of 'complete negation' that denies any possibility of the Danes being sorrowful at Grendel's death. Other forms of syntactic negation that employ terms suggesting quantity – *lyt* ('little/few'), *fea* ('few') and negated *fela* ('many')[16] – can also be used to achieve what Jespersen calls 'incomplete negation'.[17] Negation can also occur morphologically, through the use of the prefix *un-* and suffix *-leas*,[18] although critics disagree whether this kind of negation can be litotic.[19] In *Beowulf*, one use of the *un-* prefix demonstrates the extent to which the interpretation of a negated reference to emotion relies upon more than just knowledge of emotional oppositions. It is a reference that is not usually considered litotic, although, as will be demonstrated, it may well be. The term is *unleof*, and it occurs in the description of Wiglaf's reprimand of the *Geats* who abandon Beowulf as he goes to face the dragon:

> Þa wæs æt ðam geongan   grim ondswaru
> eðbegete   þam ðe ær his elne forleas.
> Wiglaf maðelode,   Weohstanes sunu,
> sec sarigferð   seah on unleofe:
> 'Þæt, la, mæg secgan   se ðe wyle soð specan
> þæt se mondryhten   se eow ða maðmas geaf,
> eoredgeatwe,   þe ge þær on standað,
> þonne he on ealubence   oft gesealde
> healsittendum   helm ond byrnan,
> þeoden his þegnum,   swylce he þrydlicost
> ower feor oððe neah   findan meahte –
> þæt he genunga   guðgewædu
> wraðe forwurpe,   ða hyne wig beget.
>
> (*Beowulf*, ll. 2860–72)

---

[16] Bracher, p. 916; Fulk, Bjork and Niles, p. cxi.

[17] Otto Jespersen, *Negation in English and Other Languages* (Copenhagen, 1917), pp. 39–42.

[18] *leas*, as both suffix and free-standing adjective, commonly describes emotional states (e.g. *dream(a)-leas*; *wyn(na)-leas*; *sorhleas*; *hyht(a)-leas*). However, as Storms notes, even when not explicitly referring to emotional states *-leas* compounds can have an 'emotional ... function in that they give expression to a pronounced subjective, personal point of view'. Storms argues that 'all the *-leas* compounds in *Beowulf* are emotional'. See G. Storms, 'The Subjectivity of the Style of *Beowulf*', in Stanley B. Greenfield (ed.), *Studies in Old English Literature in Honor of Arthur G. Brodeur* (Eugene, 1973), pp. 171–86, at 175.

[19] Bracher (pp. 916–17) believes there is little clear evidence for it; the current editors of *Klaeber's Beowulf* (p. cxi) disagree, as do R. Baird Shuman and H. Charles Hutchings II, 'The *Un-* Prefix: A Means of Germanic Irony in *Beowulf*', *Modern Philology* 57 (1960): 217–22, at 220–22.

[It was then easy to obtain a grim answer to the one whose courage had earlier forsaken them. Wiglaf spoke, Weohstan's son, a man sad at heart, he looked at the unloved ones: 'Listen, a man who might wish to speak the truth will say that the lord who gave you those treasures, the war-gear which you stand in here – when he often gave to the hall-sitters on the ale bench, helmet and corselet, a prince to his thanes, the greatest anywhere far or near such as he could find – that he completely rashly threw away that war-gear when war befell him.]

In their discussion of the *un-* prefix in *Beowulf*, Shuman and Hutchings argue that in this passage '*unleofe* ... is quite properly glossed "unloved". To gloss it "hated" would be to exceed the meaning implied by *un-* plus *leofe*. *Unleofe* implies a passive rather than active state.'[20] This seems like a sensible reading of this particular reference, especially alongside the description of Wiglaf as *sarigferð*, which suggests a weary resignation on his part. *Unleof* seems to be used here to indicate the absence of one emotion (love) rather than the presence of another (hate).

Unleof, however, only occurs on two other occasions in the corpus, both in *Genesis*, and on both occasions implies an emotional state noticeably different from a passive lack of love. The first use of *unleof* occurs when the *Genesis*-poet says of the 'kin of Giants' ('gigantmæcgas', l. 1268) that they were 'gode unleofe'. This phrase is used in apposition to 'metode laðe' ('hateful to the Creator'), which occupies the same verse in the following line. *Unleof* in this instance is clearly an active hatred rather than a simple lack of affection. In the second instance, the word refers to the inhabitants of Sodom, who are again described as 'gode unleofe' (l. 2454). They too are also referred to elsewhere in *Genesis* as 'metode laðe' (l. 1934), which again suggests they are 'hated' rather than 'not loved' by God.

Leof has a range of meanings so it is perhaps unnecessary to expect that *unleof* have a single meaning. Yet it seems significant that the word occurs only three times in the entire corpus and on each occasion refers to a group rather than an individual, and on each occasion that group has in some way abandoned their lord. This similarity raises the possibility that this reference may have been intended as a more pointed rebuke than it at first seems, and a contemporary audience may have understood it that way. The term could have been taken literally as 'unloved' but carrying the connotation of the more intense and active 'hated'. If it was understood this way, it would constitute understatement and would, therefore, be considered litotic.

However it was intended, it is clear that, in the absence of other references to this term, an appreciation of what *unleof* could mean here relies heavily on an understanding of the relationship between lord and retainer and the emotions associated with that relationship. The time spent by the *Beowulf*-poet on the

---

[20] Shuman and Hutchings, p. 220.

disloyalty of the Geats (ll. 2631–60, 2845–91), as well as evidence from elsewhere in the corpus, conveys a sense of how negatively the duplicity of retainers was viewed in Anglo-Saxon society, yet our understanding is necessarily imperfect.[21] While a contemporary audience might have also experienced the poem at a remove from this relationship, a modern audience's understanding of what *unleof* can mean is limited by the fact that the relationship between lord and retainer – where all social authority, justice, and hope of security arises from a relationship to a single individual – is entirely foreign to modern experience. An audience with a first-hand, or near first-hand, knowledge of such a relationship would arguably have a better-informed understanding of what *unleof* could mean in this instance.

Whether or not Wiglaf's companions are seen as the 'unloved ones' or the 'hated ones', the example of *unleof* illustrates that understanding a negated reference to an emotion cannot simply rely on knowledge of emotional oppositions. It is also necessary to consider the appropriateness of an emotion to a particular context. In justifying his choice of joyfulness in the Danish-reaction passage, Bracher says that the emotion 'is what the context demands'.[22] As Bracher's own experience demonstrates, however, this is too narrow an understanding of the relationship between context and emotion. The Danish-reaction passage does not 'demand' any emotion; rather, it permits a range of emotions as long as those emotions can be seen to stand in opposition to the one mentioned by the poet.

Ne þurfan – The Production and Propriety of Emotional States

Examining emotions in terms of the context in which they occur represents a different approach to emotion, though one equally relevant for understanding the Danish reaction to Grendel's death. Bracher's linking of emotion and context highlights that central to this approach is the idea that emotion is in some way produced by circumstances. Like emotional polarity, this is another theoretical concept that features prominently in contemporary emotional theory. Nico Frijda argues, for example, that 'emotions arise in response to the meaning structures of given situations; different emotions arise in response to different meaning structures.'[23] Social circumstances can also be understood as producing emotions less directly: 'cultural ideologies, beliefs, and norms as they impinge

---

[21] Concerns about the disloyalty of retainers are articulated most forcefully in the second-half of *The Battle of Maldon*, esp. ll. 185–97.

[22] Bracher, p. 916.

[23] Nico H. Frijda, 'The Laws of Emotion', *American Psychologist* 43 (1988): 349–58, at 349.

on social structures define what emotions are to be experienced, and how these culturally defined emotions are to be expressed.'[24]

One phrase common in Old English poetry indicates that Anglo-Saxons also believed that emotions were produced by circumstances. Throughout the poetic corpus, the phrase *ne þurfan* is commonly used to refer to emotions, both ironically and non-ironically. Forms of *ne þurfan* describe a variety of states that, in a given situation, a poet says 'do not need' to be felt: to be fearful or anxious;[25] to boast, exult or deride;[26] to rejoice;[27] to be ashamed;[28] to regret;[29] to hope.[30] The following are two examples of *ne þurfan* being used litotically; in both cases the statement that someone 'did not need' to feel one emotion infers that they felt, or were free to feel, the opposite emotion:

> Mære maðþumsweord manige gesawon
> beforan beorn beran. Beowulf geþah
> ful on flette; no he þære feohgyfte
> for sceotendum scamigan ðorfte.
> (*Beowulf*, ll. 1023–6)

[Many saw a famous precious sword brought before the warrior. Beowulf took the cup on the hall-floor. He did not need to be ashamed of that gift before the warriors.]

> Costontinus,
> har hilderinc, hreman ne þorfte
> mæca gemanan; he wæs his mæga sceard,
> freonda gefylled on folcstede
> (*The Battle of Brunanburh*, ll. 38b–41)

[Constantine, the old warrior, did not need to exult at the meeting of swords; he was deprived of his kinsmen, his friends killed on the battlefield.]

---

[24] Turner and Stets, p. 2.
[25] *ondrædan*: *Christ*, l.779, *Beowulf*, l. 1674, *Genesis*, ll. 1037, 2169; *an/forht wesan*: *Genesis*, l. 2172, *Dream of the Rood*, l. 117; *beon cearie*: *Soul and Body I*, l. 160.
[26] *gilpan/begylpan*: *Beowulf*, ll. 2006, 2874, *The Battle of Brunanburh*, l. 44; *hryman*: *The Battle of Brunanburh*, l. 39; *hlehhan/bihlyhhan*: *The Battle of Brunanburh*, l. 47, *Guthlac*, ll. 1356–7, *Juliana*, l. 526, *Genesis*, ll. 72–3.
[27] *gefeon*: *Guthlac*, l. 421, *Genesis*, l. 1523.
[28] *sceamian*: *Soul and Body I*, l. 145, *Genesis*, l. 2339, *Beowulf*, l. 1025.
[29] *hreowan*: *Soul and Body I*, l. 148.
[30] *hopian*: *Judith*, l. 117.

The widespread use of *ne þurfan* has two implications for understanding Anglo-Saxon attitudes to emotion. The first relates to causality and how emotions arise. This phrase confirms that Anglo-Saxons were deeply aware that emotions were produced by social situations. Saying that someone did not need to feel something in a particular situation is premised on the idea that there are situations where people 'need' to feel things. The phrase seems to hint at an awareness (or even fear) of a profound sense of powerlessness in the face of emotions. Clemoes notes that at least one Anglo-Saxon attitude to emotions was to see them as something that imposed themselves on the individual, as being 'essentially a force outside the individual, acting on him (or her) of their own accord or cooperated with by him/her as an act of will ... They were a raw material in his/her dramatic encounter with external forces.'[31] The abiding interest in containing and managing emotion found elsewhere in the corpus, with its language and imagery of locking emotions in the chest, appears almost to be a response to the sense of impotence implied by the use of *ne þurfan*.[32] Concerned that they could not stop feeling something, they could, by an effort of will, at least control their response to it.[33]

The second implication relates again to the appropriateness of emotions to particular social situations. While a certain feeling might not need to be felt by an individual in the context under discussion, the use of *ne þurfan* implies that the feeling is appropriate to those circumstances. In being told, for example, that Constantine did not need to exult after the battle at Brunanburh, an audience is reminded of the feelings that are appropriate after a battle; in being told that Beowulf did not need to be ashamed in the hall before the warriors, an audience is told that shame is a feeling appropriate to the warrior who stands before other warriors in a hall, particularly if that warrior is poorly equipped. *Ne þurfan* thus not only indicates that Anglo-Saxons understood emotions as being produced by social circumstances; it also suggests they associated certain emotions with certain social situations.[34]

---

[31] Peter Clemoes, *Interactions of Thought and Language in Old English Poetry* (Cambridge, 1995), p. 365.

[32] Malcolm Godden, 'Anglo-Saxons on the Mind', in Michael Lapidge and Helmut Gneuss (eds), *Learning and Literature in Anglo-Saxon England: Studies Presented to Peter Clemoes on the Occasion of his Sixty-fifth Birthday* (Cambridge, 1985), pp. 271–98, at 287–8; Clemoes, pp. 79–80; Antonina Harbus, *The Life of the Mind in Old English Poetry* (Amsterdam and New York, 2002), pp. 155–9; Leslie Lockett, *Anglo-Saxon Psychologies in the Vernacular and Latin Traditions* (Toronto, 2011), pp. 79–83.

[33] An ability to exercise emotional control could be seen as 'a sign of moral character' and could, therefore, form part of Anglo-Saxon definitions of heroism. See Michael Matto, 'A War of Containment: The Heroic Image in *The Battle of Maldon*', *Studia Neophilologica* 74 (2002): 60–75, at 69.

[34] A. Leslie Harris has similarly argued that in *Beowulf* litotes is used to stresses the propriety of certain behaviours to certain contexts by referencing social rituals that Grendel

Litotes and the Correlative

Underlying the Danish-reaction passage, therefore, are two distinct Anglo-Saxon attitudes to emotion. The first recognises that emotions exist in opposition to each other, the second that emotions arise from, and are appropriate to, the circumstances that produced them. Understanding what the Danes felt about Grendel's death depends upon the way these attitudes are brought together in the litotic statement itself. Litotes could be used in many different ways by Anglo-Saxon poets, but Bracher's experience demonstrates that fundamental to litotes, however it was used, was the participation of the audience. Carl Weyman, who wrote on the origins of litotes in Latin, highlights the importance of the audience's role when he describes litotes in terms of the cooperation between poet and audience, about both parties contributing information to make litotic statements meaningful:

> The figure is due to the effort, in the earlier stages of the language, to render an expression as unambiguous and impressive as possible. This is done, at first, by stating the thought twice – once by a positive, and once by a negative, clause. These are joined by some particle or used asyndetically. Later, when the pleonasm is felt, the positive part is omitted but still tacitly demands a correlative. The reader or hearer is thus compelled to cooperate actively with speaker or writer. This is stimulating and lends the expression far more force than is inherent in the simple positive predication.[35]

The kind of 'correlative' required by litotes differs depending on how a poet uses the device, how much information they provide to an audience and how much is left for an audience to contribute themselves. One method of categorising litotic statements is to divide them according to their relationship with the narrative that precedes them. On this basis, examples of litotes in the Old English corpus can be divided into one of two groups, with each group represented by one of the two *ne þurfan* passages above. The passage from *Beowulf*, for example, that describes the sword the hero receives from Hrothgar is part of a description of the gifts (ll. 1020–49) that are presented to him after his defeat of Grendel. This passage is the first and only mention of the sword. Here litotes characterises an object that, apart from the phrase 'mære maðþumsweord', is not otherwise described. Following the litotic statement this passage continues with a more detailed description of the helmet (ll. 1030–34) and the other items (ll. 1035–42)

---

does not observe (e.g. ll. 156, 168). See A. Leslie Harris, 'Litotes and Superlative in *Beowulf*', *English Studies* 69 (1988): 1–11, at 1–4.

[35] Weyman's views as summarised by Lee M. Hollander, 'Litotes in Old Norse', *PMLA* 53 (1938): 1–33, at 1.

given to Beowulf. This example of litotes seems to function as a way of providing a description of the sword's quality by appealing to the audience's imagination: if Beowulf did not need to be ashamed about the sword, if he could take pride in it, then an audience can only imagine how glorious it must have been. This kind of litotic statement does not rely on anything specific in the preceding narrative. It could be argued that a treasured sword given out by a king like Hrothgar might be expected to be a good weapon; after all, the Danish king is generous with his gifts (ll. 71–3, 80–81, 660–61, 949–53); but this information is not essential. Another example of this kind of 'free-standing' litotic statement occurs later in *Beowulf* when the poet describes how Beowulf strikes Grendel's mother with his sword; he says, 'hond sweng ne ofteah' (l. 1520).[36] This phrase effectively gives a sense of Beowulf's violence here without needing to refer back to anything else in the narrative.

In *The Battle of Brunanburh*, however, litotes functions differently. It directly follows thirty-seven lines of narrative that describe in exhaustive detail how Constantine and the other enemies of Athelstan and Edmund were beaten in battle. By the time an audience reaches the litotic statement they already have clear and well-formed expectations about how a defeated enemy would feel in such circumstances.[37] Although litotes in this passage alludes to Constantine's emotional state it is not characterising it in the way that the passage from *Beowulf* characterises the quality of the sword – the audience already has a good idea what Constantine's emotional state is likely to be; they already know from the preceding narrative that he has been utterly humiliated in battle. Litotes is thus addressing an audience's expectations and confirming existing information rather than providing new information. Instead of asking them to marvel at something novel, it invites them to become aware of the congruity between their own expectations and the emotional state being suggested by the poet.[38]

This latter kind of litotic statement is the type that forms the basis of the Danish-reaction passage in *Beowulf*. The two distinct approaches to emotion mentioned above – one based on oppositions, the other on circumstances – come together here as the audience recognises the similarity between the emotion alluded to by the poet and the emotion they believe would have been produced in the circumstances in which the Danes found themselves. Here, as in the *Brunanburh*-passage, the litotic statement is not the beginning of a weighing

---

[36] 'The hand did not withhold the stroke.'

[37] The reference to Constantine is one of three adjacent examples (ll. 44–6, 47–52) of litotes in *The Battle of Brunanburh*. All three statements are 'mocking, exulting, or scornful' (Bracher, p. 922) of Constantine and his allies. This density highlights the importance of the device in this poem as a means of celebrating the prowess of the English in battle (Bracher, p. 923).

[38] The inherent comparativeness of ironic statements is discussed in Rachel Giora, 'On Irony and Negation', *Discourse Processes* 19 (1995): 239–64.

of possible emotional oppositions or the consequences of negation. Rather it is the end of a process, the moment of recognition when the poet indirectly refers to an emotional state that the audience has already identified.

So What Did the Danes Feel?

So what did the Danes feel as they looked over Grendel's tracks? There is no single answer to this question – the answer will depend on the individual reader or listener and their response to what has preceded the litotic statement itself. The Danes could conceivably have felt any emotion that would be considered appropriate to the context described, and which could be seen as representing the opposite of sorrow. Any emotional state that satisfies both these conditions is permissible, whether that is a single emotion, a combination of emotions, or a complex emotional reaction. For each individual reader or listener, the specific character of the Danish reaction will depend on how they have approached the earlier narrative, although there is plenty of evidence in *Beowulf* to suggest that from the start of the poem the poet has been guiding them toward the kind of response evoked in Bracher.

Unlike the *Brunanburh*-passage, the emotional state of the Danes the morning after the fight at Heorot is the product of a much larger and more varied set of experiences than a single episode such as a battle. From the outset, Grendel's attacks against the Danes have focused exclusively on Heorot, and it is arguably an audience's interpretation of what this building represents to the Danes, and what they are deprived of by Grendel's attacks, that provide the basis for understanding their reaction to the creature's death. Throughout the poem the hall is associated with both earthly joy and physical security. It is, as Hume notes, the 'circle of light and peace enclosed by darkness, discomfort and danger'.[39] The poet states, for example, that Heorot's inhabitants 'lived in gladness' ('dreamum lifdon', l. 99), that they 'didn't know sorrow' ('sorge ne cuðon', l. 119), that Grendel is enraged by the 'loud rejoicing in the hall' ('dream ... / hludne in healle', ll. 88b–9a). Grendel, by contrast, represents the absence of joy: he is 'deprived of joys' ('dreamum bedæled', l. 721), a creature who lives in a 'joyless home' ('wynleas wic', l. 821). Through his attacks on Heorot, Grendel infects the Danes with his misery and joylessness. In a passage that parallels the structure of the Danish-reaction passage, the poet describes Hrothgar's emotional state on the morning following Grendel's first attack:

---

[39] Kathryn Hume, 'The Concept of the Hall in Old English Poetry', *Anglo-Saxon England* 3 (1974): 63–74, at 64; on the symbolism of the hall in *Beowulf* see also Edward B. Irving Jr., *Rereading Beowulf* (Philadelphia, 1989), pp. 133–67.

> Mære þeoden,
> æþeling ærgod, unbliðe sæt,
> þolode ðryðswyð, þegnsorge dreah,
> syðþan hie þæs laðan last sceawedon,
> wergan gastes.
>
> (ll. 129b–33)

[The famous prince, the long-proven nobleman, sat joyless, the strong one suffered, endured sorrow for his thanes, after they [i.e. the Danes] inspected the tracks of the hateful one.]

Heorot is also a symbol of security, or at least it should be; because of Grendel's persistent attacks, however, many of the Danes abandon the hall, and seek their night's rest 'further away [from Heorot] and more secure' ('fyr ond fæstor', l. 143). The *Beowulf*-poet describes at length Grendel's relentless persecution of the Danes over many years and his unwillingness to be bought off:

> Wæs seo hwil micel:
> twelf wintra tid torn geþolode
> wine Scyldinga, weana gehwelcne,
> sidra sorga. Forðam gesyne wearð,
> ylda bearnum, undyrne cuð,
> gyddum geomore, þætte Grendel wan
> hwile wið Hroþgar, heteniðas wæg,
> fyrene ond fæhðe fela missera,
> singale sæce; sibbe ne wolde
> wið manna hwone mægenes Deniga,
> feorhbealo feorran, fea þingian.
>
> (*Beowulf*, ll. 147b–56)

[It was a long time: over a twelve-year period the friend of the Scyldings endured every misery, every great sorrow. It became, therefore, evident to the children of men, revealed openly in mournful songs, that for a time, Grendel fought against Hrothgar, carried on hostilities, enmity and violence for many seasons, continual strife; he did not want friendship with any man of the Danish host, to withdraw his deadly attack, to pay compensation.]

Here *sibb* is usually translated as 'friendship', but in this context it also arguably carries the sense of 'peace', since it is being used in parallel with other methods of Grendel settling his 'feud' and bringing his attacks to an end. Along with the many references to joy it establishes the unthreatened hall as the embodiment of these two emotions. Grendel's activities deprive the Danes of both the joy and sense of peace that they experience in the hall. Thus, when an audience learns of Grendel's death and must ascribe feeling to the Danes, it is perhaps unsurprising that they would see his removal as offering a return to the emotional states that have been violated by his presence.

In guiding the audience in this way, the *Beowulf*-poet expects an audience to have the 'capacity to analyse emotions, appreciate their probable trends over time, and understand their outcomes', criteria that are considered essential to at least one modern definition of 'emotional intelligence'.[40] It may sound trite to suggest that it is necessary for the audience of this or any other poem to exercise emotional intelligence, but it seems fundamental to this type of litotes that the audience can reason and draw inferences about emotions. The conclusions to be drawn from this kind of emotional work will depend on which parts of the preceding narrative resonate most with an audience. It might be argued, for example, that a reader or hearer who places a greater value on the sense of security offered by Heorot will be more likely to believe that the Danes were relieved when a threat to that security was removed. Thus, each person's response to this passage will be uniquely their own; the information provided by the poet will at most be a guide to a conclusion they must reach alone.[41]

Conclusion

Paradoxically, in not describing an emotion, the use of litotes in the Danish-reaction passage provides much information about Anglo-Saxon attitudes to emotion. Litotes calls attention to emotional oppositions as a feature of Anglo-Saxon psychology, something that also finds expression in the style of a variety of Old English poems. The widespread use of negation, typified by the phrase *ne þurfan*, indicates that Anglo-Saxons were also keenly aware that emotions were a product of social circumstances, and that certain emotions were appropriate to certain social situations. When it was used to describe emotion, litotes could be a means of bringing these attitudes together, by involving audiences in poetic narratives. Litotes encouraged and rewarded audiences for being attentive and becoming emotionally invested in the lives of individual characters. In terms of the oral performance of this poetry, it is not hard to imagine litotic statements eliciting nods or even shouts as a poem's audience recognise the agreement between what the poet is suggesting and what they already know. For a brief moment, the poet has made them a partner, a co-creator of the poem's meaning.

---

[40] John D. Mayer, Peter Salovey and David R. Caruso, 'Emotional Intelligence: Theory, Findings, and Implications', *Psychological Inquiry* 15 (2004): 197–215, at 199.

[41] Harris, p. 2.

Chapter 6

An Embarrassment of Clues: Interpreting Anglo-Saxon Blushes

Jonathan Wilcox

Emotion is often written on the body, signalled through such uncontrolled somatic gestures as weeping or sighing, laughing or smiling, or conveyed through intentional gestures such as kissing or winking, chest-thumping or bowing. Somatic gestures are complicatedly ambiguous, which makes them rich indicators of an emotional state, if challenging to pin down. Even casual or comic gestures provide useful access to emotional states: think of the different valences of Pandarus winking to Criseyde or of Chauntecleer's winking in front of the fox; of the lady kissing Gawain and of Gawain kissing the lord. Such gestures are freighted with meaning but hard to unpack verbally, liable to misinterpretation by both the actors and the audience, with a potential to carry much weight or to mean nothing at all. Rather than picking up on the larger indices of emotion, such as weeping or laughing, I shall focus on a relatively minor bodily expression, namely blushing, alongside attention to winking and mouth-opening. Blushing in Old English literature has received little attention, perhaps because it seems so inconsequential. Rather than keying into basic emotions like grief or pleasure, blushing seems to signal what might be termed lesser emotions – embarrassment, awkwardness, shame or self-consciousness. These lesser emotional states have themselves received only limited attention by critics of medieval culture, but may be particularly interesting to a cultural critic of the past since they are more likely to be socially constructed than their more fundamental cousins.[1]

Blushing is a relatively simple bodily motion, namely the involuntary reddening of the complexion.[2] The unwilled nature of blushes simplifies their

---

[1] William Ian Miller, *Humiliation and Other Essays on Honor, Social Discomfort, and Violence* (Ithaca, NY, 1993) is fundamental, centring on Old Norse material. I discuss embarrassment in Old English literature in relation to one specific but common trigger in 'Naked in Old English: The Embarrassed and the Shamed', in Benjamin C. Withers and Jonathan Wilcox (eds.), *Naked Before God: Uncovering the Body in Anglo-Saxon England* (Morgantown, 2003), pp. 275–309.

[2] For a good introduction to recent psychological interpretation of blushing, see W. Ray Crozier, *Blushing and the Social Emotions: The Self Unmasked* (New York, 2006), who considers it as an index of embarrassment, shame, guilt and anger, and shyness.

interpretation, removing the question of intentionality that hovers around any understanding of weeping or laughing. While the appearance of blushes may thus be straightforward, their perceived significance is much more difficult to establish. As this study will suggest, understanding this small gesture calls for extreme attentiveness to vocabulary, context and overtones. I shall use this relatively small emotional signal to ponder how to approach emotions in Anglo-Saxon literature.

Theorizing Blushing: Augustine

Groundwork for a medieval understanding of such bodily signals was laid in part by Augustine, whose discussion of signs in *De doctrina Christiana* centres on language but touches on non-verbal signs. Augustine writes:

> Among signs, some are natural and others are conventional. Those are natural which, without any desire or intention of signifying, make us aware of something beyond themselves, like smoke which signifies fire. It does this without any will to signify, for even when smoke appears alone, observation and memory of experience with things bring a recognition of an underlying fire. The track of a passing animal belongs to this class, and the face of one who is wrathful or sad signifies his emotion even when he does not wish to show that he is wrathful or sad, just as other emotions are signified by the expression even when we do not deliberately set out to show them. (Book 2, ch. 1, §2)[3]

Augustine considers that somatic signs straightforwardly give away an emotional state. He takes for granted the uncontrolled nature of such display, assuming that the face reveals a person's emotion 'even when he does not wish to show that he is wrathful or sad'. While the case of Margery Kempe demonstrates how such a display of sadness can be vexingly difficult to authenticate, since her weeping is vigorously contested throughout her book, blushing seems to present a more straightforward case of Augustine's natural signs.

Augustine engages further with such unwilled bodily signs in *The City of God*, where his extended discussion is attached not to a blushing face but to movements of sexual arousal. For Augustine, such unwilled somatic gestures result directly from man's disobedience to God in the primal lapsarian scene, suggesting that man 'may have once received from his lower members an obedience which he

---

[3] Saint Augustine, *On Christian Doctrine*, trans. D. W. Robertson, Jr. (New York, 1958), p. 34.

lost by his own disobedience'.[4] The fall from prelapsarian innocence freights the body with somatic gestures that are uncontrolled by the will of the individual. The unwilled display of the body is a punishment that brings into being the need for cover, along with all humanity's woes. While Augustine dwells on the body's loss of control of its sexual member, he would presumably see the same mechanism at work in the less-charged case of the flushing of the face, a tell-tale natural sign of an inner state that God has now moved outside of the control of the will. But what does such blushing demonstrate?

Red Faces in Medieval Literature

Red faces recur throughout medieval literature. King Harald, for example, turns deep red in *Egil's Saga* before ordering the death of an insufficiently compliant visitor.[5] In this case flushing of the face seems to particularly denote anger, one of the basic emotions that has seen significant historical study of late.[6] As often, though, the red face may connote more than one thing. In the laconic world of saga literature, manly men do not necessarily verbalize their anger but instead display it involuntarily in a tell-tale red face before they have the opportunity to enact the violence that leads to a kind of catharsis.[7] In addition to anger, there may be an interesting residue of embarrassment – real men in a male heroic culture suddenly seeing their masculine quickness to violence challenged are inclined to feel the critical squirming self-consciousness of embarrassment, even as they also feel the onset of the emotion of anger.[8] A reddening complexion signals something strikingly different, however, in the erotically charged world of a romance like *Troilus and Criseyde*, where Criseyde habitually blushes, both as she gazes at Troilus and as she is quizzed by Pandarus.[9] In these cases,

---

[4] Saint Augustine, *City of God*, Book XIV, chs 15–24; Henry Bettenson (trans.), *Concerning The City of God Against the Pagans* (Harmondsworth, 1972), pp. 574–89. Citation from Book XIV, ch. 24, p. 588.

[5] *Egil's Saga*, ch. 25, trans. Hermann Pálsson and Paul Edwards (Harmondsworth, 1976), p. 67.

[6] On anger in the Middle Ages, see the essay collection, Barbara Rosenwein (ed.), *Anger's Past: The Social Uses of an Emotion in the Middle Ages* (Ithaca, NY, 1998).

[7] This pattern is explored more fully in the case of Old English literature in Sebo's chapter in the present collection.

[8] On embarrassment, see note 1 above and the modern psychological study: Rowland S. Miller, *Embarrassment: Poise and Peril in Everyday Life* (New York, 1996).

[9] Chaucer, *Troilus and Criseyde*, Book II, ll. 645–56, where Troilus's blushing in embarrassment at praise is picked up by Criseyde blushing in love at first sight; see *The Riverside Chaucer*, 3rd edn, ed. Larry D. Benson (Boston, 1987), p. 498. See also Book II, ll. 1198, 1256, Book III, l. 956, among others.

Criseyde's blushes are not connected with anger but are still complicatedly layered – apparently signalling embarrassment, as the body movement gives away a certain self-consciousness in pondering the object of her developing affections, even if, in this context, such temporary discomfiture of acute self-revelation may not be lacking in pleasure. The blushes in *Sir Gawain and the Green Knight* interestingly balance between these two worlds, with Arthur blushing in anger (and embarrassment?) at the unanswered challenge of the Green Knight, and Gawain blushing in stymied self-realization (and a consciousness of exposure?), not to mention anger and a hint of *amour* exposed, at the end of his adventure.[10] The significance of such blushes, then, clearly varies between genres and cultures, even as such a somatic response always hints at some over-ripe emotional state that is not necessarily interchangeable with a simple verbal description.

Red faces are less common in the Anglo-Saxon record than in later medieval literature, but there are enough to raise interesting issues about the emotions they signal. Since Old English literature lacks the explicit theorizing of an Augustine or the self-conscious reflection of a Margery Kempe discussing her tears, the overtones of the blushes have to be teased out from the context. An initial example nicely demonstrates an Anglo-Saxon sense that a red face called for interpretation. Gregory's *Dialogues*, in both the sixth-century Latin original and in the ninth-century Old English translation by Bishop Wærferth, includes the story of Cassius, the Bishop of Narni (Book III, ch. 6). Cassius was apparently born with a red face: 'him wæs gecynde, þæt he symble wæs read on his andwlitan', according to the Old English.[11] That red hue is interpreted by the hostile King Totila as a sign of the bishop's bibulousness and consequent dubious judgement:

> Þa ne gelyfde na se cyning Totila, þæt hit him for his gecynda wære, ac he wende, þæt hit for singalum gedrynce wære, & eallum gemetum he hine forseah & forhogode (ed. Hecht, p. 187, ll. 16–18)

> [Then King Totila did not at all believe that it was on account of his innate nature, but he thought that it was on account of continuous drunkenness, and that he forsook and despised all moderation.]

To an Anglo-Saxon audience, a red face could reasonably be seen, then, as a sign of continuous drunkenness, even if that proves to be the wrong interpretation

---

[10] *Sir Gawain and the Green Knight*, fitt 1, ll. 317–20, and fitt 4, ll. 2369–72; ed. and trans. James Winny (Peterborough, ON, 1992), pp. 18–19, 132–33.

[11] 'And it was natural to him that he was red in his face.' Hans Hecht (ed.), *Bischofs Wærferth von Worcester Übersetzung der Dialoge Gregors des Grossen*, Bibliothek der angelsächsischen Prosa 5 (Liepzig, 1900), p. 187, ll. 15–16. Translations from Old English are my own unless otherwise indicated.

in this particular case, where the bishop duly demonstrates his efficacy by exorcising a devil from one of the king's guard and so comes to earn the king's respect, presumably leading the king to reinterpret his red visage. Like much in the *Dialogues*, the incident is gently comic, in this case setting up false expectations that are duly overcome. The comedy usefully demonstrates the potential fallibility of any reading of bodily signs.

True blushes in Old English literature generally point to two distinct emotions, marking either shame or embarrassment, although both of these prove to be complex states with porous boundaries, and the blushes themselves carry the multivalent plenitude of signification characteristic of such non-verbal signs. Blushes of shame prove more common in surviving Old English, best illustrated by blushing in the Psalms; blushes of embarrassment are best illustrated in the romance-style world of the Old English translation of *Apollonius of Tyre*. These paradigmatic examples will be considered in some detail here, with briefer reference to further examples, in a discussion that concludes by attempting to draw out a methodology useful for engaging gestures in the historical study of emotions in literature.

Blushing in the Psalms

The Psalms are richly endowed with emotional gestures, which would thereby have strongly influenced Anglo-Saxon culture, since the Psalter circulated so widely and exercised such a hold on a literate Anglo-Saxon's imagination. Monks recited and re-recited the Psalms in their daily liturgical round and pious layfolk would have followed their lead, contemplating these poems with devotional regularity, as is later demonstrated through the explosive growth of private Books of Hours. The evidence from Anglo-Saxon England lies in the large number of surviving manuscripts (40 psalters or fragments with English origin or provenance), many glossed, some incorporating commentaries, and some programmatically illustrated.[12] The presence of psalter extracts on the early seventh-century wax tablets preserved in the Springmount Bog attests to their likely ubiquity on more ephemeral media, too.[13] These are works that made it into the vernacular both through extensive glossing of Latin manuscripts and in

---

[12] See Phillip Pulsiano, 'Psalters', in Richard W. Pfaff (ed.), *The Liturgical Books of Anglo-Saxon England* (Kalamazoo, 1995), pp. 61–85; George Hardin Brown, 'The Psalms as the Foundation of Anglo-Saxon Learning', in Nancy Van Deusen (ed.), *The Place of the Psalms in the Intellectual Culture of the Middle Ages* (Albany, NY, 1999), pp. 1–24; and M. Jane Toswell, 'Psalters', in Richard Gameson (ed.), *The Cambridge History of the Book in Britain*, vol. 1, *c. 400–1100* (Cambridge, 2012), pp. 468–81.

[13] Described by Michelle P. Brown, *Manuscripts from the Anglo-Saxon Age* (London, 2007), pp. 12–13, and handsomely illustrated in colour in her plate 1.

the prose and verse translations into Old English contained in the Paris Psalter.[14] The Psalter is a deeply emotional text that must have presented a virtual lexicon of emotional gestures to an Anglo-Saxon audience.[15]

The Psalms provide plenty of red faces, although interpreting what they suggest is often challenging. Psalm 34 (KJV 35), beginning, 'Judge thou, O Lord, them that wrong me: overthrow them that fight against me', a psalm in the voice of King David, provides a particularly fruitful example for discussion. The latter part of this psalm places a blushing countenance within a rich panoply of somatic gestures as the speaker expands upon a plea to confound his enemies. I provide here the Vulgate–Septuagint version of the relevant verses (that is, Jerome's revised translation based on the Greek Septuagint, which is a version that seems to have circulated widely in Anglo-Saxon England), alongside the Douay-Rheims translation and, for comparison's sake, the King James Version:

> 19 non supergaudeant mihi qui adversantur mihi inique
> qui oderunt me gratis et annuunt oculis
> 20 quoniam mihi quidem pacifice loquebantur
> et in iracundia terrae loquentes: dolos cogitabant
> 21 et dilataverunt super me os suum
> dixerunt euge euge viderunt oculi nostri. ...
> 26 erubescant et revereantur simul qui gratulantur malis meis
> induantur confusione et reverentia qui magna loquuntur super me
> (Psalm 34:19–21, 26; Septuagint)

> 19 Let not them that are my enemies wrongfully rejoice over me: who have hated me without cause, and wink with the eyes.
> 20 For they spoke indeed peaceably to me; and speaking in the anger of the earth they devised guile.
> 21 And they opened their mouth wide against me; they said: Well done, well done, our eyes have seen it. ...
> 26 Let them blush: and be ashamed together, who rejoice at my evils.
> Let them be clothed with confusion and shame, who speak great things against me.
> (Psalm 34:19–21, 26; Douay-Rheims)

---

[14] The first fifty psalms are translated into prose and usually ascribed to King Alfred; Patrick P. O'Neill (ed.), *King Alfred's Old English Prose Translation of the First Fifty Psalms* (Cambridge, MA, 2001). The remaining psalms survive in an anonymous translation into verse; George Philip Krapp (ed.), *The Paris Psalter and the Meters of Boethius*, ASPR 5 (New York, 1933).

[15] On one such emotion, see, further, Stephen J. Harris, 'Happiness and the Psalms', in Michael Fox and Manish Sharma (eds), *Old English Literature and the Old Testament* (Toronto, 2012), pp. 292–314. See also the chapters by Jorgensen and Birnbaum in the present volume.

19 Let not them that are mine enemies wrongfully rejoice over me: neither let them wink with the eye that hate me without a cause.
20 For they speak not peace: but they devise deceitful matters against them that are quiet in the land.
21 Yea, they opened their mouth wide against me, and said, Aha, aha, our eye hath seen it. ...
26 Let them be ashamed and brought to confusion together that rejoice at mine hurt: let them be clothed with shame and dishonour that magnify themselves against me.

(Psalm 35:19–21, 26; King James Version)

This passage suggests that the enemies are to be confounded in some way that shames and embarrasses them, but what the specific gestures of those enemies has been or what gestures are being called down upon them is not entirely obvious either in the Vulgate or in the Douay-Rheims or, indeed, in the King James translations. I would like to focus on two anticipatory gestures as a context for the subsequent blushing, namely the winking with the eyes at the end of 34:19 and the opening of the mouth wide at 34:21, which lead to the call for the blushing and clothing in confusion and shame at 34:26.

The winking with the eyes in verse 19 is evidently some act of malice. Other biblical translations can help clarify a modern understanding of these moments. The American Standard Version says, 'wink maliciously', suggesting the need for an adverbial gloss to clarify the action of the eye, while the Easy-to-Read Version tackles verse 19 with 'Don't let my lying enemies keep on laughing at me', which captures the spirit of this particular winking through a thoroughly different gesture, namely derisive laughter, with a grin of the mouth substituting for a wink of the eyes.[16] If the nature of the gesture in verse 19 is unclear, even the presence of a gesture at the opening of verse 21 is uncertain. Is the mouth-opening simply a metaphor for speech or is that another gesture? It seems to relate to some kind of hypocrisy spelled out in verse 20 and leads to eyes that see, perhaps in a reverse of the winking eyes of verse 19.

A learned Anglo-Saxon audience would be helped in understanding this passage by the patristic commentators. Cassiodorus reads the whole psalm allegorically, with David's voice anticipating that of Christ who seeks to be freed from the persecution of his enemies. He provides a particularly useful interpretation of the winking gesture: '*Winking with the eyes* is what we do when we declare our wish with a silent and crafty gesture; and when we do not wish to

---

[16] 'Easy-to-Read Version' published by the World Bible Translation Center, 2006, and available freely online at www.BibleGateway.com (accessed 1 May 2013).

betray our presence with words, we warn an individual with a wink of the eyes.'[17] Winking, then, is a gesture full of intent, if deliberately non-verbal. Cassiodorus's Christological reading sees the guileful of verse 20 as the 'sacrilegious cunning of the Jews', and so he sees the mouths opening wide in verse 21 as the open condemnation in shouting, 'Crucify, crucify'. He continues to lay the groundwork for the blush by remarking on the wonder of Christ rising from the tomb on the third day rather than reacting to such abusive words, 'for they were to blush all the more when all that was foretold came to pass'. Cassiodorus therefore sees the blushing of verse 26 as a gesture of embarrassment resulting from malice turned back upon itself: 'He who blushes at his own deeds is condemned on his own assessment; he who is enchained with the bonds of embarrassment is tortured by the vengeance which he exacts from himself.'[18] Apparently the invocation is a calling-down of embarrassment, presumably at the covert malice that gets openly revealed, even if what is usually a situational and slight emotion is here seen as a kind of *Schadenfreude*: an appropriate expression of shame, imagined in the powerful language of being tortured by vengeance for those who fail to convert to the Christian story.

Augustine provides a similar treatment, proceeding at greater leisure through most of the psalm, but hurrying through these final verses. He explains winking with the eyes as the gesture of hypocrites who make pretence: 'Their faces simulate feelings which have no place in their hearts.' Ironically, then, this is the opposite of the uncontrolled gesture that he described in *De doctrina Christiana*. The opening of the mouths wide is a matching mockery of praise, another sign deliberately perverted.[19] Augustine comments but briefly on verse 26, where he seems to imagine blushing as an index of confusion and shame.

A fuller sense of an Anglo-Saxon understanding of these verses may be provided by the Anglo-Saxon glosses to the key terms, and this is material that is explicated more fully by Birnbaum elsewhere in this volume. I briefly present the evidence for the English glosses to each of these gestures here in a simplified form:[20]

19 annuunt [*or* annuebant] oculis: **bicnedon mid eagum** [in various spellings]

21 dilataverunt super [*or* in] me os suum: **gebræddon** or **tobræddon** or **gebblæddon on** or **ofer me muð heora** [in various spellings]

---

[17] *Cassiodorus: Explanation of the Psalms*, trans. P.G. Walsh, 3 vols (New York, 1990–92), I, p. 346.

[18] Walsh, I, p. 348.

[19] *St. Augustine on the Psalms*, trans. Scholastica Hebgin and Felicitas Corrigan, 2 vols (London, 1960–61), II, pp. 218–19.

[20] Relevant glosses drawn from Phillip Pulsiano (ed.), *Old English Glossed Psalters: Psalms 1–50* (Toronto, 2001), pp. 471–9.

26 erubescant et revereantur simul: sceamien or ablysien or syn gescynde [ve]
l ablysian [ve]l scamian ⁊ onscunien or arwyrþian or aðracian samod or ætgædere
[in various spellings]

induantur confusione [*or* pudore] et reverentia syn gescrydde or gegyryde
mid sceame or gescendnysse or gescildnesse or forwandunge or sceame [ve]l
gescændnysse ⁊ æwiscnysse or arweorþunge or unwurþunge or anðracunge

The Old English gloss to *annuunt oculis* 'to wink with the eyes', is consistently *bicnedon mid eagum* (with various spelling variants), a phrase building on *bicnian*, 'to beckon, make a mute signal or gesture', according to the Dictionary of Old English's first definition, with senses that also range towards 'to summon' as well as 'to signify, to indicate'.[21] In the case of verse 21, at least one Old English gloss seems to imagine a more explicit bodily gesture: while most are variant spellings of *gebrædan*, meaning 'to spread, enlarge, magnify', defined only here by the DOE as 'to open the mouth: with the sense of denouncing' (is that suggesting a gesture or not?), the one instance of *geblædan*, if not an error, is defined by DOE as 'to inflate, puff up', placing more emphasis on a visually registered movement of the mouth than just on speech.[22] As with the Modern English translations, winking and mouth-gaping appear to be hostile acts, perhaps of derision, perhaps equivalent to laughing at.

These gestures of derision lead the speaker to invoke blushes on his enemies in verse 26. Here blushing is clearly paired with being ashamed. Old English glosses for *erubescant* cluster on *scamian*, 'to put to shame', and *ablysian*, 'to blush, be ashamed'.[23] The Lambeth Psalter version nicely captures the multivalence here by providing multiple glosses: 'syn gescynde l. ablysian l. scamian 7 anðracian samod', with signals of both humiliation and shame.[24] Glosses on *revereantur* suggest the different understandings of 'to be ashamed' (as in Douai-Rheims) or 'to reverence' (as in Cassiodorus and Augustine).

The second half of verse 26 provides a further helpful (?) amplification on the blushing and shame: *induantur confusione et reverentia*. *Confusione* is glossed by words that get at the idea of shame: *sceame*, here presumably 'shame' in a

---

[21] DOE, s.v. *bicnan, bicnian, beacnian*, a verb attested some 70 times; cf. also *gebicnan, gebicnian, gebeacnian*, with a similar range of senses, attested approximately a further 55 times. *Mid eagum bicnan* is defined more narrowly as 'to wink'.

[22] DOE, s.v. *gebrædan* 2, sense 5 and 5a, a fairly common verb with c. 35 occurrences; s.v. *geblædan*, which occurs just twice.

[23] BT s.v. *scamian*; DOE s.v. *ablysian*.

[24] 'Let them be humiliated (*gescynde*) or blush for shame (*ablysian*) or shamed (*scamian*) and afraid (*anðracian*) together.' U. Lindelöf (ed.), *Der Lambeth-Psalter; I Text und Glossar* (Helsinki, 1909), p. 55.

negative sense;[25] *gescendynsse*, 'a confounding'; *gescildnesse*, 'protection, defense, shielding'; *forwandunge*, 'turning away in shame'. The context of covering and uncovering picked up in the clothing imagery of this verse suggests that the involuntary gesture of blushing is providing some kind of physically grounded and involuntary sign of shame – a concept that itself needs further explanation. Birnbaum demonstrates how the Royal Psalter's understanding of the term derives from Cassiodorus's commentary and conjures up the idea of humiliation and fear, awe and reverence, all in service of a dynamic of conversion, while Jorgensen shows the complex range the term shame holds for a thoughtful writer of the Benedictine reform like Ælfric.[26]

Another Old English understanding of this scene is apparent in the continuous translation in the Paris Psalter.[27] This uses a different verb to convey the winking: *wincettað mid heora eagum*, a unique frequentative form of the verb *wincian*.[28] The context clarifies the gesture a little by suggesting such winking is not aimed specifically at the speaker: *betwuh him*, 'among themselves', suggests a wink of complicity among the in-group, albeit one that is seen and named by the excluded object of their derision. The translator leaves no doubt that the opening of the mouth in verse 21 is for insulting (*hi me bysmredon*), a causation that is explicitly reinforced with the additional explanatory phrase *for leahtre*, poised ambiguously between sin and (derisive) laughter, even if it still remains unclear whether this is speech or a gaping gesture.[29] These hostile, but hypocritical, acts of the enemies provide the context for the imagined turn in verse 26, where the blush is de-emphasized for the emotion that it encodes: *sceamien hy*, 'let them be ashamed', which is yoked to the following verb of dread even more fully than in the Latin, with both *eac*, 'also', and *ægðer endemes*, 'both together'. The translator keeps up such yoking and balance by providing two verbs and two nouns in the second half of verse 26 where the Latin has but one verb with two nouns:

---

[25] BT s.v. *sceamu*, sense I: 'the emotion caused by consciousness of unworthiness or of disgrace, in a good sense … modesty, bashfulness; in a bad sense, shame, confusion'

[26] See Birnbaum's chapter in this volume; Alice Jorgensen, '"It Shames Me to Say It": Ælfric and the Concept and Vocabulary of Shame', *Anglo-Saxon England* 41 (2013 for 2012): 249–76; and 'Historicizing Emotion: The Shame–Rage Spiral in Ælfric's *Life of St Agatha*', *English Studies* 93 (2012): 529–38.

[27] O'Neill, p. 140.

[28] *Wincettan*, 'to wink', occurs here only, but is related to *wincian*, defined by BT as 'to wink, make a sign' and 'to close the eyes, blink'.

[29] *Leahtre* here exemplifies the uneasy spelling confusion of *leahtor*, 'sin', and *hleahtor*, 'laughter', discussed generally (without reference to this example) by Donald Scragg, 'Sin and Laughter in Late Anglo-Saxon England: The Case of Old English *(h)leahtor*', in Stuart McWilliams (ed.), *Saints and Scholars: New Perspectives on Anglo-Saxon Literature and Culture* (Cambridge, 2012), pp. 213–23. O'Neill lemmatizes this form under *hleahtor*, but glosses that word as *(object of) derision*.

'beslepen hi on hy bysmor and gegyrion hy mid sceame'.[30] Explicit reference to the blush itself may have vanished in the prose translation, but the emotions of shame and dread have been clarified and the gesture of blushing may yet stand implicitly in the idea of being clothed in such emotions. The vocabulary of blushing repeatedly raises the porous boundary between interior and exterior, bodily sign and fundamental emotion.

As with other psalms, the events of Psalm 34 are depicted in the illustrated psalters, but these prove less useful for understanding the gestures than the glosses. Such programmes of illustration are modelled on the Utrecht Psalter, which became available in Canterbury in the tenth century, where it was drawn upon for the Harley Psalter (London, British Library, MS Harley 603).[31] While these illustrations are literal, they generally do not present bodies with enough detail to read facial gestures. In the case of Psalm 34, illustrated on fol. 19v, the group of enemies on the right illustrates how 'scourges were gathered together upon me' – note the whips in the hands of the leaders – and the angels with sword and spears at mid-right are clearly confounding the legions of enemies at the lower centre, who are finding their hidden snares and nets turned against them, and sending them to hell, but blushing or even clothing in confusion are not visible here.[32]

The association of blushing with shame is evident in other red faces present in the Psalter,[33] and one further example generates a term that nicely captures the somatic/emotional balance. Psalm 68, another Psalm of David that ponders the idea of shame, includes at verse 8 (KJV 69:7) the idea 'quoniam propter te sustinui obprobrium operuit confusio faciem meam' ('Because for thy sake I have borne reproach; shame hath covered my face' (Douay-Rheims)). In the verse translation of the Paris Psalter this comes out as:

> Forþon ic edwit for þe   oft aræfnade
> and me hleorsceame   hearde becwoman.
>
> (ll. 25–26)[34]

---

[30] 'Put on themselves reproach and dress them with shame'. DOE s.v. *beslypan, beslepan*, shows that the verb occurs just three times, always in Alfredian translations.

[31] See William Noel, *The Harley Psalter* (Cambridge, 1995). The illustrations are freely available in digitized form through the British Library website, 'Catalogue of Illuminated Manuscripts': http://www.bl.uk/catalogues/illuminatedmanuscripts/record.asp?MSID=18402&CollID=8&NStart=603 (accessed 1 May 2013).

[32] Full size reproduction freely available at http://www.bl.uk/catalogues/illuminatedmanuscripts/ILLUMINBig.ASP?size=big&IllID=15339 (accessed 1 May 2013).

[33] Other possible blushes associated with shame occur in Psalms 68, 69:3–5, 82:17–19, 88:46

[34] Krapp, p. 24.

[Because for you I often suffered reproach
and hard cheek-shame came on me.]

Hleorsceamu, 'cheek-shame', translates *confusio faciem* with a unique poetic term that captures in its compounding the gesture of the blush by collocating its bodily seat and the emotion that it signals.[35] In what is often within the Psalms an aggressive invocation of revenge, turning red is strongly associated with shame, signalling a fundamental failing of inner worth to be turned about through the process of conversion, even as blushing also carries an element of the social discomfiture of exposure that is the mark of embarrassment.

Such associations are also invoked outside the Psalms. At the end of the *Rule of St. Benedict*, for example, another Latin text available in both an Old English translation and an Old English gloss, Benedict reflects on the wealth of materials available to those interested in the perfection of the monastic life through a first-person modesty formula –

> nobis autem desidiosis et male viventibus atque neglegentibus rubor confusionis est. (*Rule of St. Benedict*, ch. 73)

[but as for us, they make us blush for shame at being so slothful, so unobservant, so negligent.]

– which sees translation into Old English as:

> To sceame and to ablysunge hi sint us, þe asolcene synd and yfele and gymeleaslice mid unrihte lybbað.[36]

[They are a cause of shame and blushing for us, who are indolent and bad and live heedlessly unjustly.]

Rubor confusionis, 'blush for shame', is closely translated in the glossed version as *scame gescyndnysse*,[37] but the translation sets up a doublet (*to sceame and to ablysunge*), with the resultant question of whether 'shame' and 'blushing' are seen as synonyms or discrete reflexes, one emotional, one gestural. Blushing is clearly associated with shame, although once again the valence of this emotion itself requires further interpretation. The emotion at failing to keep up with the

---

[35] 'Shame or confusion of face', according to BT, s.v. *hleorsceamu*.
[36] Arnold Schröer (ed.), *Die angelsächsischen Prosabearbeitungen der Benediktinerregel*, Bibliothek der angelsächsischen Prosa 2 (Kassel, 1885–88), p. 133, ll. 11–12.
[37] H. Logeman (ed.), *The Rule of S. Benet: Latin and Anglo-Saxon Interlinear Version*, EETS o.s. 90 (London, 1888), p. 118, l. 11: 'the confusion or confounding of shame'.

literature on the subject (familiar, perhaps, to academics) is not so much the fundamental lack of self-worth from a moral failing – shame as conjured up on the psalm-speaker's enemies – as temporary discomfiture at weakness exposed, more along the lines of embarrassment.[38] Blushing in religious works is strongly connected with shame, even as the valence of the emotion incorporates at times serious retribution and at times more lightweight discomfiture.

Blushing in Apollonius of Tyre

If Old English religious texts associate blushing primarily with shame, there is at least one example of a red-faced hero in Old English who anticipates the red-cheeked lovers of *Troilus and Criseyde* more than King David's enemies. The Old English *Apollonius of Tyre*, with its story of a wandering hero, of love and incest, loss and recovery, adventure and coincidence, told in an extended prose narrative, translated (presumably) from a lost Greek romance through a Latin intermediary, presents a story that focuses on psychology and identity to an extent that is unusual in the Old English corpus.[39] This romance text is rich for the study of gestures of all kinds, not least because characters travel to unknown cultures where their activities have to be interpreted, as do the riddles that abound in the story, starting with the foundational riddle of Antiochus the king's incest with his daughter that is used as an explicit riddle to test, and keep at bay, suitors. Understanding the lability of the body within this story provides a necessary context for understanding its portrayal of a blush.

The story is full of doublings, and court protocols are dwelled on further at the corresponding court of the good king Arcestrates in Pentapolis. Here clothes make the man – and Apollonius is traumatized to enter this world naked from his shipwreck. Although not yet triggered, the audience's gaze upon his body and its social discomfiture anticipates the subsequent blush. A kind fisherman who discovers him shares half of his cloak (ch. 12) – an outfit in which Apollonius would be socially embarrassed were it not for the games in the bathplace/gymnasium, where nakedness is legitimate and he can thus reveal his inner talents (ch. 13). Post-baths, Apollonius returns to his sartorial predicament: he is so embarrassed when he returns to his dirty cloak that, even when called upon to join the king, he will not re-enter the company 'for scame' (22/8) until the king orders for him to be re-dressed.

---

[38] On the distinction, see my essay in n. 1: 'Naked in Old English'.
[39] Peter Goolden (ed.), *The Old English Apollonius of Tyre* (Oxford, 1958), edits both the Old English text and a recreation of the Latin source. (Citations within the text are by page/line number.) For a particularly good study, see David Townsend, 'The Naked Truth of the King's Affection in the Old English *Apollonius of Tyre*', *Journal of Medieval and Early Modern Studies* 34 (2004): 173–95.

The love story at Arcestrates's court again contrasts with that of Antiochus. At Antioch the daughter had no volition, raped by her father, and was silent except for lamenting to her maid. At Pentapolis, Arcestrates's daughter gazes on the shipwrecked man, articulates her concerns, perceives his underlying nobility despite his changed outward appearance, and gets her father's encouragement to go and talk to him (ch. 15), mostly controlling the subsequent courtship scene (ch. 15).[40] Within that courtship, Arcestrate explains her desire for the shipwrecked man with a forwardness that hints at blushes, although these get deflected. She explains in riddling fashion the boldness of her assertion:

and gif ðu wundrige þæt swa scamfæst fæmne swa unforwandigendlice ðas word awrat, þonne wite þu þæt ic hæbbe þurh weax aboden, ðe nane scame ne can, þæt ic silf ðe for scame secgan ne mihte. (ch. 20, 32/14–17)

[and if you should wonder that a woman so *scamfæst* (modest, secure in respect of shameful things) wrote these words so *unforwandigendlice* (shamelessly, un-turning-away-in-shame), then know that I have declared by means of wax, which knows no *scame* (shame/embarrassment), what I could not say to you myself for *scame*.

Si miraris ... quod tam pudica virgo tam impudenter scripserim, scito quia quod pudore indicare non potui per ceram mandavi, quae pudorem non habet. (Latin source as recreated by Goolden, 33/10–12)]

Clearly, Arcestrate is self-conscious here about the potential embarrassment of her advances, even if she deflects this embarrassment by articulating rather than performing it. The potential for her emotion to be written on her body – with a blush? – is deflected to the wax on which she writes – putty in her hands and an exteriorization of the lability of the body, with its potential to *weaxan reod*. Performed embarrassment is instead transferred to the male object of desire, Apollonius. The king goes through the comedy of asking the three initial suitors which is the shipwrecked man, with one of them, the opportunistic Arcadius, volunteering for the role until slapped down by his rival suitors. The comedy of embarrassment is played out as the king turns to Apollonius for interpretation, and the finally conscious Apollonius reads the tablet and enacts the bodily gesture that encodes self-consciousness:

---

[40] On the noteworthy, if limited, female role here, see Anita R. Riedinger, 'The Englishing of Arcestrate: Woman in *Apollonius of Tyre*', in Helen Damico and Alexandra Hennessey Olsen (eds), *New Readings on Women in Old English Literature* (Bloomington, 1990), pp. 292–306.

and sona swa he ongeat þæt he gelufod wæs from ðam mædene, his andwlita eal areodode (ch. 21, 32/29–30)

[and as soon as he perceived that he was loved by the maiden, his face completely reddened.

et ut sensit se a regina amari, erubuit. (33/22)]

The king rightly interprets both the gesture and the writing. His further observation of Apollonius allows the narrator to expand upon the hero's discomfiture:

Ða geseah se cyngc þæt Apollonius mid rosan rude wæs eal oferbræded, þa ongeat he þone cwyde (34/1–3)

[When the king saw that Apollonius was completely suffused with a rosy red glow, then he understood the writing

Et his dictis videns rex faciem eius roseo rubore perfusam intellexit dictum (35/1–2)]

As Augustine's reading of involuntary signs would suggest, the body in this romance text is an unreliable mask that gives away what is going on inside. Ironically, though, it does this not when Apollonius is naked on the shore or in the baths, nor even when dressed and controlling his performance in the court, but rather when fully and appropriately dressed but taken unawares – by the inverted power of his pupil who is a woman? or by suddenly being love struck? or by having his private feelings exposed in the public setting of the court etiquette? The blush is multivalent as ever, but clearly includes embarrassment among its connotations. To some extent, it is another doubling, standing in for Arcestrates's lack of blushing as she set the whole scene up. Its valence is akin to the world of later Middle English romances, with their concentration on the nexus of private emotion and public perception, falling in love and dynastic marriage, manly men and empowered women. It differs from and yet is related to the blushing in shame and perplexity of the Psalms, a more corporate, and more aggressive activity, which yet implies something of the same world of interiority inadvertently exteriorized.

Once such blushing of embarrassment has been identified in Old English literature, it is intriguing to ponder whether it is also encoded elsewhere. Could the riddler be playing on a somewhat similar, if more explicit, idea of inverted gender roles in Riddle 25 (the onion double entendre), when the haughty maiden grabs the first-person object and 'ræseð mec on reodne' ('rushes onto red (blushing?) me', l. 8). Is the first-person onion here, like Apollonius, a lover taken by surprise at the sudden exposure to the maiden's wishes? Is a riddler playing at suggesting self-consciousness and interiority through giving a 'bodily' gesture of hue to a garden vegetable? Examining the portrayal of blushes in the corpus of Old English attunes a reader to the possibility of playful counterparts.

Conclusion

While it would be fruitful to historicize the understanding of the bodily movements that underlie blushing in terms of the model uncovered in Lockett's recent study of Anglo-Saxon psychology, it is also valuable to consider in detail the literary representations of such a gesture.[41] Both the gesture and the emotions to which it points take significant effort to interpret, requiring considerable attention to lexis and context. Let me conclude by suggesting certain methodological inferences for the study of gesture in pursuit of emotion in historical literature:

1. Overtones of gestures need to be understood through particular attentiveness to vocabulary, and yet establishing the semantic range of any Old English term is difficult. As the range of possibilities in Psalm 34 shows, both variation and glosses help to build up the overtones of a single word, but since the meaning of synonyms (if that is what they are) are also hard to interpret, certainty is often difficult to attain. While this is true of all Old English vocabulary, the issue is particularly acute in dealing with emotion, where lexis and the concept itself are in a complex dialectic.[42] In the examples considered here, what if *sceamu* is understood to mean *embarrassment*, rather than its cognate term, *shame*?[43] And what if the term may also reasonably be understood in the sense *blush* or *blushing*? At that point, it is not clear if an Old English usage is signalling an emotion or the somatic response triggered by that emotion, or whether that is a meaningful distinction. This satisfyingly embroils emotion and gesture, even as it exasperates any desire for simple comprehension.

---

[41] See Leslie Lockett, *Anglo-Saxon Psychologies in the Vernacular and Latin Traditions* (Toronto, 2011), and also her chapter in this volume. The underlying emotion can also be usefully understood through contemporary cognitive psychology, as seen in Antonina Harbus, *Cognitive Approaches to Old English Poetry* (Cambridge, 2012), and her chapter in this volume.

[42] See, further Izdebska's chapter in this volume about the lexical challenges of emotion terms.

[43] As it demonstrably does at times, as I have suggested in 'Naked in Old English' (as n. 1).

2. Latin linguistic equivalents help, but the question of semantic range and unknowable overtones remains for the Latin terms, as seen throughout the examples in this chapter.
3. Broad context is crucial for understanding the arena within which the emotions and gestures ought to be interpreted. It is the whole romance world of *Apollonius of Tyre* that makes probable a pleasurable play on exposed interiority in the blush, whereas in Psalm 34 the extensive engagement with enemies suggests an adversarial stance in which shame is key.
4. Gestures tend to cluster, and understanding one often means being attentive to the sequence. Thus the winking and mouth-gaping of Psalm 34 need pondering in relation to the blushing, and in each case the complexity of linguistic understanding and the porous boundary between gesture and emotion applies.
5. A lexicon of Anglo-Saxon gestures would help, but each case is likely to require extensive discussion. This chapter has made a start on blushing, and such a lexicon could also usefully attend to winking and mouth-opening, among many others.
6. Pictures rarely help in reading somatic gestures since Anglo-Saxon illustrations are more iconic than literalistic, and it is in portraits of the body that such a distinction is most clear. Nevertheless, pictures have their own lexicon of gestures, which is worth considering.[44]

Pursuing red faces in Old English literature is productive for getting at a cluster of awkward emotions, centring on shame, exposure and embarrassment. Blushing keys into a public/private dichotomy, not only because it is associated with exposure, but also because the surface of the body involuntarily reveals an internal state. Psalm 34:26 calls for the satisfaction of seeing on the bodies of the speaker's enemies something of their blighted internal state. *Apollonius of Tyre* shows how such involuntary exposure can reveal something pleasurable. In both cases, this particular somatic gesture appears to be uncontrolled – a natural sign in Augustine's terms, which collapses distinctions between the external (a gesture) and the internal (an emotion) and therefore constitutes *both* gesture and emotion. Reading the sign is not as straightforward as Augustine's model suggests, since the internal state that is revealed is hard to capture in language. The presentation of blushes reminds us that the body will reveal certain emotions, pointing to meanings that extend beyond the verbal for those willing to attend to such deliciously charged gestures.

---

[44] See, in particular, C.R. Dodwell, *Anglo-Saxon Gestures and the Roman Stage* (Cambridge, 2000).

Chapter 7

Naming Shame: Translating Emotion in the Old English Psalter Glosses[1]

Tahlia Birnbaum

The Book of Psalms is a unique resource for understanding the experience and performance of emotions in Anglo-Saxon England. Its first-person perspective provides a model for experiencing specifically Christian emotions, and its recitation as part of the monastic office ensured its place in the emotional fabric of monastic life. Evidence of this specific religious interpretation of emotion is made available to us by the translation of the psalter text into Old English. This chapter will examine Old English glosses of certain words associated with shame in the Psalms to determine how the Anglo-Saxons understood this emotion and its role in religious experience. The focus will be two word groups, *wandian/forwandian/forwandung* and *aswarnian/aswarnung*, first employed as glosses in the tenth-century Royal Psalter (London, British Library, Royal 2 B. V).[2] Through contextual analysis of the Latin *lemmata* and comparison with *interpretamenta* in the other Old English glossed psalters, and in consultation with Cassiodorus' *Expositio Psalmorum*, the chapter concludes that the shame conveyed in the Psalms had a wide emotional range, incorporating not only humiliation and humility, but also reverence, confusion and fear. For Cassiodorus, whose commentary is quoted in the margins of the Royal Psalter, such shame was a vital emotion for non-Christians in the conversion process. In these contexts, shame was concerned with repentance for sin and, ultimately, the salvation of one's soul on Judgement Day.

The psalter was one of the most important biblical texts in early medieval Europe, no less so in Anglo-Saxon England. Recitation of specified psalms occurred on a daily basis in monasteries, and psalter glossing is attested throughout the period in at least fourteen different manuscripts. The ninth-

---

[1] This contribution derives from a chapter of my PhD dissertation, for completion in 2015. I wish to thank the Medieval and Early Modern Centre of Sydney University for funding my attendance at the workshop in Dublin.

[2] For the edition, see *Der altenglische Regius-Psalter; eine Interlinearversion in H.S. Royal 2. B. 5 des Brit. Mus.*, ed. Fritz Roeder, Studien zur englischen Philologie 18 (Halle, 1904).

century Vespasian Psalter contains the earliest continuous interlinear Old English gloss, and the twelfth-century Eadwine Psalter the most recent.[3] The psalter text and associated commentaries contain valuable information about ideas of shame in a Christian context and its role in conversion and penance. As discussed elsewhere in this volume, words are not always directly translatable across cultures.[4] The tradition of vernacular glossing provides evidence of how Latin Christian culture was appropriated and expressed in native vocabulary – specifically, how certain Latin words were understood by those living in monastic communities. As will be seen, this vocabulary was often considered inadequate by the glossators, and new words were developed to convey concepts that had not previously required verbal expression. The transmission of new ideas and ways of expressing emotions demanded the expansion of Old English to accommodate these concepts. The variety of words used for different kinds of shame in both the Latin text and Old English glosses indicates the complexity of this emotion and its role in religious devotion.

The Royal Psalter (D) contains the *Romanum* version of the Psalms, and is the earliest extant copy of the D-type gloss.[5] It is dated to the first half of the tenth century, when the Latin psalter, marginal Latin commentary and interlinear Old English glosses were all written by the same scribe.[6] The commentary is chiefly derived from Cassiodorus' sixth-century *Expositio Psalmorum*.[7] Although it is widely accepted that the Royal Psalter is a copy of a now-lost D-type exemplar, there is debate as to whether or not the commentary was related to the original gloss.[8] Davey has convincingly argued for the direct influence of the

---

[3] N.R. Ker, *Catalogue of Manuscripts containing Anglo-Saxon* (Oxford, 1957), nos. 203 and 91. The list of glossed psalters from Anglo-Saxon England (each assigned an alphabetical *siglum*) is as follows: A, Vespasian Psalter; B, Junius Psalter; C, Cambridge Psalter; D, Royal Psalter; E, Eadwine or Canterbury Psalter; F, Stowe Psalter; G, Vitellius Psalter; H, Tiberius Psalter; I, Lambeth Psalter; J, Arundel Psalter; K, Salisbury Psalter; L, Bosworth Psalter; M, Blickling Psalter; P, Paris Psalter. For a full list of editions, dates and further references, see Mechthild Gretsch, *The Intellectual Foundations of the English Benedictine Reform* (Cambridge, 1999), pp. 18–21.

[4] See Izdebska, above.

[5] The other D-type glosses are psalters K, parts of F, G, H, J, L and M, and the corrections to E. Except for E, L and M, these are all based on the *Gallicanum* Psalter (Gretsch, pp. 26–7). The earlier glossing tradition, known as the A-type gloss, is based on the Vespasian Psalter.

[6] Ker, no. 249.

[7] Davey holds that 75 per cent of the 4280 comments show a direct influence (William Davey, 'The Commentary of the Regius Psalter: Its Main Source and Influence on the Old English Gloss', *Mediaeval Studies* 49 (1987): 335–51, at 338).

[8] *The Salisbury Psalter*, eds Celia Sisam and Kenneth Sisam, EETS o.s. 242 (Oxford, 1959), pp. 54–5.

commentary upon the gloss – an argument I endorse, and upon which I shall expand.[9] Whenever these textual elements (Latin psalter, Old English gloss and commentary) came together, they each constituted tools that would have been available for the compilation of a manuscript to aid study of the Psalms.[10] It is highly likely that a glossator creating a fresh interlinear gloss in his vernacular would have consulted Cassiodorus' work and, even if it were the Royal scribe (rather than the original glossator) who brought these elements together, the connections between Cassiodorus' commentary and the Old English gloss would have been discernible.[11]

Cassiodorus' interpretation of the Psalms values shame for its role in recognising sin and encouraging a reaction of either penance (for the faithful) or conversion (for the impious). Pleas for the shaming of one's enemies are recurrent throughout the Psalms, and interpreted by Cassiodorus as integral to the Christian mission. According to Cassiodorus, the experiences of shame, confounding, blushing and confusion are part of an integrated process that enables recognition of sin and the need to turn to God, usually with the expectation of complete conversion. Cassiodorus also explains a related theme: those who are confounded on earth will be able to repent and the punishment for their sins will be minimal. Those who do not convert, however, will be confounded forever, and condemned to eternal damnation at Judgement Day. Cassiodorus explains this interpretation repeatedly throughout his commentary for the same group of Latin words, leaving no room for ambiguity of interpretation. The way these themes influenced the Royal glossator's expression of the Latin text in Old English is the focus of this discussion.

The words used frequently in the psalter to describe these experiences are *confundere* and *reuereri*. *Confundere* occurs twenty-three times in the *Romanum* text of the Royal Psalter, and is usually glossed with a variation of *scamian/ascamian* or *gescendan*, and once with *aswarnian*. The Lewis and Short definition of *confundere* that best suits the psalter context is 'to confound, confuse, jumble

---

[9] Davey, 'The Commentary of the Regius Psalter'.

[10] A companion volume, London, British Library, Royal 4 A. XIV, contains Jerome's commentary on Ps. 109–149, written in the same hand. Along with the extensive notes in D itself, this suggests that the Royal Psalter was used in scholarship; Sisam and Sisam (eds), p. 52.

[11] The differentiation between 'scribe' and 'glossator' applies throughout this chapter. The popularity of Cassiodorus is well attested in Anglo-Saxon England, with 181 total references or reminiscences (see Michael Lapidge, *The Anglo-Saxon Library* (Oxford, 2006), p. 296). The only complete extant manuscript of the *Expositio* from Anglo-Saxon England represents a breviate version of the text (Durham, Cathedral Library, B. II. 30). Nevertheless, evidence from Bede suggests that the full text was circulated (see Richard N. Bailey, 'Bede's Text of Cassiodorus' Commentary on the Psalms', *Journal of Theological Studies* 34.1 (1983): 89–193, at 191).

together, bring into disorder'.[12] Niermeyer's *Mediae Latinitatis Lexicon Minus* gives the definition 'to be ashamed' for its passive uses in the psalter, and Souter's *Glossary of Later Latin*, based on words used by Cassiodorus and his Late Antique contemporaries, defines the deponent *confundor* in this way: 'be ashamed (of); brought to ruin, etc.'.[13] *Reuereri* is primarily glossed with *forwandian* and occasionally with *aswarnian*, and is defined in Lewis and Short as 'to stand in awe or fear of; to regard, respect, honor; to fear, be afraid of; to reverence, revere'; it is omitted from Souter and Niermeyer. This range of glosses and definitions alerts us to the difficulty of translating these words with a single equivalent, especially in such a complex text as the Psalms. It would have proven even more difficult to find such equivalents in a vernacular relatively new to the culture and emotions of Christianity. The precise meaning of these words was a concern for Cassiodorus, reflected in extensive discussions throughout his commentary. Likewise, translating the experience was of concern to the Royal glossator, as reflected in the range of verbs employed as glosses and in his use of the unusual verbs *forwandian* and *aswarnian*.

Wandian/forwandian/forwandung

The first word group under scrutiny includes two verbs, *wandian* and *forwandian*, and one noun, *forwandung*. The standard definition of *wandian*, 'to turn aside from something', is uncomplicated, and the word can be grouped with the more common *wendan* 'to turn', and *windan* 'to twist, roll'.[14] These are derived from the Proto-Indo-European form **uendh*, 'to turn, wind, wend', and have survived as the Modern English cognates 'wend', 'wind', 'went'. The use of *wandian* in this psalter context is innovative as the glossator expands the semantic field of the verb to incorporate conversion. This word is related to *forwandian*, for which the *Dictionary of Old English* provides two meanings: 'to be in awe of, revere, respect; to fear (someone acc.)', and 'to hesitate (from fear), be afraid'.[15] The nominal *forwandung* is defined simply as 'turning away in shame' (DOE). This physical sense of turning away is implicit in the verbal definition 'to hesitate', and is integrated into the verb through the component '-*wandian*'. This aspect is crucial to the way the verb is used in all contexts in the Royal gloss, as it always

---

[12] Charlton T. Lewis and Charles Short, *A Latin Dictionary* (Oxford, 1879).

[13] J.F. Niermeyer, *Mediae Latinitatis Lexicon Minus* (Leiden, 1976); Alexander Souter, *Glossary of Later Latin to 600A.D.* (Oxford, 1949).

[14] These definitions are from Joseph Bosworth and T. Northcote Toller, *An Anglo-Saxon Dictionary* (Oxford, 1898) and *Supplement* (Oxford, 1921); hereafter BT.

[15] Angus Cameron, Ashley Crandell Amos, Antonette diPaolo Healey et al., *Dictionary of Old English: A to G online* (http://www.doe.utoronto.ca, accessed 24 July 2013) (Toronto, 2007); hereafter DOE.

describes a process of change – usually conversion. I shall argue, and Cassiodorus' explanations will show, that the semantic ranges of *forwandian* and *forwandung* can incorporate almost all of the aforementioned meanings (reverence, fear, shame and conversion) in a single use.[16]

Before an analysis of the glosses, brief attention must be given to the uses of *forwandian/forwandung* elsewhere in the corpus, particularly in texts dated prior to the Royal Psalter.[17] *Forwandian, forwandung* and the related adverbial and adjectival forms *unforwandodlice* and *unforwandodlic* occur sixty-six times in the Old English corpus, primarily in translations of Latin texts, all of which (with the exception of *Apollonius of Tyre*) concern religious subject matter.[18] The fact that these words were not widely used in contexts in which a layperson may have encountered them (secular poetry, for example) suggests that their use was restricted to religious communities.[19] The restricted use of these words is suggestive of an 'emotional community' (to borrow Rosenwein's terminology) within Anglo-Saxon England, whose verbal expression of emotions differed to that of the general population.[20] The vernacular words used more commonly to express shame are *scamu, scand* and *bismer*, which also appear as glosses in psalter texts, but appear more frequently in homilies, saint's lives and secular poetry.[21] As my investigation will show, *forwandian* and associated terms formed part of a technical vocabulary, conveying a specific religious experience described in the Psalms.

Forwandian and its variants first appeared in the late ninth century, when the translation of Gregory the Great's *Regula Pastoralis* was made. Most occurrences of these forms are translated by Sweet as 'neglected', 'hesitated' and variations thereof, and represent a range of Latin words, including *non emendare, fugit, formidant, noluit* and *subterfugi*.[22] Although there may be an underlying complexity to the type of hesitation described, such as arising from humility, or

---

[16] Although 'awe' is listed as a definition for *reuereri* and *forwandian*, this aspect does not feature in Cassiodorus' descriptions.

[17] Occurrences of *wandian* are peripheral to this discussion as its use is consistent throughout the corpus.

[18] All corpus search-data comes from Antonette diPaolo Healey (ed.), *The Dictionary of Old English Corpus in Electronic Form* (Toronto, 2004).

[19] *Forwandian* occurs twice in Ælfric's homilies. *Unforwandodlic* occurs three times, and also in two anonymous homilies. These homiletic examples provide the only evidence that these words were conveyed to laypeople.

[20] See Barbara Rosenwein, *Emotional Communities in the Early Middle Ages* (Ithaca, NY, 2006).

[21] These words are the only 'shame' words to occur in the Paris Psalter, supporting Jorgensen's theory that it was designed for use by a wealthy layperson, rather than for monastic study. See Jorgensen, below.

[22] *King Alfred's West Saxon Version of Gregory's Pastoral Care*, ed. Henry Sweet, EETS o.s. 45 and 50, 2 vols (London, 1871); see chapters XXVIII, XL, XLI and XLIX.

a desire to avoid sin,[23] emotional nuances cannot be gleaned from the individual translated Latin words. Similarly, nor does each *lemma* glossed by *forwandian* in the Royal Psalter necessarily convey shame. It is only when one examines those occurrences in close comparison with Cassiodorus that the semantic nuances of this vocabulary are apparent. *Forwandian* and its variants become intensely emotional, describing a complex religious experience. These words occur in the Royal gloss nine times, as shown in Table 1:

Table 1   Occurrences of '*wandian/forwandian/forwandung*' in the Royal Psalter

Verse	Lemma	Interpretamentum
34.4	reuereantur	wandien
34.26	pudore	forwandunge
39.15	reuereantur	hy forwandian
68.7	reuereantur	hy forwandien
68.8	reuerentia	forwandung
68.20	uerecundiam	forwandunga
69.3	reuereantur	forwandien
108.29	reuerentia	of forwandunga
128.5	reuereantur	forwandien

The verb is used on all five occasions to gloss *reuereri*, whilst the nominal form is used four times, as a gloss for three different nouns: *pudor*, *reuerentia* and *uerecundia*.[24] By comparison, each occurrence of *reuereri* in the earlier A-type glosses based on the Vespasian Psalter is glossed with *onscunian*, 'to regard with fear' (BT), whilst each occurrence of the nominal *reuerentia* is glossed with *scom*.[25] This brief comparison with the A-type gloss evinces an overlap between fear and shame in the semantic range of this Latin word group. The Royal glossator rejects this separation of meaning, instead conveying a simultaneous sense of fear, shame, reverence and conversion through his development of *forwandian/forwandung*.

For comparison with the Latin text, see Gregory the Great, *Regula Pastoralis*, ed. Floribert Rommel, Sources Chrétiennes 381–382, 2 vols (Paris, 1992).

[23]   See especially XLIX, which conveys fear.

[24]   *Reuereri* is glossed differently on three other occasions; *reuerentia*, once. See below, and Table 2.

[25]   *The Vespasian Psalter*, ed. Sherman M. Kuhn (Ann Arbor, MI, 1965).

Wandian is the first of this group to occur, and glosses the Latin *reuereri* at 34.4:

> gescamigen & wandien fynd mine þa ðe secað sawle sin gecyrrede underbecling & hy ablysygen þa ðe þencað yfelu
>
> Confundantur et reuereantur inimici mei qui querunt animam meam; Auertantur retrorsum et erubescant qui cogitant mihi mala[26]
>
> [Let them be confounded and ashamed that seek after my soul. Let them be turned back and be confounded that devise against me.][27]

This verse introduces the two Latin verbs of crucial importance to the construction of shame: *confundere* and *reuereri*. In his commentary for 34.4, Cassiodorus provides a definition for each of these verbs, beginning with *confundere*:

> *Confundi* est facta sua erubescere et in meliorem sententiam commutare; nam et illi confusi dicuntur, qui conuincuntur ad poenam. Sed ut hoc magis ad conuersionem intellegere debuisses ....[28]
>
> [To be *confounded* means to blush at their deeds, and to change so as to obtain a better judgement, for men are said to be confounded when sentenced to punishment. So that you should understand the word rather in the sense of conversion ....][29]

Confounding here incorporates shame as a feeling and physical reaction, simultaneously conveyed by the verb *erubescere*. This shame causes a shift in one's judgement or understanding, and the experience results in conversion. Cassiodorus subsequently explains *reuereantur*: 'Revereantur, id est, emendati colant, quem persequendum esse putauerant.'[30] These explanations describe different elements of the same process. They both contain descriptions of change

---

[26] All quotes come from Roeder's edition. All *signes de renvoi* are replaced by semi-colons, and Tironian *et* is replaced by the ampersand.

[27] For all biblical quotations I have included the Douay-Rheims translation (based on the *Gallicanum* psalter) for comparison only, due to the difficulty of producing a translation that adequately captures both the *Romanum* text and Old English gloss.

[28] Cassiodorus, *Expositio Psalmorum*, ed. M. Adriaen, CCSL 97–98, 2 vols (Turnhout, 1958), I, p. 306.

[29] P.G. Walsh (ed.), *Cassiodorus, Explanation of the Psalms*, Ancient Christian Writers 51–53, 3 vols (New York, 1990–1991), I, p. 338.

[30] Cassiodorus, p. 306. '*And show reverence*, in other words, become changed and worship the One who they thought should be persecuted': Walsh (ed.), I, p. 338.

(*commutare, emendere*) leading to conversion, which we are told begins with shame (*erubescere*). Each time this process is described throughout the Psalter the vocabulary is interchangeable, with *erubescere, confundere, reuereri* and *conturbare* occurring in variant subjunctive pairs at 6.11, 34.4 (this example), 34.26, 39.15, 69.3, 70.24 and 128.5 – all expressing a desire to convert one's enemies.[31] *Wandian/forwandian* is used in four of these verses, and *aswarnian* is used in the remaining three.[32] The experience is highly complex, and shame takes a central role in converting the wicked.

The glossator is thus presented with the challenge of conveying all aspects of this process in his gloss. The marginal commentary associated with 34.4 reads, 'id est sua mala facta erubescant et emendati me colant',[33] paraphrasing Cassiodorus' definitions of *confundere* and *reuereri* and unambiguously linking them with *emendere*. The glossator conveys this complex combination of blushing, confounding and conversion through the verb *wandian*, imbuing the literal interpretation with a spiritual aspect. One would not simply change or turn away, but undergo spiritual change – that is, conversion. Both Cassiodorus and the Royal glossator have understood this verse as an experience of confounding and shame, leading to conversion.

A number of verses later, at 34.26, the association between *forwandian/forwandung* and shame is unambiguous, with the noun used as a gloss for the Latin *pudor*. This verse repeats the sentiment of shaming one's enemies, and shame is imbued with a similar functionality to that described previously:

> ablysigen arweorðien ætgædere þa ðe þanciað yfelum minum syn gescrydde forwandunge arweorþunge þe mætu specað ongean me

> Erubescant et reuereantur simul qui gratulantur malis meis. induantur pudore et reuerentia qui maligna loquuntur aduersum me.

> [Let them blush: and be ashamed together, who rejoice at my evils. Let them be clothed with confusion and shame, who speak great [bad] things against me.]

Cassiodorus explains these *lemmata* once again in his commentary:

---

[31] The *Gallicanum* text also switches between verbs in this group.
[32] See tables 1 and 2.
[33] 'that is they blush at their own bad deeds and corrected they honour me'. The text of the marginal commentary comes from William J. Davey, *An Edition of the Regius Psalter and its Latin Commentary*, unpublished dissertation, University of Ottawa (Canada) 1979. This has been checked against the microfiche facsimile of the manuscript: *Anglo-Saxon Manuscripts in Microfiche Facsimile, Volume Two: Psalters*, ed. Phillip Pulsiano (Binghampton, NY, 1994). Translations are my own.

Digna uindicta, poena sufficiens. Nam qui erubescit actus suos, propria aestimatione damnatus est, et se ultore torquetur, qui uinculo confusionis inuoluitur. Potest tamen aliquis *erubescere*, et reuerentiam non habere. Hic autem addidit *et reuereantur simul*, ut conuersionis eorum indicia declararet. *Reuerentia* est enim Domini timor cum amore permixtus; quod illis prouenit qui uoluntate sincerissima confessionis munera consequuntur.[34]

[The revenge is worthy, the punishment sufficient. He who blushes at his own deeds is condemned on his own assessment; he who is enchained with the bonds of embarrassment is tortured by the vengeance which he exacts from himself. Yet a man can blush and still not have reverence; here however He added: *And have reverence as well*, so that He might announce the signs of their conversion. *Reverence* is fear of the Lord mingled with love. It springs up in men who through most pure desire obtain the gifts of confession.][35]

The similarity between this explanation and that of 34.4 is striking, and the Royal scribe repeats Cassiodorus' most illuminating phrases. The marginal commentary adjacent to this verse reads: 'id est ut timeant et ament',[36] and 'id est conuersionis eorum indicia declararentur, id est conuertantur et agnoscant me',[37] which together paraphrase Cassiodorus' commentary. Once again the verse is concerned with conversion, and incorporates blushing (*erubescit*), confusion (*confusionis*) and fear (*timor*). Yet this verse includes two of the three occasions in which the glossator selects a different gloss for *reuereri/reuerentia*, instead using *arwurðian*, 'to honour, hold in honour; revere, treat with reverence' (DOE), and the nominal *arwurðung*.[38] Whilst this conveys something of Cassiodorus' explanation, the glossator evidently deems it inadequate, as it is not repeated. Instead, he settles on *forwandian* for later verses, the semantic range of which is expanded to incorporate the meaning reflected in Cassiodorus' commentary.

The glossator makes his first use of this verb at 39.15. This psalm explores the already-familiar themes associated with shame found in other verses, specifically, praying for shame upon one's enemies to instigate their conversion:

---

[34] Cassiodorus, p. 316.
[35] Walsh (ed.), I, p. 348.
[36] 'that is they may fear and love'.
[37] 'that is the evidence of their conversion may be demonstrated, that is that they be converted and believe in me'.
[38] These words occur ten times in D, elsewhere glossing *honorare / honor*. The DOE definition for *arwurðian* in this context, 'glossing *revereri* in sense "to be abashed / ashamed" as if in sense "to revere, honour"', only refers to D-type glosses for this verse and should not be accepted as commonplace. This definition would, in fact, be more appropriate for *forwandian*.

sien gescende & hy forwandian somod þe þe secað sawle mine syn gecyrred underbecling ablysien ⁒ forscamien þa ðe þohton me yfelu³⁹

Confundantur et reuereantur simul qui querunt animam meam; Auertantur retrorsum et erubescant qui cogitant mihi mala;

[Let them be confounded and ashamed together, that seek after my soul to take it away. Let them be turned backward and be ashamed, that desire evils to me.]

Cassiodorus' interpretation also explores a familiar theme:

Confundantur, dixit, mirabilium operatione turbentur. *Reuereantur* autem, resurrectionis gloria corrigantur, ut illum confiteantur Deum, quem dudum putauerant esse trucidandum.⁴⁰

[*Let them be confounded* means 'Let them be thrown into confusion by the working of miracles'; *let them be ashamed* means 'Let them be corrected by the glory of the resurrection, so that they may confess to that God who they had long believed should be slaughtered.']⁴¹

Both of these explanations are offered in the margins by the glossator: 'mirabiliorum perturbatione conturbentur',⁴² and for *reuereantur*, 'resurrexionis gloria'.⁴³ Again we are given a description of conversion that incorporates shame and confusion. In light of the similar explanations accompanying verses 34.4 and 34.26, we must assume that the verb *corrigere*, explaining *reuereri*, represents the same process.⁴⁴ The similarity in both interpretation and Latin *lemmata* suggests that, up to this point, the glossator has been experimenting with Old English vocabulary to produce glosses incorporating concepts specifically described in Cassiodorus' commentary. After testing *wandian* first, at 34.4, he then tries *arwurðian* at 34.26, in which he also makes his first use of the nominal *forwandung* for *reuerentia*. He finally settles on *forwandian* at 39.15, which he uses for all remaining glosses of *reuereri/reuerentia*, aside from two attempts at another unusual verb, *aswarnian*, at 70.24 and 82.18.⁴⁵ His experimentation has

---

³⁹ ⁒ indicates a double gloss.
⁴⁰ Cassiodorus, pp. 369–70.
⁴¹ Walsh (ed.), I, p. 405.
⁴² 'Let them be confounded by a disturbance of miracles.'
⁴³ 'glory of the resurrection'.
⁴⁴ This similarity is reinforced by the phrase *auertantur retrorsum et erubescant*, repeated in the Psalter text at 6.11, 34.4 and 69.4.
⁴⁵ The Lambeth glossator also had difficulty translating *reuereri*, selecting the unusual verb *anðracian* (to fear). See my discussion below.

led him to develop new words (*aswarnian*), and to redefine words that existed in other contexts (*wandian/forwandian*).

Aswarnian/aswarnung

Aswarnian/aswarnung occurs six times in the Royal Psalter, glossing five separate *lemmata* (see Table 2).

Table 2   Occurrences of 'aswarnian/aswarnung' in the Royal Psalter

Verse	Lemma	Interpretamentum
6.11	*erubescant*	*aswarnien*
43.16	*uerecundia*	*aswarnung*
70.24	*reueriti*	*aswarcode*[46]
82.18	*reuereantur*	*hy aswarnien*
85.17	*confundantur*	*aswarnien*
87.16	*confusus*	*aswarnod*

It occurs twice as a noun, and four times as a verb, glossing many of the words discussed above. It is unsurprising, therefore, that its meaning is closely associated with *forwandian*, especially as it is used twice as a gloss for *reuereri*. The definitions for *aswarnian/aswarnung*, 'to be confounded; be ashamed' / 'shame, confusion' (DOE), are based exclusively on occurrences in the psalter glosses (the only place these words occur) and they fail to incorporate the sense of reverence and conversion that, like *forwandian*, is also conveyed by this word group. Unlike *forwandian*, however, *aswarnian/aswarnung* is used to gloss five different word groups associated with shame, suggesting that the glossator attempted to convey an underlying interpretation associated with each verse, rather than the specific meaning of each *lemma*. This variety of *lemmata*, along with the exclusion of *aswarnian/aswarnung* from non-psalter texts, suggests that comprehension of this word was more exclusive than *forwandian*, and that its use was restricted to the 'emotional community' of monastics who had access to psalter texts.

The first use of *aswarnian* occurs well before the first use of *wandian/forwandian*, at verse 6.11, but conveys strikingly similar ideas:

---

[46] This should be the same verb. See below, p. 121.

ablysigen ł scamien & syn drefed ealle fynd mine syn gecerred on hinder & aswarnien swiþe hredlice ł anunga

> Erubescant et conturbentur omnes inimici mei. auertantur retrorsum et erubescant ualde uelociter;

> [Let all my enemies be ashamed and be very much troubled: let them be turned back and be ashamed very speedily.]

Cassiodorus' explanation is also similar:

> Et intuere quod sancta conscientia paenitentis, a peccatis suis facta libera, ecclesiasticis regulis obsecundans, mox pro inimicis suis, ut conuertantur, exorat; ut, sicut ille suscepit ueniam, ita et inimicos eius carnales ad Domini gratiam redire contingat. Nam cum dicit: *Erubescant*, uult eos tanta compunctione illuminari, ut pro his quae agebant, ipsi potius erubescant et intellegant perniciosos actus, quos pridem sibi putabant esse proficuos.[47]

> [Notice too that once the penitent is freed of his sins and obedient to the Church's rules, he then in holy awareness prays for the conversion of his enemies, that his enemies in the flesh may return to God's grace as he himself has gained pardon. When he says: *Let them be ashamed*, he wants them to be enlightened by such contrition as to be ashamed of their previous acts, and to realise that the deeds which they long considered beneficial are wicked.][48]

Cassiodorus makes a direct correlation between the penance of the sinner and conversion of one's enemies. He describes what is meant by *erubescant* as a process of enlightenment through compunction, suggesting a more complex interpretation of *aswarnian* than the DOE definition allows, and assigning a functional value to the emotion.[49] It does not simply convey shame, as suggested by the *lemma*, but incorporates the range of experiences described by Cassiodorus, which ultimately results in conversion. The scribe includes these aspects of Cassiodorus' commentary in the margins, conveying a similar experience to the later verses in which *forwandian* occurs. The phrases 'id est timore future iudicii'[50] and 'facere mala',[51] quoted by the scribe, associate this

---

[47] Cassiodorus, p. 78.
[48] Walsh (ed.), I, p. 97.
[49] For more on compunction, see McCormack, below.
[50] 'that is, by fear of future judgement'.
[51] 'to carry out bad deeds'.

verse with sin and Judgement.[52] The phrase in this psalm taken to express the act of conversion is *auertantur retrorsum*, explained in the margins: 'malus cum auertit retrorsum emendat; bonus cum auerterit retrorsum cadit in peccatum'. This paraphrases Cassiodorus' 'Malus enim, cum retrorsum redit, emendatur; cum iustus, offendit',[53] further explicating the link to conversion, and reinforcing the link between the other verses that repeat this phrase.[54]

Nonetheless, in later verses where this phrase occurs, *aswarnian* is not used as a gloss, but replaced by *ablysian* (also used at 6.11 for the first occurrence of *erubescant*). The glossator therefore selects *ablysian* to convey the physical reaction of blushing associated with the metaphorical 'turning back' of conversion. In later verses, *aswarnian* appears in contexts relating more closely to those experiences described by *forwandian*, conveying reverence and fear, as well as shame.

This link with *forwandian* is apparent at 70.24, where *aswarcode* glosses *reueriti*, a verb usually reserved for *forwandian*. Whilst the DOE differentiates *aswarcan* from *aswarnian*, the use of *aswarcan* in this context appears to be a scribal error.

> ac tunge min smeað rihtwisnesse þine þonne gescynde aswarcode beoð þa ðe secað yfelu me
>
> Sed et lingua mea meditabitur iustitiam tuam. dum confusi et reueriti fuerint. qui querunt mala mihi;
>
> [Yea and my tongue shall meditate on thy justice all the day: when they shall be confounded and put to shame that seek evils to me.]

This verse represents the only occurrence in the entire corpus for which *aswarcan* is listed with the specific meaning, 'to stand in awe, be put to shame' (DOE), suggesting that it is a likely scribal error, with 'n' mistakenly written 'c'. Cassiodorus' comments and the phrases repeated by the Royal scribe reinforce the likelihood of scribal error, due to similarities with other verses, including the reiteration of sentiments regarding the conversion of enemies:

---

[52] The first phrase quotes Cassiodorus' explanation of *conturbentur*: '*Conturbentur* autem dictum est timore futuri iudicii' (Cassiodorus, p. 78).

[53] Cassiodorus, p. 78 ('... for when an evil person turns back, he is reformed, but when it is a just man, he stumbles'; Walsh (ed.), I, pp. 97–8). Cassiodorus' commentary for this verse is heavily summarised in the breviate 'Durham Cassiodorus', and includes none of the quotes from the Royal Psalter, suggesting that whoever incorporated the commentary had access to a more complete version of the *Expositio*.

[54] See note 44.

> Duobus enim modis *confunduntur et reuerentur* inimici, quando aut hic paenitentiam gerunt, et se errasse cognoscunt; aut certe in aduentu Saluatoris, dum illa quae fieri non credebant, suis oculis manifesta conspexerint.[55]
>
> [Enemies are confounded and put to shame in two ways, either when they show repentance and realise that they have sinned, or at any rate at the coming of the Saviour, when with their own eyes they shall see clearly what they did not think could happen.][56]

The Royal scribe again emphasises Judgement Day, adding the comment: 'id est cum aduenerit dies iudicii'.[57]

The likelihood that scribal error produced *aswarcode* is supported by the use of *aswarnian* (spelt correctly) as a gloss for the same verb *reuereri* at 82.18:

> hy syn gescend & hy syn gedrefed on worulde woruld & hy aswarnien & hy forweorþen
>
> Confundantur et conturbentur in seculum seculi. et reuereantur et pereant.
>
> [Let them be ashamed and troubled for ever and ever: and let them be confounded and perish.]

Cassiodorus' commentary does not enable us to see any distinction between the *interpretamenta*, suggesting that *aswarcan* was a mistake, and that the verb should have been *aswarnian*:

> Redit iterum ad pertinaces, qui Dei munera non habebunt. Possunt enim aliqui in hoc saeculo salutariter confundi et erubescere, quando conuersionis dona percipiunt. *Confunduntur* autem *et conturbantur in saeculum saeculi*, qui aeterna ultione damnandi sunt.[58]
>
> [He turns back to the obstinate who will not possess God's gifts. Some persons can be confounded and ashamed for their salvation in this world, when they accept the gifts of conversion; but those who will be condemned to eternal vengeance *are confounded and troubled for ever and ever.*][59]

---

[55] Cassiodorus, p. 639.
[56] Walsh (ed.), II, p. 178.
[57] 'that is with the coming of Judgement Day'.
[58] Cassiodorus, p. 766.
[59] Walsh (ed.), II, p. 312.

In this verse, Cassiodorus draws out the contrast between shame in this world and shame of the unrepentant at Judgement Day. Confounding can be either positive or negative, depending on when it is experienced, yet there remains considerable overlap in the use of vocabulary. According to Cassiodorus, it is the experience associated with *erubescere* that will have a positive outcome, and the experience associated with *conturbare* that will be negative, whilst *confundere* has a role in both. We are reminded of Cassiodorus' commentary at 34.4, where he uses *erubescere* to explain *confundi*, emphasising the overlap in the meanings of these verbs and their positive functionality. The only phrase quoted by the Royal glossator for this verse is *de peccatis*, repeated both in the interlinear space and in the margin, emphasising the close link between the entire process of confounding/shame/reverence, and the concept of sin.[60]

Despite the variety of *lemmata* glossed by *aswarnian*, the contexts both of the Psalter itself and Cassiodorus' commentary suggest a similarity in interpretation between each occurrence, and also with those of *forwandian*. Distinguishing between these words presents great difficulty, and it is unclear whether differentiation was the glossator's intention. The development of two different word groups to gloss the variety of *lemmata* exemplified suggests the glossator's purpose was experimental, producing a vernacular vocabulary to describe specific religious experiences expressed in the Psalms and by Cassiodorus.

Reception in the Lambeth Psalter[61]

The innovative Lambeth Psalter (I) of the eleventh century, which incorporates more new vocabulary and almost 1500 double and triple glosses, offers the possibility of studying the later reception of these lexical innovations.[62]

---

[60] The reference to the eternal damnation of unrepentant sinners is similar to a penitential motif discussed by Malcolm Godden: 'it is better to be shamed for one's sins before one man (the confessor) in this life than to be shamed before God and before all angels and before all men and before all devils at the Last Judgement'. Godden cites this motif in fifteen Old English texts, including homilies and prayers, through which the ideas were undoubtedly conveyed to a wide audience (M. R. Godden, 'An Old English Penitential Motif', *Anglo-Saxon England* 2 (1973): 221–39).

[61] Space is inadequate here for a comparison with subsequent D-type glosses. Comments questioning the Latin knowledge of the glossators of F, G, J and K, by F's editor, Kimmens, render such analysis irrelevant to the present discussion (*The Stowe Psalter*, ed. Andrew C. Kimmens (Toronto, 1979), p. xx).

[62] The edition is *Der Lambeth-Psalter*, ed. Uno Lindelöf, Acta Societatis Scientiarum Fennicae 35.1 and 43.3, 2 vols (Helsinki, 1909–14), I. I must thank Brian Taylor for his assistance with reading the German text. For these figures, see Gretsch, p. 27.

For *aswarnian*, the Lambeth glossator accepts the first two occurrences in which the *Gallicanum* text agrees with the *Romanum* of the Royal Psalter (6.11 and 43.16). He then rejects all subsequent uses of *aswarnian/aswarnung*, two of which occur where the *Gallicanum* text differs, a practice that is consistent among other D-type psalters.[63] However, the fact that this accounts for only two of four rejections suggests other factors are involved. Both occurrences of the word in I form part of a double gloss, with *scamien* used to gloss *erubescant* at 6.11, and *scamu* at 43.16 for *uerecundia*. Whilst this may suggest the glossator feared the word could be misunderstood, or required clarification, this is an unlikely reason for its subsequent rejection. In fact, both these glosses simply combine the A-type and D-type glosses, a practice that was standard for the Lambeth glossator and relates more to the encyclopaedic nature of his gloss than to questions of meaning or understanding.[64]

There is a range of possible explanations for this pattern of repetition and rejection.[65] The simplest, albeit unsatisfying, explanation is that, after copying the first two occurrences from D, the glossator deemed the word inadequate to represent such a variety of *lemmata*. A more compelling explanation is that he felt it was too similar in form to another verb that he develops, *aswarcan*. As noted, *aswarcode* was first used by the Royal glossator at 70.24 as a gloss for *reuereri*;[66] however, this gloss is rejected by the Lambeth glossator in favour of *gebismerade*. Instead, the Lambeth glossator employs *aswarcan*, meaning 'to waste/pine away' (DOE), exclusively as a gloss for *tabescere*, at 38.12 and 138.21. The potential for confusion between these two verbs could account for the Lambeth glossator's rejection of *aswarnian*.

Another possible explanation could be the suggested standardisation of Old English under Æthelwold. Gneuss argues that the Lambeth glossator chose glosses to reflect this standard, citing a consistency with vocabulary in the works of Ælfric.[67] In this way, the first two occurrences of *aswarnian/aswarnung* were included as evidence of the alternative D-type vocabulary, and placed alongside A-type glosses that may have been more consistent with this 'Winchester vocabulary'.[68]

---

[63] F, G, H, J and L all reject *aswarnian* at 82.18 and 87.16. H alone repeats all four occurrences where the *Gallicanum* text remains the same.

[64] Helmut Gneuss, 'The Origin of Standard Old English and Æthelwold's school at Winchester', *Anglo-Saxon England* 1 (1972): 63–83, at 77.

[65] The following explanations remain relevant whether or not the Lambeth gloss was composed by an individual or numerous glossators. See *Lambeth-Psalter*, Lindelöf, II, pp. 3–10. The occurrences of *aswarnian/aswarnung* occur within what Lindelöf categorises as section one of the manuscript.

[66] See above, p. 121.

[67] Gneuss, p. 77.

[68] The common nature of *scamian* and *scamu* in the corpus makes it difficult to determine whether these words were included in the Winchester vocabulary.

Whatever its origins, the use of *aswarnian* in D to gloss multiple *lemmata*, its repetition in other glosses, and its subsequent inclusion in double glosses in I suggest that the glossators (or at least those of D and I) thought deeply about the meaning of shame and its nuanced expressions in a religious context. Initially incorporated by the Royal glossator into a technical vocabulary specifically associated with the Psalms, its nuances were understood for over a century by monastic communities with access to these D-type psalters.[69] The best explanation for its rejection in I is its exclusion from the Winchester vocabulary.

This could also explain the Lambeth glossator's wholesale rejection of *forwandian/forwandung*, which he replaces with *anðracian*, 'to fear, to be afraid, to dread' (BT), a word used sporadically by Ælfric and repeated only once in F.[70] *Anðracian* glosses four of five occurrences of the verb *reuereri*, and *anðracung* one of two occurrences of the noun, *reuerentia*. The glossator apparently rejected the semantic modification of *forwandian*, instead choosing a more unusual verb that nonetheless conformed to the Winchester standard.

The rejection of *forwandian* due to its exclusion from the Winchester vocabulary is supported by subsequent uses of the word in other texts, particularly again in the works of Ælfric.[71] Ælfric's uses of *forwandian* do not necessarily incorporate the nuances of the Royal gloss, and convey the simpler meaning of 'hesitation' consistent with the Old English *Pastoral Care*. This suggests that it did not form part of this vocabulary, and that the meaning assigned to it in the Royal Psalter did not extend beyond the psalter glosses.[72] It seems that neither *aswarnian* nor *forwandian* were accepted into the Winchester vocabulary, but this rejection only emphasises their nuanced meanings in the Royal Psalter.

Concluding Remarks

The creation of original glossed psalters in the eighth (Vespasian), tenth (Royal) and eleventh centuries (Lambeth) indicates an ongoing project of

---

[69] Excluding 87.16 and 82.18, *aswarnian/aswarnung* is repeated 10 out of a possible 20 occasions in the subsequent D-type glosses (E, F, G, H and K), suggesting that its meaning was understood in this specific psalter context.

[70] This verb also occurs in the corpus as *onðracian*, producing very limited results. It does not yet appear in the DOE, and will be presumably listed under 'o'. *Anðracian* occurs seven times in the works of Ælfric. This includes four glosses in his 'Grammar', including *ic anðracige* as a gloss for *uereor*, which supports the connection between his writing and the Lambeth Psalter as outlined by Gneuss (see above, note 67). Its use in a teaching text also suggests its inclusion in the Winchester vocabulary.

[71] The word group occurs six times in Ælfric's work.

[72] *Wandian/forwandian/forwandung* is repeated at least once in all subsequent D-type psalters.

incorporating Latin Christian concepts into the English language during the Anglo-Saxon period. The idea of shame having a positive outcome arrived at via fear, confusion and reverence demanded a new vocabulary, which led to the experimental use of such words as *forwandian/forwandung* and *aswarnian/aswarnung*. The variety of *lemmata* glossed by these word groups and the comprehensive explanations underlying each *lemma* enable us to access the complex meaning of these Old English glosses. Cassiodorus had ample space in his extensive commentary to unpack the meaning behind each individual Latin *lemma*; however, the challenge for the Anglo-Saxon glossators to incorporate his ideas within an individual *interpretamentum* would have been great indeed. The Royal Psalter in particular, with its expansive marginal and interlinear notes, provides evidence of the commentaries consulted by the glossators during the composition of their works. The Latin text in conjunction with Cassiodorus' commentary demonstrates that shame could involve a range of emotions, including fear, confusion, humility and reverence, leading to conversion. The initial use of *wandian* and subsequent uses of *forwandian* to convey all of these emotions, implicit in the individual Latin verb *reuereri*, can only be ascertained through close study of Cassiodorus' explanations. Without his commentary, the superficial inconsistency of the uses of *aswarnian* as a gloss for five separate words would make little sense. It is only when reading Cassiodorus that we are able to understand the process of glossing, and the complex of ideas behind each word. Reading Cassiodorus brings us closer to the 'emotional community' of the cloister, and closer to an understanding of the emotional language developed for translating the psalter. The process of developing and reinterpreting words for use in psalter glosses is indicative of a religious community grappling with the problem of expressing complex theological ideas in their vernacular. An appreciation of this vocabulary and the complex emotional process it represents, incorporating shame, fear, confusion and reverence, leading to conversion, is of fundamental importance for understanding representations of religious shame in other Anglo-Saxon texts and contexts.

Chapter 8

Learning about Emotion from the Old English Prose Psalms of the Paris Psalter

Alice Jorgensen

How did people in Anglo-Saxon England learn about emotion? Although built on neurological and hormonal processes, emotion has a substantial cultural component. The term brackets a complex of perceptions, judgements, and automatic and learned responses, and individuals must learn how to organise and relate these elements, both with respect to their own and others' behaviour. They must learn what events are appropriate triggers for what emotions, what gestures or actions are expected, and how to label and evaluate their own emotions and those of others. In short, they must acquire emotion 'scripts': 'prototypical sequence[s] of causally connected and temporally ordered subevents',[1] 'the little scenarios that we play out – as sequences of cause and effect, of perception, evaluation and response – when we experience any emotion'.[2] Emotion scripts encode both how emotions ought to unfold and how they typically do, and they help to structure both memories and behaviours.[3] Psychologists focus chiefly on childhood as the period when such scripts are acquired, and they emphasise the key role played by interactions with caregivers and peers.[4] For Anglo-Saxon England, we can investigate some of the culturally specific factors conditioning emotional learning by, for example, considering child-rearing practices such as fostering and oblation.[5] However, emotional learning can also take place through other kinds of interaction, including interaction with texts; and it continues

---

[1] James A. Russell and Ghyslaine Lemay, 'Emotion Concepts', in Michael Lewis and Jeannette M. Haviland-Jones (eds), *Handbook of Emotions*, 2nd edn (London, 2000), pp. 491–503, at 496.
[2] Robert A. Kaster, *Emotion, Restraint, and Community in Ancient Rome* (Oxford, 2005), p. 29.
[3] Donald E. Gibson, 'Emotion Scripts in Organizations: A Multi-Level Model', in Neal Ashkanasy and Cary L. Cooper (eds), *Research Companion to Emotion in Organizations* (Cheltenham, 2008), pp. 263–83, at 263–5.
[4] Russell and Lemay, 'Emotion Concepts', p. 498; Merry Bullock and James A. Russell, 'Concepts of Emotion in Developmental Psychology', in Carroll E. Izard and Peter B. Read (eds), *Measuring Emotions in Infants and Children*, 2 vols (Cambridge, 1986), II. pp. 203–27.
[5] See for example Mary Garrison's chapter in the present volume.

into adult life.[6] We can hypothesise that textual representations reflect the emotion scripts prevailing within a culture and that they may have functioned to reinforce and refine such scripts. Script theory thus suggests a direction for the historical investigation of emotional learning.

The Psalter was in Anglo-Saxon England a shared and ubiquitous text with vast potential to shape vocabularies, understandings, and indeed feelings and performances of emotion. Those in religious life were expected to know it by heart, and the work of committing the Psalter to memory would have begun in childhood; it was among the first texts studied in the course of a Latin education; it was the main devotional resource also for the pious laity. The Psalms are emotion scripts in the literal sense that they tell people what to say: they are not simply for reading and comprehending but for praying and performing, and they are well known for depth of feeling. The present chapter looks at one particular Psalter-text from Anglo-Saxon England, the Old English prose translation of the first fifty Psalms in the Paris Psalter (Paris, Bibliothèque Nationale, Fonds latin 8824, fols 1–63v).[7] The OE Prose Psalms constitute a particularly rich piece of evidence for how one might learn about emotion from the Psalms.[8]

---

[6] See Patrick Colm Hogan, *What Literature Teaches Us About Emotion* (Cambridge, 2011), pp. 67–8 on how reading literature develops skills in 'emotion categorization' and 'emotion modelling'.

[7] Edition: *King Alfred's Old English Prose Translation of the First Fifty Psalms*, ed. Patrick O'Neill (Cambridge, MA, 2001). O'Neill gives both the Vulgate verse numbers and numbers based on paragraphing in the manuscript; I use the former, for ease of cross-referencing. I have also found the following useful, especially for its introduction and its edition of the Paris Psalter Latin: *The Paris Prose: Edition of the Latin and English of the First Fifty Psalms in the Paris Psalter, MS. Bibliothèque Nationale Fonds Latin 8824*, prepared by Richard Stracke, 1999, revised 2002, at http://www.aug.edu/augusta/psalms/ (accessed 25 May 2013). The Vulgate is cited from Robert Weber et al. (eds), *Biblia Sacra iuxta Vulgatam Versionem*, 4th edn (Stuttgart: Deutsche Bibelgesellschaft, 1994). The Douay-Rheims translation of the Vulgate is cited from *The Unbound Bible*, Biola University 2005–2006, at http://unbound.biola.edu/ (accessed 25 May 2013). Psalms are cited according to the Vulgate numbering.

[8] It was fairly late in the preparation of this chapter that I encountered M. J. Toswell's excellent discussion of the lament psalms and their influence on OE vernacular literature, 'Structures of Sorrow: The Lament Psalms in Medieval England', in Jane Tolmie and M. J. Toswell (eds), *Laments for the Lost in Medieval Literature*, Medieval Texts and Cultures of Northern Europe 19 (Turnhout, 2010), pp. 21–44. Toswell also stresses the capacity of the Psalms to be a vehicle of personal emotion and to influence patterns of expression, and she also makes use of the Prose Psalms of the Paris Psalter, but her focus is specifically on sorrow and she does not address the mechanisms of emotional learning.

The OE Prose Psalms and the Paris Psalter

The Paris Psalter can be dated to the mid-eleventh century on the basis of script, the style of the drawings and the inclusion of St Martial of Limoges among the Apostles in the litany; various indications point to Canterbury and perhaps more precisely St Augustine's as the place of production.[9] It is clear that the Prose Psalms pre-existed the compilation of the manuscript. Although the Latin text of the Paris Psalter is a Romanum text (which is unusual at this date: by the eleventh century most Anglo-Saxon Psalters contain the Gallicanum version), the OE prose is derived from an earlier variety of Romanum, with an admixture of Gallicanum readings.[10] This source-evidence dovetails nicely with the customary attribution of the OE Prose Psalms to King Alfred on the basis of similarities of expression and technique to other Alfredian works.[11] It is also pleasing to associate the translation with Alfred's personal devotion to the Psalms as attested by his biographer Asser, who mentions psalms among the texts in Alfred's *enchiridion*.[12] However, Malcolm Godden has cast our sense of the Alfredian canon into disarray by arguing vigorously against Alfred's authorship of the *Boethius*, and the question of the authorship of the Prose Psalms must therefore be considered open.[13]

Even if the translation context of the Prose Psalms is uncertain, the Paris Psalter itself provides a context in which to reconstruct their use by a reader. It is the only Anglo-Saxon psalter to provide, not an interlinear Old English gloss such as might be used in the schoolroom, but a full translation.[14] The Latin and Old English are presented in parallel columns throughout with the Latin on the left and the Old English on the right; after the prose rendition finishes at Psalm 50 the remaining psalms are translated into verse. The Psalms are followed by Latin canticles, prayers and a litany, but there is no calendar such as any clerical or monastic user would have required. Though it is a very odd tall, thin shape,

---

[9] *Prose Translation*, ed. O'Neill, pp. 5, 17 and 20–22; Richard Emms, 'The Scribe of the Paris Psalter', *Anglo-Saxon England* 28 (1999): 179–83.

[10] *Prose Translation*, ed. O'Neill, pp. 31–4.

[11] Ibid., pp. 73–96, for the case for Alfredian authorship; also Janet Bately, 'Lexical Evidence for the Authorship of the Prose Psalms in the Paris Psalter', *Anglo-Saxon England* 10 (1982): 69–95.

[12] *Asser's Life of King Alfred*, ed. William Henry Stevenson (Oxford, 1959), ch. 88, p. 73.

[13] Malcolm Godden, 'Did King Alfred Write Anything?' *Medium Ævum* 76 (2007): 49–61; *The Old English Boethius: An Edition of the Old English Versions of Boethius's De Consolatione Philosophiae*, eds Malcolm Godden and Susan Irvine, 2 vols (Oxford, 2009), I, pp. 140–51.

[14] On schoolroom use of the Psalter, see George H. Brown, 'The Psalms as the Foundation of Anglo-Saxon Learning', in Nancy Van Deusen (ed.), *The Place of the Psalms in the Intellectual Culture of the Middle Ages* (Albany, 1999), pp. 1–24, at 1–5.

the Paris Psalter was extensively illustrated, with nine full-page illustrations (now excised) as well as the small interlinear drawings that survive in the opening folios.[15] The full-page illustrations divided the psalter according to the Roman office, though the Benedictine office was usual at this date even among the secular clergy; like the Romanum psalter, it is a conservative feature. On all these grounds O'Neill argues that the Paris Psalter was intended for devotional use by a wealthy layperson.[16] Brown suggests it 'served for private reading and study'.[17]

Interpreting Emotion in the Psalms: The Arguments

The Paris Psalter is a particularly rich source through which to think about emotional learning for three main reasons. The first is its vernacular text. Not only does the translation offer fascinating scope for comparison with the Latin, but research into modern multilingual speakers suggests the mother tongue is often experienced as more emotionally intense and authentic than languages acquired later, especially where competence is lower in the second language.[18] Second, the likely context of personal devotion and meditation licenses us to focus on verbal detail. Within the monastic horarium, while the meaning of the words is not irrelevant, a large part of the emotional impact of the psalms must have been generated by the wider liturgical context and also by the sheer discipline and effort involved. The Benedictine Rule was mild compared to the practices of the early ascetics, but it still prescribed the recitation of the whole Psalter each week, and some psalms were repeated far more often than that (for example, in Anglo-Saxon reformed monasteries, the psalms used in the *trina oratio*).[19] Third, the OE Prose Psalms are almost all accompanied by commentary

---

[15] On the excised illustrations see Francis Wormald, 'The Decoration', in Bertram Colgrave (ed.), *The Paris Psalter: MS Bibliothèque Nationale Fonds Latin 8824*, EEMF 8 (Copenhagen, 1958), pp. 14–15; on the format of the manuscript see M. J. Toswell, 'The Format of Bibliothèque Nationale MS Lat. 8824: The Paris Psalter', *Notes and Queries* 43 (1996): 130–33. The entire manuscript has been digitised and can be viewed at http://gallica.bnf.fr/ark:/12148/btv1b8451636f (accessed 14 April 2014).

[16] *Prose Translation*, ed. O'Neill, pp. 19–20. One might attribute the conservative text and office divisions to an exemplar were there not signs that the manuscript is a first attempt at arranging this combination of materials: Toswell, 'The Format', p. 133.

[17] Brown, p. 12.

[18] Aneta Pavlenko, *Emotions and Multilingualism* (Cambridge, 2005), pp. 132–5.

[19] Joseph Dyer, 'The Psalms in Monastic Prayer', in Van Deusen (ed.), *The Place of the Psalms*, pp. 59–89 (though note his remarks on how liturgical practice was sometimes designed to promote meditation: pp. 73–7); for the *trina oratio* see *Regularis concordia anglicae nationis monachorum sanctimonialiumque*, trans. Thomas Symons (London, 1963),

material that foregrounds the literal sense of the text and orientates the reader to its emotional content.

Each of the first fifty psalms of the Paris Psalter (excepting only 1, 21 and 26) is preceded by an argument summarising its meaning. The arguments are presented not simply as part of the Old English crib but as introductions to each psalm: they are written across the width of both columns of the manuscript page, preceding the Latin *tituli*. They were composed by the same person as the OE prose translations, as is evident from their shared sources and interpretations and their close verbal correspondences.[20] Besides the Paris Psalter, the arguments survive in one other copy, the mid-eleventh-century Vitellius Psalter, in which they are written into the margins; this copy is now heavily fire-damaged but it is an additional witness to interest in the OE text.[21] The arguments take a predominantly historical approach that directs attention to the literal sense of the Psalms. This literal sense is frequently identified as one of emotional expression. In the Psalms the speaker laments (*seofian*, Pss. 2, 3, 7, 10, 11, 12, 13, 14, 30, 34, 37, 38, 39, 43) and bewails (*mænan*, Pss. 2, 7, 11, 37), he marvels (*wundrian*, Pss. 8, 31) and gives thanks (*þancian*, Pss. 9, 17, 22, 28, 32, 45, 47; *þancung*, Pss. 18, 29), and he contemplates the troubles from which he prays to be or has been delivered (*earfoðas*, Pss. 2, 3, 6, 7, 14, 15, 17, 19, 22, 23, 24, 27, 29, 30, 32, 35, 39, 40, 43, 45, 46) and the comfort that he has received or will receive (*frofer*, Pss. 5, 15, 38, 41).

As Patrick O'Neill has shown, the main source for the arguments is the Pseudo-Bedan *Argumenta*, printed by Migne as one element of a composite work entitled *De Psalmorum libro exegesis*; another element, the *Explanationes*, is also used by the translator in producing the prose translations.[22] The *Argumenta* draw on the psalm commentary of Theodore of Mopsuestia translated into

---

chs. 16–17, and literature cited by Christopher A. Jones, Ælfric's *Letter to the Monks of Eynsham*, CSASE 24 (Cambridge, 1998), p. 153.

[20] Patrick P. O'Neill, 'The Old English Introductions to the Prose Psalms of the Paris Psalter: Sources, Structure and Composition', *Studies in Philology* 78 (1981): 20–38, at 20–26; Stracke, *Paris Prose*, http://www.aug.edu/augusta/psalms/intro3.htm

[21] London, BL, MS Cotton Vitellius E.xviii.

[22] On the sources and structure of the arguments see O'Neill, 'Old English Introductions'; *Prose Translation*, ed. O'Neill, pp. 23–6; Pádraig Ó Néill, 'Irish Transmission of Late Antique Learning: The Case of Theodore of Mopsuestia's Commentary on the Psalms', in Próinséas Ní Catháin and Michael Richter (eds), *Ireland and Europe in the Early Middle Ages: Texts and Transmission / Irland und Europa im früheren Mittelalter: Texte und Überlieferung* (Dublin, 2002), pp. 68–77. Earlier discussions include J. Douglas Bruce, 'Immediate and Ultimate Source of the Rubrics and Introductions to the Psalms in the Paris Psalter', *MLN* 8 (1893): 36–41, and 'The Anglo-Saxon Version of the Book of Psalms Commonly Known as the Paris Psalter', *PMLA* 9 (1894): 43–164, at 63–131. On the pseudo-Bedan *Argumenta*, Bonifatius Fischer, 'Bedae de Titulis Psalmorum Liber', in

Latin by Julian, bishop of Eclanum. They reflect Theodore's Antiochene, historical method of exegesis: for each psalm they offer an account situating the text in the life of David or of another Old Testament figure, plus, sometimes, a Christological and/or a moral interpretation. The Old English arguments are built chiefly on the historical interpretations in the *Argumenta*, but they fit the material into a fourfold exegetical scheme otherwise witnessed in three eighth-century Irish sources – the Old Irish Treatise on the Psalter, the Hiberno-Latin Reference Bible and the partial psalm commentary in Rome, BAV Pal. Lat. 68.

The OE argument for Psalm 5 exemplifies the structure:

> Ðe fifta sealm ys gecweden Davides sealm, þone he sang be his sylfes frofre and be herenesse ealra ðæra rihtwisena ðe secað yrfeweardnesse on Heofonrice mid Criste, se ys ende ealra ðinga. And ælc mann þe þisne sealm singð, he hine singð be his sylfes frofre. And swa dyde Ezechias þa he alysed wæs of his mettrumnesse. And swa dyde Crist þa he alysed wæs fram Iudeum.
>
> [The fifth psalm is called David's psalm, which he sang about his own consolation and about the praise of all the righteous who seek a heritage in the Kingdom of Heaven with Christ, who is the end of all things. And each man who sings this psalm sings it about his own consolation. And so did Ezechias when he was delivered from his infirmity. And so did Christ when he was delivered from the Jews.]

There are two historical interpretations, relating the psalm first to King David and then to another Old Testament figure, in this case King Ezechias (Hezekiah) but often the Israelites in the Babylonian exile. Some examples give more detail about events than this one. There is a Christological interpretation, usually reading the psalm as a prayer of Christ or a prophecy concerning his relationship with the Jews. Most significantly for the present discussion, there is also a moral interpretation, applying the psalm to every righteous man, everyone who sings the psalm, or a similar generic Christian figure. Earlier in the sequence of the OE Prose Psalms the usual phrasing is that all those who sing the psalm do likewise (*swa deð* – that is, they do as David or Ezechias or the Babylonian exiles did), but from around Psalm 28 onwards we are usually told that David prophesied (*witegode*) that the righteous would act or sing in this way. Occasionally David's singing of the psalm is presented explicitly as an example to be followed ('he lærde eac on þæm sealme ælcne man ... þæt he þæt ylce dyde',[23] Ps. 33, and see also Pss. 39 and 47) or as a vehicle for teaching ('Dauid witegode and rehte mid

---

J. Autenrieth and F. Brunhölzl (eds), *Festschrift Bernhard Bischoff zu seinem 65 Geburtstag* (Stuttgart, 1971), pp. 90–110.

[23] 'In that psalm he also taught every man that he should do the same.'

hwylcum geearnungum gehwylc man hine mæg alysan of his earfoðum,'[24] Ps. 23, and see also Ps. 48).

What are the implications of introductions like these for the use of the Psalms in personal prayer? The message that emerges powerfully, repeated in argument after argument, is that the Psalms function as expressions of the experiences and feelings of the person praying, whether that person is David or an Anglo-Saxon Christian. The pious are encouraged to approach each psalm as a way of both interpreting and performing their own emotions. The psalm thus has an authenticating or validating effect. Personal feelings of sadness, anger, or conversely gratitude and joy are given an authoritative language; the experiences so voiced are seen as universal among the righteous and as shared with Old Testament figures and with Christ himself. The psalm also has clear potential to shape emotion as well as vent it. The psalm provides a script – a sequence of perception, feeling and response – that both encourages the Christian to classify emotion in a particular way and directs the progression from situation to behaviour.

For an illuminating parallel to the approach encouraged by the OE arguments we may turn to the preface to *De psalmorum usu*. *De psalmorum usu* is printed by Migne as a work of Alcuin, though, as André Wilmart points out, it is a compilation made at some point in the first half of the ninth century, following Alcuin's death;[25] the preface, however, is genuinely Alcuin's and has been edited separately by Jonathan Black under the title *De laude psalmorum*.[26] In *De laude psalmorum* Alcuin sets out eight ways to use the Psalms in personal devotion, identifying texts appropriate for particular situations, with an accent on the psychological state of the believer. For example, in his sixth section he recommends psalms to say when feeling abandoned by God: 'Si te in tribulationibus a Deo derelictum intellegas, compuncto corde decanta hos psalmos: Usquequo Domine; Deus, auribus nostris; Miserere mihi, Domine, quoniam conculcavit; Exaudi, Deus, orationem meam et ne despexeris; In te, Domine, speravi; et te Deus statim laetificet in omnibus angustiis tuis.'[27] The

---

[24] 'David prophesied and explained with what deserts each man can release himself from his troubles.'

[25] André Wilmart, 'Le manuel de prières de Saint Jean Gualbert', *Revue bénédictine* 48 (1936): 259–99, at 262–5.

[26] Jonathan Black, 'Psalm Uses in Carolingian Prayerbooks: Alcuin and the Preface to *De psalmorum usu*', *Mediaeval Studies* 64 (2002): 1–60, edition at 45–60.

[27] 'If you perceive yourself to have been abandoned by God in your troubles, with compunction of heart repeat these psalms: *How long, O Lord; We have heard, O God, with our ears; Have mercy on me, O God; Hear, O God, my prayer, and despise not my supplication; In thee, O Lord, have I hoped*. And let God at once cheer you in all your difficulties.' Black, 'Psalm Uses', p. 57. My translation; for the sake of sense the incipits are supplied from Douay-Rheims rather than translated directly from Alcuin's Latin. The Psalms are 12, 43, 56, 54 and 30.

first of these is Psalm 12, and this psalm will serve as an illustration of how the text, considered as personal expression, does not simply reflect but shape and redirect emotion. The psalm opens with a plangent complaint:

> Usquequo Domine oblivisceris me in finem
> usquequo avertis faciem tuam a me[?][28]
>
> [How long, O Lord, wilt thou forget me unto the end? how long dost thou turn away thy face from me?]

But Alcuin promises that God will turn the feeling of abandonment to joy, and as the psalm progresses it enacts this process. In the final verse the speaker declares:

> Ego autem in misericordia tua speravi
> exultabit cor meum in salutari tuo
> cantabo Domino qui bona tribuit mihi
> et psallam nomini Domini altissimi.
>
> [But I have trusted in thy mercy. My heart shall rejoice in thy salvation: I will sing to the Lord, who giveth me good things: yea I will sing to the name of the Lord the most high.]

Psalm 12 carries the Christian from lonely desolation to renewed hope and joy, reminded of God's mercy.

Alcuin thus helps us to observe the relationship between psalm and emotion that is implied in the arguments of the OE Prose Psalms: on the one hand, the psalm is a vehicle for pre-existing emotions, but on the other it can reshape or even generate emotion. Although most of the arguments go no further than to say righteous men *do* feel and/or behave in a particular way, or that David prophesied that they *would* so feel and/or behave, the Psalms are implicitly conceived as having a normative dimension.

The conjunction of the arguments with a full vernacular translation makes the OE Prose Psalms a uniquely rich resource for thinking about emotional learning in Anglo-Saxon England. Alcuin parallels and illuminates them, but they offer more than Alcuin in that they give detailed evidence for engagement with the full text of individual psalms. Of some thirty-seven other surviving psalters or psalter-fragments written or owned in England before 1100, twelve contain Old English glosses, four contain psalter collects, most contain Latin tituli of either the 'Biblical' or 'Christian' type, and eight contain psalter

---

[28] Latin: Weber, *Biblia Sacra*, septuagint text (i.e. Gallicanum); English: Douay-Rheims.

prefaces.[29] There is also plenty of evidence, both in surviving manuscripts and from source-study, of knowledge of other psalm-commentaries such as the great works of Augustine and Cassiodorus. However, the Prose Psalms of the Paris Psalter offer a unique combination of the mother tongue, a devotional context, and a wealth of commentary focusing attention above all on the literal, experiential sense of the text.

Learning Emotion from the Psalm Text

The arguments teach us that praying the Psalms can express emotion but also shape and redirect it. Remaining with Psalm 5 as our example, let us examine in more detail how this shaping takes place when we turn from the summary view of the argument to the more complex and dynamic perspective evinced in the Psalms themselves. The most obvious and important way in which the Psalms script emotion is their presentation of all experience and all attitudes to experience in terms of the central relationship with God; Psalm 5 shows us several facets of how this works.

The argument tells us that Psalm 5 is about praise (*herenes*) and about comfort or consolation (*frofer*). The psalm itself reveals consolation to be a process not a state, and it shows praise developing out of petition. At first the speaker gives voice to his lamentation ('min gehrop', v. 2); by the end he is calling on all God's people to rejoice ('And blissian ealle þa þe to ðe hopiað ... Forþam þu eart se Drihten þe gebletsast and geblissast rihtwise', vv. 12 and 13).[30] The movement from sorrow to joy is very common in the psalms (we have already seen it in Psalm 12).

An important vehicle for the emotional progression in Psalm 5 is the idea of God's presence. This draws on a powerfully emotive vein of imagery; God's face being turned away or God not hearing the psalmist are recurrent images of anguish and abjection in the psalms (for example, Ps. 26.9 'Ne awend þu þine ansyne fram me, ne þe næfre yrringa acyr fram þinum þeowe';[31] and see also 12.1, 29.8, 43.24, 50.13). At the opening of Psalm 5 the psalmist stands in God's presence as a petitioner: 'Drihten, onfoh min word mid þinum earum ... Forðam

---

[29] Phillip Pulsiano, 'Psalters', in Richard W. Pfaff (ed.), *The Liturgical Books of Anglo-Saxon England* (Kalamazoo, MI, 1995), pp. 61–85, at 64–6, 71, 72–3 and 79. From Pulsiano's figures I have subtracted two twelfth-century Psalters as well as the Paris Psalter itself. For the tituli see Pierre Salmon, *Les 'Tituli Psalmorum' des manuscrits latins*, Collectanea Biblica Latina XII (Rome, 1959).

[30] 'And let all those who put their trust in you rejoice ... Because you are the Lord who blesses and makes glad the righteous.'

[31] 'Do not avert your face away from me, nor ever wrathfully turn away from your servant.'

ic gebidde on dægred to ðe; ac gedo þæt þu gehyre min gebed, Drihten ... Ic stande on ærmergen beforan ðe æt gebede, and seo þe' (vv. 2, 4 and 5).[32] Repeated requests to be heard convey a sense of need and anxiety; in the Anglo-Saxon context, the early morning setting resonates with scenes of loneliness and sorrow at daybreak in the elegies (*The Wife's Lament* ll. 7 and 35; *The Wanderer* ll. 8–9). The idea of needy petition is reinforced in the manuscript by the interlinear drawing that fills in space beneath the Latin text of v. 5. The psalmist, hands spread out in supplication and face turned upwards with an anxious expression, gazes towards God's hand, which emerges out of the clouds holding a pair of dividers symbolic of His creative power; the psalmist sees God (*Ic ... seo þe*), but only just. However, the psalm proceeds to explore the idea of God's presence in other ways that convey increasing confidence. The wicked have no place with God: 'Ne mid þe ne wunað se yfelwillenda, ne þa unrihtwisan ne wuniað beforan þinum eagum' (v. 6).[33] By contrast, the psalmist seeks God's presence as a place of refuge, balances due fear against faith in divine mercy, and prays for God's direction: 'Ic þonne hopiende to þinre þære myclan mildheortnesse ic gange to þinum huse, Drihten, and me gebidde to þinum halgan altare on ðinum ege. Drihten, læd me on þine rihtwisnesse fram minra feonda willan. Geriht minne weg beforan þinre ansyne' (vv. 8–9).[34] The spatial imagery is given an aggressive twist in verse 11 in the psalmist's prayer to God to 'drive out' the enemies ('be þære andefne heora unrihtwisnesse fordrif hi'[35]). Admission to God's presence is a sign of His favour given to the righteous.

The emotional resonance of God's presence is coloured by the basic human experience of utter dependence in infancy; the portrayal of God as a father and humans as his children is, of course, prevalent in scripture, especially in the New Testament. In Kleinian terms, God is the Good Breast, source of all comfort, nourishment and safety.[36] We should note, however, that dependency is accompanied by reverent fear, because of God's awesome majesty and powers of judgement: 'Ic ... me gebidde to þinum halgan altare on ðinum ege' (v. 8).[37] This

---

[32] 'Oh Lord, receive my word with your ears ... For I pray at daybreak to you; but grant that you hear my prayer, Lord ... I stand in the early morning before you at prayer and see you.'

[33] 'The evil-willed one does not dwell with you, nor do the unrighteous dwell before your eyes.'

[34] 'I then trusting in your great mercy go to your house, Lord, and pray to your holy altar in fear of you. Lord, lead me in your righteousness out of the power of my enemies. Direct my path before your face.'

[35] 'Drive them out according to the measure of their wickedness.'

[36] M. Klein, 'Love, Guilt and Reparation (1939)', *Love, Guilt and Reparation and Other Works 1921–1945*, with an introduction by R.E. Money-Kyrle (London, 1981), pp. 306–43, at 306–8.

[37] 'I ... pray to your holy altar in fear of you.'

is an image that leads us to think about the way the shaping pressure of the psalm must interact with both individual development (especially the particularities of early relationships with caregivers) and culture-specific meanings, for example to do with entry into the presence of the human lord or king.[38] The idea of God's presence is thus keyed to a complex of emotions rather than a single one.

While the psalm relates both sorrow and joy to God, with sorrow being the lack of the joy God will provide, it also has a third point of triangulation in the enemies. These appear first as the unrighteous whom God hates ('Þu hatast ealle þa þe unriht wyrcað' v. 7[39]), but they quickly morph into the personal enemies of the psalmist, while still being identified in terms of their sinfulness: 'læd me ... fram minra feonda willan ... Forðam on minra feonda muðe is leasuncg, and heora mod is swiðe idel' (vv. 9–10).[40] Richard Stracke has shown how the translator extends the already prominent role of the enemies in the course of rendering the first fifty psalms into Old English.[41] God's hatred of the enemies is an affirmation of his love of the righteous. The enemies also support the construction of identity by functioning as an outgroup; the believer, aligned with the psalmist, belongs to God's people rather than the sinners.

Altogether, Psalm 5 provides a combination of concrete spatial imagery (presence and absence, paths, God's altar, God's face) and a somewhat generalised but highly emotive scenario: the psalmist, persecuted by enemies, calls on God in the hour of need. It is built around a set of complementary emotional states, sorrow and joy on the psalmist's part, hatred and merciful benevolence on God's, but the multiple resonances of the imagery allow for these binaries to be nuanced. Anyone experiencing anxiety, isolation, spiritual oppression or external hostility, or even simply meditating on the condition of being a mortal in a fallen world, could enter into the emotional trajectory of Psalm 5. The psalm scripts such experiences in terms of dependency on God and the conflict of the righteous and the wicked, and it moves the person praying from sorrowful petition towards joy and praise.

The Difficulty of the Text and Learning about Emotion

As examined so far, the process of emotional learning indicated by the argument and the progression of the psalm is experiential and active. One is given not simply ways to think about one's own feelings but ways to enact them. Both petition and

---

[38] Stephen Jaeger stresses the emotional intensity of a face-to-face encounter with the king in *Ennobling Love: In Search of a Lost Sensibility* (Philadelphia, 1999), p. 21.

[39] 'You hate all who bring about injustice.'

[40] 'Lead me ... out of the power of my enemies ... Because in the mouth of my enemies is falsehood, and their heart is very empty.'

[41] Stracke, *Paris Prose*, http://www.aug.edu/augusta/psalms/intro3.htm#enemies

praise are matters of performative language: in saying 'hear my prayer' or 'you are the Lord who blesses and makes glad the righteous',[42] the believer petitions and praises. This is learning through practice. However, the psalms are often difficult texts and, even with the help of the Old English arguments, they present puzzles that impede the kind of inhabitation of a drama that has been envisaged so far in this chapter. Two kinds of difficulty deserve mention, both of which can be occasions for a more conscious kind of learning about emotion. The first allows us to sketch in another aspect to the potential emotional learning of the user of the Paris Psalter. The second points rather to the ways the pre-existing emotion concepts of the translator affected the treatment of the Latin text, and allows us as modern readers to learn more about Anglo-Saxon emotion scripts.

Periodically throughout the OE Prose Psalms we encounter what we might call a 'glossing voice' that provides exegesis and clarification, frequently drawing on commentaries such as those of Cassiodorus, Jerome and Augustine as well as Theodore of Mopsuestia and the *Argumenta*.[43] Returning to Psalm 5, a good example occurs in verse 5: 'Ic stande on ærmergen beforan ðe æt gebede, and seo þe (þæt is, þæt ic ongite þinne willan butan tweon and eac þone wyrce), for ðam þu eart se ylca God þe nan unriht nelt.'[44] Here there are in fact three expansions of the Latin, which reads, 'Mane adstabo tibi et videbo, quoniam non volens Deus iniquitatem tu es'.[45] By specifying that the psalmist is 'at prayer' and that he sees 'you', the translator renders the situation more concrete (drawing on Theodore of Mopsuestia in the first instance and Jerome in the second).[46] However, the portion O'Neill has placed in parentheses – and for which he finds no source in the commentaries, though he suggests a parallel in the OE version of Augustine's *Soliloquies*[47] – constitutes a marked change of tone and also strikingly repositions the reader of the psalm. In 'Ic stande...', 'I' can be the person praying, but (unless we envisage believers explaining their words to a possibly puzzled God) 'þæt is' marks the intrusion of another voice that pushes the reader out of the subject-position. It presents the psalm as a text that needs to be studied rather than

---

[42] 'Þu eart se Drihten þe gebletsast and geblissast rihtwise', v. 13.

[43] *Prose Translation*, ed. O'Neill, pp. 34–40 (in the Introduction) and pp. 165–271 (Commentary).

[44] 'I stand before you in the early morning at prayer, and see you (that is, that I perceive your will without hesitation and also perform it), because you are the same God who desires no injustice.'

[45] 'In the morning I shall stand before you and see, for you are a God who does not desire iniquity.' The Latin *adstabo* and *videbo* are both future tense. It would be possible to translate OE *stande* and *seo* as future, since the present tense also functions as a future in OE, but the OE itself provides no clear cue for this. A reader's understanding of the OE would depend on how well they understood the Latin alongside it.

[46] *Prose Translation*, ed. O'Neill, p. 173.

[47] Ibid.

just ardently poured out. Other such more-or-less intrusive comments appear at verses 7 and 9 (translator's additions in bold): 'Þu hatast ealle þa þe unriht wyrcað, **and þæt ne forlætað ne his ne hreowsiað**';[48] 'Geriht minne weg beforan þinre ansyne. **Se weg ys min weorc**.'[49]

In verse 5, the interpretation of seeing God as perceiving and performing His will jars against the resonances of the imagery of God's presence as they play out at the start of the psalm. We have seen earlier how the opening verses convey a sense of anxious petition and of being vulnerable and needy before the all-powerful Father. The gloss reworks literal beholding of God into something more abstract and also presents the psalmist in a much more positive and active guise. However, it anticipates the idea, which emerges as the psalm progresses, that admission to God's presence is a sign of righteousness and God's favour. It also offers a lesson in how the believer should respond to sorrow and need – in how feeling should issue in action. The gloss can be read in more than one way. It can be related to *seo þe* alone and taken to mean that the one who truly sees God is the one who is conformed to His will through righteous deeds. Alternatively, it can be taken as a comment on the whole earlier part of the verse: prayer itself is an action in conformity with God's will. In either case, meditation on the OE version of this verse, incorporating the contribution of the 'glossing voice', yields a lesson about how the *frofer* of the argument is to be achieved. It interrupts the emotional trajectory of the psalm, but it provides another way of aiming at its eventual goal, presenting both the meaning of the text and closeness to God as things that must be actively worked for.

This examination of an instance of the 'glossing voice' in the Old English Prose Psalms points to how engagement with the Psalms might entail conscious modification of emotion scripts (in the case of Ps. 5.5, replacing a perhaps rather passive model of the individual who receives *frofer* with a more active one). Elsewhere the translations modify the Latin text in the direction of more culturally familiar concepts and images of emotion. This evidence relates more directly to the (Alfredian?) composition context than the eleventh-century manuscript context.

A literally visceral image that does not survive into the Old English text is that of the kidneys or reins as the seat of emotion. Although Anglo-Saxon authors commonly view powerful feelings as welling up in the torso they associate them with the breast or heart and not the lower viscera.[50] In Ps. 15.7 the Latin reads 'usque ad noctem increpaverunt me renes mei',[51] but the OE has 'þeah he me þara

---

[48] 'You hate all those who perform wrong, and do not abandon or repent of it.'
[49] 'Direct my path before your face. The path is my works.'
[50] See Leslie Lockett, *Anglo-Saxon Psychologies in the Vernacular and Latin Traditions* (Toronto, 2011).
[51] 'Until night my kidneys have reproved me.'

uterrena gewinna gefreode, þeah winnað wið me þa inran unrihtlustas dæges and nihtes.'[52] The fact that O'Neill identifies Theodore of Mopsuestia as the source of this interpretation does not take away the implication that reproving kidneys were a puzzle to the translator, who felt the need to consult a commentary for clarification.[53] Similarly, in Ps. 25.2 'ure renes meos et cor meum'[54] is translated as 'smea mine geþohtas'.[55] In these instances the moral and psychological language of the OE is likely to strike a modern reader as decidedly paler than the bodily imagery of the Latin, but we must remember the prominence of terms like *mod*, *hige* and *gemynd* in Old English poetry.[56]

In Ps. 6.3–4 we find an instance where the translator has used a verbal and conceptual formula well known in Old English poetry in a way that clarifies an odd image – perhaps the initial impetus for the modification – but also indicates the wider interpretative approach to the passage: 'ac miltsa me, Dryhten, for þam ic eom unhal; and gehæl me for þam eall min mægn and eal min ban synt gebrytt and gedrefed, and min sawl and min mod ys swyðe gedrefed.'[57] The Paris Psalter Romanum text here reads: 'miserere michi, Domine, quoniam infirmus sum. Sana me, Domine, quoniam conturbata sunt ossa mea, et anima mea turbata est valde.'[58] The introduction of *mægn* apparently reflects a sense going back to the commentaries that *ossa mea* is an odd image in need of interpretation. O'Neill cites a likely source in the *Glosa ... ex traditionem seniorem*: 'omnes uirtutes, quae ossa appellauit.'[59] The capacious term *uirtus* is transparently related to *uir* and carries the sense 'manliness', but can also convey physical strength, moral goodness, or courage; other instances where it is translated as *mægen* are cited by Bosworth and Toller.[60] However, in this context the full range of implications of *uirtus* is perhaps not felt. *Mægn* and *ban* – for the translator supplements the

---

[52] 'Though he freed me from outward struggles, yet inward wrong desires contend against me day and night.'

[53] *Prose Translation*, ed. O'Neill, p. 192.

[54] 'Burn my reins and my heart'. This is usually read as an image of purgation, as for example by Augustine: *Sancti Aurelii Augustini Enarrationes in Psalmos*, ed. E. Dekkers and I. Fraipont, CCSL 38–40, 3 vols (Turnhout, 1956), I, p. 140.

[55] 'Examine my thoughts.'

[56] Antonina Harbus, *The Life of the Mind in Old English Poetry* (Amsterdam and New York, 2002), pp. 3 and 23.

[57] 'But have mercy on me, Lord, because I am infirm; and heal me because all my strength and all my bones are broken up and troubled, and my soul and my mind is greatly troubled.'

[58] 'Have mercy on me, Lord, for I am infirm. Heal me, Lord, for my bones are disordered, and my soul is greatly troubled.'

[59] 'All powers/strengths/virtues, which were called bones'. *Prose Translation*, ed. O'Neill, p. 174.

[60] Joseph Bosworth and T. Northcote Toller, *An Anglo-Saxon Dictionary* (Oxford, 1898), p. 655, s.v. *mægen*.

image of the Latin rather than replacing it – are balanced against *sawl* and *mod*; the opposition of *mægen* 'physical strength' to *mod* 'mental strength, courage' is most famously exemplified in *The Battle of Maldon* l. 313 ('mod sceal þe mare, þe ure mægen lytlað').[61] Physical affliction is balanced against mental, emotional and spiritual affliction. Other key terms in these verses are chosen to carry both a physical and a spiritual/psychological sense: *gehæl*, like *sana*, can mean 'save' as well as 'heal', and *gedrefed*, like *(con)turbata*, can refer to both physical disturbance (for example of water or the ground) and mental agitation. The pairing of physical and emotional suffering is also explicit in the OE argument: 'Dauid sang þysne sextan sealm be his mettrumnesse and be his earfoðum, and eac be þam ege þæs domes on Domesdæge.'[62] I would suggest that what is happening here is not simply that the argument influences the translation, but that the argument, the glossing tradition, and the cultural knowledge crystallised in the formula *mod and mægen* all in conjunction produce the translator's approach to the passage.

Conclusion

The chapter began with the question of emotional learning and has proceeded both to argue for the importance of the OE Prose Psalms as a source and to explore three different kinds of learning that it facilitates: learning by approaching the text as personal expression, learning from glosses, and the modern student's learning about Anglo-Saxon emotional culture from the decisions of the translator. Though the stress in much of the discussion has been on the potential of the text to change the reader's emotion scripts, the final section has drawn attention to how the reception of a text is itself affected by the reader's pre-existing folk psychology. In addition to specific insight into concepts such as *frofer*, which we have seen elaborated in Psalm 5, investigation of the OE Prose Psalms reminds us that emotional life, even as it can be reconstructed from such a force for continuity as a sacred text, entails an evolving interchange between the personal and the cultural. The scripts provided in the psalms, though constrained within certain limits by the arguments, are sufficiently open to be bent to the needs of believers at the same time as encouraging the believers to conceptualise their needs in certain ways. Poetry and lexis have proved the richest sources for Anglo-Saxon emotion so far; but it is hoped that this chapter has indicated something of the potential yet untapped in liturgy, biblical texts and prayers.

---

[61] 'Our courage must be the greater, the more our strength diminishes.' See Norma J. Engberg, '*Mod-mægen* Balance in *Elene*, *The Battle of Maldon* and *The Wanderer*', *Neuphilologische Mitteilungen* 85 (1985): 212–26.

[62] 'David sang this sixth psalm about his sickness and about his afflictions, and also about the fear of the judgement on Doomsday.'

Chapter 9
Those Bloody Trees: The Affectivity of *Christ*

Frances McCormack

The tradition of affective piety in both literature and art is usually seen as emerging in the high Middle Ages, and as flourishing after the Fourth Lateran Council made confession an annual requirement:[1]

> For more than half of a century now, scholarship on the history of medieval spirituality has drawn attention to a profound shift in the patterns of devotion that took place in western Europe around the middle of the eleventh century. In this era, we witness the emergence of a radically new form of piety centred on compassionate devotion to the suffering of Christ. ... Suddenly, pious reflection turned to contemplate, with increasing fervour, the excruciating pains endured by Christ in the crucifixion, inviting the faithful to share mentally in the torment and sorrow.[2]

Meditation on the sufferings of Christ or his mother was thought to elicit contrition and lead to a deepened faith, thereby avoiding the passive and mechanical devotion that was likely in a church that dictated when and how one demonstrated repentance for one's sins.

This type of affective faith is not absent from Old English literature, though. Scott DeGregorio notes that,

> Bede ... speaks of being 'inflamed with God's love until there is an effusion of tears' ('amore illius usque ad lacrimarum fusionem inflammari'), of being 'enkindled

---

[1] See, for example, T.H. Bestul, *Texts of the Passion: Latin Devotional Literature and Medieval Society* (Philadelphia, 1996); R. Kieckhefer, 'Convention and Conversion: Patterns in Late-Medieval Piety', *Church History* 67 (1998): 32–51; S. McNamer, *Affective Meditation and the Invention of Medieval Compassion* (Philadelphia, 2010); R.A. Powell, 'Margery Kempe: An Exemplar of Late Medieval English Piety', *The Catholic Historical Review* 89 (2003): 1–23; O.D. Watkins, *A History of Penance*, 2 vols (London, 1920).

[2] S.J. Shoemaker, 'Mary at the Cross, East and West: Maternal Compassion and Affective Piety in the Earliest *Life of the Virgin* and the High Middle Ages', *Journal of Theological Studies*, 62 (2011): 570–606, at 570–71.

with desire for things eternal and longing for the face of our Creator' ('aeternorum desideriis accensi atque eius quem nondum uidemus conditoris nostri faciem suspirantes') and of what he calls 'the opening of secret compunction' ('foramen secretae compunctionis'), which causes those who experience it to 'become warm' ('incaluit'), 'melt' ('liquefuit'), and 'dissolve in tears' ('in lacrimis resolui'). Such language, and more so the range of emotional experience it seeks to trigger in the individual believer, should be all too familiar to scholars of later medieval devotion, who, bypassing Anglo-Saxon England, rush to make the eleventh and twelfth centuries the *terminus post quem* for the emergence of affective elements in western devotional literature.[3]

In this chapter, I shall focus on one specific passage and the startling imagery contained therein to shed new light on the way in which emotion is expected and practised in Anglo-Saxon England. I shall explore how *Christ* (and in particular what many editors consider to be the third of three poems) constructs an affective devotion in order to effect compunction in the audience. In particular, I wish to demonstrate how this poem evokes affective response not through images of human suffering (as we see in the later Middle Ages), but through the image of a tree as metonym for the cross.

A certain theological unity seems to underpin much of the Exeter Book. Exposition on salvation history – and, in particular, the end of days – receives a highly personalised treatment with the focus on the individual's faith and his unique relationship with God. Whether detailing the effects of grace (as do *The Gifts of Men* and *The Wanderer*), charting the life of an individual working towards salvation (*Guthlac* and *Juliana*), or affectively depicting the apocalypse (*Christ* and *Judgement Day I*), there is a prevailing mood of penitence, and of mindfulness of the proximity of Final Judgement. It is, though, in *Christ*, that the soteriological themes are more fully realised, and the already-revealed salvific plan is designed to evoke a sense of compunction. Much attention has been drawn recently to the doctrine of compunction in Old English literature, with Sandra McEntire devoting an entire chapter of her book-length study of compunction to the topic,[4] and James M. Palmer[5] analysing how the doctrine manifests itself in *The Wanderer*. Significant treatment of compunction in *Christ* has been lacking, however, and yet this poem presents an interesting take on the doctrine, using rich imagery and sophisticated rhetoric to establish a fresh and powerful way of both depicting,

---

[3] S. DeGregorio, 'Affective Spirituality: Theory and Practice in Bede and Alfred the Great', *Essays in Medieval Studies* 22 (2005): 129–39, at 131.

[4] S. McEntire, *The Doctrine of Compunction in Medieval England: Holy Tears* (Lewiston, NY, 1990).

[5] J.M. Palmer, '*Compunctio* and the Heart in the Old English Poem *The Wanderer*', *Neophilologus* 88 (2004): 447–60.

and indeed evoking, the emotive effects of compunction. In this chapter, I shall look at compunctive tears (on which much has already been written) in order to understand more about the comparatively lesser-studied motif of tears of blood in Anglo-Saxon literature.

Compunction is traditionally seen as a grace or charism by which the individual, through a pricking of the heart, may strengthen his relationship with God and effect his own salvation. It is often depicted as the physical condition of weeping ('Holy Tears' is the term that is most often used). As Sandra McEntire elaborates:

> Compunction is a grace, gratuitously given, with which the beneficiary must cooperate. ... Tears are the exterior expression of the greater activity, prayer between the individual and God. The grace of tears is never sought for its own sake, but as the abiding sign of the deep interior sorrow one feels before the greatness and mercy of God. The interior attitude is expressed in the outward sign of tears; both tears and compunction are elements of grace being given.[6]

These tears are thought to be the most readily identifiable feature of compunction, and the written testaments to compunctive tears are manifold: in the *Vita Sancti Gregorii* the weeping of Gregory the Great for the soul of Trajan, for example, results in the baptism and spiritual cleansing of the dead emperor.[7] Monastic mourning is a main theme of ascetic literature, with John Gale asserting that monastic life at the time is characterised by compunction and tears.[8]

Images of tears abound in *Christ*, some compunctive, and some not: the tears shed by those on earth awaiting the *Paraousia* (ll. 150b–152); the tears of Joseph at the scorning of Mary's reputation upon the revelation of her pregnancy (ll. 172–3); the tears of the damned who are exiled from heaven (ll. 530–540a). In the early stages of the development of the doctrine of compunction, according to McEntire, mourning was encouraged. Later, however, compunction is

---

[6] McEntire, p. 55.

[7] Should read 'Quidam quoque de nostris dicunt narratum a Romanis, sancti Gregorii lacrimis animam Traiani imperatoris regrigeratam uel baptizatam, quod est dictum mirabile et auditu.' (*S. Gregorii Papae vita* II, 44 (PL 75, cols 105–6) ['Some of our people also tell a story related by the Romans of how the soul of the Emperor Trajan was refreshed and even baptized by St Gregory's tears, a story marvellous to tell and marvellous to hear.'] (*The Earliest Life of Gregory the Great*, ed. B. Colgrave (Cambridge, 1985), pp. 126–8)).

[8] J. Gale, 'The Divine Office: Aid and Hindrance to Penthos', *Studia Monastica* 27 (1985): 13–30, at 15.

distinguished from other forms of weeping. McEntire quotes Chromatius' distinction between compunctive and non-compunctive tears:

> Quis nobis iste luctus intellegendus est salutaris? Vtique non ille qui ex rerum nascitur detrimentis, non qui ex amissione carorum, nec qui ex iactura saecularium dignitatum, quae utique omnia iam paper factus spiritu non dolebit.[9]

> [What mourning must be understood by us as healthy? Surely not that which is born of the loss of things, nor from the loss of dear ones, nor from the loss of earthly dignities, all things which will not hurt a man who has been made poor in spirit.]

One of the most interesting examples of compunctive tears in *Christ*, though, occurs in an account of the day of doom at the moment when the trees recall Christ's crucifixion, when he mounted one of their number in preparation for his death:

> Ða wearð beam monig   blodigum tearum
> Birunnen under rindum   reade ond þicce;
> sæp wearð to swate.[10]   Þæt asecgan ne magum
> foldbuende   þurh frod gewit,
> hu fela þa onfundun   þa gefelan ne magun
> dryhtnes þrowinga,   deade gesceafte.
>
>   (ll. 1174–9)[11]

> [Then, many a tree became bedewed under the bark with bloody tears, red and thick; sap became blood. So that no one of the earth dwellers may tell, through wise understanding, how much those lifeless of creation, which cannot feel, sensed the suffering of the Lord.]

The startling prosopopoeia of this description of bloody tears is clearly affective in outcome: the contrast between the lack of feeling and understanding of the sentient *foldbuende* and the empathy of the *deade gesceafte* points to the failure of compunction among humankind in general. In fact, the passage is set in stark contrast against the refusal of mankind to acknowledge its salvation and to renounce sin:

---

[9]   *CCSL*, 1953ff. Cited and translated in McEntire, p. 35.
[10] Bosworth and Toller define swat, in sense II.2, as 'blood'.
[11] All Old English translations are my own, unless otherwise stated.

Þa þe æþelast sind   eorðan gecynda,
ond heofones eac   heahgetimbro,
eall fore þam anum   unrot gewearð,
forhtafongen.
...
Hwæs weneð se   þe mid gewitte nyle
gemunan þa mildan   Meotudes lare,
ond eal ða earfeðu   þe he fore ældum adreag,
forþon þe he wolde   þæt we wuldres eard
in ecnesse   agan mosten?
Swa þam bið grorne,   on þam grimman dæge
domes þæs miclan,   þam þe dryhtnes sceal
deaðfirenum forden   dolg sceawian,
wunde ond wite.   On werigum sefan
geseoð sorga mæste: hy se sylfa cyning
mid sine lichoman   lysde of firenum,
þurh milde mod,   þæt hy mostun manweorca
tome lifgan,   ond tires blæd
ecne agan.   Hy þæs eðles þonc
hyra waldende   wihte ne cuþon;
forþon þær to teonum   þa tacen geseoð
orgeatu on gode   ungesælge.

(ll. 1180–83a, 1199–215)

[Those who are the noblest of earth's kind, and of the high edifice of heaven too, all because of that one became sorrowful, seized with fear. ... What does he know who has no understanding and is not mindful of the gentle teachings of the creator, and of all the misery that he suffered in the presence of men, because he wished that we might possess a heavenly home forever. Thus it will be miserable, on the grim day of the great judgement for the one who, with deadly sin, has to gaze upon the Lord's scars, wounds and punishment. In dejected mood they will see the greatest of sorrows: how the same king with his flesh released them from transgressions through his merciful spirit, so that they might live free from sins, and possess the everlasting abundance of glory; for that gentility they did not express thanks to their ruler; because of this they will see the inauspicious signs of affliction plainly visible on God.]

The bloody tears of the trees that are witness to Christ's passion, then, become a model for human compunction: a model that is not, at this point, emulated by the unfeeling earth-dwellers, but which, it is implied, should produce an affective response in the listeners of the poem itself – the lamentation of the inanimate is surely a reproach to those who do not feel. These tears are significantly different from those discussed by McEntire: the presence of the blood adds a new layer of significance to this emotive manifestation. If tears are a physical manifestation of a psychological state, then bloody tears are that state intensified. The body's shedding of blood is associated with physical injury, and the bloody tears absorb the significance from this, suggesting not only grief, but also wounding.

The Old English period reconceptualised the material world in most interesting ways. In the Riddles, inanimate objects speak to us, introduce themselves obliquely to us, reconfigure themselves in metaphorical relation to other objects (a chopping board may pretend to be a shield, for example, or a key a phallus), and then they ask us, as listeners, to locate and define their 'true' (and I use that word cautiously) identity. 'Saga hwæt ic hatte', or 'say what I am called', is the phrase that is most often used. In Riddle 30, for instance, one object takes on the form of three: a tree in a grove becomes a devotional crucifix and a symbol of Christ's cross. Arnold Talentino, writing on this Riddle (the solution to which was first proposed to be *beam* by F.A. Blackburn in 1901),[12] states:

> I agree ... that the central idea of Riddle 30 is description of a cross; however, the imagery adds up to 'cross' in a way that makes the whole greater than the sum of its parts. In Riddle 30 we have a cross with a difference, for the poem goes beyond just projecting the symbol and lays the significance of the symbol bare. As well as calling to mind the cross, Riddle 30 adumbrates its qualities and power.[13]

Talentino reads the opening four lines as pointing towards what he refers to as the 'cosmic transcendence of the world of men': the potential power of the tree to effect salvation. The tree of the opening lines of the poem therefore points out beyond itself to the devotional cross that is passed from hand to hand, and both of these assumed forms of the riddlic object transcend the physical to denote the crucifixion and connote salvation. Into this one riddle, then, are packed layers upon layers of significance, and the riddle becomes a locus for the transference of meaning from one object to another, from the material to the spiritual, from the animate to the inanimate.

Prosopopoeia creates a further transference of meaning. Through this rhetorical device the interlocutor shifts shape, adopts the form of something else, points out beyond its own immediate signification, and compels the audience to interpret the metaphor that it has formed around itself. Aldhelm himself commented on the transformative nature of prosopopoeia when he wrote:

---

[12] F.A. Blackburn, 'The Husband's Message and the Accompanying Riddles of the Exeter Book', *JEGP* 3 (1901): 1–13.

[13] A. Talentino, 'Riddle 30: The Vehicle of the Cross', *Neophilologus* 65 (1981): 129–36 at 130.

> Quia nonnumquam rationabilis creatura irrationabilium gestu et personis utitur et a diverso irrationabilis sensusque vivacitate carnes intellectualium gestu et voce futitur.[14]

> [For sometimes a rational creature adopts the behaviour and persona of irrational things and, on the other hand, an irrational thing is endowed with the vital force, behaviour and voice of creatures with the capacity of understanding.]

Prosopopoeia therefore relies on the vicarious identification of the audience with the object being described, and thereby invites the audience into participation in what Craig Williamson (writing on prosopopoeia in the Riddles in particular) describes as an ontological game:

> In half of the riddles, the reader identifies with the 'I' of the human riddler; in half with the 'I' of the creature. The two narrative stances constitute poles of a perceptual game. Sometimes we escape the bone-house and embody the world; sometimes we see what the world charged with metaphor means. This is an ontological game – the challenge is either, 'Say what I mean', or 'Say who I am'. Meaning depends upon our manipulation in images of the Other.[15]

If effective, this device will challenge the reader to enter into a process of self-investigation and will intensify the emotive effect of the text, as Quintilian notes in his *Institutio Oratoria*:

> His et adversariorum cogitationes, velut secum loquentium protrahimus: quæ tamen ita demum a fide non abhorreant, si ea locutos finxerimus quæ cogitasse eos non sit absurdum: et nostros cum aliis sermones, et aliorum inter se credibiliter introducimus, et *suadendo, obiurgando, querendo, laudando, miserando*, personas idoneas damus. Quin deducere deos in hoc genere dicendi, et inferos excitare, concessum est; urbes etiam populique vocem accipiunt: ac sunt quidam, qui has demum προσωποποιΐας dicant, in quibus et corpora et verba fingimus; sermones hominum assimulatos dicere διαλόγους malunt, quod Latinorum quidam dixerunt *sermocinationem*. ... Commode etiam aut nobis aliquas ante oculos esse rerum, personarum, vocum imagines fingimus, aut eadem adversariis aut judicibus non accidere miramur: qualia sunt *Videtur mihi* et *Nonne videtur tibi?* Sed magna

---

[14] Aldhelm, *De metris et enigmatibus ac pedum regulis*, ch. 7, in *Aldhelmi opera*, ed. R. Ehwald, *MGH* AA 15 (Berlin, 1919, rpt 1961), p. 76.

[15] *A Feast of Creatures: Anglo-Saxon Riddle-Songs*, trans. C. Williamson (Philadelphia, PA, 1982), p. 25.

quædam vis eloquentiæ desideratur: falsa enim et incredibilia natura necesse est aut magis moveant, quia supra vera sunt, aut pro vanis accipiantur, quia vera non sunt.[16]

[By this means we display the inner thoughts of our adversaries as though they were talking with themselves (but we shall only carry conviction if we represent them as uttering what they may reasonably be supposed to have had in their minds); or without sacrifice of credibility we may introduce conversations between ourselves and others, or of others among themselves, and put words of advice, reproach, complaint, praise or pity into the mouths of appropriate persons. Nay, we are even allowed in this form of speech to bring down the gods from heaven and raise the dead, while cities also and peoples may find a voice. ... With things which are false and incredible by nature there are but two alternatives: either they will move our hearers with exceptional force because they are beyond the truth, or they will be regarded as empty nothings because they are not the truth.]

Poems frequently participate in this ontological game in Old English literature. In *The Dream of the Rood*, for example, one object is clearly transformed into another: the tree becomes a cross, which in turn becomes a synecdoche for salvation. In fact, throughout the text, it straddles the distinction between the two. It even redefines itself metaphorically –

    Ne þearf ðær þonne ænig   anforht wesan
    þe him ær in breostum bereð   beacna selest.
                                           (ll. 117–18)

[None of them will need to be afraid who bears before him in his breast the best of signs.]

– and it creates the double meaning of a cross that is carried on the breast (as material devotional object) and one that is carried in the heart (as a reminder of the promise of eternal life). But, of course, the most remarkable transformation is of that from the inanimate to the animate, the silent to the articulate. Margaret Schlauch asserts that,

to endow the Cross with the power of locution was to use a device of unexampled effectiveness in making a vivid event about which, for all devout Christians, the entire history of the world revolved. The object most intimately associated with that breath-taking moment when 'the veil of the temple was rent in twain from the top to the bottom; and the earth did quake, and the rocks were rent'

---

[16] Quintilian, *Institutio Oratoria* in *Institution oratoire de Quintilien*, ed. C. V. Ouizille (Paris, 1832), IX.2.30–31 and 33.

might well be given speech with profound literary effectiveness. Yet this was not commonly done at the time.[17]

The tradition of anthropomorphised *beams*, though – whether trees or crosses – is clearly not uncommon to the Anglo-Saxon imagination, and enables the reader to investigate more thoroughly the relationship between spiritual and material, real and imagined, signified and interpreted.

But what of trees that shed bloody tears? The *beam* of *The Dream of the Rood* bleeds from its right side (ll. 18–20a), in imitation of the wound endured by Christ when his side was pierced by the soldiers. But the bloody tears of the trees in *Christ* are an entirely different sort of emission. They are not imitative of the blood of Christ, but rather a subjective response to the Passion. St Gregory of Nyssa writes of tears of repentance that they are like 'blood from the wounds of our soul',[18] and the motif of an impassioned weeping that causes so much grief that it rends the soul has an interesting history in the western tradition, with images of bloody tears becoming a recurring trope in cultural artefacts such as literature, visual art, film, and so on. In *Ragnars Saga Loðbrókar*, when Queen Áslaug finds out about the death of her sons, Eirik and Agnar, she cries a single tear of blood:

> Ok nú kvað hann þá vísu, er Eirekr hafði kveðit, er hann sendi henni hringinn. Nú sjá þeir, at hún felldi tár, en þat var sem blóð væri álits, en hart sem haglkorn. Þat hafði engi maðr sét, at hún hefði tár fellt, hvárki áðr né síðan.[19]
>
> [And then he quoted the verse, which Eirik had spoken, when he had sent the ring to her. Now, they say that she let fall a tear, and that it looked like blood, and yet seemed as hard as a hailstone. No man had seen that, that she had let fall a tear, either before or after.] (translation my own)

Here, the image of a single tear encapsulates the reach and complexity of Áslaug's grief – the blood perhaps representing how harrowing the news, its hardness her resolve to seek vengeance. Interestingly, the motif of the heedless bystander (seen as the uncomprehending *foldbuende* in *Christ*), reappears, emphasising the singularity of her experience, and the individualised and experiental nature of its expression.

---

[17] M. Schlauch, 'The "Dream of the Rood" as Prosopopoeia', in P.W. Long (ed.), *Essays and Studies in Honour of Carleton Brown* (New York, 1940), pp. 23–34 at 24.

[18] St Gregory of Nyssa, 'Funeral Oration on the Empress Flacilla', in *Gregorii Nysseni opera* IX, ed. A. Spira (Leiden, 1967), p. 477.

[19] *Ragnars Saga Loðbrókar ok Sona Hans*, ed. G. Jónsson and B. Vilhjálmsson, Perseus Digital Library, http://nlp.perseus.tufts.edu/hopper/text;jsessionid=2A93873BC88772 661AAEE61643DEFA56?doc=Perseus%3Atext%3A2003.02.0029%3Achapter%3D10 [accessed 10 April 2013], Bk. X.

The *Annals of Ulster* recount the battle of Imlech Pich, culminating in a description of overwhelming, albeit hypothetical, grief:

> Bronaigh Conailli indiu,
> deithbir doaibh iar nUaircridiu,
> niba ellmhu bias gen
> i nAird iar nDubh da Inbher.
>
> Sirechtach
> bronan file for tir Taidhgg
> cen Dub Cuile cen macc mBrain,
> cen Dub da Inber ar Aird.
>
> Sirechtach
> sella fria lecht leacca,
> for coin, for milcoin, for mna
> do buid la far n-echtrata.
>
> Mona·icad dam amne
> mac Crunnmael dom' siricht-sa,
> roptis fula ocus cro
> mo der do marb Imblecho.[20]

[Sad are the Conaille today, fittingly indeed after the death of Uarchride; a smile will come to none too readily in Ard after the death of Dub dá Inber. Wistful is the grief which afflicts Tadc's land without Dub Cúile, without Bran's son, without Dub dá Inber in Ard. Sorrowful are your glances at their grave-stones, with your hounds, your hunting-dogs, your women in the possession of your enemies. If Crunnmael's son should fail to requite me thus for my yearning my tears for the dead of Imblech would be tears of blood and gore.]

Once again, tears of blood are representative of heart-rending grief and suffering. This physicalised description of mourning contrasts starkly with the internalised grief in the earlier part of the poem, and once again, the motif of the observance of the grief of others serves to intensify the emotion of the passage.

In the *Hêliand*, Peter sheds bloody tears of compunction upon his realisation of the significance of his third denial of Christ:

---

[20] *The Annals of Ulster (to A.D. 1131)*, ed. and transl. S. Mac Airt and G. Mac Niocall, Part I: Text and Translation (Dublin, 1983).

> Thes thram imu an innan môd
> bittro an is breostun,   endi geng imu thô gibolgan thanen
> the man fer theru menigi   an môdkaru,
> suiðo an sorgun,   endi is selbes uuord,
> uuamscefti uueop,   antat imu uuallan quâmun
> thurh thea hertcara   hête trahni,
> blôdaga fan is breostun.[21]
>
> (ll. 5000b–5006)

[This swelled up in his mind, bitterly in his breast, and thus he went thence, swollen; the man went from the crowd in grief, with great sorry, and he lamented his own words, his misery, until hot and bloody tears came welling up from his breast through his heartbreak.]

Leslie Lockett, reading this passage, notes the intensity of the description of Peter's *hertcara* and *môdkara*:

> Peter himself is also said to be swollen (*gibolgan*) as he goes away to weep in solitude. In this context *gibolgen* seems much more likely to mean 'swollen' than 'enraged,' since Peter's state of mind is more sorrowful and anxious than angry, as indicated by the words *môdkaru*, *sorgum*, and *hertcara*. ... The tears, in fact, are not only hot but bloody, emphasizing the severity of pain and injury that his heart endures during this crisis.[22]

All of the aforementioned instances of bloody tears accompany depictions of profound affectivity: the tears representing grief, the blood signifying a wound. Such physical representations of an emotional state intensify the description of the experience and render it more palpable. Nevertheless, the fact that such images of bloody tears are not uncommon in medieval literature suggests that this was a depiction of intense emotion that was not unfamiliar to the medieval mind. The aforementioned examples draw on the image of haemolacria for both secular and religious purposes, but all are brought about by an awareness of death, whether past or impending. Bloody tears, then, in the medieval mind at least, seem to indicate some sense of grief, if not necessarily compunction.

The motif of bloody tears may also be familiar to the modern imagination, as it has permeated Catholic and Eastern Orthodox traditions, with haemolacria becoming an increasingly common feature of religious iconography. Much

---

[21] *Hêliand*, ed. J.E. Cathey, Medieval European Studies 12 (Morgantown, 2002). Translation my own.

[22] L. Lockett, *Anglo-Saxon Psychologies in the Vernacular and Latin Traditions* (Toronto, 2011), pp. 140–41.

recent attention in religious communities has been given to sightings of statues (often of the Virgin Mary) that appear to weep blood.[23] The common interpretation of such bloody tears is that they represent moral censure for the plight of the contemporary church and of the corruption of the age. However one interprets these images, though, they are clearly a modern form of affective piety. An issue of the Medjugorje[24] newsletter, *Echo of Mary*, from the 1990s (a decade in which sightings of lacrimating statues were frequently reported) uses affective language to explain why one small statue of the Virgin, brought from Medjugorje to Rome, appeared to weep tears of blood:

> Each apparition – or similar event – never brings anything new, but serves as a warning light, like that of a machine to say something is not working correctly. Warning lights from heaven are being sent to us; and happy are those who know how to read them.[25]

The affectivity of the images of haemolacria has carried on through to modern Goth and Fantasy art, where depictions of young women (and, less frequently, men) weeping bloody tears is almost iconic. The figures who weep tears of blood in the portraits by Valencian artist Victoria Francés exhibit a duality of character: a vulnerability, but also a moral and spiritual darkness. When the vampires in Charlaine Harris's *Southern Vampire Mysteries* weep, their tears are of blood,[26] and Le Chiffre, in the most recent film adaptation of Ian Fleming's *Casino Royale*, is depicted as suffering from haemolacria (probably as a sign of underlying moral corruption).[27] Furthermore, in Zadie Smith's novel, *White Teeth*, Dr Marc-Pierre Perret (known to the children in the novel as Dr Sick), a former Nazi collaborator who assisted in eugenics projects, cries tears of blood due to diabetic retinopathy.[28] These tears are, like those of Le Chiffre, a

---

[23] There are websites such as 'Visions of Jesus Christ' (http://www.visionsofjesuschrist.com/ weepingstatuesandicons.htm [accessed 10 April 2013]) that provide a catalogue of sightings and locations, and even photographs of the statues in question.

[24] Medjugorje is a town in Bosnia and Herzegovina, where the Virgin Mary is first said to have appeared to six Herzegovinian Croat children in 1981. These children reported seeing daily apparitions of the Virgin Mary for several years, and the town became a pilgrimage site. Three of the former children claim that they still receive the daily apparitions. The Vatican began a formal investigation of the apparitions in 2010, but has yet to announce its findings.

[25] Fr A. Mutti, 'Why Does our Mother Cry Tears of Blood', *Echo of Mary, Queen of Peace* 118 (March–April, 1995): 1–2 (http://www.medjugorje.ws/en/echo/echo-118/ [accessed 10 April 2013]).

[26] C. Harris, *The Southern Vampire Mysteries* (series) (New York, 2001–present).

[27] M. Campbell, dir., *Casino Royale* (MGM-Columbia, 2006).

[28] Z. Smith, *White Teeth* (London, 2000). I am grateful to Jonathan Wilcox for drawing my attention to this instance of haemolacria.

further example of how haemolacria in contemporary culture may be read as a physiological manifestation of ethical degeneracy.

Heart-rending bloody tears are, however, most notably linked with the later medieval tradition of affective piety and its depictions of the Virgin Mary. One such appearance of the bloody tears of the Virgin is in the thirteenth-century lyric *Stond wel, Moder, under rode*, in which Christ looks down from the cross and addresses his mother thus:

> 'Moder, thou rewe all of thy bern,
> Thou woshe away the blody tern;
> It doth me worse then my ded.'[29]

Mary replies,

> 'Sone, how may I teres werne?
> I see the blody stremes erne
> From thin herte to my fet.'

In yet another, *Thou synfull man of resoun*, the bloody tears of the Virgin are clearly intended to evoke compunction:

> Thou synfull man of resoun þat walkest here vp & downe,
> Cast þy respeccyoun one my mortall countenaunce.
> Se my blody terys fro my herte roote rebowne,
>
> Loke one my sorofull chere & haue therof pytee,
> Bewailynge my woo & payne, & lerne to wepe wyth me.[30]
>
> (ll. 1–3, 6–7)

In *M and A and R and I*, the bloody tears of the Virgin are once again apparent at the Passion:

> Our swete lady stod hym by,
> With M and A, and R and I,
> Che wept water with here ey,
> And alwey the blod folwyd among.[31]
>
> (ll. 11–14)

---

[29] M.S. Luria and R.L. Hoffman (eds), *Middle English Lyrics* (London, 1974), p. 216.
[30] C. Brown (ed.), *Religious Lyrics of the Fifteenth Century* (Oxford, 1939), no. 8.
[31] T. Wright (ed.), *Songs and Carols from a Manuscript in the British Museum of the Fifteenth Century* (London, 1856).

The images of blood and water resonate with the blood and water that flow from the side of Christ after his death on the cross, and therefore represent an active participation in his sacrifice. These affective depictions of Mary in Middle English literature, these images of a weeping, dejected Theotokos therefore emphasised the humanity of Christ and brought home to the penitent how much Christ, and his mother as intercessor, had suffered for his sins; furthermore, the humanity of the Virgin transforms her experience into exempla for the penitent.

It is not the Virgin Mary, though, who weeps tears of blood in *Christ*: in fact, whenever she features she is figured as a vehicle of the grace of the Holy Spirit. Her duties include bringing comfort to others: she begs Joseph to stop mourning her condition and she inspires joy in the hearts of the angels in heaven. In fact, throughout the poems, she is exalted, described as 'seo clæneste cwen ofer eorþan' ('the most spotless woman on earth', l. 276), 'þa æþelan cwenn' ('the noble lady', l. 1198), and

> mægða weolman,
> mærre meowlan, mundheals geceas.
> (ll. 445b–446)

[the flower of virgins, glorious maiden, chosen protection.]

Little else is to be expected from the poem in its depiction of Mary: the Anglo-Saxon tradition of the virgin places much more emphasis (following, perhaps, the lead of Ambrose) on her glory and grace.[32]

Even *The Dream of the Rood*, with its intensely affective images, manages to depict the Virgin in glory, oblivious to the cruel tortures being inflicted on earth:

> Swylce swa he his modor eac, Marian sylfe,
> ælmihtig god for ealle menn
> geweorðode ofer eall wifa cynn.
> (ll. 92–5)

[Thus he, Almighty God, has honoured his mother Mary herself, for all people, above all womankind.]

This sense of grace, though, only serves to enhance the compunctive element of the poems, with the humiliation and physical torture intensified by contrast with the glory and spiritual honour of the company of heaven.

---

[32] See, for example, M. Dockray Miller, 'The Maternal Performance of the Virgin Mary in the Old English *Advent*', *NWSA* 14/2 (Summer, 2002): 38–55, at 49.

Instead of choosing a human agent for these bloody tears, then, the poet of *Christ* creates a figurative context for the affectivity of his text. The trees become anthropomorphised in order to highlight the shortcomings of human piety, and the text opens itself up metaphorically to ask us to interpret the trees (as devotional objects or as instruments of torture) and the substance that they shed. Just as anthropomorphised beams were not unfamiliar to the Anglo-Saxon imagination, nor were natural phenomena combining blood and water. The *Anglo-Saxon Chronicle* contains examples of what is now known as 'blood rain': rain with a reddish hue due to the presence of sand carried in from desert regions. In the *Chronicle*, and elsewhere, these bloody rains are omens of doom. The entry for A.D. 685 in London, British Library, Cotton Domitian A. VIII reads, 'Her wearþ in Brytene blodi ren. ⁊ meolc ⁊ butere wurdon gewend to blode',[33] while the entry for 979 in London, British Library, Cotton Tiberius B.I reads:

> On þys geare wæs Æþelred to cininge gehalgod on þone sunnandæig feowertyne niht ofer Eastron at Cingestune; ond þær wæron æt his halgunge twegen ercebisceopas ond tyn leodbisceopas. Þy ilcan geare wæs gesewen blodig wolcen on oftsiðas on fyres gelicnesse; ond þæt wæs swyðost on middeniht oþywed, ond swa on mistlice beamas wæs gehiwod; þonne hit dagian wolde, þonne toglad hit.[34]

> [In this year, Æthelred was consecrated as king, on the Sunday fortnight after Easter, at Kingston. And there were two archbishops and ten suffragan bishops at his consecration. In the same year, a bloody welkin was often seen in the likeness of fire; and that was most apparent at midnight, and thus in misty beams was shown; but when it became day, then dispersed.]

The homily for Easter Day in the *Blickling Homilies* describes how the eschaton will be accompanied by a mixture of blood and water:

> Þa ærestan dæge on midne dæg gelimpeþ mycel gnornung ealra gesceafta, ond men gehyraþ myccle stefne on heofonum swylce þær man fyrde trymme and samnige. Þonne astigeþ blodig wolcen mycel from norþdæle ond oforþecþ ealne þysne heofon, ond æfter þæm wolcne cymeþ legetu and þunor ealne þone dæg. Ond rineþ blodig regn æt æfen.[35]

---

[33] 'In this year there was a bloody rain in Britain. And milk and butter were turned to blood.' In B. Thorpe (ed.), *The Anglo-Saxon Chronicle, According to Several Original Authorities*, 2 vols (London, 1861), I, p. 63.

[34] For an analysis of blood-rain in medieval writings, see J.S.P. Tatlock, 'Some Mediæval Cases of Blood-Rain', *Classical Philology* 9 (1914): 442–7.

[35] 'Dominica Pascha', in R. Kelly (ed.), *The Blickling Homilies: Edition and Translation* (London and New York, 2003), pp. 57–67 at ll. 136–40.

> [At midday on the first day a great mourning of all creation will occur, and men will hear a great summons from heaven as though an army is being recruited and assembled. Then a great bloody cloud will proceed from the northern regions and cover all this heaven, and after this cloud will come lightning and thunder all day. And it will rain bloody rain in the evening.]

This rain is a portent of doom – a sign of the impending eschaton, accompanying the earth being consumed by a conflagration, the sea drying up, and the skies becoming agitated. These examples of bloody rain, though, are of a very different sort of phenomenon than that described in *Christ*, where the trees emit this bloody substance, and where the emanations are said to be not a sign or *tacn* (as they are in the *Blickling Homily*), but an instinctive, yet emotive, response.

Of course, blood and water are closely linked throughout Christianity. For a start, there is an intermingling of water and wine during the Eucharist: a practice that is believed to have been common in the Mediterranean at the time of Jesus. There is a further intermingling of the two substances on the Mount of Olives in the gospel of Luke, as the trepidatious perspiration shed by Christ is streaked with blood.[36] Finally, the blood and water that flow from the side of the crucified Christ when pierced by a spear helps to reinforce the blending of the two substances in the Christian imagination.

This linking of blood and water takes one set of biblical symbols and juxtaposes them with another. Blood, in the bible, symbolises existence: in it lies the vitality of life, whether animal or human – hence the dietary prohibitions against the eating of meat in which blood is present (Lev. 17:10–12; Deut. 12:23–4). We also see how blood, when shed and distributed, can have positive effects: the Israelites escaping from Egypt mark their doors with blood to protect themselves from God's vengeful angel (Exod. 12); blood also comes to be symbolic of atonement, of sacrifice, and of promise: it is through blood that the covenant between God and the Israelite people is sealed on Mount Sinai (Lev. 1), and it is through the shedding of the blood of Christ that mankind is

---

[36] 'Et egressus ibat secundum consuetudinem in monte Olivarum. Secuti sunt autem illum et discipuli. Et cum pervinisset ad locum, dixit illis: Orate ne intretis in temptacionem. Et ipse avulsus est ab eis quantum jactus est lapidis: et positis genibus orabat, dicens: Pater, si vis, transfer calicem istum a me: verumtamen non mea voluntas, sed tua fiat. Apparuit autem illi angelus de cælo, confortans eum. Et factus in agonia, prolixius orabat. Et factus est sudor ejus sicut guttæ sanguinis decurrentis in terram.' [And going out, he went, according to custom, to the Mount of Olives. And his disciples also followed him. And when he had reached the place he said to them: Pray, so that you do not enter into temptation. And he withdrew himself a stone's throw from them, and kneeling he prayed, saying: Father, if you wish, remove this chalice from me; however, let not my will, but yours, be done. And an angel from heaven appeared to him, comforting him. And being in agony, he prayed at great length. And his sweat became as drops of blood, flowing onto the ground.] (Luke 22:39–44)

saved and, according to tradition, bought out of any punishment it owes for its sins. Water, on the other hand, is life-sustaining, cleansing and purifying. Baptism with water brings all of these benefits. The fusion of these two substances, then, has absorbed a broad significance from scripture, but with more specific points in Christ's life: his baptism and his Passion.

The image of the bloody tears in *Christ* therefore resonates with the three points of Christ's ministry and mystery through which blood and water come to be associated: the Eucharistic celebration of Christ's sacrifice, the anguished prayer on the Mount of Olives, and the death of Christ on the cross. In these three episodes, the intermingling of blood and water is clearly an echo of Christ's Passion – as it is in the poem itself. The bloody tears of the poem are, in fact, anticipated in these lines:

> Ond eac þa ealdan wunde   ond þa openan dolg
> on hyre dryhtne geseoð   dreorigferðe,
> swa him mid næglum þurhdrifan   niðhycgende
> þa hwitan honda   ond þa halgan fet,
> ond of his sidan swa some   swat forletan,
> þær blod ond wæter   bu tu ætsomne
> ut bicwoman   fore eagna gesyhð,
> rinnan fore rincum,   þa he on rode wæs.
>   (ll. 1107–14).

[And also they, dejected in spirit, will see the old wound and the open sore on their lord, as men of malicious thought pierced with nails those white hands and the holy feet, and caused to issue forth blood from his side – there blood and water both together came out, before the sight of all, gushing before the men when he was on the cross.]

The depiction of the injured body of the dead Christ will pre-empt and resonate with the portrayal of the trees that shed tears of blood at the sight of the Passion. In fact, it is the prosopopoeia of the poem that enhances the affectiveness of the tears, just as the prosopopoeia of *The Dream of the Rood* produces a similar effect. Here, though, the fusion of blood and water points out beyond its own immediate signification – as a manifestation of soul-rending emotion and piety – to the signification of these two substances in their scriptural and liturgical antecedents. The bloody tears in *Christ* therefore become an ultimate compunctive act, but also serve a reminder to those who have not yet wept for their souls to make haste and do so immediately. To borrow the words of the Vercelli homilist:

> Men þa leofestan, ic eow bidde and eað modlice lære, þæt ʒe wepen and forhtien on þysse med-miclan tide for eowrum synnum. Forþan ne bioð eowre tearas and eowre hreowsunga for noht ʒetealde on þære towearden worulde.[37]
>
> [Most beloved men, I ask and humbly teach you, that you weep and fear for your sins in this short space of time. Because your tears and your repentance will not avail in the next world.]

While *Christ* is what we might call 'affective', then, its affectivity is of quite a different character to that which we might traditionally associate with the term. The affectivity is directed more to evoking shame in humankind than pity, and through this emotion, experiencing compunction. While the apocalypticism of the triad is both terrifying and horrific in equal measure, this is secondary to the sorrow one ought to feel at the absence of a loved one – in this case, God. Furthermore, the suggestion that this sorrow itself may lead to salvation provides further motivation for compunction where no further motivation is necessary. So those bloody tears may seem horrific to the modern mind, but interpreted in the light of the kind of compunction that the poems attempt to evoke, it is evident that they are testament to exactly this kind of heart-wrenching, soul-rending compunction that is less reliant on eliciting fear of the terror of hell and judgement day, and more on emphasising the brutal sadness of separation from God.

If, as Williamson notes, prosopopoeia serves as a mirror in which the listener can identify himself, the use of this device in *Christ* highlights the desired compunctive state and asks the listener to measure himself against it. The deep affectivity of the outward signs of compunction, when transferred to an inanimate object, is intensified by virtue of the nature of that inanimate object. Richard C. Payne, writing on *The Dream of the Rood*, asserts that,

> when we turn to a consideration of the dreamer's reaction to the vision as it is presented in lines 13ff., we arrive at the thematic core of the poem, and we can begin to see the intended effect of the poem's eschatological locus. ... The dreamer's reaction to the vision of the cross is undoubtedly intended as a 'touchstone' of the response expected from the poems' audience.[38]

If the response of the dreamer to the vision of the Rood is a touchstone of that which is to be expected from the audience, then that of the trees in *Christ* is merely a glimmer of that which is to be expected from inanimate beings.

---

[37] 'Vercelli Homily IV', in M. Föster (ed.), *Die Vercelli-Homilien: I–VIII Homilie* (Hamburg, 1932). Cited in McEntire, p. 96.

[38] R.C. Payne, 'Convention and Originality in the Vision Framework of *The Dream of the Rood*', *Modern Philology* 73 (1976): 329–41, at 334.

Not only this, though, but the weeping trees become a metaphor for the crucifixion itself, taking on all the layers of signification bound up with arboreality in Anglo-Saxon thought, and affectively demonstrating the barbarity of the event while highlighting how it has facilitated salvation. The poem mediates between the spiritual and the material worlds in order to compel the listener to explore the Passion from a range of perspectives. Through the trees taking on human characteristics, the listener takes on the viewpoint of the anthropomorphised trees, comes to experience the Passion vicariously as a participant, and reconfigures his understanding of the psychological process of grief into a concrete, material, vivid, brutal image of bloody tears. Arner and Stegner write,

> the key innovation of *Christ III* is the implication that the pleasure derived from the act of reading is continued in the afterlife. The *Christ III* poet establishes the connection between the vision and the act of reading by presenting the Crucifixion as a spectacle occurring 'fore eagna gesyhð' (before the sight of their eyes, l. 1113); it is not simply a self-evident visual event, but one performed and dependent on the interpretation of signs. Consequently, the blessed's visual apprehension and interpretation of signs on the bodies of the damned is figured in terms of the reader's engagement with the words of a text. ... The *Christ III* poet underscores that the blessed are engaged in an ongoing, pleasurable hermeneutic process. Consequently he proposes that the blessed will continue to be readers in heaven.[39]

The text creates an ontological game, as Williamson asserts – a tree bears multiple identities from organic entity to devotional object to instrument of torture. Its tears absorb a wealth of scriptural and theological significance, and the listener, through the comparison created by the prosopopoeia of the text, is urged to hasten to define *himself* spiritually before the Day of Doom.

---

[39] T.D. Arner and P.D. Stegner, '"Of þam him aweaxeð wynsum gefea": The Voyeuristic Appeal of *Christ III*', *JEGP* 106 (2007): 428–46, at 429.

Chapter 10
Emotion and Gesture in Hroðgar's Farewell to Beowulf

Kristen Mills

When Beowulf leaves Heorot after defeating Grendel and his mother, he takes his leave of Hroðgar before returning to Hygelac's court. The king bids Beowulf farewell and gifts him with treasures, before kissing him and enfolding him in a tearful embrace:

> Gecyste þa   cyning æþelum god,
> þeoden Scyldinga   ðegn bet[e]stan
> Ond be healse genam;   hruron him tearas
> blondenfeaxum.   Him wæs bega wen
> ealdum infrodum,   oþres swiðor,
> þæt h[i]e seoðða[n no]   geseon moston,
> modige on meþle.   (W)æs him se man to þon leof
> þæt he þone breostwylm   forberan ne mehte,
> ac him on hreþre   hygebendum fæst
> æfter deorum men   dyrne langað
> born wið blode.[1]
>
> (*Beowulf*, ll. 1870–80a)

[The king kissed the good noble,
The lord of the Scyldings, the best thegn,
and took him by the neck; he shed tears,
grey-haired. There were both expectations for
the very old man, one of them stronger,
that afterward they would not have the opportunity
to see him, brave in council. That man was so dear to him,
that he could not restrain that breast-surge,
but secret longing, bound fast in his breast with mind-fetters,
burned against his blood after the dear man.]

---

[1] *Klaeber's Beowulf*, 4th edn, ed. R.D. Fulk, Robert E. Bjork, and John D. Niles (Toronto, 2008).

This scene takes place at a pivotal point in the narrative, as Beowulf, his heroic stature firmly established by his exploits at the Danish court and his youthful potential stretching before him, leaves behind the spectres of death and helplessness that have long haunted Heorot. Hroðgar's tears, his grief and his anxieties, look ahead to the ending of the poem, when the Geats mourn for Beowulf with an elaborate funeral. Here, one old man weeps for Beowulf's absence; there, an entire nation mourns his death. The poet takes eleven lines to describe Hroðgar's sorrow during the farewell scene, suggesting that his emotional state is significant. How should one read this scene? It is a commonplace of *Beowulf*-scholarship to observe that Hroðgar serves as a foil to Beowulf, and thus one's interpretation of Hroðgar's behaviour will depend largely on how one views Beowulf. In this scene Beowulf appears unmoved, his emotions opaque. All of the action, all of the feeling, belongs to Hroðgar. Such a lack of emotion on Beowulf's part may suggest a heroic stoicism, but it may also reflect the brashness of undefeated youth; he is as yet unaware of the full weight of loss and grief. Is Hroðgar's behaviour a sentimental display of weakness, indicative of an overall decline in his masculinity and his ability to rule as king, as has been suggested?[2] Or do his tears and cares fall within the range of acceptable emotional norms for a man in Anglo-Saxon culture?[3] In this chapter, I shall re-examine the farewell

---

[2] Mary Dockray-Miller has offered the most extensive recent critique along these lines. She posits that the old king's weeping is a sign of his growing weakness and effeminacy, and describes Hroðgar's decline in terms of Freudian and Lacanian psychoanalysis. She argues that 'the emotional and homoerotic nature of the farewell scene shows that the "normal" male–male relationship of the *comitatus*, with which the Danes have been having so much trouble since Grendel's coming, has been broken down to the point where Hroðgar cannot find an unambiguously masculine gesture of parting from the younger man.' (Mary Dockray-Miller, '*Beowulf*'s Tears of Fatherhood,' *Exemplaria* 10 (1998): 1–28, at 2.) According to Dockray-Miller, 'editors and critics ... have interpreted this part of the text in such a way that it glosses over the homoerotics of the scene. The emotional and physical presentation of Hroðgar's farewell underscores the fragility of Hroðgar's masculinity as he tries to assert himself as a Father figure but ends up positioning himself as an effeminate Other. The erotics in the farewell scene are intense beyond the norm of male-male social relations ...' (p. 18).

[3] In the context of a nuanced discussion on the idea of emotional restraint in Old English texts, in which he argues that stoicism was one of a range of approaches to emotional expression circulating in Anglo-Saxon England, Thomas D. Hill takes Hroðgar's tears as evidence that 'we may assume that Anglo-Saxons were free from the prejudice that it is somehow dishonourable for a man to cry' (Thomas D. Hill, 'The Unchanging Hero: A Stoic Maxim in "The Wanderer" and its Contexts', *Studies in Philology* 101 (2004): 233–49, at 239). Teresa Pároli finds the scene 'particularly moving', although she later qualifies this by observing that, while most male mourning in the poem is collective, 'only the ancient Hroðgar is allowed to indulge without shame in open and profoundly felt tears in a farewell which is a prelude to his not too distant death' (Teresa Pàroli, 'The Tears of the Heroes in Germanic Epic Poetry', in Hermann Reichert and Günter Zimmermann (eds),

scene in light of other texts where the formula of a man falling on another's neck, kissing him, and weeping occurs. By analysing the social contexts and power dynamics in a number of scenes involving gestures parallel to Hroðgar's, I shall provide a new framework for interpreting this scene. As part of my analysis, I shall address the cultural biases of previous criticism that have tended to obscure the meaning of this scene, paying attention to the manner in which Victorian and modern views on masculinity have inflected the critical dialogue on male emotions in Anglo-Saxon texts. Finally, having argued for the acceptability and masculinity of Hroðgar's gestures during the farewell scene, I shall conclude by considering the emotions that Hroðgar conceals.

A full engagement with the question of whether Hroðgar is a strong or a weak king falls beyond the scope of the present chapter;[4] while I shall argue that the farewell scene does not present Hroðgar as an emasculated figure, I believe that the poem as a whole may be read in a variety of ways to yield a number of different interpretations. The complexity of *Beowulf* defies attempts to make definitive statements about the meaning of the poem, and any interpretation seeking to be comprehensive must take into account not only the worldview of the *Beowulf*-poet, but also that of the scribes who copied the poem, that of the society depicted within the poem, and that of the Anglo-Saxon audiences of the poem from its time of composition until it passed out of circulation and comprehension. Certainly, Hroðgar's inability to protect the Danes from Grendel, his unwillingness to fight the monster himself, does not seem particularly heroic. However, is it therefore more admirable to die battling a monster, thus leaving one's people vulnerable, as Beowulf does? Is Hroðgar as heroic as Beowulf? No, but then, who is? Beowulf is singular, his strength and daring unparalleled, but surely the heroic masculinity of Beowulf is not the only masculinity esteemed by the Anglo-Saxon cultural milieu.

Despite the fact that they are only one component of a complex interaction involving gestures and emotions, Hroðgar's tears have dominated critical comment on this scene. As the study of the history of emotions has expanded in recent decades, the cultural and historical contexts of weeping have increasingly attracted attention.[5] The act of weeping 'constitutes a challenging intersection

---

Helden und Helden- sage: Otto Gschwantler zum 60. Geburtstag, Philologica Germanica 11 (Wien, 1990), pp. 233–66, at 242, 244). Thomas L. Wright concludes that the king's tears do not stem from grief; rather, they 'acknowledge, not gratitude and regret, but fellowship and the sense of destined succession' (Thomas L. Wright, 'Hrothgar's Tears', *Modern Philology* 65 (1967): 39–44, at 44).

[4] For a valuable overview of critical perspectives on Hroðgar, see Dockray-Miller, pp. 5–8.

[5] See *Crying in the Middle Ages: Tears of History*, ed. Elina Gertsman (New York, 2011); Thomas O'Loughlin and Helen Conrad-O'Briain, 'The "Baptism of Tears" in Early Anglo-Saxon Sources', *Anglo-Saxon England* 22 (1993): 65–84; Thomas M. Greene, 'The Natural

between emotion and behaviour';[6] tears are a medium by which interior emotion is rendered externally visible, a bridge between feeling and flesh, the physical distillation of intangible sentiment. Produced within and proceeding outward from the body, tears offer, or appear to offer, particular insight into the internal emotional state of the weeper. Weeping may be performed as a consequence of grief, loss, physical pain, anger, regret, or penitence, among other causes, and may be used to feign any of the above; 'weeping, after all, is a gesture, a behavioural and performative act open to manipulation.'[7]

Victorian and modern views on masculinity have influenced the critical reception and interpretation of male tears in the corpus of Old English literature; examples of weeping men are often ignored or viewed as aberrant, while instances of women's weeping are taken as normative behaviour. The amount of scholarly attention paid to the unnamed woman who mourns at Beowulf's funeral exemplifies this tendency. As Helen Bennett observes, the 'passage ... does not actually exist', allowing 'patriarchal scholars' 'to insert their own inverted reflection to fulfill the supposed desire of the text while confirming their own ideologies'.[8] Robin Norris has considered the mourning for Beowulf's death as a site of interest not only for what it suggests about the associations between grief and gender in *Beowulf*, but also for what it reveals about the tendency of scholars to neglect accounts of male grief in the poem, while simultaneously lavishing attention upon the one woman depicted mourning the hero. The female lamenter dominates the discussion of Beowulf's funeral rites, but for the most part, the men who mourn for their dead king have been ignored.[9] Despite Bennett's and Norris's powerful critiques of the emphasis placed on mourning women in Anglo-Saxon texts, the notion that men who adhered to the 'heroic code' were not permitted to openly express grief retains currency. In a recent discussion of weeping in Anglo-Saxon texts, Tracey-Anne Cooper argues that 'the pagan-themed poems anachronistically gender the shedding of tears, which

---

Tears of Epic', in Margaret Beissinger, Jane Tylus, and Susanne Wofford (eds), *Epic Traditions in the Contemporary World: The Poetics of Community* (Berkeley, 1999), pp. 189–202; Tom Lutz, *Crying: The Natural and Cultural History of Tears* (New York, 1999); Andrew Lynch, '"Now, Fye on Youre Wepynge!": Tears in Medieval English Romance', *Parergon* 9/1 (1991): 43–62; Sandra J. McEntire, *The Doctrine of Compunction in Medieval England: Holy Tears* (Lewiston, NY, 1991); Piroska Nagy, *Le don des larmes au Moyen Age. Un instrument spirituel en quête d'institution, Ve–XIIIe siècle* (Paris, 2000).

[6] Lyn A. Blanchfield, 'Prolegomenon: Considerations of Weeping and Sincerity in the Middle Ages', in Gertsman (ed.), *Crying in the Middle Ages*, pp. xxi–xxx, at xxi.

[7] Blanchfield, p. xxii.

[8] Helen Bennett, 'The Female Mourner at Beowulf's Funeral: Filling in the Blanks / Hearing the Spaces', *Exemplaria* 4 (1992): 35–50 at 35.

[9] Robin Norris, 'Deathbed Confessors: Mourning and Genre in Anglo-Saxon Hagiography' (PhD diss., University of Toronto, 2003), pp. 5–10.

was especially disdained in men who must keep their emotions inside, and was ritualized in women for the purposes of funeral lamentation.'[10] Cooper supports this assertion by citing the prohibitions on speaking one's mind in ll. 1–16 of *The Wanderer*, and with two instances in *Beowulf* where grief is described as contained, within the *mod* and *sefa*.[11] Based on this evidence, she concludes that 'men must keep their grief inside, but women, in the heroic culture described in *Beowulf*, have more opportunity to mourn outwardly' during funerary rituals.[12] In making this argument, Cooper leaves out a number of men who publicly grieve for Beowulf's death: Beowulf's followers observe his corpse 'wollenteare' ('with welling tears', l. 3032), and the roaring fire is 'wope bewunden' ('wound about with weeping', l. 3146) with the tears of those watching the pyre. In a surprising omission, Cooper also neglects to acknowledge or discuss Hroðgar's tears at Beowulf's departure.

Heroic poetry offers admittedly few parallels to the farewell scene in *Beowulf*. On the difficulties of interpreting this scene, John M. Hill observes that '[w]e have so little heroic poetry outside of *Beowulf* that what is in *Beowulf* may well reflect the normative possibilities of emotion in heroic life literarily rendered ... Still, the combination of gesture and intense emotion is unusual in this passage. How is it presented to us and what can we say about its inspiriting causes?'[13] *The Wanderer* offers a close, but not exact, parallel, when the narrator,

> þinceð him on mode　　þæt he his mondryhten
> clyppe ond cysse,　　ond on cneo lecge
> honda ond heafod.[14]
>
> (*The Wanderer*, ll. 41–43a)

[imagines that he embraces and kisses his lord, and lays his hand and head on his knee.]

The fact that the narrator of the poem chooses *this* scene as a representation of an ideal lord–retainer relationship suggests its significance: the tableau of the kiss,

---

[10] Tracey-Anne Cooper, 'The Shedding of Tears in Late Anglo-Saxon England', in Gertsman (ed.), *Crying in the Middle Ages*, pp. 175–92 at 176.

[11] Cooper, p. 176. Cooper, using Sidney A.J. Bradley's translation in his *Anglo-Saxon Poetry* (London, 1995), takes *sefa* in l. 49 as 'spirit', *mod* in l. 50 as 'heart', *hreðerbealo* as 'affliction of spirit', and *sefan* in l. 1342 as 'heart'. See Leslie Lockett, *Anglo-Saxon Psychologies in the Vernacular and Latin Traditions* (Toronto, 2011), pp. 33–41, for an insightful discussion of Old English vocabulary for the mind.

[12] Cooper, p. 177.

[13] John M. Hill, *The Narrative Pulse of Beowulf* (Toronto, 2008), p. 60.

[14] George Phillip Krapp and Elliot Van Kirk Dobbie (eds), *The Exeter Book*, ASPR 3 (New York, 1936).

the embrace, and the placing of hand and head on the lord's knee encapsulates the essence of belonging in a community for the lonely exile. For a moment he visits the home that survives only in memory, before he is reawakened to the loneliness of the present, where such joys are absent. In a footnote, Mary Dockray-Miller briefly entertains, but ultimately dismisses as irrelevant, this scene as a possible parallel for *Beowulf*'s farewell scene: 'one possible exception could be the fantasy of the narrator of *The Wanderer*, who imagines laying his head in his lord's lap (ll. 41–4); this emotionally charged moment, however, exists only in the narrator's mind, while the farewell scene occurs within the textual "reality" of *Beowulf*.'[15] This 'fantasy' involves more intimate physical contact than Dockray-Miller's summation of it would indicate, as she omits the fact that he *clyppe ond cysse* his lord before he lays both his head and his hand in the lord's lap in her discussion. Despite the degree of physical intimacy in *The Wanderer*, there is no suggestion that the author viewed this behaviour as aberrant. If the author found such behaviour shameful or effeminizing, he would have chosen a different range of gestures to illustrate the bond between lord and retainer. The poet of *The Wanderer*, like the *Beowulf*-poet, intends to portray a scene of great emotion, but this does not mean that the intensity of the feeling is inappropriate, or the gestures outside the standards of masculine behaviour. Still, *The Wanderer* provides only a partial parallel to *Beowulf*. The gestures overlap but are not identical, and there is no context through which one may interpret the scene: does the narrator imagine a greeting, a farewell, a pledge of loyalty, or some other ritual? What the audience glimpses through the narrator's description is undoubtedly meaningful, but its meaning is obscured.

If one looks outside the corpus of Old English heroic verse, the combination of weeping, embracing, and kissing, while not widespread in Anglo-Saxon texts, is not unique to *Beowulf*. In a recent examination of the portrayal of Joseph's weeping in the Old English *Heptateuch*, Jonathan Wilcox draws attention to the close parallels between the weeping of Hroðgar and Joseph.[16] Before considering Wilcox's interpretation, it will be helpful to cite the relevant portion of the Old English text, which relates that, when Joseph is reunited with his brothers in Egypt, 'he clypte hira ælcne and cyste hig and weop' (Gen. 45:15).[17] This corresponds to 'Osculatusque est Ioseph omnes fratres suos et ploravit super

---

[15] Dockray-Miller, p. 19.

[16] Jonathan Wilcox, 'A Place to Weep: Joseph in the Beer-Room and Anglo-Saxon Gestures of Emotion', in Stuart McWilliams (ed.), *Saints and Scholars: New Perspectives on Anglo-Saxon Literature and Culture in Honour of Hugh Magennis* (Cambridge, 2012), pp. 14–32. I am indebted to Jonathan Wilcox for providing me with a copy of his article.

[17] 'He embraced each of them, and kissed them and wept.' *The Old English Heptateuch and Ælfric's Libellus de Veteri Testamento et Novo*, I, *Introduction and Text*, ed. Richard Marsden, EETS o.s. 330 (Oxford, 2008), p. 80.

singulos'[18] in the Vulgate. As Wilcox points out, the Old English translations omit verse 14, which reads, 'amplexatus recidisset in collum Beniamin fratris sui flevit illo quoque flente similiter super collum eius.'[19] Wilcox suggests several possible reasons for the omission: the translator may be 'downplaying ... so much weeping and embracing in a male authority figure'; joyful weeping may 'be too much for an Anglo-Saxon sense of decorum'; or there may be 'something too vulnerable in the full range of gestures from the Vulgate scene that the translator wanted to shield his clearly powerful protagonist from.'[20] Wilcox's main focus throughout is on the version of the narrative preserved in Cambridge, Corpus Christi College, MS 201, which has several significant variations from the other Old English translations, chief of which is the alteration of the location of an earlier bout of weeping when Joseph first sees his favourite brother, Benjamin, who does not recognize him. While the Vulgate and one of the Old English versions have Joseph retreat to his own chamber to weep, in CCCC 201 Joseph goes to the *beorclyfa*, 'beer-room,' to weep in private.[21] The weeping in the beer-room is one of several occasions of weeping discussed by Wilcox. Space does not permit a full examination of Wilcox's nuanced examination of the portrayals of public and private weeping in the narrative of Joseph in the present chapter; thus I shall confine my discussion to his interpretation of the weeping and embracing that occurs when Joseph reveals his identity to his brothers.

Wilcox suggests reading Joseph's reunion with his brothers alongside Beowulf's departure from Heorot. He argues that 'the climactic gestures in the "Story of Joseph" provide an analogous emotional highpoint' to Hroðgar's parting from Beowulf, and suggests that 'shared weeping' encouraged communal bonds.[22] In his conclusion, Wilcox proposes that,

> Male weeping by an admired figure of authority is a gesture reclaimed through this biblical narrative. At its most meaningful, the weeping is suppressed but builds up in scenes of tension where recognition and affection is also suppressed but anticipating an outlet. When the weeping bursts forth it is multi-valenced, suggesting, among other things, joy in the relief of finally acknowledging intense emotions and the creation of community among those who share the weeping. Such a handling of weeping is thinkable but not common in more clearly native Old English heroic literature, as is seen in the tears of Hroðgar and the interpretative conundrum they present to critics.[23]

---

[18] 'And Joseph kissed all of his brothers, and wept upon each of them.' All quotations from the Vulgate are cited by chapter and verse from the *Biblia Sacra iuxta Vulgatam Versionem*, ed. Robertus Weber, 2 vols (Stuttgart, 1969).

[19] 'Falling upon the neck of his brother Benjamin, he embraced him and wept, and he (Benjamin) likewise wept upon his neck.'

[20] Wilcox, pp. 29–30.

[21] Ibid., p. 23.

[22] Ibid., p. 30.

[23] Ibid., p. 31.

Wilcox points out that Joseph is 'marked as a virile and desirable subject' in the narrative,[24] bestowed with 'confident masculine power.'[25] Wilcox's analysis of the portrayal of Joseph in these texts suggests an alternative model for considering Hroðgar's characterization in *Beowulf*. Once one ceases to assume that weeping, kissing, and embracing were a *de facto* sign of weakness in Anglo-Saxon England, or in the world of Old English heroic poetry, what evidence is there that they were not considered an acceptable form of expression? Or, to approach the problem from another direction, is there evidence, aside from the Joseph-narrative, that the performance of such gestures by men would have been considered acceptable behaviour?

Besides the account of Joseph's reunion with his father and brothers, the formula of a man falling on another's neck, kissing him, and weeping occurs elsewhere in the Bible. When Jacob is reunited with his brother Esau, 'currens itaque Esau obviam fratri suo amplexatus est eum stringensque collum et osculans flevit' (Gen 22:4).[26] The Old English translation of Jacob's meeting with Esau retains the embrace and kiss, but omits the weeping: 'Esau arn ongen his broþur and clipte hine and cyste hine' (Gen. 33:4).[27] In the Book of Tobit, when Raguhel is informed that Tobias is his kinsman, 'cum lacrimis osculatus est eum et plorans super collum eius' (Tob. 7:6).[28]

The Old English version of the legend of St. Eustace, based on the Latin *Passio Sancti Eustachii*, also uses this formula or variants of it several times.[29] Eustace, his wife, and their two sons were all separated when the sons were in infancy. The sons meet later as adults, unaware of their relationship. The older son tells the tale of his separation from his family to his brother, who realizes their kinship: 'þa aras he and gelæhte hine be þam swuran, and cyste and clypte, and sæde, "þurh þone God þe Cristene wurðað, ic eom þin broðor be þire (sic) tale"'.[30] Soon after this their mother is reunited with their father, who 'beheold

---

[24] Ibid., p. 24.
[25] Ibid., p. 25.
[26] 'And then Esau, running to meet his brother, embraced him and gripped his neck and, kissing him, wept.'
[27] 'Esau met his brother and embraced him and kissed him.' Marsden (ed.), p. 62.
[28] 'Tearfully he kissed him and wept upon his neck.'
[29] Hugh Magennis discusses the Latin sources for the Old English Life of St Eustace in 'On the Sources of Non-Ælfrician Lives in the Old English *Lives of Saints*, with Reference to the Cotton-Corpus Legendary', *Notes and Queries* 230 (1985): 292–9. For a wide-ranging discussion of the Eustace legend and analogues, see Gordon Hall Gerould, 'Forerunners, Congeners, and Derivatives of the Eustace Legend', *PMLA* 19 (1904): 335–448.
[30] 'Then he arose and caught him by the neck, and kissed and embraced him, and said, "By the God whom Christians worship I am thy brother by thy tale."' *Ælfric's Lives of Saints*, ed. Walter W. Skeat, EETS o.s. 76, 82, 94, 114, 4 parts in 2 vols (Oxford, 1881–1900), II, pp. 210–11.

… hi and gecneow hi be hyre wlite, and for micelre blisse weop and hi cyste'.[31] Eustace's wife had overheard their sons speaking of their separation, and told Eustace that she suspected they were their children. Eustace summons the youths and they tell their tale, 'And he þa gecneow þæt hi his suna wæron, and hi to him genam, and clypte and cyste'.[32] The Old English *Apollonius of Tyre* contains a similar reunion scene, although there is no mention of kissing. When Apollonius is reunited with his wife, whom he has long thought dead, she 'up aras and hine ymbclypte'.[33] Apollonius does not recognize her and pushes her away, causing her to declare her identity 'mid wope' ('with weeping').[34] Their daughter is presented to her, and 'hig weopon ða ealle'.[35]

A passage from the eleventh-century *Encomium Emmae Reginae* also depicts a family reunion that features embracing, weeping, and kissing. After the death of Sveinn Forkbeard, king of Denmark and conqueror of England, his son Knútr, whom he had intended to succeed him as ruler of England, is driven from the island. Sveinn's other son, Haraldr, now rules in Denmark, and it is to his brother's court that Knútr flees. When Haraldr learns of his brother's approach, he sends an entourage to escort him: 'a latere regis milites diriguntur delecti, paratique in occursum transmittuntur equi. Fraternus siquidem amor fratris eum monebat inseruire decori'.[36] The Encomiast (literally) frames the brothers' meeting, as they are reunited on the threshold of Haraldr's court: 'Cumque tandem honorifice, utpote regem decet, fraterna subintraret limina, frater ipse in primo aditu occurrit'.[37] Each brother advances with care towards the other. Knútr is respectful in his entrance (*honorifice*), but his reserve dissolves as Haraldr meets him at the threshold. The Encomiast may have chosen this particular location to show that the brothers meet as equals: Knútr is not a supplicant, but a ruler in his own right, albeit temporarily dispossessed of his kingdom. Haraldr does not require his brother to formally approach him, and I think it would not be amiss

---

[31] 'beheld her and recognised her by her beauty, and for great bliss wept and kissed her'. Ibid., II, pp. 212–13.

[32] 'And he then knew that they were his sons, and took them to him, and embraced and kissed them.' Ibid.

[33] 'She rose up and embraced him.' *The Old English Apollonius of Tyre*, ed. Peter Goolden (Oxford, 1958), p. 38. The Latin has 'levavit … et rapuit eum in amplexu', p. 39.

[34] Goolden (ed.), p. 38. The Latin is 'cum lacrimis voce', p. 39.

[35] 'They all wept.' Ibid., p. 38. The Latin has 'Et flebant ad invicem omnes', p. 39.

[36] 'Chosen soldiers were sent from attendance on the king, and horses ready for use were dispatched to meet him, for brotherly love prompted the king to regard the dignity of his brother.' *Encomium Emmae Reginae*, ed. and trans. Alistair Campbell (Cambridge, 1998), p. 16; Campbell's translation, p. 17.

[37] 'When at length Knútr, exhibiting the respect due to a king, entered his brother's doors, his brother himself met him at the very entrance', ibid.; Campbell's translation, ibid.

to read this as arising from eagerness to see his brother. Strong fraternal affection is amply evidenced by what follows: 'mutuoque brachiorum conexione pressis corporibus sibi inuicem pia quam saepe defigunt oscula. Collum utriusque partim pro amore partimque pro patris morte fusae madefecere lacrimae; quibus uix extinctis, mutuo refocillantur affamine'.[38] Cooper points out that the Encomiast presents this emotional greeting in a positive light: 'these were battle-hardened and often ruthless men, but there was no apparent censure of their tearful display.'[39] The Encomiast, Cooper suggests, 'is certainly not trying to evoke feeling of embarrassment or disdain in his audience, nor does it seem that the kings expect any kind of rebuke for their public lachrymation. Their tears do not unman them: they feel and they weep without public shame or cultural emasculation.'[40] Of course, given that Knútr later marries the eponymous Emma who commissioned the *Encomium*, it would have been extremely impolitic for the Encomiast to portray him in a negative fashion.

In none of the examples above is there any suggestion of abnormality or effeminacy when men embrace, kiss, and weep during a reunion. On the contrary, it seems to indicate high levels of affection, and the majority of the instances are between men. It is frequently, though not always, the case in these reunions that the man who does the embracing, kissing, and weeping is the individual with a higher social status. When Joseph is reunited with his brothers and his father, he has risen high in the Egyptian court, and they are destitute foreigners seeking aid. Eustace, as father, husband, and military officer, is of greater status in relation to his wife and sons. In all the examples, the reunion scene takes place after much tribulation, in some cases after decades of suffering and separation. Deliverance from woeful circumstances and the re-establishment of kinship bonds mark these scenes.

Hroðgar's initiation of physical intimacy need not be interpreted as an indication of weakness next to the taciturn Beowulf, but can be read as a sign of his authority in Heorot: he is the one determining how the social ritual of their relationship will be played out in public. Admittedly, Beowulf's lack of response may pose a problem for this interpretation. It is possible that the poet, who was focused far more on Hroðgar's actions and emotional state during the farewell scene, simply did not feel that Beowulf's response was worthy of note, or perhaps he thought that the hero's reciprocation of the gestures was assumed. Nonetheless, the range of close parallels strongly indicates that Hroðgar's actions

---

[38] 'And they, with their bodies mutually locked in an embrace, impressed tender kisses upon each other many times. Tears shed partly for love, and partly for their father's death moistened the neck of each, and when these were scarcely dry, the exchange of words brought on more', ibid.; Campbell's translation, ibid.

[39] Cooper, p. 177.

[40] Ibid.

at Beowulf's departure did not condemn the king as a man whose masculinity was in decline.

There is, however, one point on which Hroðgar's farewell to Beowulf differs markedly from the majority of the parallels cited above: all feature joyful greetings between kin, the majority of whom never expected to be reunited, either because of distance, exile, or presumed death. The men of the Old Testament shed tears of joy as they embrace brothers, sons, fathers, and cousins; Apollonius and Eustace weep over long-lost wives and children; Knútr and Haraldr combine the pleasure of reunion with the pain of a father's death. In contrast, Hroðgar's tears are tears of sorrow at Beowulf's departure. If the poet or the poem's audience would have been familiar with this trope from these or other examples, its occurrence not at the time of Beowulf's arrival, but at his departure, might have added extra poignancy to the scene.

I have found one Biblical parallel that depicts weeping, embracing, and kissing at a farewell. When travelling through Asia Minor, the Apostle Paul hopes to return to Jerusalem by Pentecost, and thus decides to bypass Ephesus. Stopping in Miletus, he sends for the church elders of Ephesus, whom he informs of his plans. Paul's announcement of his immediate departure to Jerusalem is met with great sorrow by the Ephesian clergy: 'magnus autem fletus factus est omnium et procumbentes super collum Pauli osculabantur eum. Dolentes maxime in verbo quo dixerat quoniam amplius faciem eius non essent visuri et deducebant eum ad navem' (Acts 20:37–8).[41] There are several striking parallels between this scene in the Book of Acts and the farewell scene in *Beowulf*. Like Beowulf, Paul is setting out on a sea voyage, leaving behind a group whom he has aided and who hold him in great esteem. Like Hroðgar, the elders weep, embrace, and kiss the traveller. Hroðgar's fear that he will not see Beowulf again is paralleled by the Ephesian clergy's sorrow that they will not look upon Paul's countenance in the future. Unlike the clergy and Hroðgar, Paul and Beowulf seem unmoved by sorrow. The clergy, while grieved by Paul's impending absence, are not portrayed as weak. As in the sources discussed above, the kissing, embracing, and weeping are indications of affection.

An argument could be made that these sources – religious, often translations of Latin if not composed in Latin – offer an imperfect means of assessing emotional norms and expectations for Old English 'heroic' poetry. This would not be an invalid criticism, but the dearth of Old English poetry that resembles *Beowulf* in length or subject matter, and the small corpus of extant Old English poetry that is secular and heroic, makes it impossible to compare like with like. Like its hero, *Beowulf* is *sui generis*. However, the copy of *Beowulf* that survives

---

[41] 'A great weeping was made by all and, falling upon Paul's neck, they kissed him. They were greatly sorrowful for the statement he had made, that they would not see his face again, and they led him to the ship.'

dates from the late Anglo-Saxon period, and is found in a manuscript containing Old English translations of Latin texts. For the compilers of the manuscript, the distinct genres and origins of the texts included within seem to have offered no great conceptual difficulty, and it does a disservice to imagine that an Anglo-Saxon audience would have been unable to draw meaningful connections between Latin and Old English texts.

The assumption that Hroðgar's behaviour during the farewell scene was somehow 'unmanly' is further undermined by the fact that he does successfully conceal some aspects of his emotional state. If he were at the mercy of his emotions, unable to hold back effeminate tears or resist unmanly embraces, would he not also be unable to keep his *dyrne langað* safely tethered within his breast? Leslie Lockett interprets this passage in light of the 'hydraulic model' of the mind, which she convincingly argues underlies many of the descriptions of the mind in Anglo-Saxon texts. Lockett acknowledges that the *breostwylm* that Hroðgar *forberan ne mehte* could refer to the tears he shed, but points out that this contradicts the next lines, which state that Hroðgar bound his *dyrne langað* in his breast, thus concealing his emotion.[42] Wright also found this contradiction puzzling, and attempted to solve it by arguing that the accepted understanding of the syntax was incorrect.[43] Lockett takes a simpler approach. She translates *breostwylm* literally, as 'boiling in the breast', and interprets the line to mean that Hroðgar cannot prevent this seething brought on by his emotions, but he does not openly display it.[44]

This distinction is intriguing for the interpretation of the emotions in this scene, as it equates the *langað* with the emotion causing the *breostwylm*, and suggests that the emotion causing the tears is separate from that which causes the *breostwylm*. I find Lockett's interpretation of the lines persuasive; however, it is also possible to understand the *breostwylm* as distinct from the *dyrne langað*, so that, while the *breostwylm* is unrestrained, either within the chest, in the form of

---

[42] Lockett, p. 83.

[43] Wright is troubled by *dyrne* in l. 1879, which is usually taken as an adjective modifying *langað*. Wright asks how *dyrne* can mean hidden, mysterious, or dark in this line, when Hroðgar's 'tears hardly leave his affection for Beowulf either secret or hidden?' (Wright, p. 42). He attempts to solve this issue by taking *dyrne* as an adverb modifying *langað*, which Wright argues is not a noun but 'probably an inflected form of a verb that means "to belong to", "to be proper to", to befit"', even though such a verb is otherwise unattested. He translates *dyrne* as '"inwardly" or "deeply" or even "uniquely and specially"' (p. 42). He renders the final two lines of this passage as 'in the custom that belongs to dear men, / as a warrior of the same blood' (p. 41). The most recent editors of Klaeber's *Beowulf* uphold the traditional emendation of *beorn* to *born*, and find that Wright's rejection of the emendation, along with his reading of *langað* as a verb, 'makes for a strained interpretation of **wið blode**' (Fulk, Bjork, and Niles, p. 221, note on l. 1880).

[44] Lockett, p. 83.

emotion, or without, in the form the tears, the *langað* remained safely tethered. In this reading, the *breostwylm* may refer back to the weeping, but may also refer to Hroðgar's expectation that he will never meet Beowulf again (the statement of which precedes the reference to the *breostwylm* in the text). It would also be possible to read Hroðgar's concern that he will not see Beowulf again as the cause of his tears, as the cause of the *breostwylm*, or as the cause of both.

I propose that the poet is depicting Hroðgar as experiencing several intersecting emotions in this passage: sorrow at Beowulf's departure, which causes him to weep and embrace the hero; fear that they will not meet again; strong affection (*Wæs him se man to þon leof*), causing the *breostwylm*; and *langað* for Beowulf, which he confines within his breast. David Clark suggests that the *dyrne langað* is 'implicitly that the hero remain as his son',[45] a suggestion that strikes me as highly plausible, and would fit neatly with the pattern of fathers weeping, kissing, and embracing sons given above. Both Hroðgar's sorrow that Beowulf is leaving and his concern that they will not meet again must be connected to his strong affection for the younger man, and this affection could contribute to his desire that Beowulf take on a filial role.

This complex interplay of feelings in the farewell scene indicates an appreciation on the part of the poet and audience for the intricacies of emotional states. If *Beowulf* is structured like a diptych, as some have argued,[46] then the farewell scene is carefully placed at the hinge. At a joyous moment in the poem, where optimism, briefly, holds sway, the poem lingers on Hroðgar's response to loss. His grief subtly connects this moment to other moments where the poet articulates death and loss more clearly: the funerals of Scyld Scefing, Hildeburh's male kin, and Beowulf; the 'Lay of the Last Survivor'; the deaths of Hreðel's son and Hreðel himself; the sorrowing lament of the old man whose son is hanged. Even at the outset of Beowulf's triumphal return to his homeland, the poem is inscribed with an awareness of loss. Hroðgar's sorrow during the farewell scene is not the passive, helpless grief he felt at Æschere's death; it is decorous, restrained. He is in control, publicly performing the emotions he wishes to display, while hiding the emotions he prefers not to reveal. This does not suggest weakness and decline. By assigning this set of gestures to Hroðgar, the poet aligns him with patriarchs, saints, and exiles, strong figures that endured suffering and were delivered by divine will. Had the poet's intent been to depict Hroðgar as a weak king, he need not have sketched such an intricate portrait of competing – even conflicting – emotions and desires.

---

[45] David Clark, *Between Medieval Men: Male Friendship and Desire in Early Medieval English Literature* (Oxford, 2009), p. 137.

[46] J.R.R. Tolkien, 'Beowulf: The Monsters and the Critics', *Proceedings of the British Academy* 22 (1936): 245–95 at 271–2; Charles Donahue, '*Beowulf* and Christian Tradition: A Reconsideration from a Celtic Stance', *Traditio* 21 (1965): 55–116, at 86.

Chapter 11

Ne Sorga: Grief and Revenge in *Beowulf*

Erin Sebo

The idea for this chapter first came from reading Jurasinski's recent work on legal history and Old English literature. In his stimulating monograph, *Ancestral Privileges*, he examines how contemporary assumptions coloured the scholarship of early Anglo-Saxonists and how this continues to affect the scholarly tradition. In particular, he devotes a chapter of the book to tracing the origin of the view (held first by nineteenth-century historians and then by literary scholars) that vengeance was a 'sacred duty'[1] in Germanic cultures, and he suggests that, while honour is clearly a central element of these cultures, its importance has, at times, been over-stated.[2] Of particular interest to us here, he writes extensively on the Hrethel episode, attempting to find a definite legal precedent for the poet's assertion that the killing of the king's son, Herebeald, is a 'feohleas gefeoht' (l. 2441).[3] Significantly, he claims, 'it might be said that the Hrethel episode is one of the few portions of *Beowulf* whose standard interpretation is ultimately derived from legal-historical and not literary studies.'[4] And yet, as recent scholars such as John M. Hill, Paul Hyams, and Gale Owen-Crocker have demonstrated, Anglo-Saxon revenge culture cannot be understood exclusively in terms of what Day calls 'the economy of honour'.[5] Hyams notes that 'the actors, including bystanders, always have at their disposal more than one choice of how to respond,'[6] while Hill notes the profoundly emotional nature of the drive for vengeance when he describes Beowulf

---

[1] S. Jurasinski, *Ancestral Privileges:* Beowulf, *Law, and the Making of Germanic Antiquity* (Morgantown, WV, 2006), p. 97.

[2] Ibid., p. 90. Moreover, it has been an influential body of scholarship. Jurasinski notes that 'Strafrecht de Isländersagas (1911) – a major influence on the work of William Ian Miller – shows its deep indebtedness to the tradition originated by Wilda' in its assessment of feud and revenge in Germanic societies (p. 98).

[3] '... conflict without compensation'.

[4] Ibid., p. 115.

[5] D. Day, '*Hwanan sio fæhð aras*: Defining the Feud in *Beowulf*', *Philological Quarterly* 78 (1999): 77–96, at 77.

[6] P. Hyams, 'Was there Really Such a Thing as Feud in the High Middle Ages?' in S. Troop and P. Hyams (eds), *Vengeance in the Middle Ages: Emotion, Religion and Feud* (Farnham, 2010), pp. 151–76, at 153.

as 'grief-enraged'.[7] So, here I want to leave to one side the question of the role of honour in revenge and focus on the role played by grief. In particular, I shall explore the observation made by Owen-Crocker that King Hrethel, as the father of both the killer and the slain, cannot take revenge and that, 'deprived of his heroic role of avenger, can only die of grief.'[8] I make my study through the examples of four grieving figures: Hrothgar, Hrethel, the unnamed thief's father, and finally, Grendel's mother. These four have in common that their grief is extreme, and that the death that provokes it is in some way unexpected and therefore (at least from the perspective of the victims' loved ones) cruel and unusual. Their grievances are personal.

Recent scholarship on revenge culture has stressed the importance of the distinction between individual, personal grievances and group grievances against 'national enemies'[9] born out of conflicts between kingdoms, tribes, or peoples,[10] so I have chosen examples where the conflict does not have a political dimension. Further, scholars of revenge culture such as Hudson and Halsall have stressed that the concept of feud[11] may be used cynically under certain circumstances. Hudson notes that it may act as a 'legitimizing narrative',[12] while Halsall comments that some 'feuds are actually periodically reinvented to justify discrete acts of violence.'[13] So, in focusing on these four, I have chosen examples in which the mourner suffered a profound personal loss. Finally, and perhaps most significantly in terms of Owen-Crocker's comment on the consequences of being unable to assume the role of avenger, two of the four are able to exact revenge while two are not. This allows for an exploration of the emotional effect of vengeance, at least as it is depicted in a literary text. For, while literature is not necessarily an indicator of reality, it is often an indicator of cultural assumptions. Narratives express a stylised and, in the case of heroic figures, idealised version of human behaviour, but not one beyond the reach of our understanding. That Anglo-Saxon kings had their family trees interwoven with mythic narrative, that *Beowulf* itself freely entwines historical with mythic figures, or that Hrothgar's

---

[7] J.M. Hill, *The Narrative Pulse of Beowulf* (Toronto, 2008), pp. 79, 86.

[8] G. Owen-Crocker, *The Four Funerals of Beowulf* (Manchester, 2000), p. 224.

[9] Ibid.

[10] See J. Hudson, 'Feud, Vengeance and Violence in England from the Tenth to the Twelfth Centuries', in B. Tuten and T. Billado (eds), *Feud, Violence and Practice: Essays in Medieval Studies in Honour of Stephen D. White* (Burlington, VT, 2010), pp. 29–54, and G. Halsall, 'Violence and Society in the Early Medieval West: an Introduction', in G. Halsall (ed.), *Violence and Society in the Early Medieval West* (Woodbridge, 1998), pp. 1–45.

[11] As Day demonstrates, it is not entirely clear what the Anglo-Saxons meant by *fæhðe* except that it almost certainly does not coincide perfectly with modern understandings of 'feud'. See Day, '*Hwanan sio fæhð aras*'. Indeed, Hyams suggests that feud was not a rigid or precisely defined concept and further that 'words like *fæhðe* often take on a quite general meaning of conflict with no evident limitation to any particular kinds of situation.' Hyams, p. 167.

[12] Hudson, p. 33.

[13] Halsall, p. 20.

bard compares Beowulf to Sigemund are not simply examples of glorification. They also suggest that the Anglo-Saxons compared themselves and their actions with literary models to which they aspired.

I begin with Hrothgar and his reaction to the death of his friend, Æschere. In a narrative that has already told of so many deaths and murders, Hrothgar's extraordinary outpouring of grief arrests the poem. Æschere's death comes the night after Grendel has eaten one of Beowulf's men, Hondscio, who is unmourned and unmentioned by either his Geatish companions or his Danish hosts. Indeed, it is only when Beowulf has returned home and is retelling the story to Hygelac that Hondscio is referred to by name, and even then only once. To add insult to (fatal) injury, when Beowulf is eventually confronted with the corpse of Hondscio's killer and is seized with anger and lust for revenge, the poet enumerates the crimes for which Beowulf wishes to take vengeance on Grendel but, startlingly, the death of Hondscio – a member of his own war band – is not amongst them.[14] Hrothgar's consuming, passionate grief, then, stands in stark contrast to Beowulf's emotional reaction to the death of his warrior. Despite the sorrows Hrothgar has suffered over the years at Grendel's hands, Beowulf says that Æschere's death:

> ... wæs Hroðgare   hreowa tornost
> þara þe leodfruman   lange begeate.
> (ll. 2129–30)[15]

[... was for Hrothgar the cruellest grief that the people's king had long received.]

In his distress, Hrothgar speaks to Beowulf in what is in part a eulogy for his friend and in part a call for vengeance. The speech extends over sixty lines. It charts a progression from Hrothgar's kingly anger at the violence against his peace, people, and power, to his personal grief, and finally to a desire for vengeance. Earlier raids by Grendel on Heorot are described in terms of an almost existential wound to the humanity and community of the Danes and Hrothgar's speech begins by locating Æschere's death in that sorrow:

>   Sorh is geniwod
> Denigea leodum: dead is Æschere.
> (ll. 1322–3)

[Sorrow is renewed for the Danish people: Æschere is dead]

---

[14] This takes place at lines 1576–84. For a fuller discussion of this passage, see below.

[15] All quotations from *Beowulf* are taken from *Klaeber's Beowulf and the Fight at Finnsburg*, 4th edn, ed. R.D. Fulk, Robert E. Bjork, and John D. Niles (Toronto, 2008). All translations are my own.

However, it is not only a grief to the Danish people. Hrothgar's grief is personal. He recounts his friendship with Æschere:

> Yrmenlafes   yldra broþor,
> min runwita   ond min rædbora,
> eaxlgestealla   ðonne we on orlege
> hafelan weredon,   þonne hniton feþan,
> eoferas cnysedan.   Swylc scolde eorl wesan,
> æþeling ærgod   swylc Æschere wæs.
>   (ll. 1325–9)

[Yrmenlaf's elder brother, my confidante and my counsellor, my shoulder-companion when we shielded our heads in battle, when war-bands clashed, striking the boar crests. So a warrior should be – a prince proved worthy – so Æschere was.]

For the rest of the speech, the next thirty-four lines, Hrothgar's mind is bent solely on revenge and he gives Beowulf as much information as he can to assist with the tracking and killing of Grendel's mother.

At the end of his outpouring of grief he tells Beowulf, 'nu is se ræd gelang / eft æt þe anum' (ll. 1376b–7a),[16] and Beowulf famously responds:

> Ne sorga, snotor guma.   Selre bið æghwæm
> þæt he his freond wrece,   þonne he fela murne.
>   (ll. 1385–7)

[Do not grieve wise man! Better be it that each man avenges his friend than that he mourns much.]

This utterance, which is phrased like a maxim, implies that vengeance assuages grief – an idea to which Beowulf returns at the end of his speech where, having committed himself to avenge Æschere for Hrothgar, Beowulf asks the king to be patient in his misery and grant him the time he requires to remedy the situation and exact revenge:

> Ðys dogor þu   geþyld hafa
> weana gehwylces,   swa ic þe wene to.
>   (ll. 1395–6)

[This day you must have patience in each of the woes, as I expect you to.]

---

[16] 'Now the remedy rests once more with you alone.'

As Hill notes, the very prospect of vengeance has an immediate effect:[17] the promise alone appears to ease Hrothgar's grief and he leaps up ('ahleop', l. 1397) at Beowulf's words. Here, as elsewhere in the poem, action proves 'an alternative to the prison of lament'.[18] Once Beowulf has taken revenge, Hrothgar's grief seems resolved. There is no further mention of Æschere and no further mourning. Moreover, though a banquet held in celebration of Beowulf's victory is necessarily a joyous occasion, it is noticeable that Hrothgar seems quite free of sadness. For, as we shall see, grief in *Beowulf* is an emotion that has the power to dominate the mourner's mind to the exclusion of all else; those in its grasp seem both unable and unwilling to hide their distress, even when they are given no avenue for expressing it.

This is the situation of King Hrethel. In contrast to Hrothgar, he dies of his grief. For, unlike those able to take vengeance, his grief is all-encompassing, all-consuming, and unending. One of his sons, Haethcyn, accidentally kills his brother, Herebeald. The accident is unavengable, a *feohleas gefeoht* (l. 2441), and so Herebeald dies *unwrecen* (l. 2443). The deeply ambiguous language describing the incident stresses 'contradictory sides of the event'.[19] At first the poet seems to imply malice towards Herebeald on the part of his brother, and perhaps even a degree of planning:

> Wæs þam yldestan   ungedefelice
> mæges dædum   morþorbed stred.
>
> (ll. 2435–6)

[For the eldest a murder-bed was spread, unfittingly, by a kinsman's deed.]

As Morey writes, the phrase 'implies something more than accident'.[20] However, the poet then proceeds to tell us the opposite: that it was an accident. He stresses that Herebeald is Haethcyn's *freawine*, his friend and lord – not merely his lord – and says that, far from intending to kill his brother, Haethcyn 'miste mercelses ond his mæg ofscet' (l. 2439).[21] The more sinister word *morþor* is replaced here with the ambiguous verb *ofsceotan*, which may imply only striking or shooting. However, no sooner has he done this than the poet again refers to the incident as 'fyrenum gesyngad' ('a crime sinfully committed', l. 2441), which 'conveys the

---

[17] Hill, p. 51.
[18] Ibid., p. 76.
[19] L. Georgianna, 'King Hrethel's Sorrow and the Limits of Heroic Action in Beowulf', *Speculum* 62 (1987), 829–50, at 836.
[20] J. Morey, 'The Fates of Men in *Beowulf*', in C. Wright et al. (eds), *Source of Wisdom: Old English and Early Medieval Latin Studies in Honour of Thomas D. Hill* (Toronto, 2007), pp. 26–51, at 31.
[21] 'missed his mark and struck down his kinsman'.

moral import'[22] of the action. As Georgianna puts it, 'the poet simply refuses to let us have it one way or the other, either as tragic mishap or as wicked crime.'[23] She adopts the long-standing interpretation that this ambiguity is born of a confusion of legal categories; a reflection of the fact that Anglo-Saxon law treats both intentional and accidental homicide as punishable and therefore the distinction between an accident and crime is not part of the cultural discourse. However, Jurasinski has challenged this reading;[24] and indeed, Georgianna herself concedes that Anglo-Saxon law does recognise distinctions in the seriousness of crimes and punishments.[25]

Rather, then, I would suggest that the 'dual presentation,'[26] as Georgianna puts it, enacts – through oscillating, contradictory language – Hrethel's conflicted emotional state and the impossibility of any kind of resolution of his grief. The alternating assessments of the incident might perhaps be seen as enacting phases of grief; a reflection of Hrethel's own successive subjective responses as he attempts to come to terms with an irreconcilable event, at first struck by anger at the death of Herebeald and then pity for Haethcyn, divided by the claims of each. An interesting comparison might be made here with Ovid's[27] description of Althea, who, like Hrethel, has suffered the death of kin at the hands of kin: her son has killed her brothers, though significantly there is no question of the act being accidental here. Ovid describes her as alternating between grief and anger:

> Pugnat materque sororque,
> et diversa trahunt unum duo nomina pectus.
>
> (Ov. Met. 8.463–4)

[The mother and the sister fight and her two different roles drag at one heart.]

Unlike Hrethel, she takes revenge and, in one of Ovid's most famous phrases:

> et consanguineas ut sanguine leniat umbras,
> inpietate pia est.
>
> (8.474–5)

---

[22] Morey, p. 31.
[23] Georgianna, p. 837.
[24] See Jurasinski, pp. 113–48.
[25] Georgianna, p. 837.
[26] Ibid., p. 836.
[27] Rauer, who suggests the possibility of the *Metamorphoses* as a direct influence on *Beowulf*, notes the 'verbal similarities'. C. Rauer, *Beowulf and the Dragon: Analogies and Parallels* (Cambridge, 2000), p. 45. Orchard has noted the influence of Ovid in Anglo-Saxon literature more generally, see A. Orchard, *The Poetic Art of Aldhelm* (Cambridge, 1994), pp. 145–9. All quotations from *Metamorphoses* are taken from *Ovid: Metamorphoses*, 1, Books 1–8, trans. F. Miller (London, 1971).

[... in order to appease with blood the ghosts of her flesh-and-blood, she is dutiful in her violation of duty.]

As Hardie notes of the play on *pia* and *inpietate* and more particularly on *consanguines* and *sanguine*, 'these pointed formulations focus the underlying conflict in the episode between competing duties, a dilemma of a kind that informs the plots of many Attic tragedies, as well as the plot of the Aeneid.'[28] Though it has long been interpreted (and perhaps sometimes dismissed) as a legal term,[29] the aural repetition in the phrase *feohleas gefeoht* performs a similar function.

This phrase is at the centre of Hrethel's conflict and there has been lively and prolonged debate as to why the event is irresolvable – why neither revenge nor wergild can be taken.[30] Each of the various theories is problematic and scholars have wandered farther and farther afield in search of an explanation. Jurasinski, frustrated by the absence of anything in English legal codes that prohibits recompense in such a situation, goes as far as Montenegro – unsuccessfully – in search of a Germanic legal code from any pre-modern period which might throw some light on this problem.[31] Georgianna outlines the standard interpretation of the event when she writes that:

> Insofar as this event is considered a fight, it does have its price or wergild, but because the deed was done by a kinsman, there is no appropriate person of whom to demand the price. King Hrethel, whose duty as the victim's kin is to exact vengeance or compensation from the killer's family, is also the killer's father.[32]

This analysis, then, does not allow for the notion that the killer, and not just the killer's family, might make recompense. While, according to Miller, this principle did exist in Icelandic law,[33] in our earliest English codes (as well as some Continental codes, such as Charlemagne's[34]) there is an assumption that persists throughout the Anglo-Saxon period that the killer himself should make restitution, if he is

---

[28] P. Hardie, *The Cambridge Companion to Ovid* (Cambridge, 2002), p. 43. For a fuller discussion of the use of paradox to express irreconcilable emotions and duties, see G. Tissol, *The Face of Nature: Wit, Narrative, and Cosmic Origins in Ovid's Metamorphoses* (Princeton, 1997).
[29] Jurasinski, p. 114.
[30] For an account of this debate see Jurasinski, pp. 113–48.
[31] Ibid., p. 145.
[32] Georgianna, p. 837.
[33] W.I. Miller, 'Choosing the Avenger: Some Aspects of the Bloodfeud in Medieval Iceland and England', *Law and History Review* 1 (1983): 159–204, fn 7.
[34] T.B. Lambert, 'Theft, Homicide and Crime in Late Anglo-Saxon Law', *Past and Present* 214 (2012): 3–43, at 10. Again, if we accept North's dating of Beowulf, Charlemagne's code would be roughly contemporary.

able. So Æthelbert's seventh-century code states, 'Gif man mannan ofslæhð, medume leodgeld C scillinga gebete' (*Atb* 21).[35] Edmund I's legal code, complied in the tenth century towards the end of the Anglo-Saxon period, specifies that *only* the killer is liable unless others agree to involve themselves.[36] Moreover, as Jurasinski points out, what is really significant in this episode is that in the absence of revenge Hrethel does not substitute some lesser punishment such as exile, which 'most modern anthropological studies consider the standard punishment for intra-group slaying in feud societies'.[37] Interestingly, the ninth-century *Historia Brittonum* relates that Brutus was exiled for killing his father in a hunting accident and the story must have had some currency since it appears in several sources in England during the Anglo-Saxon period – though, perhaps significantly, none by an Anglo-Saxon writer. In any event, Hrethel does not exile his son. In fact, not only does he not seek a *feoh*, he does not even disinherit Heathcyn; rather, he leaves his property to both his sons and the poet makes a point of telling us so at lines 2470–71. If Hrethel's desire was for justice to be done, punishment inflicted, or honour satisfied, he could have gone some way to achieving these through such a measure. But though Herebeald's death is inextricably associated with Haethcyn for Hrethel and he is angry with his son – we are told 'him leof ne wæs' (l. 2467)[38] – Hrethel does not blame his son either: 'hatian ne meahte' (l. 2466) Haethcyn.[39] It seems that the problem is not that the king cannot impose a vengeful punishment – since his son is not dear to him, exile would seem all the more appropriate – but that revenge in this case would be meaningless because there is no guilty party. Rather, the twist of fate is *hygemeðe* ('soul-wearying', l. 2442). It is an extraordinary depiction of emotion internalised and eventually Hrethel is simply unable to live with his grief.

The poet focuses this insight into Hrethel's emotion through the analogy of the thief's father. In many ways it is an odd analogy and we might wonder why the poet should choose an example so entirely different from the original situation to illustrate it. For, where the innocent Herebeald dies unavenged through no fault of his own, the thief must die unavenged because of his own crime. If the poet intended to emphasise the injustice that an honourable prince should have to die unavenged, he could hardly have chosen a more unsuitable parallel. Rather, the analogy centres attention on the nature of grief where there can be no possibility of revenge. This is the point of similarity between the two situations. The analogy, then, is only concerned with emotion; it offers no

---

[35] 'If anyone kills a man, he is to pay as an ordinary wergild one hundred shillings.' F. Liebermann (ed.), *Die Gesetze der Angelsachsen*, 3 vols (Halle, 1903–16; Clark, NJ, 2007), vol. 1, p. 4.
[36] Ibid., vol. 1, p. 186 (II Em. 1).
[37] Jurasinski, p. 126.
[38] 'He [Haethcyn] was not dear to him.'
[39] 'He could not hate.'

judgement as to the validity of the fathers' emotional reactions or to the nature of the circumstances. The poet's preoccupation is underlined linguistically through a play on the word *wrecan,* which may mean either 'avenge' or 'recite' and which acts here to construct grief and revenge, again, as alternative. As we have seen, at line 2443, Herebeald is *unwrecan* ('unavenged'). The thief must also die *unwrecan* so the thief's father *wrece* ('recites', l. 2446) dirges. The father who cannot have an avenger's reckoning is reduced to the other kind of reckoning. Unlike Hrethel, he does not internalise his sorrow but instead attempts, unsuccessfully, to assuage his grief by mourning. This is an interesting point since we might have been tempted to read Hrethel's death as the result of suppressing fierce emotion. However, the thief's father mourns excessively and still dies of his grief. Just as the dissimilarity between the two situations is illuminating, so is the dissimilarity between the two fathers. The thief's father and King Hrethel do not have in common their circumstances, or their reactions, or their dispositions, or their social responsibilities. What they do have in common, however, is the fact that they cannot take revenge, and die of their grief.

This brings us back to Æschere's death and to our last and, perhaps, most controversial figure: Grendel's mother. There has been a sense that, in pursuing vengeance, Grendel's mother transgresses cultural norms. The most seminal statement of this position was made by Jane Chance, who argues that revenge is solely the province of a kinsman and that from an Anglo-Saxon point of view Grendel's mother does not have the right to avenge.[40] For Chance it is an expression of her monstrosity that Grendel's mother takes revenge: '[s]uch a woman might be wretched or monstrous to an Anglo-Saxon audience because she blurs the sexual and social categories of roles.'[41] This reading remains influential and informs the work of critics such as Acker, Oswald, and Schrader.[42] However, it has been challenged by others. Most recently, Weber has argued for a wide-ranging cultural bias in the translation of passages across Germanic literature that deal with gender,[43] while Hennequin argues that,

---

[40] As William Ian Miller has demonstrated, this is the case in Icelandic culture where degrees of kinship and corresponding degrees of obligation are observed with almost equal strictness in both legal codes and in the sagas. Miller, fn 20. In the same article in 1983, Miller argues that Grendel's mother is monstrous; however, I argue that English laws and literature suggest that the Anglo-Saxons were less rigid on this point (see below).

[41] J. Chance, 'Grendel's Mother as Epic Anti-Type of the Virgin and Queen', in R.D. Fulk, (ed.), *Interpretations of Beowulf* (Bloomington, 1991), pp. 251–63, at 252.

[42] P. Acker, 'Horror and the Maternal in *Beowulf*', *PMLA* 121/3 (2006): 702–16; D. Oswald, *Monsters, Gender, and Sexuality in Medieval English Literature* (New York, 2010); and R. Schrader, 'Succession and Glory in *Beowulf*', *JEGP* 90 (1991): 491–504.

[43] See W. Weber, 'Transmitting Fantasies: Sexist Glossing, Scholarly Desires, and Translating the Heroic Woman in Medieval Germanic Literature', *Translation Studies* 5 (2012): 312–26.

True, she crosses gender lines and performs the functions of warrior, avenger, and king, all generally associated only with men, and she is certainly depicted as supernatural. Despite these qualities, however, neither the poem nor its characters demonize her or even criticize her actions; rather she is presented as a noble and brave opponent and even as a somewhat sympathetic character.[44]

Certainly, the poet describes Grendel's Mother as a 'wrecend' ('an avenger', l. 1256), and Hrothgar himself seems to acknowledge her right of vengeance when he says:

>   Heo þa fæhðe wræc
> þe þu gystran niht   Grendel cwealdest
> þurh hæstne had.
>   (ll. 1333b–5a)

[She avenged the feud in which last night you killed Grendel by violent means.]

The conflict is seen as tragic and mournful but not improper or unusual. The poet seems to imply that circumstances forced both sides equally into sad fates and his language implies not only a validity but, as Day notes, a 'dignity':[45]

>   Ne wæs þæt gewrixle til,
> þæt hie on ba healfa   bicgan scoldon
> freonda feorum.
>   (ll.1304b–6a)

[That was no good bargain, that on both sides they had to trade in the lives of their friends.]

Despite this, Schrader describes Grendel's mother's vengeance as a 'much remarked role and gender reversal'.[46] Yet, one of the more surprising aspects of the four figures considered in this chapter is that, faced with grief, none of them adopts the role we think of as typical for their gender. There is a long-standing view that, 'absent from the field of action, women surround the action with their words: urging before and officially mourning after'.[47] Yet, of the four grievers it is only the woman who

---

[44] M.W. Hennequin, 'We've Created a Monster: the Strange Case of Grendel's Mother', *English Studies* 89 (2008): 503–23, at 504.
[45] Day, p. 79.
[46] Schrader, p. 499.
[47] H. Bennett, 'The Female Mourner at Beowulf's Funeral: Filling in the Blanks / Hearing the Spaces', *Exemplaria* 4 (1992): 35–50, at 42. Though it should be noted that

takes the field of action, while it is the men who either urge before (Hrothgar) or mourn after (the thief's father and to a lesser extent, Hrethel).

Like that of Hrothgar, Hrethel, and the thief's father, the grief of Grendel's mother is extreme. The poet tells us she is driven, wretched, desperate with grief:

> Gifre ond galgmod   gegan wolde
> sorhfulne sið,   sunu deoð wrecan.
>   (ll. 1277–8)

[Voracious and miserable in mind, she wished to take the sorrowful journey to avenge the death of her son.]

Grendel's death and her own grief dominate her mind, excluding all other thoughts. So much so that it is only once she arrives at Heorot and the warriors wake in terror that the danger of the situation strikes her and she wants to 'feore beorgan' ('to protect her life', l. 1293). In some ways this is rather puzzling,[48] but for our purposes the significant fact is that it is *after* the onset of this fear she stops, first to exact her revenge by killing Æschere (ll. 1294–5a) and then to retrieve her son's hand (ll. 1302b–3a). For the moment her drive for vengeance outweighs her desire to live and it is a measure of the strength of her determination for revenge that, despite her overwhelming impulse to flee, she does not leave until she is avenged. However, the wish to survive is also illuminating. The grief of the unavenged Hrethel and of the thief's father causes them to retreat from the world and lose all interest in living. But once Grendel's mother is avenged, her grief is no longer all-consuming and she fights to live.[49] When next we see her she is making a pre-emptive attack against Beowulf, dragging him back to her hall. Here she is given another chance to avenge her child (l. 1546), which she takes eagerly, but she is no longer described as wracked or driven by grief, though

---

a more recent scholar comments more cautiously, 'it seems that women may have played a ceremonial role in pagan cremation funerals', Owen-Crocker, p. 48.

[48] The poem describes her contemplating the journey to Heorot so it seems odd that it only occurs to her half way through her raid that attacking a hall of warriors might be dangerous, especially given that this is how her fearsome son died. Moreover, as Hennequin has remarked, there is no sign of this fearfulness when Beowulf attacks her in the mere. Hennequin, p. 505.

[49] In this, she is also unlike the most famous female avenger of Germanic tradition, Signy – an intertext the poet establishes at the beginning of this episode implicitly through his comparison of Beowulf and Sigemund at lines 874–902. For once the Scandinavian Signy is avenged and honour satisfied, she has no further interest in life. This perhaps reflects the more strictly defined understandings and requirements of revenge and honour that may be found in Icelandic society. However, it also demonstrates, by contrast, how telling a fact it is that Grendel's mother does wish to live.

it is so soon after the death of her beloved son. (Beowulf's attack comes within twenty-four hours of Grendel's death and within twelve hours of her revenge.) In contrast to the conflicted, dismal figure she presents in her grief, she is now the aggressor, always advancing, while, despite having sought her out, Beowulf is, at least initially, defensive. Here we may only judge her emotions through the description of her actions. Her emotional state – which dominates the account of her attack on Heorot – is not mentioned at all, a telling expression of the resolution of her grief.

Instead, attention is focused on Beowulf, who is now the avenger, and in this passage it is his emotions that are described. Having been caught off guard, he thinks of his honour in an effort to recover and spur himself on:

> Eft wæs anræd,   nalas elnes læt
> mærða gemyndig.
>
> (ll. 1529–30a)

[Again he was resolute, not at all slackening in courage, mindful of glorious deeds.]

Despite the fact that his sword has broken and Grendel's mother seems to have the best of the fight, 'nalas for fæhðe mearn' (l. 1537),[50] as the fight progresses, he becomes more aggressive and lunges at her 'þa he gebolgen wæs' (l.1539).[51] Yet the poet also describes him as 'werigmod' (l. 1543), an emotion like the *hygemeðnes* that struck those connected to the death of Herebeald. In the final moments of the fight, 'aldres orwena yrringa sloh' (l. 1565).[52] Then, standing in the hall having killed Grendel's mother, Beowulf sees Grendel's corpse and is seized with a sudden and violent desire to have revenge on him: 'he hraþe wolde / Grendle forgyldan' (ll. 1576b–7a).[53] This is uncharacteristic for the circumspect Beowulf, who distinguishes himself throughout the poem by his reluctance to pursue feuds unless there is a political necessity. Nevertheless, here, still enraged from the fight, 'wæpen hafenade / heard be hiltum' (ll. 1573b–4a),[54] and moves towards the corpse, 'yrre ond anræd' ('angry and single-minded', l. 1575). Over eight lines the poet lists the grievances for which Beowulf wants revenge and yet the murder of one of his own men is not amongst them. Instead, he is concerned with avenging Grendel's attacks against the Danes. Beowulf travels to Heorot in order to end these attacks so perhaps it makes sense that this is his preoccupation now. Still, it seems strange that Hondscio does not cross his mind. We might

---

[50] 'He did not regret the feud.'
[51] 'Now he was enraged'.
[52] 'Without hope of life, he struck angrily.'
[53] 'Quickly he wished to pay Grendel back.'
[54] 'He grasped the sword hard by the hilt.'

surmise that since Hondscio has come to Denmark in search of a fight he cannot be considered to have been wronged when he finds one. Yet, when Hygelac dies in a skirmish leading a raiding party against the Frisians, Beowulf avenges him at lines 2363–4 and 2503–8a. Hygelac is Beowulf's lord and especially dear to him, and this seems to be the key to the difference. Perhaps, despite being one of Beowulf's war band, Hondscio was not especially close to his leader. After all, Hrothgar demand's vengeance for a member of his war band, Æschere, but not on the grounds that he is one of Hrothgar's warrior. Rather, it is because Æschere is dear to the king.

As we have seen, the poem describes a wide range of personalities and an equally various range of emotional responses. Despite the sense that, as Day puts it, 'the heroic "economy of honour" ... demands certain behavioural choices of its inhabitants',[55] the characters of *Beowulf* seem to have surprisingly personal reactions and make individualistic decisions, often driven by emotion. Ties of emotion such as friendship seem in many instances as strong as the obligations of kinship; and indeed, this flexible approach to situations directed by emotional reactions is reflected in the English legal codes. In contrast to our earliest source for Scandinavian laws, the Icelandic *Grágás*, which emphasise the rights[56] of kin in feuds and which specify rigidly and precisely 'who may take action for [an injury] and when',[57] the situation in England does not seem so clear cut. English law codes make no such specifications and vengeance seems to be exacted by whoever has the inclination.[58] English legal codes tend to assume that avengers will be related to the victim, but they do not specify this.[59] On the contrary, they

---

[55] Day, p. 77.

[56] In fact, even the *Grágás*, which are more bloodthirsty than their English counterparts, are keen to underline the idea that revenge is not an obligation but rather a right that 'the principal', the next of kin, may pursue, 'if he wishes'. J. Byock, *Medieval Iceland: Society, Sagas, and Power* (Los Angeles, 1990), p. 26. This appears to be a means of limiting violence. However, by specifying who holds the right of revenge, these laws place some sort of onus on that man to avenge.

[57] A. Lanpher, 'The Problem of Revenge in Medieval Literature: *Beowulf*, *The Canterbury Tales*, and *Ljosvetninga Saga*' (PhD Thesis, University of Toronto, 2010), p. 36.

[58] Interestingly, Edmund's homicide laws occasionally use 'family' and 'friends' interchangeably (II Em. 1). This comparatively lesser status of kin is reflected in the fact that the rise of agnatic kinship happens only quite late in the Anglo-Saxon period. Andrew Wareham, 'The Transformation of Kinship and the Family in Late Anglo-Saxon England', *Early Medieval Europe* 10 (2001): 375–99, at 376.

[59] In the late seventh century, Theodore of Tarsus outlines more lenient penitence for those who avenge a brother than for those who avenge more distant kin, which perhaps implies some recognition, at least from a religious point of view, of a conception of kinship honour obligations. On the other hand, Theodore arrived in England in his late sixties with the express purpose of changing Anglo-Saxon culture, so he is perhaps not a good barometer of Anglo-Saxon sentiment. The emphasis on the fraternal relationship is also interesting since

are concerned to stress that it is the obligation of all to avoid revenge killing. The laws of both Alfred and Eadmund I assume that friends may be involved in feuds,[60] a situation borne out by the description of feuds in *Beowulf*. In fact, Miller suggests that 'friendship ties cut across kinship obligations.'[61] Philpott cites the famous eighth-century example in which friendship is privileged over kinship in the settling of a feud – the Cynewulf and Cyneheard episode in the *Anglo-Saxon Chronicle* – when she notes that in *Beowulf* the practice of friends taking vengeance is apparently regarded as unremarkable: the feuds surrounding both Æschere and Ecgtheow are adopted by friends, not kin.[62] Bede, too, implies that affection plays a role in feuds. When relating the potential feud between the kings of Mercia and Northumbria in 679 occasioned by the death of Ælfwine, Bede comments that Ælfwine was 'multum amabilis' ('much loved').[63] For Bede, it is the strength of Ælfwine's friendship that virtually ensures vicious and bloody retribution.[64]

Such an understanding of the role of emotion in feud here is in line with anthropological studies.[65] However, this last example from Bede has another intriguing aspect that sheds light on another facet of emotion in feud. Even though Bede clearly regarded the circumstances of the conflict between Æthelred of Mercia and Ecgfrith of Northumbria as explosive, reconciliation was possible. Despite Ælfwine's death, Theodore, Archbishop of Canterbury, was able to broker peace. All the English law codes urge the resolution of feuds and reconciliation between the parties, and though this has largely been treated as reflective of an aspiration rather than a reality, historical evidence demonstrates some basis for it. As Halsall has argued, 'the evidence as it stands almost invariably shows us tales of violence in one or, at most, two acts. There is

---

it is at odds with the filial emphasis in the *Grágás*. Here it is the victim's son who has the right to avenge and a brother may only avenge in the event that there is no son or that sons are underage.

[60] Liebermann, vol. 1, p. 76.
[61] Miller, p. 169.
[62] B. Philpott, *Kindred and Clan in the Middle Ages and After* (Cambridge, 1913), p. 237.
[63] *Bede's Ecclesiastical History of the English People*, ed. B. Colgrave and R.A.B. Mynors (Oxford, 1969), pp. 400–401.
[64] Interestingly, that the death occurred in battle does not seem to alter the sense of grievance. By the time of Alfred's laws there is the principle – in Wessex, at least – that any man fighting for his lord ought to be considered *orwige*, but Bede's account suggests that this principle was not current in Northumbria in the seventh and eighth centuries. See Liebermann, vol. 1, p. 76: (Af 42, 5–7).
[65] See C. Boehm, 'The Natural History of Blood Revenge', in Jeppe Büchert Netterstrøm and Bjørn Poulsen (eds), *Feud in Medieval and Early Modern Europe* (Aarhus, 2007), pp. 189–204.

scant reference to long standing enmities producing the recorded outbreaks and little or no indication that, after the narrated outbursts, lasting hostility led to further violence.'[66]

Not only, it seems, was reconciliation and the suspension of hostilities possible, but there are also examples of close friendships developing between old enemies. Thus, in one of Anglo-Saxon England's most famous feuds, Uhtred's son, Ealdred, avenged his father by killing his murderer, Thurbrand. Thurbrand's son, Carl, and Ealdred, each attempt to murder the other. However, remarkably, they were reconciled and became great friends. Gregory of Tours gives a Continental example of the same phenomenon in his account of the late sixth-century feud between Sichar and Chramnesind[67] – another feud, incidentally, in which the avenger adopts the feud out of friendship (Greg. *LH* VII.47) – where, after prodigious bloodshed, these two were also reconciled and became very close friends.

What is intriguing in terms of our understanding of emotion in the early medieval period is that these episodes suggest that it was possible for the intense anger, fear, and grief caused by the extreme violence of a feud to be resolved, perhaps even dissolved, at least for a time. The chroniclers who relate these episodes do not seem to have found implausible the notion that the violent and consuming emotions that drove feuds could be resolved and replaced with more positive emotions. In the historical examples listed above, the feuds are resolved through wergild; in *Beowulf*, they are resolved through revenge killing. However, the result is the same: there is only resolution in those cases where restitution has been made. Each of the four grieving figures considered in this article reacts differently. Each is of a markedly different disposition with different emotional responses. Hrothgar, as we have seen, delegates the responsibility for exacting revenge to a proxy. Hrethel internalises his grief. The thief's father mourns, lamenting dirges for his son. Grendel's mother acts. The commonality is that the two who are able to avenge are relieved of their grief, while the two who are not, die of it. Thus, despite the extremity of their mourning, the grief of both Grendel's mother and Hrothgar seems almost instantly assuaged once revenge has been taken, while for those who are not able to take revenge, the grief never lessens or resolves.

Emotion, as much as anything else, seems to underpin even the drive for honour in revenge. Thus, in the cases of Ealdred and Carl, Sichar and Chramnesind, though the feud is resolved and replaced with friendship, the parties eventually fall out again, fatally. In the latter example, as in the feud between the Heathobards and the Danes in *Beowulf*, it is only *after* having been goaded into anger that the revenger reflects that his failure to act is shameful

---

[66] Halsall, p. 22.
[67] W. Arndt (ed.), *Decem Libri Historiarium*, MGH SRM I (Hanover, 1885, 1951).

(Greg. *LH* IX.19). Even the level-headed Beowulf is seized by the desire for revenge once his anger and blood-lust is raised by the fight with Grendel's mother. This is particularly interesting, since of all the conflicts in the poem this is the one with which he has, arguably, least personal involvement. Moreover, he is usually strategic and circumspect in his attitude to revenge. Indeed, his tone in the discussion of the Heathobard–Danish feud with Hygelac suggests that he is perhaps even faintly disapproving of those who pursue rash feuds in the heat of emotion. After all, the poet says in his eulogy to Beowulf's reign, that 'nealles druncne slog / heorðgeneatas' (ll. 2179–80),[68] where drunkenness does play a part in the inflamed emotions that lead to the rekindling of both Sichar and Chramnesind's feud and that between the Danes and Heathobards, just as it plays a role in Unferth's flytings with Beowulf, though Beowulf's circumspection and self-possession prevent matters from escalating.

Beowulf begins with an invocation to the glorious lives lead by warriors seeking fame and ends with the judgement of Beowulf's people that he was *lofgeornost* ('most eager for fame', l. 3182). The hope to which Beowulf appeals throughout the poem, that men should live bravely so that their deeds will be remembered by future generations, is enacted and fulfilled by the poet, who uses the poem to do just that. However, grief, at least in the four cases examined here, seems to be an emotion that turns the griever's focus inward. These four show little interest in how others view the revenge or in how it will make others feel. They do not plot or savour punishments that would be fitting repayment for their own loss, nor do they gloat over the misery they have inflicted as reciprocation for their own misery. Instead, they are consumed by their own emotions.

---

[68] 'He never in drunkenness killed his companions.'

Chapter 12
Maxims I: In the 'Mod' for Life

Judith Kaup

This chapter proposes a reading of *Maxims I* that is informed by recent contributions to emotion studies. I shall show that the central topic and purpose of the poem is the development of the mental faculty, which has to be understood as a unit comprising emotional and intellectual qualities. This concept of a joined faculty explains how a distinction of emotional and rational effects of the poem would have appeared artificial to an Anglo-Saxon audience. The difficulties critics have with this poem stem, to a great extent, from the anachronistic concept of an opposition of the rational and the emotional.[1] Once *Maxims I* is recognized as dealing with the education of the Anglo-Saxon mind, which I shall refer to as *mod* in this chapter to keep it free from associations with the modern term, the structural principles of the text become clear. Shippey includes *Maxims I* in a group of 'poems which aim primarily neither at narrative nor at self-expression, but deal instead with the central concerns of human life'.[2] The description fits *Maxims I* accurately, and I shall show how the poem[3] is ultimately directed towards probably the most central concern of human life – the pursuit of happiness. A short introduction to ideas of happiness will show how the development of the mental faculty serves the purpose of achieving a fulfilled, happy existence in an Anglo-Saxon sense.

While many philosophical schools propagate the pursuit of happiness as the goal of all human beings,[4] opinions as to the definition of this happiness

---

[1] Both an alleged lack of coherence (cf. George Phillip Krapp and Elliot Van Kirk Dobbie (eds), *The Exeter Book*, ASPR 3 (New York, 1936), pp. xlvi–xlvii), and the assumed absence of a noteworthy purpose (see T. A. Shippey, *Poems of Wisdom and Learning in Old English* (Cambridge, 1976), p. 18) can be explained as results of this fundamental misconception.

[2] Shippey, p. 1.

[3] On account of the structural and thematic interrelations, I shall treat *Maxims I* as one poem with three sections rather than as three different poems, as has also been suggested (Paul Cavill, *Maxims in Old English Poetry* (Cambridge, 1999), p. 166; Carl T. Berkhout, Jr., *A Critical Edition of the Old English Gnomic Poems* (PhD Thesis, University of Notre Dame, 1975)).

[4] See Dan Haybron, 'Happiness', in Edward N. Zalta (ed.), *The Stanford Encyclopedia of Philosophy* (Fall 2011 Edition), http://plato.stanford.edu/archives/fall2011/entries/

differ widely. Harris discusses concepts of happiness in Anglo-Saxon culture and points out the greatest pitfalls for an accurate understanding of early medieval happiness: modern concepts of happiness 'tend to equate happiness with pleasure',[5] while earlier concepts attached a sense of purpose and direction to the term and thus to the idea of the pursuit of happiness. He points out that 'Greek philosophers like Aristotle and Plato spoke of *eudaimonia*, which refers to long-term happiness, the sort of happiness one means when speaking of enjoying a happy life.'[6] While the concept of *eudaimonia* comes closer to the type of happiness sought after in *Maxims I*, the most fitting definition of Anglo-Saxon happiness can be found in Alfred's translation of Boethius' *De Consolatione Philosophiae*. Harris establishes that 'Alfred links proximity to God with wisdom, and wisdom with happiness.'[7] Furthermore, Frantzen observes how the figure of Reason/Wisdom (*gesceadwisness/wisdom*), who is instructing *mod* in Alfred's translation, makes the central point that 'true power and happiness cannot be found in the rewards of the world, but only in the strength of the soul.'[8] This chapter will show how *Maxims I* uses a tripartite structure to enhance the intellectual and emotional stability of its audience and thus actively contributes to the achievement of a strong soul – a well-developed, balanced and stable mental faculty that includes emotional as well as rational/intellectual dimensions, namely the *mod*.

Scholars analysing *Maxims I* tend to look at only one component of this tripartite structure, thus failing to recognize how the three levels complement each other. Positive evaluations of *Maxims I* have seen the poem as a 'prescribed action list',[9] the work of a dedicated scholar but a less-than-genial poet who wished to stress the importance of the wise man's role in securing order in this world,[10] a catalogue poem meant to collect a large quantity of maxims,[11] and a memory aid organized along principles comparable to the modern literary

---

happiness/ (accessed 6 April 2013) for a discussion of happiness and its pursuit in philosophy. See Stephen J. Harris, 'Happiness and the Psalms', in Michael Fox and Manish Sharma (eds), *Old English Literature and the Old Testament* (Toronto, 2012), pp. 292–314, at 304–6 for developments in modern philosophy that often equate the search for happiness with the search for pleasure.

[5] Harris, p. 304.
[6] Ibid., p. 307.
[7] Ibid., p. 309.
[8] Allen J. Frantzen, *King Alfred* (Boston, 1986), p. 56. The essential role of wisdom in the achievement of happiness is highlighted by the change of Lady Philosophy's person.
[9] Elizabeth Jackson, 'From the Seat of the Pyle? A Reading of *Maxims I*, Lines 138–40', *JEGP* 99 (2000): 170–87, at 181.
[10] James W. Earl, '*Maxims I*, Part I', *Neophilologus* 67 (1983): 277–83, at 278, 280.
[11] Nicholas Howe, *The Old English Catalogue Poems* (Copenhagen, 1985), p. 152.

stream of consciousness technique.[12] In addition, the poem has been interpreted as either the subversive voice of a female poet talking about power relations between men and women, or the work of a male poet afraid of the female supremacy in these relations.[13] All of these interpretations offer valuable insights on individual aspects but fail to integrate them into a holistic reading.

The first study to advocate a broader significance that goes beyond personal, didactic or collective purposes was Remley's 1971 essay 'The Anglo-Saxon Gnomes as Sacred Poetry', which also recognizes features of the text designed to create emotional co-experience in the audience.[14] An intended effect of *Maxims I* on its audience is also thematized by Cavill, who attributes to it the purpose to 'structure reality as perceived by a society, and in turn, construct the reality the society perceives'.[15] I agree with his findings, but think *Maxims I* is aimed at achieving more than that. This twofold effect of at once describing and constructing the reality experienced by the society is only one of several techniques employed to achieve an emotional response in an (ideal) reader.[16] The emotional response directly serves the development of the mental faculty that houses emotion and reason. They are not only situated together but comprise one unit. When Harbus states that *Maxims I* and *II* are 'texts which predominantly function as discourses of advice',[17] and sees the 'valorisation of the mental world' as the 'single most prevalent characteristic of the gnomic literature',[18] her focus is based on the assumption that the mind in *Maxims I* is predominantly the place of reflection and understanding. This is slightly at odds with her observation elsewhere that, 'unlike our compartmentalised construction of the mind, the Anglo-Saxon conception seems to place greater emphasis on the interaction of mental functions than on their discrete activities. The mind is an integrated whole, essentially the individual rather than purely the rational or perceptive faculty implicated in the control of the self.'[19] Though she moves further towards an inclusive approach in her 2012 monograph *Cognitive Approaches to Old English Poetry*, where she argues for a close interaction of

---

[12] R. McGregor Dawson, 'The Structure of the Old English Gnomic Poems', *JEGP* 61 (1962): 14–22, at 15.

[13] Murray McGillivray, 'The Exeter Book *Maxims I B*: An Anglo-Saxon Woman's View of Marriage', *English Studies in Canada* 15 (1989): 383–97, especially 392–3.

[14] Lynn L. Remley, 'The Anglo-Saxon Gnomes as Sacred Poetry', *Folklore* 82 (1971): 147–58, at 153.

[15] Cavill, p. 10.

[16] Or on an ideal listener.

[17] Antonina Harbus, *The Life of the Mind in Old English Poetry* (Amsterdam, 2002), p. 61.

[18] Ibid., p. 65.

[19] Ibid., p. 187.

emotional and cognitive reactions in the reception process,[20] she still essentially retains a differentiation between emotion and reason. Harbus argues that the

> affective power [of *Wulf and Eadwacer*] derives in part from the investment required on the part of the audience, and on the capacity for emotional co-experience. More specifically, it draws on the acknowledged role of emotions as managers of the inner life and controllers of cognitive functioning, and on the capacity of poetry to behave as emotion realised in aesthetic form.[21]

A closer look at the relationship of mind and emotion in Anglo-Saxon times will help to show why it is unduly reductive to concentrate on the formation of the mind without taking into account the emotional entity integrated in this same faculty.

In her ground-breaking recent study, *Anglo-Saxon Psychologies in the Vernacular and Latin Tradition*, Lockett shows that the division of heart and mind, or emotion and brain (which is intimately connected to the concept of an oppositional mind–body relationship) is a concept alien to the vast majority of Anglo-Saxons.[22] She observes that 'the distinction between the cognitive and the emotional is a conceptual opposition that the Anglo-Saxons invoked very rarely.'[23] Lockett further specifies that 'in fact, the OE lexicon evidently includes no precise equivalents for MnE "emotion" or "emotional" as non-pejorative alternatives to "reason" or "rational".'[24] In the light of these observations it can be assumed that a strict distinction between a text valuable for the development of the rational mind and one beneficial for the emotional well-being of its audience is rather artificial with respect to Old English literature. Instead of anachronistically dividing the rational and emotional dimensions of the mind into oppositions we need to realize their intimate relationship and the intricate make-up of the *mod*. This unitary model of the *mod* is visible in the terms used to refer to it in *Maxims I*. Terms for heart and mind appear in clusters and

---

[20] Antonina Harbus, *Cognitive Approaches to Old English Poetry* (Cambridge, 2012), especially pp. 162–76.

[21] Ibid., p. 173.

[22] Leslie Lockett, *Anglo-Saxon Psychologies in the Vernacular and Latin Traditions* (Toronto, 2011), p. 9: 'scholarly readers ... are prone to read "Christian Literature", including literature merely copied by Christians, through the lens of Augustine's psychology, which emphasizes the oppositional relationship between the body and the incorporate soul, while treating the transcendent soul and the rational mind as a single entity.'

[23] Ibid., p. 5.

[24] Ibid., p. 34; there, she also points out: 'Beyond a very small group of discursive texts that replicate the Platonic tripartition of the soul into the rational, the irascible, and the concupiscible, the Anglo-Saxons did not conceive of emotion as a different class of thought or localize them in different bodily seats.'

wisdom and positive emotions as well as foolishness and negative emotions are repeatedly paired.[25] The categories of mind, emotion and intellect should be thought of as much more flexible and fluid than they tend to be understood today. Especially for a reading of *Maxims I*, a less rigid division between rational mental activity and emotional state proves rewarding and helps to overcome much of the confusion regarding the purpose of the poem and its appeal to a contemporary audience.

The unifying structural principle of *Maxims I* is its concern with the development of the *mod*, for which it offers guidance and support on three levels. On a basic level, the poem describes instances of order and stability in this world, affirming the reliable framework given to humankind by the benevolent God who created everything that exists. Disturbances and apparent flaws are accounted for and thus stripped of their potential for confusion and fear. A second strand of the poem is concerned with the positive and joyful aspects of human existence that can flourish on this solid foundation. Again, disruptions and problems are not excluded but their causes are explained and solutions are offered. The third strand develops the governing theme of *Maxims I*, which is the inherent ability of all humans to work towards the achievement of happiness by the right use of their *mod*.[26] The development of the *mod*, which is necessary to realize its full potential emotionally as well as mentally, is grounded in communication.[27]

These three aspects are not neatly separated in the poem, but are woven into a pattern that makes frequent use of juxtaposition and cross-reference. This structure is in itself a congenial representation of an idea of the mind as an entity that includes various aspects comprising what could be called the 'self'.[28] From the point of view of its effect on the (ideal) reader, it is certainly an adequate structure to aid in the development of this entity as it simultaneously stimulates the mind in its various functions. I would also like to point out that this structure, which appears logical and unified if analysed in the context of the poem's concern with the formation of the *mod*, probably accounts for the various interpretations of the text mentioned in the beginning. If the first strand, as mentioned above, is not set into context, the poem is a mere catalogue, often stating the obvious. If the second strand is taken by itself, the descriptions of human community appear as either relating individual experiences or simply describing ordinary events. Parts of the third strand convey an impression of a solely didactic purpose.

---

[25] For example ll. 1–4, 'ferð', 'hygecræft', 'heort', 'geþohtas'; ll. 35–7, 'dol', 'nat', 'snotre', 'eadig', 'soð'; ll. 18–20, 'frod', 'ferð', 'sibbe'.

[26] 'Happiness' is used in this chapter solely in the Anglo-Saxon sense detailed at the beginning.

[27] See Earl, p. 278, on the importance of communication in *Maxims I*.

[28] See Harbus, *Life of the Mind*, p. 187.

The following analysis of *Maxims I* is structured according to these three strands. It starts with the governing theme, then turns to the descriptions of human experience and finally to the basic assertive statements. The introductory lines set the scene for the poem's governing theme:

> Frige mec frodum wordum! Ne læt þinne ferð onhælne,
> degol þæt þu deopost cunne! Nelle ic þe min dyrne gesecgan,
> gif þu me þinne hygecræft hylest ond þine heortan geþohtas.
> Gleawe men sceolon gieddum wrixlan.
>
> (ll. 1–4)[29]

[Question me with wise words! Don't let your heart/mind be hidden, [be] hidden what you know most deeply! I shall not tell you my secret, if you conceal the strength of your heart/mind from me and the thoughts of your heart/mind. Wise men must exchange learned speech.[30]]

A cluster of heart/mind terms is paired with references to communication and understanding on the one hand and the possible refusal of interaction on the other hand. The message of the poem is presented in a nutshell: successful communication is the basis of the acquisition of knowledge and is therefore the way to happiness. As heart and mind, emotion and intellect, are not considered to be separate entities, so the terms in this passage do not refer solely to either one or the other. If understood in its cultural context, the passage is an invitation to engage with the text on its various levels in an act of communicative understanding. The 'exchange of speech' (that is, mutual communication) is the appropriate activity of wise people. The direct address that instantly offers the reader the option to become part of the group of wise men by engaging in the adequate action seems intended to stress the ability of all humans to use and develop their *mod*. The activity of *mod*-formation is not reserved for an exclusive circle and will be furthered by the text that follows. The option to become a wise man – to develop one's *mod* and thus acquire the means to seek wisdom and thus happiness – is available to more than an elect few.

The development of the *mod* is a task issued to everyone, as the *mod* is one of God's gifts to humankind. He endows people with this capacity for

---

[29] The Old English text and line numbering follows the ASPR edition. Translations are my own, though I consulted the following translations: Louis Rodrigues, *Anglo-Saxon Verse Charms, Maxims and Heroic Legends* (Middlesex, 1993); Shippey, *Poems of Wisdom and Learning in Old English*.

[30] I settle for the translation 'learned speech' because it has fewer connotations than 'song' or 'proverb'. The distribution of terms in ll. 165–6 also suggests that *gied* is not necessarily paired with wise men.

thought and emotion: 'He us geþonc syleð / missenlicu mod' (ll. 12b–13a).[31] The poet notes a potential hindrance to communication, as God also gave the people 'monge reorde' ('different languages', l. 13). However, the poet goes on to stress that communication and peace between the different people is possible through the interaction of the wise, who are alike with regard to their emotional and mental make-up:

>   Þing sceal gehegan
> frod wiþ frodne;   biþ hyra ferð gelic.
>   (ll. 18b–19)

[The wise shall hold counsel together, their *mod* is alike.]

The difference in language and culture is overcome by the universal sameness of the *mod*. The *mod* is essentially shared by all humans and it is the instrument by which to achieve the universal goal of happiness in the sense of leading a life directed towards God, who is the ultimate source of wisdom. Therefore it is only natural that problems in the positive order of things and in the harmonious communication between people are caused by the 'wonsælge' (l. 21), the ones lacking in happiness, who bring about strife. I translate *wonsælge* literally as 'lacking in happiness' to draw attention to the opposition of the *wonsælge* and the wise men. The happiness these people are lacking is of the kind that can only be brought about by the development of the *mod*. It is frequently stated in Old English literature that the possession of a well-working capacity for thought and emotion ensures happiness and the juxtaposition with the wise men, who can enable reconciliation (l. 20), serves to highlight the point.[32] Later in the poem, the unhappy man who takes wolves for companions is also called 'wonsælig' (l. 146). The fact that these companions are likely to slay him creates a fitting reference to the topic of the connection of happiness and communication, with the latter always enabled by a well-functioning *mod*. Companionship is not possible without communication, and as real communication in *Maxims I* takes place among people trained in the use of their *mod*, it is not possible with animals (even less so with beasts such as wolves who are representative of outlawry and thus anti-social conduct).

The topic of anguish that comes from inadequate communication is taken up again in lines 41b–42. The passage speaks of the sorrow of the blind man who suffers in various ways but most from the fact that he alone knows his affliction:

---

[31] 'He gives us reflection, various sensations of the mind.'
[32] See Harbus, *Life of the Mind*, p. 67: 'Within the Old English poetic corpus ... wisdom is ... a necessary ingredient of a full and happy life.'

>   Þæt him biþ sar in his mode,
> onge þonne he hit ana wat,   ne weneþ þæt him þæs edhwyrft cyme.[33]

[This is painful to him in his heart and thoughts, causing anxiety since he alone knows it, he does not think that there will be a change in this state.]

While the man in the company of wolves cannot communicate with them due to lack of social ability on their part, the blind man is isolated from society by his inability to see and, even more, by his inability to share the experience with others. The passage also asserts that the blind man is accountable for his state and God would heal him if his heart were pure (ll. 43–4). This notion ties in well with the concept voiced at the beginning of the poem that it is everyone's responsibility to work towards improvement of the self (ll. 4 ff.).

The key passage for the poem's understanding is the description of the education of the young man, beginning in line 45:

> Lef mon læces behofað.   Læran sceal mon geongne monnan,
> trymman ond tyhtan þæt he teala cunne,   oþþæt hine mon atemedne hæbbe,
> sylle him wist ond wædo,   oþþæt hine mon on gewitte alæde.
> Ne sceal hine mon cildgeongne forcweþan,   ær he hine acyþan mote;
> þy sceal on þeode geþeon,   þæt he wese þristhycgende.
> Styran sceal mon strongum mode.   Storm oft holm gebringeþ,
> geofen in grimmum sælum;   onginnað grome fundian
> fealwe on feorran to londe,   hwæþer he fæste stonde.
> Weallas him wiþre healdað,   him biþ wind gemæne.
> Swa biþ sæ smilte,   þonne hy wind ne weceð;
> swa beoþ þeoda geþwære,   þonne hy geþingad habbað,
> gesittað him on gesundum þingum,   ond þonne mid gesiþum healdaþ
> cene men gecynde rice.
>
>   (ll. 45–58a)

[A sick man needs a doctor. A young man needs to be taught, encouraged and urged to know well, until he is tamed (i.e. his *mod* has been shaped to meet cultural standards). He shall be given food and clothing till he is brought to understanding. He shall not be insulted while still a boy, before he can reveal himself; he shall then prosper among people, in order to become firm and confident in his *mod*. A man shall govern with a strong *mod*. The storm often takes hold of the sea, (grips) the ocean with fierce weather. From far off the angry grey waves come to hurry to

---

[33] A parallel is found in *The Seafarer*, ll. 53–7, whose speaker also describes the suffering of the one that cannot communicate his thoughts and emotions to someone who has not shared his experiences.

the land, to see if it will stand firm. The cliffs hold them back, they both feel the wind. As the sea is calm when the wind does not steer it, so peoples are peaceful when they come to terms. They settle in safety, and then amid comrades, brave men hold a natural sovereignty.]

The passage reads like an elaborate variation on the topic of the wise men who can bring about peace among people. Just as a sick man needs a doctor, a young man needs instruction to make him *þristhycgende*.[34] The *mod* of the young man is 'firm and confident'; he is 'bold-minded' in the positive sense of being prepared to bravely withstand troubles.[35] Then, the poet implies, just as the cliffs withstand the waves until the sea is calm again, the young man will be able to rely on this well-developed and stable *mod* to work towards reaching agreements between people and to re-establish a positive, harmonious and happy state. The emotional dimension of this passage is again, as at the beginning of the poem, one of reassurance that peace, unity and a life in accordance with the divine order, and therefore happiness, can be actively brought about by communication. The essential point of this passage is the educational aspect: the *mod* needs to be trained to function well. Though inherent to all humans it is not fully developed from the outset. The ability to communicate successfully in difficult situations depends on its appropriate development, which is such an essential task for everyone that it is equal in urgency to seeing a doctor if ill. Thus the underdeveloped *mod* is described as not only a deficiency but an illness. A well-tended *mod*, on the other hand, will be strong and confident. It is achieved by nurturing both body and *mod*, the latter clearly including emotional dimensions, as it is not only important to convey learning to the young man but also essential not to injure his spirit (l. 48). If the mod was a simple rational faculty the warning against injuring the young man's spirit would seem superfluous. Rationality is not so much impaired by pressure in the education process.

Further references to communication stress its importance *ex negativo* as they point out consequences of failed communication and lack of understanding: gossip and slander can endanger the happiness of a couple (l. 100) and the unity of a band of warriors can be destroyed by bad talk (ll. 179–80). The unguided one is in danger of failing to distinguish good from bad counsel (ll. 118b–119), which exemplifies why it is so important to attain a strong *mod* that is not easily deceived. Especially in Anglo-Saxon culture, relying on the stability of social

---

[34] Earl, p. 280, points out that the teacher as physician is a keynote image in Gregory's *Pastoral Care*, where the teacher is also referred to as 'modes laece' and 'heortan laece' – another example of the concept of the unitary *mod*. See also R. McGregor Dawson, 16: 'Young men need to be taught, that they may develop their characters, especially the quality of firmness of mind.'

[35] Cf. the use of terms like *stiðmod* ('strong-minded') and *swiðmod* ('stout-hearted') to characterize positive as well as negative protagonists in Old English literature.

bonds, the ability for proper, undisturbed communication within one's social group is a matter of vital importance. Sadly, strife breaks out easily, occasioned by harsh words exchanged among men who will then turn away from each other (ll. 189–90). Misdirected or failed communication is a source of disturbance and unhappiness, just as positive communication ensures happiness.

I shall now turn to passages of the second strand describing instances of positive human experience. The first emotion directly mentioned in the poem is pleasure. After the four introductory lines, which supply the governing theme, the poet states that men should first and foremost praise God who granted us life and its transitory joy:

> God sceal mon ærest hergan
> fægre, fæder userne,   forþon þe he us æt frymþe geteode
> lif ond lænne willan.[36]
>
> (ll. 4b–6a)

[God is to be praised first, fittingly, our father, because in the beginning He granted us life and transitory pleasure.]

The pleasure in this world is defined as resulting from positive social interaction and community throughout *Maxims I*. Very much like the governing theme, the second strand is introduced by a passage defining the thematic spectre. Joy and community are thematically brought together in recalling the first and most important of bonds – the reliable bond between God and His people (l. 6). Pleasure in this world results from bonds among weak humans and is necessarily transitory and prone to disturbances. Lasting happiness can only be achieved by the training of the *mod* and the resulting acquisition of wisdom, which means closer proximity to God. There, stability is guaranteed as God is eternal, unchanging, almighty and patient.[37]

---

[36] I translate *willa* here as 'pleasure' rather than 'will' because these lines introduce the second strand much in the way the introductory lines set the scene for the governing strand. It also ties in well with the following reference to ageing, as the pleasures in this world are transitory because we have to die and subsequently leave them. The meaning of 'pleasure' for *willa* is attested, though admittedly not as frequently as 'will, wish, desire'. See for example *Andreas*, l. 356; *Beowulf*, l. 1711; *Judith*, l. 296 for clear instances of the meaning 'joy, pleasure'. Loren C. Gruber translates it as 'transitory delights' ('The Agnostic Anglo-Saxon Gnomes: *Maxims I* and *II*, *Germania*, and the Boundaries of Northern Wisdom', *Poetica* 4 (1976): 22–47, at 27). Dawson, p. 15, has 'transitory pleasures'.

[37] 'ece' ('eternal', l. 8); 'ne wendaþ hine wyrda, ne hine with dreceþ / adl ne yldo' ('what is happening does not change him, nor is he afflicted by sickness or age', ll. 9–10); 'ne gomelaþ he in gæste, ac he is gen swa he wæs' ('he does not grow old in spirit, but he is still as he was', l. 11); 'almihtig' ('almighty', l. 10); 'geþyldig' ('unchanging', l. 12).

The topic of marital union as a source of worldly joy is important to the poet, featuring in the first part and dominating the second (ll. 81–206). Positive feelings of community and belonging are evoked by line 23 'Tu beoþ gemæccan',[38] which immediately follows the positive description of peace between people brought about by the communication between wise men. A disturbance of this harmony by the premature death of a couple's children, the emotional impact of which is illustrated by the example of the tree mourning its limbs when it loses leaves (ll. 25–6), is integrated into the established context of God's working in the world. God needs to let people die to avoid overcrowding (ll. 27–34). Though sadness is unavoidable in this world, all events form part of a balanced system that is ultimately devised by God. The main focus in this passage is on the couple as parents. Birth and possible death of children are of central concern to communal aspects of life and the joy of having children is defined by the negative, that is by the sadness experienced at their loss. However, the naturalness of the experience is made explicit by the comparison of the human couple's mourning to the mourning of the tree. King and queen in part two of the poem are described with a stress on the mutual nature and positive bond of their relationship. Their marital union is set in the context of societal bonds: the queen is 'loved by her people' ('leof mid hyre leodum', l. 85); she is firmly established in her community. To be *leohtmod* (of cheerful/positive spirit[39]) goes together with keeping counsel (*rune healdan*) – emotional and rational traits again being closely associated. The positive emotions described here are the result of functioning community, brought about by appropriate actions and emotions (ll. 81–92). The well-known ensuing passage speaks of a mundane couple, the sailor and his Frisian wife. Their mutual relationship is characterized by love.[40] While, unlike the queen, the Frisian wife does not fulfil a representative role within society, there is still a recommended mode of conduct that strengthens the marital community. Trust is the foundation of this bond and the poet urges people to be true to one another and wait for their beloved.[41] Faithfulness is due to the power of a strong *mod* as those who wait are characterized as *fæsthydig* (firm of thought), and opposed to the one's who are *fyrwetgeorn* (eager with curiosity).

Friendship is another source of happiness that can also not be taken for granted: 'Eadig biþ se þe in his eþle geþihþ, earm se him his frynd geswicaþ' (l. 37).[42] Possibly the following reference to lack of food can be explained within the context of companionship under a common lord because the one

---

[38] 'Two are mates.'
[39] 'leohtmod'(l. 85); 'rune healdan' (l. 86).
[40] 'leof wilcuma / Frysan wife' ('dear is the loved one to the Frysian wife', ll. 94b–5a); 'his lufu' ('his love', l. 99).
[41] 'Wif sceal wiþ wer wære gehealda' ('a woman shall be true to her man' l. 100); 'a mon sceal seþeah leofes wenan' ('one shall wait for the beloved', l. 104).
[42] 'Blessed is he who thrives in his native land, wretched is he whom his friends abandon.'

abandoned by his friends is also without the other benefits of life in the hall.[43] I believe that a parallel between food as nourishment for the body and friendship as nourishment for the *mod* is also intended. The comparison of starving and deprivation of social interaction functions along similar lines as the comparison of the sad parents and the sad tree.

The last section of *Maxims I* is predominantly concerned with instances of disturbed social interaction, and it elaborates upon the theme of lack of companionship as a source of desperation for the individual.[44] A particularly drastic example is the unhappy friendless man, who is driven into the company of wolves. Desperate to amend his lonely state, the man seeks company that is not to be trusted, and which will probably kill him (ll. 146–7). It is highly unnatural for a man to socialize with wolves, as he should feel fear ('gryre', l. 148), and he thus appears dehumanized by lack of appropriate involvement in communication. In addition, the association of the beasts with outlawry stresses the exclusion of the friendless man from society. The poet returns to the topic of loneliness and the resulting sadness in lines 172–3: 'Earm biþ se þe sceal ana lifgan, wineleas wunian hafaþ him wyrd geteod.'[45] This lamentation of being alone is juxtaposed with a positive description of the desirable state of not being alone, either because one has a brother (l. 174) or is a member of a band of warriors (ll. 175–6). The value of community is further stressed in the passage immediately following, where the poet describes the elevating and reconciling effect of two men playing a board game together:

> Hy twegen sceolon tæfle ymbsittan,   þenden him hyra torn toglide,
> forgietan þara geocran gesceafta,   habban him gomen on boarde.
>
> (ll. 181–2)

> [Two shall sit together at the game-board, while their anger fades away, forget the sad things, take their pleasure at the board.]

The interaction of playing a game together is seen as a valid form of communication because playing has the power to reconcile – a feature elsewhere in the poem attributed to the communication of wise men. The shared features

---

[43] Though there are more references to lack of food as a cause of illness in different contexts in *Maxims I*. Hugh Magennis, *Anglo-Saxon Appetites: Food and Drink and Their Consumption in Old English and Related Literature* (Dublin, 1999), pp. 44–5, suggests a combination of the recognition of the necessity of food with a concept of domestic order for l. 124, which could support the notion of lack of food as representative of lack of inclusion in the social order. See also *Proverbs* 15:15: 'All days of the afflicted are evil but he that is of a merry heart hath a continual feast'.

[44] e.g. ll. 144–5.

[45] 'Sad is he who lives alone, dwells friendless as fate dealt to him.'

of playing and the training of the *mod* also portray the latter as an activity not devoid of entertainment.

There are a number of negative emotions endangering the positive community experience and thus the positive emotions resulting from it:

> Cyning biþ anwealdes georn;
> lað se þe londes monað, leof se þe mare beodeð
>
> (ll. 58b–9)

[A king is eager for sovereignty; hated is he who claims land, loved who gives more.]

To avoid hateful emotions of his subjects and ensure their love, the king should give freely (probably in order to gain and keep the sovereignty he is eager for). The king's eagerness for sovereignty could be a reference to pride, thus portraying how a negative trait of the mind occasions negative emotional responses. A woman who wants to avoid becoming the focus of negative emotions such as contempt and disrespect from her people has to avoid walking about too much (ll. 64–5). That a bad reputation is circulated by people talking is nothing new, but in the context of *Maxims I* serves as an additional reminder of the power of communication to achieve good as well as evil. A person already shamed has to hide in the shadows (l. 66) and even someone engaged in the positive social practice of gift-giving could become 'gifre' ('greedy', l. 69).

The underlying reason for all disturbances of positive community is revealed in the last section of *Maxims I*. It is ultimately caused by a lack of understanding, communication and an astute *mod*. The origin of strife among men is placed at the time of the brother-slaying of Cain:

> Wearð fæhþo fyra cynne,   siþþan furþum swealg
> eorðe Abeles blode.   Næs þæt andæge nið,
> of þam wrohtdropan   wide gesprungon,
> micel mon ældum,   monegum þeodum
> bealoblonden niþ.   Slog his broðor swæsne
> Cain, þone cwealm nerede;   cuþ wæs wide siþþan,
> þæt ece nið ældum scod.
>
> (ll. 192–8a)

[Violence came to the human race, since the moment the earth swallowed Abel's blood. That was no one-day strife, from the enmity-drops came much evil to men, malice-infected violence to many peoples. His beloved/own brother slew Cain, whom the death [of Abel] saved; it has been widely known ever since that the eternal violence harms men.]

Violence spread from this condemnable event like a disease, infecting humankind. It is disconcerting that, apart from God, 'violence' is the only thing called explicitly eternal in *Maxims I*. However, as the failure to communicate, to understand, and to use and develop one's mental faculty always leads to violence, it is an ever-present option as the opposite of happiness, resulting in distance from God as opposed to proximity to Him. While *nerede* ('saved') in line 197 has often been emended, I think that the manuscript reading makes perfect sense here. Cain slew Abel because he envied him for his apparently more favourable treatment by God at the sacrifice. His slaying of his brother was thus an act of removing an obstacle in his way to God's attention. While we know that it did not improve his standing, the motivation for the deed remains. This passage offers a reasonable explanation for the discrepancy between the ordering powers of God and the often-disturbed state of human relationships that is repeatedly thematized in the poem. Lack of understanding and failed communication (between Cain and Abel, and between Cain and God), both the result of a poorly trained *mod*, even brought the first murder (and subsequently all other evil) into the world. The last lines accept the inevitable reality of ongoing conflict between human beings and offer what looks like recommendations for dealing with this harsh reality: 'the shield must be ready, a spear be on the shaft, the sword have an edge, the spear a point and the stern man spirit' (ll. 201–3). An element of justice is added by the statement that a man lacking in spirit will have the least treasure (l. 204).

These last lines can of course also be allotted to what I have called the basic or foundation level of meaning in *Maxims I*. They state general, observable facts about life in a warrior culture, thus putting the framework of ordinary, daily life just after the religious explanation of the initial reason for violence in the world. The following examples finish my analysis of the tripartite pattern in *Maxims I*. The basic strand contains all the famously obvious gnomic sayings of *Maxims I*. The ritualistic function of repeating what is already known, such as

> Winter sceal geweorpan,   weder eft cuman,
> sumor swegle hat
>
> (ll. 76-7a)

[Winter passes, fair weather returns, sun-hot summer.]

has been recognized.[46] The use of repetition, especially of verse, as a device to assert and calm is universal and very old.[47] This does not, however, imply that

---

[46] For example, see Cavill.
[47] At the workshop on Anglo-Saxon Emotions at Trinity College Dublin in 2012, the topic of the calming properties of sameness were mentioned. Especially Erin Sebo's and

there are archaic and modern strata at odds with each other or simply mingled in *Maxims I*. On the contrary, the basic level provides the emotional stability needed to deal with the more emotionally challenging passages.[48] Comforting emotions are conveyed by stressing the orderly nature of the natural and social world, even though the latter is always subject to the influence of men, who can reinforce or disturb order.[49] Some of these general observations are not positive, which is in line with the overall technique of pairing or juxtaposing positive and negative aspects and emotions in *Maxims I*. For example, even God's gifts to the happy man are not as reliable, because He may give them and also take them back again:

> Mæg god syllan
> eadgum æhte   ond eft niman
>
> (ll. 155b–6)

[God may give riches to the happy man and take them [away] again.]

The exemplifying of positive values or emotions *ex negativo* is a common device in Old English poetry and also frequently used in *Maxims I*. Thus, the statement that God does not like a faithless man with an inadequately developed mind, who is venomous-minded and false –

> Wærleas mon ond wonhydig,
> ætrenmod ond ungetreow,
> þæs ne gymeð god
>
> (ll. 161–3)

[A faithless man and of deficient *mod*, venomous-minded and false, God does not care for him.]

– really also serves to define what kind of person is loved by God, i.e. one possessing the opposite traits of mind.

In my brief analysis of the three strands within the poem, I have established the following observations regarding emotions in *Maxims I*:

Mary Garrison's papers dealt with order as a comforting measure (Garrison) and the comfort found in the universal nature of, for example, death (Sebo). See also Remley, p. 152, on the chant-character of *Maxims I*. The use of the singing of mantras to influence the state of mind is of course also a feature of Yoga.

[48] McGillivray, p. 393: 'First, the "gnomic" statements in the poem serve the purpose of asseveration.'

[49] If *willa* in l. 6 was to be understood as will, it would refer to this fact, i.e. that the free will of humankind can disturb the order intended by God.

1. Joyful and positive feelings are always connected with instances of community. The topic of bonds between humans pervades the whole poem.
2. Happiness in *Maxims I* is necessarily linked to positive social interaction and sad feelings are likewise connected to failed or lacking social interaction.
3. The bond between humans and God prepares the ground and forms the backdrop for all other modes of interaction. God as the creator of everything alone understands everything and His capacity for order is visible everywhere in the natural world.
4. While the natural world functions according to the divine plan, the social world of humans can be disturbed by their own actions.

The most powerful remedy against such disturbance is a well-trained mind that enables communication and peace. The mind is thus valued extremely highly (as Harbus has pointed out), but it is not the training of the mind in a didactic sense that is the purpose of the poem. When employing an inclusive mind/emotion concept, the strengthening of a person must include other aspects. The poem gives the example of a young man in lines 45–50, who should explicitly not be broken in spirit but brought up to be *pristhycgende*, which I would argue means emotionally as well as rationally strong. The *mod* in its entirety needs to be strengthened. But *Maxims I* does not only lay out the educational concept, it also actively works on the training of the *mod* and thus the achievement of happiness. Harbus's chapter in this collection focuses on the direct cognitive and emotional effect of literature on its audience and adds to our understanding of the 'second-hand emotion' that is experienced by a reader confronted with emotionally charged texts. As I have shown, *Maxims I* contains numerous trigger-situations for emotional involvement that subsequently contribute to the development of the mind by rehearsing various emotional states. Furthermore, Harbus also highlights the particular effectiveness of emotional involvement through changing states of emotions within a text in her earlier study.[50] *Maxims I* with its adversary pairs and constant juxtaposing of positive and negative emotional aspects of certain situations should therefore have a most profound effect on the minds of its readers.

Maxims I is neither didactic in the sense of conveying wisdom nor predominantly constructing reality, but it is a text that reassures in the most literal sense of the word. It creates solid mental foundations to withstand the surging waves of life in this world. I propose that the purpose of the poem is to cause or to re-establish emotional strength and stability. Both within the text's narrative (by pointing out the ever-present order in the world, even where

---

[50] Harbus, *Cognitive Approaches*, p. 173.

one fails to detect it or where it is disturbed) and also outside of the text (by the emotional training effect it provides) *Maxims I* creates railings one can hold onto in times of trouble. It is not soothing in a naïve manner but offering support for gaining the emotional and mental stability: the strong *mod*, needed to enjoy this world.

Chapter 13

The Neurological and Physiological Effects of Emotional Duress on Memory in Two Old English Elegies

Ronald Ganze

In 'The Expression of Emotional Distress in Old English Prose and Verse', Simon Nicholson sets out to demonstrate that the Old English language possessed the vocabulary necessary to express emotional distress in psychological terms, differing with the evolutionary theory proposed by J.P. Leff, who argues that non-western and early western cultures do not differentiate between 'somatic and psychic expressions of emotional distress'.[1] While Nicholson does earn his conclusion, that 'Old English distinguished between what would now be regarded as psychological and somatic expressions of emotional distress', and 'the language differentiated between different emotional states',[2] the more important takeaway from Nicholson's essay is that so many of the Old English words used to express emotional distress do find their roots in words naming parts of the human body.

Those words, for example, that Nicholson identifies as referring only to states of mind, like *hatheortnes* and *breostcearu*, are obvious compound words indicating a bodily state: 'hot-heartedness' and 'breast-care', 'breast-sorrow', or 'breast-grief'. Nicholson acknowledges these words contain 'connotations of both mental and bodily disturbance',[3] but quickly moves on, presumably because the words are so often translated as 'anger' or 'rage' and 'anxiety' or 'grief', respectively. But despite their translation into Modern English as terms that retain no connotations of a bodily state, the Old English words provide an accurate description of bodily changes that take place when said emotions are present – changes that themselves constitute the feelings of anger and grief. Anger does cause increased blood flow, resulting in flushing, which does produce the sensation of heat. Grief can cause heart fluttering or palpitations, a physiological phenomenon that might be described as 'breast-care', which

---

[1] Simon Nicholson, 'The Expression of Emotional Distress in Old English Prose and Verse', *Culture, Medicine and Psychiatry* 19 (1995): 327–38, at 327.
[2] Ibid., p. 337.
[3] Ibid., p. 330.

Nicholson identifies as a possible meaning for the phrase 'cnyssað nu / heortan geþohtas' (*The Seafarer*, ll. 33b–34a), and which he translates as 'clash now the thoughts of the heart'. But – perhaps because Nicholson's article proceeds on Leff's assumption that strictly psychological terms indicate a superior understanding of human emotion, and somatic terms of an earlier stage of development – he does not make the connection between somatic vocabulary and modern neuroscience, which demonstrates the essentially embodied nature of emotional responses. Contrary to Leff (and Nicholson), the use of somatic terms to express emotional states is far more accurate than those terms that maintain a mind/body separation.

Since the publication of Antonio Damasio's *Descartes' Error: Emotion, Reason, and the Human Brain* in 1994, the centrality of emotions to thinking and reasoning and the relationship between emotion and somatic function – the physiological origins of 'feelings' – has become widely accepted in cognitive neuroscience. Damasio explains that the brain receives 'input' from the body via the peripheral nerves, which allow 'nearly every part of the body, every muscle, joint, and internal organ' to send signals to the brain, after which they are 'carried inside the brain, from neural station to neural station', and via chemical substances, which, 'arising from body activity[,] can reach the brain via the bloodstream and influence the brain's operation either directly or by activating special brain sites'.[4]

This process also works in the opposite direction: 'the brain can act, through nerves, on all parts of the body', using the autonomic nervous system and the musculoskeletal nervous system (the voluntary nervous system), as well as 'manufacturing or ordering the manufacture of chemical substances released in the bloodstream, among them hormones, transmitters, and modulators'.[5] The understanding of brain and body that emerges is that of an 'indissociable organism', a 'partnership [that] interacts with the environment as an ensemble, the interaction being of neither the body nor the brain alone'.[6]

Emotions are central to Damasio's model of the 'indissociable organism'. He argues that, while rationality appears to be something that takes place in the *neo*cortical region of the brain (which is evolutionarily recent), it is actually the case that older areas of the brain, responsible for biological regulation as well as drives and instincts, operate in concert with the neocortex in order to produce rational thought. Damasio does not argue for specific hard-wired emotional responses, but he does argue for the possibility that humans 'are wired to respond with an emotion, in preorganized fashion, when certain features of stimuli in

---

[4] Antonio Damasio, *Descartes' Error: Emotion, Reason, and the Human Brain* (New York, 1994), p. 88.
[5] Ibid.
[6] Ibid.

the world or in our bodies are perceived, alone or in combination'.[7] Damasio explains, 'the *essence* of emotion ... [is] the collection of changes in body state that are induced in myriad organs by nerve cell terminals, under the control of a dedicated brain system, which is responding to the content of thoughts relative to a particular entity or event.'[8]

But how can a modern, neurological understanding of emotion serve to illuminate the depiction of emotion in tenth- and eleventh-century literature? To begin, it requires us to divert our focus, at least initially, from the external causes of emotional response and to examine emotion as an internal process that involves specific neurological and physiological changes in the individual organism. This new focus can then be applied to the emotional responses we see being exhibited by the individuals depicted in the texts we have placed under scrutiny. We are thus provided with a new point of entry into the text as well as a point of contact between the contemporary reader and the medieval poet, whose understanding of emotional reactions we are reading; while the cultural causes of emotional response have certainly changed within the course of the last thousand years, the neurological and physiological components of emotion have not. The changes to the human genome required to effect so drastic a change to the human organism would take millions, not thousands, of years. As Damasio points out, 'notwithstanding the reality that learning and culture alter the expression of emotions and give emotions new meanings, emotions are biologically determined processes, depending on innately set brain devices, laid down by a long evolutionary history.'[9] While an Anglo-Saxon might not understand the term 'fight or flight reaction', were the physiological concept to be explained it would prove communicable, and narratives of such an experience could be shared. The same holds true for other emotional states, such as depression, trauma, and anxiety, all of which manifest themselves through specific neurobiological changes that have remained constant for millennia. Vocabulary and categorization may change, but the biological determinants do not, and given the somatic vocabulary used by the Anglo-Saxons to describe various emotional states, a discussion of emotions taking place between a modern neuroscientist and an Anglo-Saxon poet might reveal a greater number of shared assumptions than one between a modern neuroscientist and a psychoanalyst. Certainly members of a culture whose literature indicates that they thought of the mind as a container would be able to navigate their way from this analogy to the fact that the mind does, in a sense, act as a container for serotonin, dopamine,

---

[7] Ibid., p. 131.
[8] Ibid., p. 139.
[9] Antonio Damasio, *The Feeling of What Happens: Body and Emotion in the Making of Consciousness* (New York, San Diego, and London, 1999), p. 51.

cortisol, and a whole host of neurochemicals, the presence of which determines the emotional state of the individual.[10]

In addition, literature written by beings so neurologically different from us would likely prove as impenetrable as literature written by a completely alien species. As Antonina Harbus has pointed out, 'our very ability to create a coherent response to the [Old English] text ... requires us to deploy universal human cognitive functions that have changed very little, if any, in the [last] thousand-odd years.'[11] We can understand and relate to literary works from the past because, evolutionarily speaking, we have changed very little since the Anglo-Saxon period. We can also 'feel along with' these literary works:

> Our understanding and empathy with the emotional complexity of the subjective experience represented in this text [*Wulf and Eadwacer*] are predicated on comparable human psychological functioning shared by the creator and receiver of this text. Moreover, the apparent cross-cultural intelligibility of the text and its emotional texture points to consistency rather than variation in human apprehension of and cause for emotional pain, as well as the deep entrenchment of the reliance on poetry to represent and to engage with the emotional life.[12]

With this in mind, I would like to examine the intersection between emotion and memory in two Old English elegies, *The Wanderer* and *The Wife's Lament*. It is my contention that the speakers of these poems exhibit the characteristics of post-traumatic stress disorder (PTSD), and that by taking note of these symptoms, we can come to one explanation for why we have had such difficulties in determining their narrative and spatial contexts. In making this argument about two elegies with speakers who have been exiled from their homelands, I am well aware that some of my observations regarding memory function have been made by other scholars of exile literature, though I am unaware of any studies referencing PTSD. Domnica Radulescu's description of the subjective experience of memory in exile is a useful starting point for the discussion of the effects of emotional trauma on memory. She explains that memory of the exile is required to perform its regular day-to-day functions, but at the same time, to 'keep alive the information and experience of one's most important and formative experiences from childhood to the time of exile, without the incentive

---

[10] The Anglo-Saxon understanding of the mind as a container is the subject of three articles by Britt Mize: 'The Representation of the Mind as an Enclosure in Old English Poetry', *Anglo-Saxon England* 35 (2006): 57–90; 'Manipulations of the Mind-as-Container Motif in *Beowulf*, *Homiletic Fragment II*, and Alfred's *Metrical Epilogue to the Pastoral Care*', *JEGP* 107 (2008): 25–56; and 'The Mental Container and the Cross of Christ: Revelation and Community in *The Dream of the Rood*', *Studies in Philology* 107 (2010): 131–78.

[11] Antonina Harbus, *Cognitive Approaches to Old English Poetry* (Cambridge, 2012), p. 1.

[12] Ibid., pp. 172–3.

of the physical reality. The memory of the exile has to feed on itself to some extent, to keep creating and recreating itself in order to replace that which has been lost in the physical realm.'[13]

Radulescu's observations can be restated in terms of cognition: in order to reduce fragmentation of the self, the exile must attempt to maintain the integrity of those episodic memories that comprise autobiographical memory, but in the absence of any meaningful retrieval cues or compatriots with whom these memories might be rehearsed. I would add to this that these memories are often retrieved in a stressful and anxious environment: a place in which the exile cannot feel at home and is often explicitly made to feel other than those with whom he or she is surrounded. The emotional state of the exile at the time of retrieval is also detrimental to the ability to recall and contextualize episodic memories.

Neither *The Wanderer* nor *The Wife's Lament* directly addresses the matter of memory, but both poems depict problematic acts of retrieval performed by subjects fraught with anxiety while either negotiating or residing in confusing, alienating, and decontextualized environments. In *The Wanderer*, we are presented with a speaker who has survived his lord in battle and is left an outcast. In Augustinian terms, the poem presents the speaker's spiritual movement from the despair of an *eardstapa* ('earth-stepper') who has invested too much desire in the things of this world to a *snottor* ('wise one')[14] who has learned to invest his desire in the eternal and to receive the gift of God's grace; exiled from the City of Man, he comes to understand his true status as a citizen of the City of God. Emotionally, we are presented with a speaker suffering through an existential crisis – a temporary inability to see past the ephemeral nature of this world – before faith in God provides the spiritual solution necessary to alleviate the crisis.[15]

The *eardstapa*'s alienation and isolation are made immediately apparent in lines 9b–11a, in which he laments,

                nis nu cwicra nan
þe ic him modsefan   minne durre
sweotule asecgan.[16]

---

[13] Dominica Radulescu, 'Theorizing Exile', in Dominica Radulescu (ed.), *Realms of Exile: Nomadism, Diasporas, and Eastern European Voices* (Lanham, MD, 2002), pp. 185–204, at 189.

[14] I am reading this as a substantive, and understand line 111a, 'Swa cwæð snottor on mode', to mean, 'So spoke the wise one in his mind.'

[15] Ronald J. Ganze, 'From *anhaga* to *snottor*: The Wanderer's Kierkegaardian Epiphany', *Neophilologus* 89 (2005): 629–40. See also Dennis Chase, 'Existential Attitudes of the Old English "Wanderer"', *Language Quarterly* 26 (1987): 17–19, who makes his argument using atheistic existential philosophers, and Lawrence Beaston, 'The Wanderer's Courage', *Neophilologus* 89 (2005): 119–37, who uses the theology of Paul Tillich.

[16] All quotations from *The Wanderer* and *The Wife's Lament* are taken from Anne L. Klinck, *The Old English Elegies: A Critical Edition and Genre Study* (Montreal, 1992).

[there are now no living ones to whom I dare to tell openly my heart-thoughts.]

Our speaker clearly suffers from the inability to rehearse memories with his compatriots. This lament is followed in lines 11b–14 with,

>   Ic to soþe wat
> þæt biþ in eorle   indryhten þeaw,
> þæt he his ferðlocan   fæste binde,
> healde his hordcofan,   hycge swa he wille.

[I know it is a truth that it is a noble practice for a nobleman to bind fast his spirit-locker, hold his treasure-coffer, whatever he may think.]

Some have read lines 9b–11a as leading into lines 11b–14, taking the entire passage to be a statement of the taciturn nature of the Anglo-Saxon warrior. This is a legitimate reading, of course, because it *is* the nature of Anglo-Saxon society that prevents a nobleman from openly telling his heart to anyone outside of his lost *comitatus*, his plight that of the lordless man.[17] But the sources of the *eardstapa*'s extreme alienation are two: he seems to have no point of entry into a new social group (no one he encounters knows him or his people), but, more importantly, he has suffered through a traumatic experience that serves to separate him from those who have not, an experience difficult to communicate to others, because it is dominated by emotional memories divorced from the narrative context required to communicate them to others. Alone in his exile – both external and internal – the *eardstapa* has no one with whom to talk about the past, no one with whom to rehearse and reinforce his memories.

His lack of companionship is something with which the *eardstapa* is keenly aware. In lines 26b–29a, he wishes that he

>   findan meahte
> þone þe in meoduhealle   min mine wisse,
> oþþe mec freondleasne   frefran wolde,
> weman mid wynnum.

[might find one in a meadhall who knew me or my people, or who would console me, friendless, would console, attract me with joy.]

Translations are my own.

[17] Robert Bjork makes this argument, citing *Maxims I*, which speaks of the wretchedness and friendlessness of the one whom fate decrees must live alone, in 'Sundor æt rune: The Voluntary Exile of the Wanderer', *Neophilologus* 73 (1989): 119–29.

The *eardstapa* does not just want to find a new lord to whom he can attach himself; he also wants to find someone who knew his people, someone with whom he can reminisce and recreate the past for which he spends the first half of the poem longing. Short of this, he is willing to settle for a group of people who will accept him in his *freondleasne* state, people with whom he might create new memories and who might help him to craft a new identity.

But this lack of companions with whom to rehearse old memories does not seem to be the root cause of the fragmentary nature of the memories presented in *The Wanderer*. Is it not, I would argue, so much the environment in which the memories are retrieved that causes their fragmentation – though this certainly contributes to their *continued* fragmentation – as it is the conditions under which they were initially encoded. Simon Nicholson's article, with which I began this chapter, establishes the fact that the *eardstapa*, and many other speakers and figures in Old English poetry, is under emotional duress as he recounts the story of his life. The *eardstapa* appears to be suffering from those deficits of memory commonly associated with long-term exposure to stress and the emotional turmoil that results. These cause certain neurochemical imbalances in the hippocampus, the amygdala, the medial temporal lobe, and the prefrontal cortex. Some studies link this particular set of imbalances to post-traumatic stress disorder, though others maintain that the relationship between PTSD and memory dysfunction is unclear. Regardless, both the *eardstapa* and the speaker in *The Wife's Lament* do exhibit the types of memory dysfunction associated with emotional duress, comorbid with the depression that often accompanies alienation and isolation. For the *eardstatpa*, his current situation, the dictates of his society, and his own neuroendocrinological processes combine to create a situation in which the sharing of experience is, at least initially, impossible. It is only the salvific epiphany he has at the poem's end that changes this, and which makes his case so different from the Wife's – points to which I shall return at the end of this chapter.

However, before further examining the neurological effects of extreme emotional duress in these poems, a brief explanation of the current understanding of memory in cognitive neuroscience is necessary. The consensus view is that there are several types of memory: during the encoding of a memory of an event, that event is broken down and processed by the brain according to category. Emotional memory, for example, is generally processed by the amygdala, though the hippocampus is responsible for the 'contextual regulation of emotional responses',[18] as well as the processing of spatial and contextual memory in general. When that event is later retrieved, these memory fragments

---

[18] Mieke Verfaellie and Jennifer J. Vasterling, 'Memory in PTSD: A Neurocognitive Approach', in Peter Shiromani, Terrence Keane, and Joseph E. LeDoux (eds), *Post-Traumatic Stress Disorder: Basic Science and Clinical Practice* (New York, 2009), pp. 105–30. at 117.

are reintegrated, an operation that takes place 'in the process of an appropriate cue'.[19] When each of the brain areas involved in memory is working as it is designed to function, the various fragments making up an individual memory are properly encoded and can be successfully reintegrated; what we think of as normal remembering occurs.

When an individual is placed under emotional duress, however, various hormones are released that affect these areas of the brain in unique ways. During encoding, for example, the increase in stress hormones can impair the proper functioning of the hippocampus.[20] Since the hippocampus is responsible for the encoding of contextual memories, detailed memories, and episodic memories (including coherent and specific autobiographical memories), we can expect these types of memories to be impaired with hippocampal damage.[21] And, indeed, high levels of cortisol cause physiological damage, resulting in a pronounced decrease in the ability to encode episodic or spatial memories. The individual has the ability to recall only an overgeneralized version of events, generally devoid of specific detail or the contextual information necessary to understand and integrate the event into the individual's autobiographical memory.

The encoding of emotional memories, however, is enhanced by the presence of cortisol, as it 'facilitate[s] amygdalar functions and the emotional memories dependent on them',[22] memories that are 'unbound to the spatio-temporal context of the relevant events'.[23] The result is that coherent memories of trauma are essentially inaccessible to recall.[24] What remain accessible are memories of the gist or the centre of an event, which is enhanced by emotion, as opposed to the peripheral detail, which is not. This central information 'may represent a *concentration* of experience, where disproportionate emphasis is placed on emotion'.[25] These memories are often inaccurate, and may involve a process called 'narrative smoothing'. Events maintain a consistent 'theme', but the context and details are constructed, rather than recalled.

Returning first to our *eardstapa*, he is in exile following the death of his lord and the disintegration of his *comitatus* – an event that appears to have taken place several years before the poem's present. His mood in the beginning of the poem is definitely depressed, though as we move toward the poem's end, he is able to find consolation for his earthly loss through an Augustinian focusing of his desire on eternal things. What is curious about the poem – and what has

---

[19] Jessica D. Payne, et al., 'The Biopsychology of Trauma and Memory', in Daniel Reisberg and Paula Hertel (eds), *Memory and Emotion* (Oxford, 2003), pp. 76–128, at 95.
[20] Ibid., p. 80.
[21] Ibid., p. 94.
[22] Ibid., p. 96.
[23] Ibid.
[24] Ibid., p. 97.
[25] Ibid., p. 108.

generated so much speculation in the criticism – is that we are provided with very few specifics that allow us to contextualize the *eardstapa*'s experience. For example, we do not know why the *eardstapa* is in exile. We do know that he has survived his lord. Most readers assume that his lord and a fair number of his retainers died in battle, and that the *eardstapa* somehow escaped death, much to his own shame. But we are never actually told this. We only know that the *eardstapa*'s lord has died because he tells us that

> geara iu goldwine minne
> hrusan heolstre biwrah, ond ic hean þonan
> wod wintercearig ofer waþema gebind.
> (ll. 22–24)

[long ago I covered my generous lord in earth darkness, and thence I went, wretched and winter-sad, over the binding waves.]

The narrative is sparse; only the gist is recalled (as we might expect, given that these memories were encoded while under emotional duress). Though the context and the specifics of the burial are absent in his description, the emotional content of this passage is pronounced. The *eardstapa* leaves the place of his lord's burial *hean* ('wretched') and *wintercærig* ('winter-sad'). The latter word implies not only desolation, but also possible connections between depression and raised body temperature: the *eardstapa*'s 'winter sorrow' may include a heightened experience of the cold, caused by the disparity between his internal temperature and that of the environment.[26] Increased body temperature and the experience of 'chills' are a common somatic manifestation of depression and other negative emotions; given the understanding of somatic manifestations of emotions evidenced in the Old English corpus, it would not be surprising were this such a reference.[27] But even if this particular detail is unrelated to the *eardstapa*'s

---

[26] See for example D. Marazziti, A. Di Muro, and P. Castrogiovanni, 'Psychological Stress and Body Temperature Changes in Humans', *Physiological Behavior* 52 (1992): 393–5; D. Zhou, A.W. Kusnecov, M.R. Shurin, and B.S. Rabin, 'Exposure to Physical and Psychological Stressors Elevates Plasma Interleukin 6: Relationship to the Activation of Hypothalamic-Pituitary-Adrenal Axis', *Endocrinology* 133 (1993): 2523–30; and S. Arancibia, F. Rage, H. Astier, and L. Tapier-Arancibia,'Neuroendocrine and Autonomous Mechanisms Underlying Thermoregulation in Cold Environment', *Neuroendocrinology* 64 (1996): 257–67.

[27] A study at Aalto University in Finland (L. Nummenmaa, E. Glerean, R. Hari, and J.K. Hietanen, 'Bodily Maps of Emotions', *Proceedings of the National Academy of Sciences*, 2013, DOI: 10.1073/pnas.1321664111) asked participants from Finland, Sweden, and Taiwan to colour in bodily regions whose activity they felt either increase or decrease when presented with specific emotional cues. These 'bodily sensation maps' proved consistent across subjects,

emotional state, this is clearly an overwhelmingly emotional memory: emphasis is placed on the emotions surrounding the event, a 'concentration of experience' focusing almost solely on the decontextualized image of the burial. We can only wonder what the *eardstapa* remembers of the actual events that precipitated his lord's death; it is possible that he lacks recall for these traumatic events, because the presence of stress hormones in the brain prevented them from being properly encoded. He may be further prevented from contextualizing these memories because of the emotional duress under which they are recalled. Just prior to this passage, he explains that he must *feterum sælan'* ('seal with fetters') his *earmcearig modsefan* ('wretched and sad mind/heart'), and tell no one that he is *seledreorig* ('hall-sick/sick from the lack of a hall'). This passage is overwhelmed by the sheer number of words expressing emotional turmoil, burying any narrative context in a whirlpool of emotion locked fast in the *eardstapa*'s *modsefa*. Both encoding and recall are suspect in this case, the memory reduced to an emotion-laden, two- or three-second fragmentary image.

This emotional turmoil would seem to affect the remainder of the 'narrative' part of the poem, as we are presented with a curiosity: a poem that focuses so much of its attention on loss recounts only this single memory of the *eardstapa*'s own traumatic loss. Notwithstanding that the other memories recounted in the poem are displaced onto a hypothetical 'he' whose experiences I have always understood to parallel those of the *eardstapa*, we should take note that none of these memories is of the traumatic event; rather, they are decontextualized memories from before the tragedy that sent the *eardstapa* into exile. If we examine the second passage in which he remembers his lord, we find marked similarities to the first:

>   Ðonne sorg ond slæp   somod ætgædre
>   earmne anhogan   oft gebindað,
>   þinceð him on mode   þæt he his mondryhten
>   clyppe ond cysse   ond on cneo lecge
>   honda ond heafod,   swa he hwilum ær
>   in geardagum   giefstolas breac.
>   Ðonne onwæcneð eft   wineleas guma,
>   gesihð him biforan   fealwe wegas,
>   baþian brimfuglas,   brædan feþra,
>   hreosan hrim ond snaw,   hagle gemenged.
>   (ll. 39–48)

---

demonstrating a degree of universality in the somatic experience of emotional states. While published too late to be included in this chapter, I intend to address the relevance of this study to the Anglo-Saxon understanding of the bodily sensation of emotion in a future article.

[When sorrow and sleep both together often bind the wretched solitary one, it seems to him in his mind that he clasps and kisses his liege lord, lays head and hands on his knee, just as he sometimes before, in days gone by, enjoyed the gift-throne. Then the friendless man awakens again, and sees before him the fallow waves, seabirds bathing, spreading their feathers, frost and falling snow, mingled with hail.]

This passage begins with the sorrowful *eardstapa* falling asleep and suffering from fitful dreams in which decontextualized memories arise in his mind unbidden, leaving him wretched. The act of fealty paid his lord takes on an almost ghostly quality. There is the retainer, there is the lord, there is perhaps a throne, but there are no further details of the ceremony, the place in which it occurred, or others who were in attendance. There is only the gist of the experience, recalled under conditions of sorrow and stress, fragmented images of amygdalar memory, the same as the first recollection of his lord; we should not be at all surprised if we find the details of the ceremony confusing.

This continues in the next section of the poem, in which the *eardstapa*, awakened from the dream of his lord, is visited by the memories of his former companions:

> Þonne beoð þy hefigran   heortan benne,
> sare æfter swæsne;   sorg bið geniwad,
> þonne maga gemynd   mod geondhweorfeð:
> greteð gliwstafum,   georne geondsceawað –
> secga geseldan   swimmað eft onweg.
>
> (ll. 49–53)

[Then heavier wounds are in his heart, sore after his beloved; sorrow is renewed when the remembrance of kinsmen pervades the mind: he greets them gleefully, eagerly surveys hall-companions – they always swim away.]

Again, individuals from the *eardstapa*'s past with whom he once had strong, emotional ties are presented to memory in a disembodied manner, swimming in and out of memory like aquatic apparitions. These memories are even more decontextualized than the memories of his lord, quite possibly due to the *eardstapa*'s greater emotional investment in these hall-companions, who would have been his social peers. Some, at least, are specifically named his kinsmen; these are the people to whom he would most likely have been able to unfetter his *modsefa*. These memories also serve to intensify the sorrow and stress of his exile. 'Sorg bið geniwad', we are told: 'sorrow is renewed'. Once again, the memories called to mind are likely amygdalar; given the *eardstapa*'s current level of emotional distress and the fact that his memories of his lord and companions have all been retroactively linked to the subsequent trauma of their deaths, it is likely that his hippocampus has been flooded with cortisol at the time of recall, and his mind is thus unable to bind these highly emotional memories to any specific context. Instead, they are bound to the emotions of sorrow and grief, and their recall environment is best characterized as one of anxiety, a common symptom in post-traumatic stress disorder. It is important to remember that the phenomenon of the flashback, a PTSD symptom with which most modern readers are familiar from cinematic depictions of Vietnam War veterans, does not need to include memories of the trauma itself. In these amygdalar memories, 'emotion might be remembered in the form of intrusive fear and recurrent images of the trauma (flashback) *or* as persistent anxiety (free-floating anxiety).'[28] While it is not clear whether the *eardstapa* suffers from intrusive fear and recurrent images of the trauma – beyond the image of burying his lord – the anxiety demonstrated in the poem closely resembles existential angst, as I have already noted, a condition that may point toward some sort of generalized anxiety disorder.

Generalized anxiety disorder is commonly comorbid with the depression, and the *eardstapa* certainly presents many of the symptoms associated with depression. While the above passages provide more than enough evidence of a depressed mind, those passages in which the *eardstapa* encounters Roman ruins and projects onto them a story of sorrow and loss that we assume to be similar to his own story reveals that he has learned to read the world through that depression. Daniel Schacter points out that depressed patients 'tend to encode (and therefore retrieve) everyday episodes through a negative filter that confers a kind of repetitive and pervasive drabness on all their experiences'.[29] The landscape in which the ruins are found – indeed, the landscape of the whole poem – is repetitive and drab. The fact that the *eardstapa* assumes that these ruins indicate the destruction of a civilization through battle reveals his belief that his traumatic experiences are ones that repeat themselves throughout history, and will continue to repeat until 'eal þis eorþan gesteal idel weorþeð' (l. 110).[30]

Yet for all the elusiveness of context in *The Wanderer*, the fact that the speaker provides a few concrete details of his life allows readers to construct a very sparse narrative context for his emotional distress. *The Wife's Lament* does not provide enough contextual details to ascertain even basic assumptions about the narrative context. In her edition of the elegies, Anne L. Klinck argues that the poem is spoken by 'a living woman lamenting her confinement in the wilderness and her separation from her living husband'.[31] Yet even these simple

---

[28] Payne, et. al., p. 111.
[29] Daniel Schacter, *Searching for Memory: The Brain, the Mind, and the Past* (New York, 1996), p. 211.
[30] 'All the framework of this earth stands empty.'
[31] Klinck, p. 50.

assumptions have been questioned. Some critics have gone so far as to argue that the speaker of the poem is actually dead, and that the earthen cave from which she is making her address is actually a grave.[32] Others have argued that the speaker is a male, addressing his lord,[33] and another has argued that the speaker is 'a cast off heathen deity, addressing her converted priest.'[34] Klinck's counters these more speculative readings with one that relies upon firmly established meanings for the troublesome Old English terms included in the poem as well as a bare minimum of emendations.

What emerges in Klinck's account are a small number of plot points that are barely contextualized into a coherent narrative. We know that the wife and her husband are separated. We know that there is strife between the wife and her husband's kin, and it is possible that there is strife between the husband and his kin, though this is less certain. We know that the wife has been ordered to be seized and forced to live in a cave, and we think we know that it is the husband who has ordered this. These are the *only* concrete details that emerge from the poem. Klinck ends her introduction to the poem by concluding,

> The speaker's feelings, not the events of her life, nor even in any exact sense her physical surroundings, are the focus, and this makes the poem both highly evocative and at the same time tantalizingly laconic and elliptical. Probably the poet meant to mystify; the woman's circumstances are disturbing largely because they are strange and undefined.[35]

She also notes, 'Words for "longing," which combines desire, suffering, and anxiety form a leitmotiv.'[36] I agree with this assessment, and wish to take it a bit further. I do not think that this poem is about the presentation of concrete details, nor do I think it is an attempt to construct a verse narrative. Instead,

---

[32] Klinck lists three studies in her edition: Elinor Lench, '*The Wife's Lament*: A Poem of the Living Dead', *Comitatus* 1 (1970): 3–23; Raymond P. Tripp, 'The Narrator as Revenant: A Reconsideration of Three Old English Elegies', *PLL* 8 (1972): 339–61; and William C. Johnson, '*The Wife's Lament* as Death-Song', in Martin Green (ed.), *The Old English Elegies: New Essays in Criticism and Research* (Rutherford, NJ, 1983), pp. 69–81.

[33] Klinck lists Levin L. Schücking, 'Das angelsächsische Gedicht von der *Klage der Frau*', *Zeitschrift für Deutsches Altertum und Deutsche Literatur* 48 (1906): 436–49; Rudolf C. Bambas, 'Another View of the Old English *Wife's Lament*', *JEGP* 62.2 (1963): 303–9; Martin Stevens, 'The Narrator of *The Wife's Lament*', *Neuphilologische Mitteilungen* 69 (1968): 72–90; and Jerome Mandel, *Alternative Readings in Old English Poetry* (New York, 1987).

[34] Klinck, p. 49, referencing A.N. Doane, 'Heathen Form and Christian Function in *The Wife's Lament*', *Mediaeval Studies* 28 (1966): 77–91.

[35] Klinck., p. 54.

[36] Ibid.

I think that it is about the presentation of the speaker's emotional state, and believe that the 'mystery' that surrounds this poem can be attributed to the fact that it is an attempt to present a state of emotional duress, the lament of a speaker whose traumatic experiences have, like those of the *eardstapa*, so affected her ability to encode and retrieve memories that what remains of her experience are a few, scattered details surrounded by an incredibly larger number of words expressing her emotional state.

From the first line of the poem, in which the wife explains that she sings this song of herself *ful geomorre* ('very mournful'), we are presented with a deluge of negative emotion stemming from the speaker's *wræcsiþa*: 'torment of exile' or 'painful experience'. The possibility of existential angst or generalized anxiety disorder is raised with the word *uhtceare*, a term that Klinck translates as 'anxiety in the small hours of the morning'. This anxiety appears to be a constant in the wife's life, as she speaks of it as occurring at the beginning of her troubles, when her husband goes away, but continuing through the present, as she explains, 'eal ic eom oflongad' (l. 29),[37] waking as she does in the desolate environment to which she has been banished, missing the presence of her husband. Though Klinck links this anxiety to sexual deprivation, I think it more likely that the anxiety of waking alone is just that: a daily reminder of her alienation and isolation, and of her husband's betrayal. Her comparison of her situation with that of other lovers who lie happily in their beds also need not refer to sexuality; again, her complete lack of companionship, her status as a *wineleas wrecca*, goes far beyond mere sexuality to indicate a much more pervasive deprivation, the sort of deprivation of companionship we encounter in the *eardstapa*, with the same effects on memory, both in terms of the inability to rehearse memory, and the interference with proper encoding and retrieval associated with extreme emotional duress. The somatic elements of this duress are made clear through the use of the terms *modcearu* 'mind sorrow/anxiety' in line 40 and *breostcearu* 'breast sorrow/anxiety' in line 44.

The expression of emotion in *The Wife's Lament* provides a portrait of a remembering mind much like the one we encounter in *The Wanderer*. The wife's memories are as fragmented as the *eardstapa*'s, and seem even more inflected with emotional content than his. Only two clear images emerge from the wife's memory: that of the lord leaving his people 'ofer yþa gelac' ('over the tossing waves'), in line 7, and the lord's 'bliþe gebæro' ('smiling face'), in line 21. The description of the landscape surrounding the earth cave in which the wife has been forced to live also contains a few concrete details; however, this description is not from a memory, but rather from the wife's current existence, and she mentions only that the hills are too high and the dales too dark, most likely drawing a somewhat vague comparison with her homeland.

---

[37] 'Often I am all worn out with anxiety.'

This lack of narrative context can be attributed, in part, to the crucial difference between the speakers of *The Wanderer* and *The Wife's Lament*: one has found an answer to his distress, in the turn to God and the eternal, while the other continues to relive the memories of her past over and over again – a process that appears to prevent her from moving past the traumatic events that have so affected her emotional state. We are told, 'ful oft mec her wraþe begeat / fromsiþ frean' (ll. 32b–33a).[38] The speaker's memories do more than just rise into conscious thought: the poet uses the verb *begietan*, which the *Dictionary of Old English* indicates is, in its usage in *The Wife's Lament*, related to 'emotion, misery, temptation, etc.', and is best translated as 'to take hold of, seize, afflict'. The implication is that these memories not only manifest themselves with some regularity, contributing to the speaker's *uhtceare*, but also violently and overwhelmingly. The Wife, unlike the *eardstapa*, is unable to move past the traumatic events of her past, which continue to define and control her present existence. This becomes particularly clear in lines 39b–41, in which the Wife complains,

> forþon ic æfre ne mæg
> þære modceare   minre gerestan,
> ne ealles þæs longaþes   þe mec on þissum life begeat.

Roy Liuzza translates this passage, 'and so I may never escape from the cares of my sorrowful mind, nor all the longings that have seized my life', capturing an element of the Wife's description often missing in other translations: the notion that her very life has been seized by her memories of the past, that she is incapable of moving forward because she sits alone in her earth-cave, reliving over and over the fragmentary and decontextualized memories of her traumatic past. This is a far cry from *The Wanderer*, with its Augustinian solution to overcoming the power of trauma to cripple one's mind, but the contrast is an enlightening one: the *eardstapa* is able to put his faith in something larger than himself and the experiences through which he has suffered, whereas the Wife is not, and emerges from the poem as one who can now freely speak of his troubles, as he is witnessing the salvific power of God. But whether the differences between these poems can be attributed to the relative levels of paganism and Christianity in each is not a question to tackle as I reach the end of this chapter; I shall, however, make the observation that the Old English elegies provide us with examples of speakers who turn to God manage to successfully negotiate their traumatic experiences and speakers who do neither, and that modern patients suffering from PTSD often turn to a higher power when their own cognitive capabilities prove inadequate to dealing with their trauma. This point of contact between the Anglo-Saxon world and our own should not escape unnoticed.

---

[38] 'Here my lord's leaving very often fiercely took hold of [or seized] me.'

Yet whether we can 'diagnose' fictional characters, particularly those created more than a thousand years ago, with PTSD or any other neurological ailment is, of course, questionable. To begin, these characters are fictional depictions, created by authors who would most definitely not have been thinking in terms of neurobiology. But our Anglo-Saxon authors, working within their culture's somatic understanding of emotion, means that a neurobiological approach, grounded in a strongly somatic understanding of emotion and cognition, is going to yield a reading of the minds depicted in these works with a greater claim to historical and cultural transcendence than, say, a psychoanalytical approach (grounded as psychoanalysis is in a particular historical moment), or even a poststructuralist approach, which, though recognizing the fragmentation displayed in these poems, in the case of *The Wanderer*, attributes it to an anachronistic desire to construct an 'anonymous polyphony', rather than the fragmentation of memory and emotion that accompanies trauma in the human mind, both across time and culture.[39] True, PTSD is a diagnosis whose parameters were first defined in the 1970s, but Anglo-Saxon authors, living in a time of Viking invasions and high mortality rates, would likely have been familiar with individuals suffering from the effects of trauma, and would have been able to incorporate their observations into their depictions of the fictional speakers in their poems. And these poems would not be the earliest texts to depict individuals with the symptoms of what is now classified as PTSD: the earliest depiction of a set of conditions resembling this disorder can be found in Herodotus's account of Epizelus.[40]

When we think of the Anglo-Saxons – or the Ancient Greeks – in terms of cognitive neuroscience, the cultural differences become more easily negotiable, and the subjective experiences with which we are presented – fictional and non-fictional – more accessible to the modern reader. And this is where our experience with the literary text begins: shared subjectivity. We read literature to obtain a window into the minds of others: the minds of authors and their creations – the narrators, speakers, and characters that populate their works. A focus on the depiction of human cognition can only facilitate the opening of these windows, as any text produced during written human history – and that's all of them – will necessarily reveal minds that work much like the reader's own, despite the vast cultural differences that may separate them. In the end, the mysteries of the *eardstapa* and the Wife are a little less mysterious when we consider the effects of trauma on cognition and the formation of emotional memories; Anglo-Saxon emotions may find their external triggers in social matters foreign to the modern reader, but their manifestation in the 'indissociable organism' that is brain and body is something that has remained constant since humanity climbed to this rung on the evolutionary ladder.

---

[39] Carol Braun Pasternack, 'Anonymous Polyphony and *The Wanderer*'s Textuality', *Anglo-Saxon England* 20 (1991): 99–122.

[40] 'Shock Tactics', *Scotsman*, 25 July 2009, retrieved 23 December 2012.

Chapter 14

Early Medieval Experiences of Grief and Separation through the Eyes of Alcuin and Others: The Grief and Gratitude of the Oblate

Mary Garrison

The poignant expressions of abandonment, longing and grief in some Old English poems (especially the *Wanderer, Seafarer, Husband's Message* and *Wife's Lament*) have sometimes invited comparisons with Anglo-Latin literature, most prominently the letters of the nun Bertgyth, but also those of Alcuin and Boniface.[1] That the Latin and vernacular compositions share some characteristic images is intriguing, for it is a clue to a distinctive cultural sensibility. The emotional dimensions of this commonality have been little explored.[2]

Instead, these fictional/poetic and (auto)biographical expressions have enjoyed sharply divergent receptions. The authenticity of the feelings conveyed in the Old English elegies is unquestioned, least of all when the dramatic situation of the speakers is set out so vaguely that the emotional expression is the essence of the poem: it would be silly to ask whether the Seafarer really feels bereft, or whether the woman speaker in *Wulf and Eadwacer* is sincere. In contrast, similar sentiments and expressions in non-fictional first-person texts are subjected to misplaced critical scepticism. Thus Alcuin's longing for absent friends and his frequent requests for prayers and relics have led one commentator

---

[1] Bertgyth: see M. Tangl (ed.), *Bonifatius Epistulae*, MGH *Epistolae selectae in usum scholarum separatim editae* (Berlin, 1916), ep. 143, 147, 148 at pp. 282, 284–7.

[2] A salient exception: Peter Dronke and Ursula Dronke, *Growth of Literature: the Sea and the God of the Sea*, H.M. Chadwick Memorial Lectures, 8 (Cambridge, 1998); see also Peter Dronke, *Women Writers of the Middle Ages: A Critical Study of Texts from Perpetua (†203) to Marguerite Porete (†1310)* (Cambridge, 1984), pp. 30–34; B.K. Martin, 'Aspects of Winter in Latin and Old English Poetry', *Journal of English and Germanic Philology* 68 (1969): 375–90; Michael Lapidge, 'Beowulf, Aldhelm, the Liber Monstrorum and Wessex', *Studi medievali*, 3rd ser., 23 (1982): 151–91.

to characterize him as 'bourgeois and unheroic'.[3] Another has judged that, 'on the whole, grief was not a problem for Alcuin'.[4] Likewise, Boniface's letters have been said to offer a 'glimpse into the tortured heart of the eighth century' and one, even, is 'a pathetic swan song', revealing little of Boniface himself.[5] Finally, to take an example from one of Alcuin's continental pupils, Einhard's letters after the death of his wife have been seen as part of a world of inadequate literary expression, populated, as a result, by 'blurred and lifeless' 'figures'.[6]

The contrast in the treatment of the same emotional register in (fictional) vernacular verse and Latin epistolary sources reflects disciplinary trends, the reception of fictional as opposed to historical texts, and perhaps even the familiar human tendency to hold oneself apart from another's grief.[7] And yet the emotions expressed in the writings of the Anglo-Saxon *peregrini* and the Old English verse derive from the same literary and human background. The *Wanderer*- and *Seafarer*-poets were as steeped in biblical and patristic thought as the Anglo-Latin writers[8] and both might have been familiar with at least some further now-lost vernacular traditions of lament.[9] Anglo-Saxon poets

---

[3] Heinrich Fichtenau, *The Carolingian Empire*, trans. P. Munz (1957; rpt. Toronto, 1978), pp. 94–6 at p. 95.

[4] Peter von Moos, *Consolatio: Studien zur Mittellateinischen Trostliteratur über den Tod und zum Problem der christlichen Trauer* 4 vols (Munich, 1971–1972), III, p. 109: 'Aufs ganze gesehen erscheint in der Alkuinschen Trostkunst die Trauer kaum je als ein Problem'.

[5] Boniface: J.M.W. Wallace-Hadrill, *The Frankish Church* (Oxford, 1983), p. 161. For skepticism about Bede's regard for Ceolfrith, see Walter Goffart, *The Narrators of Barbarian History (A.D. 550–800): Jordanes, Gregory of Tours, Bede, and Paul the Deacon* (1988, rpt. with new preface, Notre Dame, 2005), p. 278, note 200; discussed below. On fictional characters as more real or credible than real people, see Janet Malcolm, *The Silent Woman: Sylvia Plath and Ted Hughes* (1993; rpt. London, 1995), p. 96.

[6] Erich Auerbach, *Literary Language and Its Public in Late Antiquity and the Middle Ages* (1958), trans. Ralph Manheim, Bollingen Series 74 (1965; rpt. with new foreword by Jan Ziolkowski, Princeton, 1993), pp. 122–5.

[7] Fuller discussion, Mary Garrison, 'The Study of Emotions in Early Medieval History: Some Starting Points', *Early Medieval Europe* 10 (2001): 243–50 at p. 249; Garrison, 'An Aspect of Alcuin: "Tuus Albinus" – Peevish Egotist? or Parrhesiast?', in Richard Corradini, Matthew Gillis, Rosamond McKitterick and Irene Renswoude (eds), *Ego Trouble: Authors and their Identities in the Early Middle Ages* (Vienna, 2010), p. 140.

[8] Peter Clemoes, '*Mens absentia cogitans* in *The Seafarer* and *The Wanderer*', in D. Pearsall and R.A. Waldron (eds), *Mediaeval Literature and Civilisation: Studies in Honour of G.N. Garmonsway* (London, 1969), 62–77; Malcolm Godden, 'Anglo-Saxons on the Mind', in Michael Lapidge and Helmut Gneuss (eds), *Learning and Literature in Anglo-Saxon England: Studies Presented to Peter Clemoes on the Occasion of his Sixty-fifth Birthday* (Cambridge, 1985), pp. 271–85.

[9] Andy Orchard, 'Oral Tradition', in Katherine O'Brien O'Keeffe (ed.), *Reading Old English Texts* (Cambridge, 1997), pp. 101–23; Joseph Harris, 'Elegy in Old English and Old

and Latin letter writers alike faced all the uncertainties of a world where radical dependence on protectors human and divine was essential. The lives of the letter writers, Boniface, Bertgyth, Alcuin and other *peregrini*, were marked by successive separations – from biological kindred, home community, homeland.

Grief is raw and complex, perhaps at times a kind of madness, which can bring moments of denial and numbness, but also rage, guilt, regret, despair and abandonment along with sorrow. For all its complexity, grieving as a response to loss is not exclusive to humans. Many animals grieve, not only primates and elephants but also even birds and turtles.[10] In the new history of the emotions, grief itself has lagged behind anger, shame, fear and sexuality. There is of course a rich older tradition of study of consolation literature and funerary art.[11]

In the account that follows, I shall be primarily though not exclusively concerned with the grief occasioned by separation and death, and with exploring its relationship to the practice of child oblation. Child oblation, as is well known, entailed the commendation of a child to a religious house with, in theory, complete separation from biological parents and kindred followed by education in a close-knit group of peers.[12] It is primarily but not exclusively associated with Benedictine monasticism and seems to have occurred around age six. The insight that oblation was understood as a meaningful gift or even sacrifice, rather than rejection or abandonment, has been crucial to recent

---

Norse: A Problem in Literary History', rpt. in Martin Green (ed.), *The Old English Elegies: New Essays in Criticism and Research* (Rutherford, NJ, 1983), pp. 46–56.

[10] B. King, *How Animals Grieve* (Chicago, 2013).

[11] To cite only four examples: Charles Favez, *La consolation latine Chrétienne* (Paris, 1937); Von Moos; Erwin Panofsky, *Tomb Sculpture: Four Lectures on its Changing Aspects from Ancient Egypt to Bernini* (London, 1964); Jill Anne Kowalik, *Theology and Dehumanization: Trauma, Grief, and Pathological Mourning in Seventeenth and Eighteenth-century German Thought and Literature*, ed. Gail Hart, Ursula Mahlendorf and Thomas P. Saine, Berliner Beiträge zur Literatur- und Kulturgeschichte (London, 2009), pp. 41–57.

[12] M. de Jong, *In Samuel's Image: Child Oblation in the Early Medieval West* (Leiden, 1996), pp. 145–55; M. Lahaye-Geusen, *Das Opfer der Kinder: Ein Beitrag zur Liturgie- und Sozialgeschichte des Mönchtums im hohen Mittelalter*, Münsteraner Theologische Abhandlungen 13 (Altenberge, 1991), both offering an alternative view to J. Boswell's construction of oblation as abandonment in his *The Kindness of Strangers: The Abandonment of Children in Western Europe from Late Antiquity to the Renaissance* (Chicago, 1988) and '*Expositio* and *Oblatio*: The Abandonment of Children and the Ancient and Medieval Family', *American Historical Review* 89 (1984): 10–33. For the later Anglo-Saxon centuries, Katherine O'Brien O'Keefe, *Stealing Obedience: Narratives of Agency in Later Anglo-Saxon England*, H.M. Chadwick Memorial Lecture (Cambridge: Department of Anglo-Saxon, Norse and Celtic, 2009) and the book of the same title (Toronto, 2012). *RB 1980: The Rule of Benedict in Latin and English with Notes*, ed. Timothy Fry (Collegeville, MN, 1981), cap. 58-9, pp. 267–73.

interpretations.[13] How would this experience affect individuals and contribute to a distinctive cultural and religious sensibility? What can modern psychological insights into attachment, separation and grief add to our understanding of medieval experience? I shall seek to illuminate what might have been distinctive about the experience of grief for Alcuin and others who had been child oblates by juxtaposing their first-hand testimonies with modern attachment theory. However, to appreciate the particularity of individual experience in a remote era also invites a broader consideration of the place of grief in the wider emotional landscape of that culture. Past cultures are not static or homogenous, so regional contrasts, turning points and some pertinent modern comparanda may be useful. The evidence for grieving (as well as for the refusal to grieve and its consequences) can be an ultra-violet lamp[14] that reveals patterns of attachment unlike those of our world.

Modern Understandings of Grief

In the past hundred years, the psychoanalytical study of mourning has been characterized by diverse, sometimes contradictory paradigms, but two crucial insights underlie most theoretical and therapeutic approaches: namely, that later griefs recapitulate earlier ones and that there is a distinction between successful mourning – the 'work' of mourning, which brings a kind of resolution – and melancholy (arrested, pathological or 'complicated' grieving), which does not.[15]

In the twentieth century, John Bowlby's pioneering studies of attachment and loss showed that secure maternal attachment (especially during the first two years) conferred resilience and the capacity to form strong connections; insecure attachment (due to inconsistent early mothering or the early loss of the mother) had long-lasting negative effects. Insecure attachment is further subdivided into anxious–preoccupied, fearful–avoidant and dismissive–avoidant style; the labels predict the way a person will experience and negotiate the later quest for intimacy. Bowlby argued that the experiences of the first two years were the most crucial.

---

[13]   Compare the views of Boswell, and de Jong.

[14]   Metaphor used of the comparative method in general, Jonathan Shay, *Achilles in Vietnam: Combat Trauma and the Undoing of Character* (New York, 1994), p. 147.

[15]   Sigmund Freud, 'Mourning and Melancholia' (1915), rpt. in A. Richards (ed.), *On Metapsychology: The Theory of Psychoanalysis. The Penguin Freud Library II*, trans. J. Strachey (Harmondsworth, 1984), pp. 245–67. For grief turned to melancholy: John R. Cole, 'Montaigne's Dead Babies', in *Montaigne Studies* 12.1–2 (2000): 167–84. Research by George Bonanno on resilience and complicated grief has revised earlier paradigms, including Elisabeth Kübler-Ross's well-known five-stages model; see his *The Other Side of Sadness: What the New Science of Bereavement tells us about Life after Loss* (New York, 2009). I leave out the matter of object relations theory and the one- or two-body viewpoints.

So very early maternal deprivation would have enduring repercussions even while there would still be a possibility for life-long development in the capacity for attachment.[16] Bowlby also established a correlation between infantile insecure attachment and subsequent enduring difficulty with loss and separation. Thus early trauma predisposes a person to later difficulty with grief, or to excessively needy, distant or ambivalent future relationships. Bowlby's insights now seem obvious; at the time they represented a controversial new direction.[17]

Recent research and practice in grief therapy holds that fully mourning adult losses can bring an opportunity to heal earlier wounds. Encountering acceptance and support during grief can enable a bereaved person to regain the capacity to feel dangerous emotions that had been suppressed during childhood; in so doing, a person becomes more whole and alive.[18] The healing comes from regaining parts of the self that had been suppressed because of pressure to be 'good' to gain the love and approval of caregivers who had been unable to be consistently present and offer unconditional love to a child, especially when it was expressing negative or disruptive emotions. In all, current psychological understandings of grieving (no matter whether based on Freudian drive theory or object relations) converge in seeing grief as a *natural* process that should progress towards some resolution; the inability to do the work of mourning is thus deemed to require therapeutic intervention. Meanwhile the larger culture remains more uncomfortable with grief than at many times in the past.

How appropriate is it to resort to modern understandings of grief in the quest for a richer understanding of fragmentary evidence about past individuals? Clearly, there are caveats. One arises from the value judgement implied by the term 'pathological grieving'. Other cultures, eras and literary traditions have not always regarded refusal to finish grieving as pathological. ('Closure' and 'moving on' are characteristically modern expressions.) In the Anglo-American ballad tradition, lovers regularly die of broken hearts; that motif normalizes the refusal

---

[16] Mary Ainsworth and John Bowlby, *Child Care and the Growth of Love* (London, 1965); John Bowlby, *Attachment and Loss*, 3 vols (New York, 1969, 1973, 1980); Nini Leick and Marianne Davidsen-Nielsen, *Healing Pain: Attachment, Loss, and Grief Therapy*, trans. D. Stoner (London, 1991); Colin Murray Parkes, 'Traditional Models and Theories of Grief', *Bereavement Care* 17.2 (1998): 21–3; Neil Small, 'Theories of Grief: A Critical Review', in Jenny Hockey, Jeanne Katz and Neil Small (eds), *Grief, Mourning and Death Ritual* (Buckingham, 2001), pp. 19–48.

[17] Christopher Reeves, 'Why Attachment? Whither Attachment?: John Bowlby's Legacy, Past and Future', *The Online Journal of the American Association for Psychoanalysis in Clinical Social Work* 2 (December 2007): http://www.beyondthecouch.org/1207/reeves.htm (accessed 31 May 2013).

[18] Leick and Davidsen-Nielsen, pp. 14–24; Alice Miller, *The Drama of the Gifted Child: The Search for the True Self*, trans. Alice Ward (1981; rpt. New York, 1997), pp. 13, 56, 61, 59–61.

to let go. The same tradition also transmits a contrasting, warning, motif: the revenant dead lover who forbids the grief-stricken living partner from a final embrace because the kiss of the dead would bring death.[19]) Prohibition of grief can also be a collective cultural norm; this has sometimes been the case for groups of elite males. As the proverb in Beowulf affirms:

> Ne sorga, snotor guma.   Selre bið æghwæm
> þæt he his freond wrece,   þonne he fela murne.[20]

> [Do not grieve, wise man. It is better for every man
> that he avenge his friend than that he mourn much.]

In many heroic literatures and cultures, male losses are correlated with violent acts of revenge. If revenge is the only outlet for the pain of loss, impossible dilemmas arise. Hence, when one of King Hrethel's sons accidentally killed his brother, the old king, unable to find release in either mourning or revenge, died of sorrow.[21] Modern psychology would suggest that these episodes, like dying of a broken heart, are pathological grieving. But the diagnosis is problematic. For some tribes or polities, the obligation of vengeance against an outside killer (sometimes associated with restrictions on mourning for the victim) might seem adaptive for group survival. The interpretative dilemma points to the importance of studying individual expressions of grief from other eras against a collective background. In a recent collection on medieval emotions, Stephen Jaeger called attention to the distinction between individual emotion and the public shared sensibility of an era.[22] Mary Douglas wrote, 'psychological explanations cannot of their nature account for what is culturally distinctive' and yet, with grief, the culturally distinctive may not foster individual well-being.[23]

---

[19] N. Würzbach and S.M. Salz, *Motif Index of the Child Corpus: The English and Scottish Popular Ballad* (Berlin, 1995), pp. 21 (death from grief at death of wife/mistress) (for rejection of love), 26–27 (ghost, encounter with; revenants, etc.), 35 (love rejected, death from).

[20] *Beowulf and the Fight at Finnsburg*, 3rd edn with first and second supplements, ed. Frederick Klaeber (1922, rpt. New York, 1950), pp. 52–3, lines 1384–5.

[21] *Beowulf*, lines 2444 and 2464;. See, *inter alia*, Linda Georgianna, 'King Hrethel's Sorrow and the Limits of Heroic Action in Beowulf', *Speculum* 62 (1987): 829–50. See also Shay, pp. 39–68, on military grief and non-grieving.

[22] Stephen Jaeger, 'Introduction', in S. Jaeger and Ingird Kasten (eds), *Codierung von Emotionen im Mittelalter* (Berlin, 2003), pp. vii–ix.

[23] Mary Douglas, *Purity and Danger: An Analysis of the Concepts of Pollution and Taboo* (1966; rpt. London, 1984), p. 121. For a challenging study of pathological grief in seventeenth- and eighteenth-century German thought, arguing that sermons about death during and after the Thirty Years' War fostered a culture of widespread pathological mourning, see Kowalik.

Second and no less important: most recent perspectives on human attachment are based on a model of child rearing that presupposes a dyadic mother–child bond and often also the nuclear family. However, through time and space, human societies have been characterized by great diversity in childrearing arrangements; the dyadic model is not a biological necessity, nor the only possible mode.[24] It is also widely recognized that the nuclear family is not and has not been universal. So to explore past testimonies about grief and separation, we shall have to reckon on the possibility that primary attachments and infantile experiences might have been very different from those of Bowlby's subjects. Accordingly, it may be useful to consider phenomena such as child oblation and monastic education, secular fosterage and court-rearing, alongside instances of *communal* childcare and parental separation from other eras. Moreover, we must give full weight to the role of religious belief. God and the saints could serve, for some, as attachment figures and protectors. The role of theism and grief is complex: dismiss the relevance of belief and risk an impoverished view of human experience. Similar reductionism results from assuming the efficacy of the consolatory discourse that holds out the joys of heaven for the departed as an instant, rather than hard-won, solution.[25]

Third, there are the familiar challenges of incomplete evidence. We know virtually nothing of eighth-century Anglo-Saxon childrearing practices, nor of the very earliest experiences of any documented individuals. Extant testimonies are third-hand or hearsay and can seem implausible – was Willibrord handed over to Ripon immediately after weaning, as Alcuin reported?[26] Had Bede really begun to love books before being given to Wearmouth?[27] Any individual's experience of oblation would have been superimposed on an already-formed but now unknowable attachment style. Is it valid to infer an attachment style from the reaction to oblation? Or to look for connections between childhood oblation and later experiences of grief and reactions to separation? For this speculative venture, Alcuin's testimonies will be our chief source.

---

[24] Sarah Hrdy, *Mothers and Others: The Evolutionary Origins of Mutual Understanding* (Cambridge, Massachusetts, 2009); on allo-mothering and the concept of cooperative breeding: *Mother Nature: Maternal Instincts and How They Shape the Human Species* (New York, 2000).

[25] Kowalik, pp. 41–57.

[26] Alcuin, *Vita Willibrordi*, cap. 3, ed. W. Wattenbach, in W. Wattenbach and E. Dümmler (eds), *Monumenta Alcuiniana a Philippo Iaffeo praeparata* (Berlin, 1873), pp. 36–79 at 42; de Jong, In *Samuel's Image*, pp. 50, 137, 241.

[27] Alcuin, *The Bishops, Kings and Saints of York*, ed. P. Godman (Oxford, 1982), lines 1291–2, pp. 102–3. (Hereafter, cited as Alcuin, *York Poem*.)

Reading Alcuin's Grief

Grief and expressions of longing for absent friends are a recurring presence in Alcuin's letters as they must have been in his life; yet, as we have seen, even a scholar as perceptive as Fichtenau saw Alcuin's anxiety about friends and concern with relics as 'bourgeois and unheroic'.[28] For all eras, expressions about loss and consolation can seem either too opaque or too transparent; a reader can be tricked into assuming either that 'we know just what they mean' or else that the feelings are not authentic. It is important to remember that our own language of consolation is no less formulaic than the medieval idiom.[29] Topoi and stock expressions can regain their power and allow a glimpse of the shared understanding of sender and receiver only when readers approach them with sensitivity to context and elaboration and with empathy from personal memories of loss. Helen Waddell explains such reading in a comment in *More Latin Lyrics*:

> Alcuin's lament for the sack of Lindisfarne by the Northmen seemed to me when I read it years ago a little trite and full of ancient platitude; now that the bombers circle over Holy Island, I read it with a kind of contemporary anguish.[30]

Expressions that appear to be flat, or else maudlin and uncontrolled, to a reader from another era may not have been so for a contemporary. Similarly, quotations and intertextual references do not necessarily detract from sincerity; rather, their meaning depends on the full individual and cultural context of the intertextual borrowing. The distribution of particular expressions must be taken into account as well as their sources. Finally, intuitions need to be informed by self-awareness and by contextual and comparative information.

We know, for example, that Alcuin's friendship with Arn was one of his closest, not so much from the supposedly passionate greetings (which are straight from Jerome, sometimes directed to others, and not necessarily erotically intended), but rather because Alcuin's letters to Arn mention missing him and arrangements for meetings far more often than his letters to other correspondents.[31] That Alcuin alone among the learned courtiers used nicknames for Charlemagne's daughters reveals as much about his special intimacy with the royal family as the tone of

---

[28] See above, note 3, and Garrison, 'Peevish Egotist', pp. 143–4.

[29] Garrison, 'Peevish Egotist', p. 142.

[30] Helen Waddell, *Medieval Latin Lyrics* (1929; rpt. New York, 1948), p. 37. For an example of flippancy, see Jonathan Jarrett's characterization of Alcuin's post-Lindisfarne letters as 'eschatological froth': http://tenthmedieval.wordpress.com/2011/09/21/the-first-viking-raid-on-england-or-francia/ (accessed 21 September 2011).

[31] Garrison, '"Praesagum nomen tibi": The Significance of Name-wordplay in Alcuin's Letters to Arn', in Meta Niederkorn-Bruck and Anton Scharer (eds), *Erzbischof Arn von Salzburg* (Vienna, 2004), pp. 107–27.

his letters to them.[32] Similarly, Alcuin's deployment, in poems to Charlemagne and one of his daughters, of the *exclusus amator* topos, the image of the lover shut out, rejected, in bad weather outside his mistress's door, reveals something about the intensity of his connection to them.[33] Alcuin's poems play on shared knowledge of Tibullan love poetry and borrow Tibullus's objective correlative of stormy weather to dramatize feelings of perceived neglect. Tibullus would have been unknown to all outside the closest court circle. An unsympathetic view of court life and the role of remembered reading might lead a reader to dismiss this as merely elitist display. But the mutual regard of Alcuin and Charlemagne and Alcuin's special status as an intimate of the royal family, combined with the stark reality of any courtier's acute dependence, bespeak a heartfelt plea intensified by the allusion to shared reading.

In these examples, expressions of attachment are intertwined with separation and loss. In the early 790s, Alcuin wrote to Paulinus of Aquileia:

> But I fear – which I cannot say without the greatest grief [in] my heart – that in this life I shall not again see the countenance of your blessedness. Since we make our toilsome journey of this life on the road of separation and we hasten through the vale of tears to an uncertain end; and perishable flesh swiftly returns to where it came from, and all its beauty withers, stricken by a burning wind.[34]

Bible quotations are a standard element in the consolatory discourse that forbids grieving. Alcuin himself often purveyed such consolation. Here, in contrast, biblical reminiscences add poignance to the expression of grief at separation and anticipated death. The start of the passage recalls Paul's tearful final farewell to the Elders of Ephesus after he had explained that he was going to Jerusalem and

---

[32] Garrison, 'Les correspondants d'Alcuin', in Philippe Depreux and Bruno Judic (eds), *Alcuin de York à Tours: Écriture, pouvoir et réseaux dans l'Europe du haut moyen âge*, Annales de Bretagne et des Pays de l'Ouest 111. 3 (Rennes, 2004): 319–32.

[33] Garrison, 'Alcuin and Tibullus', in M.C. Díaz y Díaz and J.M. Díaz de Bustamante (eds), *Poesía Latina Medieval (siglos V–XV): Actas del IV congreso del 'Internationales Mittellateinerkomitee', Santiago de Compostela, 12–15 de Septiembre de 2002* (Florence. 2005), pp. 749–59. For a most illuminating study of the distinctive nature of court relationships, see Stephen Jaeger, *Ennobling Love: In Search of a Lost Sensibility* (Philadelphia, 1999).

[34] E. Dümmler (ed.), *Alcuini epistolae*, MGH Epistolae IV, Epistolae Karolini Aevi II (Berlin, 1895), ep. 86, p. 130: Sed vereor—quod sine maximo cordis dolore non dico—me ulterius in hac vita tuae beatitudinis faciem non visurum. Quia in via divisionis iter agimus laboriosum et per vallem lacrimabilem ad incertum properamus finem; et cito fragilis caro, unde sumpta est, [Iob 27.21] revertetur; et omnis decor illius, urente percussa vento, flaccescit [Eccl 12.5.7] et ibit homo in domum aeternitatis suae et circa eum stabunt in platea plangentes, et spiritus revertetur ad Deum, qui dedit illum.

they would never see his face again; reminiscences of Job and Ecclesiastes colour the transience imagery.[35]

Alcuin's plangent longing for absent or rejecting friends can be paralleled in the writings of other *peregrini*. Some decades earlier, an eighth-century Anglo-Saxon nun in Thuringia, Bertgyth, had corresponded with her brother in England. It will be useful to juxtapose Bertgyth's three letters with Alcuin's. Her letters articulate the theme of longing for a distant correspondent no less powerfully; moreover, the final extant letter by Bertgyth encapsulates the essential theme of the grief and gratitude of the oblate into a single sentence.

In her earliest extant letter, Bertgyth wrote:

> What is it, my brother,/ that you have let pass such a long time,/ that you have delayed to come? / Why do you not want to remember,/ that I am alone on this earth/ and no other brother will visit me,/ or any other kinsman will come to me ... Oh brother, oh my brother, / How can you afflict the mind of me, who am naught,/ with constant grief, weeping and sorrow, / day and night through the absence of your love?/ .... Look, I can't suggest all this to you by letter./ Already I feel certain that you don't care about me, who am naught.[36]

As Peter Dronke observes, 'the evocation of solitude and tears and longing has precise parallels in the two extant Anglo-Saxon women's love-laments, known as "The Wife's Complaint" and "Wulf and Eadwacer"'.[37]

Near the start of a second letter, Bertgyth continued in similar vein:

---

[35] Acts 20.37–38: 'magnus autem fletus est omnium et procumbentes super collum Pauli osculabantur eum (38) dolentes maxime in verbo quo dixerat **quoniam amplius faciem eius non essent visuri**' [emphasis added]; 'And there was much weeping ... and falling on the neck of Paul they kissed him (38) being grieved most of all for all the words which he had said, that they should see his face no more' (Douai Rheims).

[36] Translation from Dronke, *Women Writers*, pp. 30–31 with essential discussion. Dronke's line divisions, indicated with slashes, evoke the metrical and sense-units of vernacular verse; *Bonifatii Epistulae*, ep. 143, p. 282: 'Quid est, frater mi, quod tam longum tempus intermisisti, quod venire tardasti? Quare non vis cogitare, quod ego sola in hac terra et nullus alius frater visitet me neque propinquorum aliquis ad me veniet? Et si ideo facis, quia adhuc nihil potui secundum quod mens mea diligenter voluisset, aliquid beneficii inpendere, tamen caritatis atque adfinitatis iura nullo alio suadente aut mens tua mutando debes obliviscere. O frater, o frater mi, cur potes mentem parvitatis meae adsiduae merore fletu atque tristitia die noctuque caritatis tuae absentia adfligere? Nonne pro verto scies, quia viventius omnium nullum aliom propono tuae caritati? Ego non possum omnia per litteras tibi indicare. Iam ergo certum teneo, quod tibi cura non est de mea parvitate'.

[37] Dronke, *Women Writers*, p. 31.

> For I am alone, forsaken and deprived of the support of kin. 'For my father and my mother have left me: but the Lord hath taken me up'. [Ps 26.10] Great are the gatherings of waters between me and you, still, let us be joined in love, since true love is never sundered by a difference of place. But still I declare that *tristitia* never departs from my soul, nor do I find peace of mind at night in sleep; 'since love is as strong as death' [Cant.8.6] ... Now therefore I ask you, O my most beloved brother, that you come to me, or make me come to you, so that I may see you before I die, since love for you never departs from my soul.[38]

We know from her third letter that Bertgyth's brother had sent a messenger who delivered some gifts and announced the brother's intention to visit; in his letter, which is lost, the brother apparently also chided Bertgyth for her attachment to him, exhorting fuller devotion to God.[39] She responded with anticipation, but also yearning. Though she wished to fulfil all he had commanded, she insisted again, slightly defensively, that her desire for a visit was the result of unceasing love.[40] Yet alongside all the powerful feelings of abandonment and longing in each of her letters (even after the brother's reply), Bertgyth's third letter also reveals that she had been able to find comfort for the anguish of early childhood abandonment in God's mercy. Even so, her warm and enduring gratitude to God for *not* having abandoned her did not dilute her anxious yearning and intense affection for her brother. From the perspective of attachment theory, the combination of Bertgyth's emphasis on her unworthiness (to receive divine comfort) and her enduring sadness and neediness seem to point to insecure attachment.[41]

> ... for I cannot by any means quell the fountain of my tears. When I see and hear that others will go to their friends, then I recall that I was entirely forsaken by my parents in my youth and have remained here alone. And yet for all that, I was not abandoned by God, but I give thanks to God for his great kindness, which he is often accustomed to grant by his tender mercies[42] to the undeserving, and thus he has saved us sound and whole. And now my brother, I adjure and beseech you, that you lift this sadness from my heart, since it hurts me greatly.[43]

---

[38] *Bonifatii epistolae*, ep. 147, p. 284.

[39] *Bonifatii epistolae*, ep. 148, p. 285, lines 24–5. Discussion Dronke, *Women Writers*.

[40] Tangl (ed.), *Bonifatii epistolae*, ep. 148, p. 286, line 15–17: 'Sin autem displicet tibi inplere petitionem meam, tunc Deum testem inuoco, quod in me numquam fit derelicta dilectio nostra'.

[41] Miller, p. 28.

[42] *Misericordie ... uiscera*: biblical *viscera* (bowels, innards) denote the part of the self that is the seat of compassion, good-heartedness, hence translation.

[43] Tangl (ed.), *Bonifatii epistolae*, ep. 149, p. 286: 'quia ullo modo fontem lacrimarum adquiescere [not us. transitive] non possum. Quando video et audio alias ituras ad amicas suas, tunc recolo quod a parentibus in iuuentute derelicta fui et sola hic permansi. Et tamen

The experiences and emotions that Bertgyth distils into just a few sentences here can be found scattered widely through Alcuin's writings. For Alcuin too, attachment theory and the psychology of grief seem to suggest a connection between the anxiety about separation from friends (evinced in adult poems and letters) and earlier experiences. As we have seen, psychoanalytical theories of grief suggest that each new occasion of loss recapitulates earlier ones; the unhealed wound of the past grief reopens, compounding present sorrow; insecure early attachment sets up the likelihood of difficulty grieving and an anxious or dismissive–avoidant attachment style. Juxtaposing Alcuin's consolation writings to others with his testimonies about his own grief and longing and with what we know of the circumstances of his life can suggest that grief was almost continuously present. Thus one might interpret the frequent expressions of sadness and anxiety about absent friends (an Alcuinian leitmotif) as a reflex of the deep infantile injury to Alcuin's sense of security, a trauma compounded when he was handed over to the *familia* of York Minster. Alcuin never mentions his biological parents; from his statements about his devotion to his teacher Ælberht, we might suspect that he transferred his insecure parental attachment to the community which had raised him, above all to Ælberht.[44]

Alcuin's total silence about his parents is significant and intriguing. That he knew something about several generations of his biological family is certain since he mentions having inherited a church at Spurn Point from Willibrord's father Wilgils.[45] Were his parents dead, so that the church came to him? Or did he choose not to mention them as a reaction to trauma? As an adult, it was his teacher Ælberht whom he regarded as a father; he addressed and described members of the cathedral community as parents, brothers and sons. The epitaph he wrote for Ælberht is steeped in filial devotion and close identification. Alcuin later used many of the same words he had used about Ælberht to describe himself in his own epitaph, evoking their shared pursuit of wisdom.[46] Unusually, he

---

a Domino derelicta non fui, sed gratias ago Deo de **inmensa** eius **pietate**, quam saepe **non merentibus** per **misericordie** suae **viscera donare consuevit** et sic nos incolumes **servavit**. Et nunc frater mi, adiuro te atque deprecor, ut auferas tristitiam ab anima mea, quia valde nocet mihi ....'

[44] Mayke de Jong, 'From Scholastici to Scioli: Alcuin and the Formation of an Intellectual Elite', in L.A.J.R. Houwen and Alasdair A. McDonald (eds), *Alcuin of York: Scholar at the Carolingian Court*, Germania Latina, vol. 3, (Groningen 1998), pp. 45–57.

[45] Alcuin, *Vita Willibrordi archiepiscopi Traiectensis*, ed. W. Levison, in *MGH Scriptores Rerum Merovingicarum 7: Passiones vitaeque sanctorum aevi Merovingici V*, ed. B. Krusch and W. Levison (Hanover, 1920), 1.1 at p. 116. For the *Vita Alcuini*'s brief allusion to commendation to York Minster, see *Vita Alcuini*, ed. Wilhelm Arndt, MGH Scriptores Rerum Germanicarum 15.1 (Hanover, 1887), cap. 4, pp. 186–7.

[46] *MGH PLAC* I, ed. Ernst Dümmler, Alcuin, carm. 2, pp. 206–7 and carm. 123, pp. 350–51.

inserted himself into six lines of the fourteen-line epitaph for Ælberht, recalling Ælberht's role as his teacher from his earliest years, his own devotion, and his willingness to follow and serve his master anywhere.[47] In short, there is a lot of autobiography in an epitaph for someone else. Together the epitaphs seem to show Alcuin's identity intertwined with Ælberht's. Here a Freudian would recall Freud's notion of melancholy as mourning stalled because of the mourner's identification with the lost object.

Alcuin's grief at Ælberht's death is conspicuous in his long poem about York. Indeed, the death is narrated or referred to no less than six times in the space of seventy lines, usually with some additional description of the associated grief.[48] The poem's editor, Peter Godman, commented, 'to the Roman foundation and occupation of York are devoted 19 lines of Alcuin's poem; the death of Ælberht alone receives 34'.[49] The apparent rawness of the grief led Louis Holtz to the strongest argument for an early date for the poem.[50] Whether the poem actually conveys fresh grief or instead 'powerful feelings... recollected in tranquility', we can safely assume that Alcuin and his intended audience, the minster *familia*, would have felt the loss acutely. Alcuin's literary representation of the emotions must relate to their shared experience, not least because he was addressing others touched by the same grief.[51] What is most telling, however, is not the number of lines devoted to the event, but rather, the impression of lack of control. Ælberht's death does not constitute a discrete thirty-four line vignette. Rather, Alcuin circles back to it again and again, sometimes protesting against it, in a meandering, recursive, non-chronological exposition.

---

[47] Ibid., Alcuin, carm. 2. See Freud, 'Mourning and Melancholia'. For the parallel between Alcuin and Hrabanus, see M.C. Ferrari, 'Alcuin und Hraban. Freundschaft und auctoritas im 9. Jahrhundert', in B. Körkel, T. Licht and J. Wiendlocha (eds), *Mentis amore ligati. Lateinische Freundschaftsdichtung und Dichterfreundschaft in Mittelalter und Neuzeit. Festgabe für Reinhard Düchting zum 65. Geburtstag* (Heidelberg, 2001), pp. 81–92, and Garrison, 'Alcuin, *carmen ix* and Hrabanus, *Ad Bonosum*: a Teacher and his Pupil Write Consolation', in John Marenbon (ed.), *Poetry and Philosophy in the Middle Ages: A Festschrift for Peter Dronke* (Leiden, 2001), pp. 70–71.

[48] Alcuin, York Poem, lines 1520–22; 1563–5; 1568; 1573–5; 1583–5; and 1590–91, indirectly.

[49] Alcuin: York Poem, p. lvii.

[50] L. Holtz, 'Alcuin et la renaissance des arts libéraux', in P. Butzer, M. Kerner and W. Oberschelp (eds), *Charlemagne and His Heritage: 1200 Years of Civilization and Science in Europe* (Brepols, 1997), p. 51, note 17: '[le poème] se termine par une lamentation sur la mort d'Ælberht, ressentie comme toute récente'.

[51] William Wordsworth, preface to the second edition of *Lyrical Ballads, with Other Poems, volume 1* (1800), p. 14, http://www.gutenberg.org/ebooks/8905 (accessed 20 August 2014).

When one looks beyond the familiarity of many of Alcuin's phrases (*O nobis, O nigra dies! O clara sed illi*, 1576), the rawness of the *depiction* of the emotions (especially in contrast to the epitaph) stands out. In combination, repetition, wrenched syntax and images enact a turmoil that hinders fluent logical speech, veering into loss and then defending against full recollection of pain. Chaos and abandonment are evoked. The image of drowning in tears is reified when Ælberht's survivors are likened to orphans on a stormy sea.[52] Grief's power to destroy creativity and hope is dramatized when the poem is envisaged, successively, as in danger of shipwreck, drowned in tears, and as a ship bereft of its pilot.[53] Would it be inferring too much to suggest that the description of the passengers adrift implies anger at the pilot who has wrongfully *deserted* his passengers? Alcuin stops short of making Ælberht the subject of the active verb *desero*, instead describing those who remain as *deserti*.[54] The state of being forsaken implies a wrongful departure. Still there is some consolation to be had: from the perpetuation of Ælberht's memory, from the image of regular seasonal change adumbrating of divine order, and above all, from the prospect of a joyous reunion in heaven.[55] For all the profusion of logical arguments in his attempts to console others, Alcuin's own most deeply felt encounter with grief required images rather than arguments or doctrine.

A glimpse from another source corroborates the severe trauma, for Alcuin, of Ælberht's death. The *Vita Alcuini*'s anonymous ninth-century author (who had had one of Alcuin's students as an informant) described '[Ælberht], whom the good Albinus wept bitterly for with his tears, as if for his mother, and would not be consoled'.[56] Here there is an additional layer of psychological complexity. Alcuin grieves for Ælberht as if a child for his mother, but at the same time, the wording of the passage recalls two biblical exempla of inconsolable parental grief: Rachel bitterly weeping for her children and Jacob lamenting for Joseph when he believed him dead.[57] The allusions do not merely escalate the grief into archetypal inconsolability. Rather, the bereft child merges with the grief-stricken parent. This fusion, or confusion, of grieving subjects and objects is significant.

---

[52] Alcuin, *York Poem*, lines 1570, 1576–8. The link between salt tears and the salt sea is widespread: for discussion, Dronke and Dronke.

[53] Alcuin, *York Poem*, lines 1589–90 and 1572–3.

[54] Alcuin, *York Poem*, lines 1590–91: 'te sine nos ferimur turbata per aequora mundi/te duce deserti variis inuoluimur undis'.

[55] Alcuin, *York Poem*, lines 1579; 1593; 1625ff.

[56] On the personal testimony of Siguulf available to the vita-author, Bullough, *Alcuin*, pp. 29 and 237; on the grief, *Vita Alcuini* cap. 8, p .189: 'quem pius Albinus ut matrem deplorans lacrimis nolebat tamen consolationem recipere'.

[57] Rachel: Jeremiah 31.15 'et nolentis consolari super eos' and Mt 2.18 'noluit consolari'. Jacob: Genesis 37.35 'noluit consolationem accipere'.

Why should the writer (who had not himself known Alcuin) choose to represent the adult subject of the *vita* as a disconsolate orphan, and why elide the images of orphan and parent?[58] The choice may reflect the author's empathy for the situation and his sense of the best way to convey the emotions and awaken sympathy. As a former oblate himself, he would have known the same deep attachment to a *nutritor*. Indeed, the pattern of such attachment can be traced across generations.[59] Alcuin's own students felt towards him the same kind of filial love that he had had for Ælberht; this is evident in the writings of Hrabanus Maurus, a former oblate who had come to study with Alcuin as a teenager. A decade after Alcuin's death, Hrabanus would describe Alcuin interceding in prayer on his behalf (again, like Alcuin, refusing to let go of the father figure) and Alcuin remained present through Hrabanus's poetic borrowings, through liturgical commemoration at Fulda, and through Hrabanus's use and explanation of his Alcuinian by-name Maurus.[60] Alcuin himself had conjured his paternal teacher's posthumous presence in his letters and, even after he had spent many years in Francia, his understanding of his destiny and Northumbrian affairs would still revolve around memories of Ælberht's statements and prophecies.[61]

The chronology of Alcuin's life invites extrapolation from these facts. Not long after Ælberht's death in November 780, Alcuin had travelled to Rome to collect the archiepiscopal pallium for Ælberht's successor, Eanbald I. On the way back, on 15 March, he met Charlemagne (not by chance, nor for the first time) in Parma and received the invitation to join the Frankish court.[62] Alcuin would later protest to his former comrades at York (perhaps protesting too much) that he still loved them despite his service to Charlemagne; he would describe Charlemagne as a friend granted to him by God.[63] Charlemagne, for his part, valued Alcuin so much that he tried to keep him with him as much as possible during Alcuin's first continental sojourn. It seems, then, both from the timing and from his subsequent devotion, that Alcuin transferred his filial attachment from Ælberht to Charlemagne.

In modern psychological terms the story could be retold thus: Alcuin suffered from unresolved grief: a primal trauma in infancy shaped an anxious

---

[58] *Vita Alcuini: orbatus*, used of death of Egberht, p. 186.

[59] De Jong, 'From Scholastici to Scioli', on the characteristic bonds. See also Sita Steckel, *Kulturen des Lehrens im Früh- und Hochmittelalter: Autorität, Wissenkonzepte und Netzwerke von Gelehrten*, Norm und Struktur: Studien zum Sozialen Wandel in Mittelalter und frühen Neuzeit 39 (Köln, 2010), pp. 110–16; 170–84.

[60] Ferrari, pp. 81–92; Garrison, 'Alcuin, cam. IX and Hrabanus', pp. 66–7.

[61] *Vita Alcuini*, cap. 7, p. 189; *inter alia*, Alcuin ep. 114, and ep. 271.

[62] Donald Bullough, *Alcuin: Achievement and Reputation* (Leiden, 2001), p. 331–6; on the meeting: Garrison, 'The Teacher and the King', *BBC History Magazine* 2.7 (July 2001): 22–5. The date of his arrival at court may have been as early as 782 or as late as 786.

[63] See *inter alia*, Alcuin ep. 42, ep. 43, ep. 44, ep. 47, ep. 48.

attachment style. So subsequently, when he was given to York Minster, Alcuin coped by clinging intensely to Ælberht, a surrogate attachment figure. who provided the warmth and security that Alcuin sought. (Hence, in reaction to the earliest unresolved trauma, Alcuin's failure to mention his parents.) Ælberht had himself been an oblate, though not at York, and well knew what kind of nurture was required for those entrusted to him. As Alcuin wrote, 'whenever he saw young men of excellent character,/ he took them to him, to teach, cherish, and love'.[64]

Decades later at Ælberht's death, Alcuin broke down; grief is clearly a problem in the York Poem, in the epitaph Alcuin wrote for Ælberht, even in the biography of Alcuin written by someone who knew him only through the account of one of his students. Indeed from all these testimonies, it is evident that Alcuin continued to identify closely with Ælberht long after his death, seemingly an instance of the Freudian *identification* of the ego with the abandoned object', the melancholic position, where the bereaved cannot, and does not wish to, let go of the deceased.[65] In this perspective it is hardly surprising that less than four months after Ælberht's death, Alcuin would choose to leave York and attach himself to a new parental figure, the king of the Franks. Hence the persistent concerns about separation and dependency, the plangent notes in letters to absent friends (or in search of royal favour), and the motivation for his remarkable effort to maintain contact with such a wide circle of correspondents. Hence too some of the recurrent tropes in his verse: the objective correlative of bad weather and the cessation of poetic creativity both arise when friends are absent or ill-will perceived; both connote melancholy or depression rather than grief and anger. In short, it seems impossible to defend von Moos's observation that grief was, on the whole, not a problem for Alcuin even if he had no trouble composing appropriate letters of consolation as often as required.[66] Instead, one might suggest that struggle with loss had a profound and ultimately creative influence on Alcuin's personality.

---

[64] Alcuin, *York Poem*, line 1402, 'orphanisque pater' and lines 1415–29, 110; line 1449–50, 114: 'Indolis egregiae iuvenes quoscumque uidebat/ hos sibi coniunxit, docuit, nutriuit, amauit.'

[65] For a discussion of melancholy identification with the deceased as a feature shaping character, Freud's views, and more recent nuancing: Jonathan Boulter, *Melancholy and the Archive: Trauma, History and Memory in the Contemporary Novel* (London, 2011), pp. 5–6, with Freud, 'Mourning and Melancholia', p. 258.

[66] Von Moos, III, p. 109; discussion, Garrison, 'The Study of Emotions'.

Comparison: Grief for Ceolfrith

It is easy to suggest that Alcuin's grief for Ælberht was complicated and excessive, a 'persever[ing] in obstinate condolement'.[67] However, comparing his reaction to the death of Ælberht with another nearly contemporary loss that was even more fully observed and documented can suggest that his 'unprevailing woe' was neither so exceptional nor so private. The accounts of this other eighth-century Anglo-Saxon example of the loss of a religious father are still more extensive and immoderate. Exploring them can suggest that no matter how easily the data about Alcuin can be interpreted to fit the categories of melancholia, complicated grief and anxious attachment, the loss of a religious surrogate father was widely regarded by contemporaries as particularly grievous. The subject in this case is Ceolfrith, abbot of Wearmouth and Jarrow, and the testimonies occur in several works of another ex-oblate, Bede, and in the Anonymous *Vita Ceolfridi*.

Ceolfrith announced on 4 June 716 that he would depart for Rome with the delegation that he had selected to deliver one of the great Wearmouth–Jarrow pandect bibles to the pope. There, he said, he would pass the rest of his days at the tombs of the apostles. The delivery of the pandect had been planned long in advance, but Ceolfrith's last-minute decision to accompany the delegation had not. The episode was recounted twice at some length by Bede[68] and again, also at great length, in the Anonymous *Vita Ceolfridi*,[69] making it one of the best-documented events in Anglo-Saxon history before Alfred.[70] As it turned out, Ceolfrith would die in Langres, *en route*, and the great pandect, now the famous *codex Amiatinus*, would lose the evidence of its Northumbrian origin when one *Petrus Langobardorum* substituted his own name for Ceolfrith's in the epigraph.[71]

Ceolfrith's announcement was a shock. The language of both accounts, Bede's and that of the Anonymous, hints at a perception of abandonment, even betrayal. Bede digressed in the preface to the fourth part of his Commentary

---

[67] Hamlet, Act 1, scene 2 line 93.
[68] Bede: *Historia abbatum*, printed in C. Plummer (ed.), *Venerabilis Baedae Opera Historica*, 2 vols (Oxford, 1896), I, cap. 16–23, 364–87; and in Christopher Grocock and Ian Wood (eds and trans.), *Abbots of Wearmouth and Jarrow* (Oxford, 2013), pp. 20–76. Hereafter the text will be cited with the editor(s) specified. Bede, preface to *Commentarius in primam partem Samuelis*, ed. David Hurst, CCSL 119 (Turnhout, 1962), p. 212. Bede also narrated the event less emotively in his *Chronicon*: Plummer, *Baedae Opera*, vol. ii, p. 366. Note Bede's silence on the topic in *Historia Ecclesiastica: Bede's Ecclesiastical History of the English People*, ed. and trans. B. Colgrave and R.A.B. Mynors (1969 rpt. corr. Oxford, 1991).
[69] Anonymous, *Vita Ceolfridi* (aka *Historia abbatum auctore anonymo*), Plummer, I, cap. 21–38, pp. 388–404, notes, II, pp. 370–88; and in Grocock and Wood, *Abbots*, pp. 77–122.
[70] Peter Hunter Blair, *The World of Bede* (1970; rpt. Cambridge, 1990), p. 190.
[71] Richard Marsden, *The Text of the Old Testament in Anglo-Saxon England*, Cambridge Studies in Anglo-Saxon England 15 (Cambridge, 1995), pp. 88–9.

on Samuel, explaining that his emotional turmoil at the departure of his most reverend abbot had diverted him from work and confounded others who had been entrusted to the abbot's care; the distress[72] was all the greater because Ceolfrith's departure had been unexpected.[73] The connotations of Bede's word for departure, *discessus*, may imply criticism or even a perception of betrayal in a way that the Anonymus's *decessus* does not.[74] This sentiment and hint of culpability, is evident elsewhere in the Anonymous *Vita Ceolfridi* and invites comparison with Alcuin's image of the ship deserted by its captain:

> Tertio in beatum Samuelem completo uolumine, putabam me aliquandiu reparata per quietem meditandi uel scribendi uoluptate, sic demum ad inchoationem quarti manum esse missurum. Uerum haec eadem mihi quies, si tamen quies dicenda est **inopinata** mentis anxietas, prolixior multo quam decreueram, noua circumstantium rerum mutatione prouenit, maxime **discessu** abbatis mei reuerendissimi, qui post longam monasterialis cura obseruantiam, subitus Romam adire, atque inter loca beatorum apostolorum ac martyrum Christi corporibus sacra, extremum senex halitum reddere disponendo, non parua commissorum sibi animos, et eo maiore, quo conturbatione stupefecit.[75] [emphasis added]

> [After I had finished the third book of my commentary, I thought that when my delight in studying and writing had been renewed by resting for a while I would at length set my hand to the beginning of the fourth. But this rest of mine, if indeed unexpected anguish of mind can be called rest, has proved to be much longer than I had intended because of a new turn in our affairs, and particularly because of the departure of my most reverend abbot. After attending to the oversight of the monastery for a long time, he suddenly decided to go to Rome and in his old age to breathe his last breath amid places made sacred by the bodies of the blessed apostles and martyrs of Christ, bringing to the minds of those who had been entrusted to his care a sense of stunned confusion which was all the greater because his departure had been unexpected.][76]

Bede's account of Ceolfrith's departure and death closely matches that of the Anonymous *Vita Ceolfridi*. Both works devote a disproportionate number

---

[72] ... *non parua commissorum sibi animos, et eo maiore, quo improvisa conturbatione stupefecit.*

[73] Hunter Blair, p. 193 from Bede, *Commentarius*, p. 112, lines 1–12; the text is also printed by Plummer in the notes to his edition of *Historia abbatum* in *Baedae Opera*, vol. II, pp. 366–7.

[74] Charlton T. Lewis and Charles Short, *A Latin Dictionary* (Oxford, 1879), s.v. *decessus* and *discessus*.

[75] Plummer, *Baedae Opera*, vol. ii, p. 366–7.

[76] Hunter Blair, p. 193.

of chapters to the episode (nearly a third and more than a half, respectively)[77] while the important but sensitive matter of the election of Ceolfrith's successor is minimally explained.[78] The Anonymous, like Alcuin, resorted to recursive narration. He mentions Ceolfrith's death then skips backwards, then turns again to his departure and death.[79] Both accounts, too, mention tears, grief and sobbing with striking frequency. In each, a vivid detail captures the particularity of the grief. For Bede, that detail is something he adds to the events at Langres:

> ... et crastino in ecclesia beatorum Geminorum martyrum honorifice sepultus est, non solum Anglis genere qui plusquam octoginta numero in eius fuerant comitatu, sed et illius loci accolis pro retardato tam reuerendi senis desiderio, in lacrimas luctusque solutis. **Neque enim facile quisquam lacrimas tenere potuit**, uidens comites ipsius partim patre amisso coeptum iter agere, partim mutata intentione qua Roman ire desiderant domum magis qua hunc sepultum nuntiarent reuerti; partim ad tumbam defuncti inter eos quorum nec linguam nouerant pro inextinguibili patris affectu residere.[80] [emphasis added]

> [The following day he was buried with all dignity and in the church of the Three Brother Martyrs amidst the tears and lamentation not only of the eighty or more English men who made up his company but also of the local inhabitants who were deeply affected at the sight of an old man being disappointed of his wish. **It was hard for anyone to restrain his tears at the sight of some of Ceolfrid's party starting out to continue their journey without their father**, while others revoked their intention of going to Rome and the rest, in their undying love for him, remained to keep watch by his tomb in the midst of a people whose language they could not understand.][81]

Bede projects onto the residents of Langres deep empathy for the whole situation – not just Ceolfrith's death, but also his grief at not fulfilling his wish. Bede supplies the unparalleled observation of the irresistible sadness, to onlookers, of the sight of the men continuing their journey without their father. The image of the bereaved remnant is charged with cultural meaning. More than the unfulfilled dream, and more than the spectacle of those who will stay by the grave in a foreign land, it is the crux here: the middle term, the masterly addition, the

---

[77] Goffart, p. 278. In Bede's account: chapters 15–23 of 23 chapters (that is 9/23 or 1/2.5); in the Anonymous, chapters 21–38 of 39 (or 18/39 or 1/2.16).

[78] For a political reading of the departure and election and the suggestion that Bede shows no warmth towards Ceolfrith: Goffart, p. 278, note 200.

[79] Anonymous, *Vita Ceolfridi*, ed. Grocock and Wood, cap. 32, p. 112 and 36, p. 116.

[80] Bede, *Historia Abbatum*, ed. Grocock and Wood, cap. 21, pp. 70–72.

[81] D.H. Farmer (ed. and trans.), 'Lives of the Abbots of Wearmouth and Jarrow', in his *The Age of Bede* (1965; revised edn, Harmondsworth, 1983), pp. 185–210 at 207.

circumstance that *demands* tears.[82] The band of monks without their abbot (no less than the men deprived of their lord in heroic literature) crystallizes *collective* attachment and *collective* dependence on a protector; it invites us to see the full depth of the grief described: this is not just a private individual bereavement, but a collective orphaning that exposes the vulnerability and filial dependence of a group on their father–abbot. This dependence extended beyond the cloister, for, the Anonymous affirms, not just Ceolfrith's immediate retinue but also the poor of the region had a filial attachment to the abbot:

> Erant in comitatu eius octaginta circiter uiriqui diuersis collecti de partibus, qui illum universi quasi patrem sequebantur et colebant eum ....

> [In his company there were about eighty men gathered from various regions who all followed him and were devoted to him as if he were their father...][83]

> Denique profecturo et profiscicente illo unanimous egenorum uagorumque gemitus, quasi patre se et altore destitutum, testabatur

> [It is reported that as he was preparing to set out and then actually leaving, destitute and vagrant men all wept, as though deprived of their father and provider.][84]

In the Anonymous account, the essential detail is Ceolfrith's own uncontrolled and disruptive tears shed amidst the weeping of his monks and other locals. I know of no other section of any work in early medieval Latin prose where so much crying by so many parties is described in so few pages. Ceolfrith himself was overcome by grief after his boat crossed the Wear: he broke down in sobbing and tears and then looked back and beseeched God to protect his monks. This moment of crying was omitted by Bede, even though he had surely been an eyewitness. Did he regard it as unseemly, or not care, or did it not suit his narrative scheme?[85] Or did Anonymous devise it to bring out the reciprocity of the sorrow and the parting, thus diminishing the sense of desertion and culpable abandonment?

> Flebant omnes, ruentes in faciem pedesque illius apprehendentes, fusis lacrimis obsecrant ne tam repentinus abscederet, sed uel una die apud eos subsisteret ....[86]

---

[82] According to Grocock and Wood, *Abbots*, p. xliv, Bede's account predates the Anonymous. It is immaterial whether Bede invented the detail, or conversely, whether it was part of the report from those who returned and the Anonymous chose to omit it.
[83] Anonymous *Vita Ceolfridi*, ed. Grocock and Wood, cap. 34, pp. 114–15.
[84] Anonymous *Vita Ceolfridi*, ed. Grocock and Wood, cap. 34, p. 114–15.
[85] Anonymous *Vita Ceolfridi*, ed. Grocock and Wood, cap. 21, pp. 98–100.
[86] Anonymous *Vita Ceolfridi*, ed. Grocock and Wood, cap. 23, p. 100.

[Then all broke down and wept, and clutched at his feet, and in floods of tears begged him not to leave quickly, but to remain with them even for just one day....][87]

The special nature of the attachment of early medieval students to their teachers and of monks to their abbots or *nutritores* can be explored through medieval sources and modern psychology alike. The points of contact between the testimonies associated with the deaths of Ælberht and Ceolfrith suggest that the grief associated with the loss of such father-figures and the associated laments, rituals and historical accounts should be understood as constituting a distinctive and recognizable cultural constellation. It is crucial to remember, too, that these father figures provided protection and material support to rival that of a secular lord.[88] Attachment theory is undeniably relevant to understanding the role of that bond in individual lives, but the commonalities here also suggest that textual evidence that can seem peculiar and idiosyncratic – Alcuin's depiction of Ælberht's death, the various accounts of Ceolfrith's – is precisely that, *common*, shared, as typical of its era but as foreign to us as, say, the literary motifs associated with consumption in the nineteenth-century novel, a cultural sensibility.

Cultural Context: England and Frankia

Leaving aside the practical questions associated with the reality of status and real material dependence on an abbot or *magister* and archbishop, how do the outpourings of grief for Ælberht and Ceolfrith fit into the broader emotional landscape of eighth-century England and Frankia? Were there differences in custom and affect between the two regions that can further nuance our understanding of Alcuin and his grief in their contemporary setting?

It is well known that the Insular *peregrini* tended to have been oblates while their continental contemporaries, before the 790s, usually had not.[89] Many of Alcuin's contacts in his first years abroad thus would not have experienced the intense bond with a religious *nutritor* that had shaped the character of the English and the Irish at court; this difference may account for some tensions at court and even at Tours. There are other significant differences as well; these pertain to secular culture and relate to the acceptability of royal anger, the literary display of mourning, and political tolerance for private revenge. The

---

[87] Anonymous *Vita Ceolfridi*, ed. Grocock and Wood, cap. 23, p. 101. Further references to tears and grief at cap. 24, p. 102; cap. 25, p. 104; cap. 26, pp. 104–6; cap. 27, p. 106.

[88] Boniface's concern for his followers after his death: *Bonifatii epistulae*, ep. 93, p. 213, lines 15–17; Wallace-Hadrill's 'swan song', p. 161. Compare Shay, pp. 14–19 on the effect of the fiduciary assumption that modern armies will provide everything necessary for subsistence and battle.

[89] De Jong, 'From Scholastici to Scioli', pp. 45–57.

associated phenomena, I shall suggest, are interrelated, and point to a gulf in sensibility between England and Frankia.

A notable shift in the prevalence of the literary representation of grief occurred during the reign of Charlemagne. Grief emerges with new prominence in the prose narrative sources and letters associated with the court. In Einhard's portrait, Charlemagne wept for his three children who died and mourned Pope Hadrian as a brother or a son, commissioning a commemorative plaque for him.[90] To Einhard, Charlemagne's grief at the death of Pope Hadrian exemplified an admirable capacity for making and sustaining friendships and for respect and loyalty.[91] The deaths of warriors Eric of Friuli and Gerold of Bavaria in 799 were likewise occasions of both public and private grief.[92]

It is interesting to juxtapose this new prominence of royal grief with what appears to be a related trend – namely, the 'caesura' that Gerd Althoff has identified in the 'depiction of royal anger' in sources for the same era. Althoff commented that 'the Carolingian royal annals ... and Einhard's *Life of Charlemagne* have no place for anger ... just the opposite' and further that 'royal gentleness, mercy and clemency are in the foreground.'[93] (Alcuin himself was remembered as the one who was never seen to be angry.)[94] Reality seems to conform to representation: Carolingian rulers carried out death sentences

---

[90] *Annales Regni Francorum inde a. 741 usque ad 829, qui dicuntur Annales Laurissenses maiores et Einhardi*, ed. G.H. Pertz; rev. edn F. Kurze, MGH Scriptores rerum Germanicarum in usum scholarum separatim editi (Hanover, 1895), s.a. 796, 98 & 99; Einhard, *Vita Karoli Magni*, ed. G.H. Pertz, G. Waitz, O. Holder-Egger, 6th edn (Hanover, 1911), II.19, 24; Alcuin, ep. 93, p. 137; Mary Garrison, 'The Emergence of Carolingian Latin Literature and the Court of Charlemagne, 780–814', in Rosamond McKitterick (ed.), *Carolingian Court Culture: Emulation and Innovation* (Cambridge, 1994), pp. 111–40, at 123. Contrast Einhard's positive depiction of Charlemagne weeping at the deaths of his children with the story of Fredegund urging Chilperic to burn the tax registers, thinking that the death of their children was God's judgement on their oppression of the poor (Gregory of Tours, *Historia Francorum*, V.26).

[91] Einhard, *Life of Charlemagne* II.19, trans. P. Dutton, *Charlemagne's Courtier: The Complete Einhard* (Toronto, 2nd revised edn, 1998), p. 29: 'Charles was by nature a good friend; for he easily made friends and firmly held on to them. Indeed he treated with greatest respect those he had bound closely to himself in a relationship of this sort'.

[92] E. Dümmler (ed.), *MGH PLAC* 1; epitaphium Geroldi, pp. 114–15; Paulinus's lament for Heric, Paulini carm. 2, pp. 131–3; epitaphium Hadriani, pp. 113–14. *Annales Regni Francorum inde a. 741 usque ad 829, qui dicunture Annales Laurissenses maiores et Einhardi*, s.a. 799, 108.

[93] G. Althoff, 'Ira Regis: Prolegomena to a History of Royal Anger', in B. Rosenwein (ed.), *Anger's Past: The Social Uses of an Emotion in the Middle Ages* (Cornell, 1998), pp. 59–74 at pp. 64–5. But note that anger as tool of political terror is attributed to Charlemagne by the Carolingian poets: Garrison, 'Emergence', p. 133.

[94] P. Neff (ed.), *Die Gedichte des Paulus Diaconus: kritische und erklärende Ausgabe* (Munich, 1908), carm. Xvii, p. 86 notes on lines 29–32.

on their relatives and Frankish nobles with reluctance and apparently far less frequently than their predecessors[95] or Northumbrian contemporaries. Charlemagne's *Admonitio Generalis* (largely written by Alcuin) sought to impose the same new gentleness on his subjects. One provision insisted that there must be peace, concord and unanimity among the whole populace, lay and ecclesiastical, great and humble. In a stringent demand for obedience to biblical precepts, all were to love their neighbours as themselves; those who did not were sons of the devil and their offerings to God would not be acceptable.[96] The coincidence of the new Carolingian restrictions on royal anger and vengeance with the new emphasis on mercy and forgiveness and the expanded opportunities for displaying the emotions of both friendship and grief points to a deep realignment of anger, grief, revenge and forgiveness and suggests a deeper change in sensibility emanating from the court.[97]

At the same time in poetry and letters, there is a new vogue for literary expression of homesickness, reflecting a new sensibility, not merely new elite mobility. Exponents of this trend include Alcuin, Paul the Deacon, court *missi*, Colman the Irishman, Hrabanus, Walahfrid and Gottschalk.[98] In earlier Latin literature there are no parallels for such a flowering of a poetry of homesickness associated with courtly taste and mainly inspired by routine absences for business or study or religious *peregrinatio* rather than political exile (as Fortunatus's had been).

These Carolingian developments mark the cultural distance between Charlemagne's court and Alcuin's England. The shocking dénouement of the Cynewulf/Cyneheard revenge saga[99] occurred in the same decade as the *Admonitio*'s radical insistence on neighbourly love. In the Anglo-Saxon kingdoms, there was no corresponding caesura in the display of royal rage, no new emphasis on mercy, nor any (extant) legislation to force people to lay aside feuds and love their neighbours comparable to the *Admonitio*'s. The literary mode associated with the late eighth-century Northumbrian rulers was not

---

[95] De Jong, *In Samuel's Image*, pp. 256–7.

[96] *Die Admonitio Generalis Karls des Grossen*, ed. Hubert Mordek, Klaus Zechiel-Eckes and Michael Glatthaar, MGH Fontes iuris Germanici antiqui in usum scholarum separatim editi XVI (Hanover, Hahn, 2012), cap. 61, p. 210, citing Matthew 5:23–4; Leviticus 19:18; Matthew 5:9; John 13.35; I John 3.10.

[97] To be sure, grief is well attested in the pages of Gregory of Tours, but there, is often followed by rage, revenge or sudden actions to avert God's wrath. Gregory, *Historia Francorum*, v. 34, p. 297, on Fredegund and Chilperic.

[98] Garrison, 'Emergence', p. 115. P. Neff (ed.), *Die Gedichte des Paulus*, pp. 53–5. Waddell: Colman to Colman, pp. 74–7. *MGH Poetae Latini Aevi Carolini II*, 403; 388–90; 412–13; Poetae IV, 731–2

[99] *Two of the Saxon Chronicles Parallel*, ed. John Earle and Charles Plummer (Oxford, 1898, repr. 1972), I, 46–8 (755) and 52 (784).

Latin court poetry of *amicitia*, court banter and homesickness, as in Francia, but heroic verse, king lists and genealogies.[100] In late eighth-century Northumbria, the frequency of royal expulsions and regicides surpasses Merovingian and Visigothic dynastic violence.

Alongside these differences, however, the continent and the Insular world shared a range of non-parental child-rearing practices, which means that in both oblation was not the only reason for extended childhood separation from biological kin. It will be useful to consider these briefly before returning to the topic of the grief and gratitude of the oblate in order to establish the point that, although oblation could be associated with a distinctive emotional constitution, childhood separation and rearing by others was unexceptional.

Fosterage meant that young aristocratic males, lay and religious alike, faced separation from their families at various ages. At a very young age, a boy in Ireland might be given for fostering to another family; ecclesiastical fosterage (distinct from oblation) was also practised there.[101] Slightly older, at puberty, youths on the continent might be sent to court for education,[102] handed over as hostages,[103] or placed in another noble household for education in worldly arts. Court training for aristocratic male youths was also practised elsewhere, including seventh-century Northumbria.[104] Such separations were not inevitably traumatic. In Ireland fostering led to close emotional bonds; indeed, it was partly undertaken to create alliances. Members of the Merovingian élite might remember their youthful educational sojourns at court with fond nostalgia. Some of these crucial secular childhood separations occurred at roughly the same time as for children destined for the religious life. In a parallel between secular and religious life, from the late eighth century onwards, former oblates might be sent away from their own monasteries in their early teens to

---

[100] H. Moisl, 'Anglo-Saxon Royal Genealogies and Germanic Oral Tradition', *Journal of Medieval History* 7 (1981): 215–48 and D.N. Dumville, 'The Anglian Collection of Royal Genealogies and Regnal Lists', *Anglo-Saxon England* 5 (1976): 23–50; Mary Garrison, 'Quid Hinieldus cum Christo', in Katherine O'Brien O'Keeffe and Andy Orchard (eds), *Latin Learning and English Lore: Studies in Anglo-Saxon Literature for Michael Lapidge*, 2 vols (Toronto, 2005), I, pp. 237–59. at 248.

[101] Peter Parkes, 'Celtic Fosterage: Adoptive Kinship and Clientage in Northwest Europe', Comparative Studies in Society and History 48.2 (2006): 359–95; Bronagh Ní Chonaill, 'Fosterage', in John Koch (ed.), *Celtic Culture: a Historical Encyclopedia* (Oxford, 2006), p. 771: the three age ranges for Irish fosterage – 0–1; 7–12; 12–17.

[102] P. Riché, *Education and Culture in the Barbarian West, Sixth through Eighth Centuries*, trans. J. Contreni (Columbia, 1976), pp. 236–46.

[103] E.g. Theodoric the Ostrogoth educated in Constantinople; Dhuoda's sons, political hostages.

[104] Thomas Charles Edwards, 'Social Structure', in Pauline Stafford (ed.), *A Companion to the Early Middle Ages: Britain and Ireland c.500–1100* (Oxford, 2009), pp. 107–25, at 113.

complete their studies at major centres with renowned masters.[105] Nonetheless, if the childhood separation of oblation was not exceptional, it differed sharply from secular patterns of upbringing because of the requirement to sever ties with the biological family.

Separations continued to characterize adult life for women (through marriage alliances) and for religious and secular men. The pain of the Irish *peregrinatio pro amore Dei*[106] qualified it as one of three grades of martyrdom. The idea that asceticism was a type of martyrdom had originated earlier on the continent, but in Ireland the idea was fully elaborated, an acknowledgement of the emotional cost.[107] Bede's *Ecclesiastical History* records numerous Anglo-Saxon princes and nobles compelled to flee into exile. Youths and adults alike are attested as hostages across the whole late antique and early medieval world, although, among the elite, life as a hostage might shade into fostering. Finally, secular and ecclesiastical administration in the new empire of Charlemagne led to short-term mobility on a new scale: *missi dominici* and other emissaries were posted across Charlemagne's realm. This increased administrative mobility of secular officials across a newly expanded realm was an innovation; in some respects it resembles aspects of the Roman imperial civil service.

There were countervailing forces to assuage the pains of distance, dislocation, separation and ever-present mortality,[108] techniques for strengthening connections in this world and beyond. It is no accident that the first synodal declaration about prayer confraternities is from 762 (Attigny); evidence for systematic recording of reciprocal prayers between monastic houses (rather than merely individuals) rises steadily from this time.[109] The earliest extant *libri vitae* (of Salzburg and Durham) date from shortly afterwards. The introduction (or reassigning from its old May date) of the Feast of All Saints is an allied

---

[105] E.g. Einhard to Alcuin at court; Hrabanus and Hatto of Fulda to Alcuin at Tours; Walahfrid of Reichenau to Hrabanus at Fulda. Sita Steckel, *Kulturen des Lehrens im Früh- und Hochmittelalter: Autorität, Wissenskonzepte und Netzwerke von Gelehrten*, Norm und Struktur. Studien zum sozialen Wandel im Mittelalter und Früher Neuzeit 39 (Köln, 2010), pp. 110–15 and 381–96.

[106] A. Angenendt, *Monachi Peregrini: Studien zu Pirmin und den monastischen Vorstellungen des frühen Mittelalters* (Munich, 1972).

[107] Clare Stancliffe, 'Red, White and Blue Martyrdom', in Dorothy Whitelock, Rosamond McKitterick, D.N. Dumville (eds), *Ireland in Early Mediaeval Europe: Studies in Memory of Kathleen Hughes* (Cambridge, 1982), pp. 21–46, at 23; Thomas M. Charles Edwards, 'The Social Background to Irish *Peregrinatio*', *Celtica* 11 (1976): 43–59.

[108] Summary of mortality statistics: Janet Nelson, 'La mort de Charles le Chauve', *Médiévales* 15.31 (1996): 53–86.

[109] Jan Gerchow, *Die Gedenküberlieferung der Angelsachsen* (Berlin, 1988); Wilhelm Levison, *England and the Continent in the Eighth Century: The Ford Lectures* (Oxford, 1946), p. 102.

phenomenon; the feast's new date was brought to the continent by Alcuin.[110] No less important were the rituals that created new networks of kinship among the living, the spiritual kinship brought about by baptismal sponsorship.[111] This created horizontal bonds between godparents and biological parents as important as biological parenthood. Alongside these were the fictions of familiarity created by the metaphorical use of kinship terms and special nicknames – 'fictions' because constructed, yet still able to constitute, not just symbolize, a non-biological network of reciprocal affection and obligation.[112] We should take full account of the emotional importance of such kin.[113]

To summarize: separations from parents for diverse religious, political and educational purposes are a shared feature of England and the continent in this era, a normal occurrence, and are a reason to avoid relying on the assumptions and expectations associated with the modern western child-centred nuclear family. Yet the cultural restraints and customary expressions of mourning, grief, anger and revenge seem to have been in flux, with some national differences clearly evident.

Modern Comparanda

Since childhood separation and upbringing away from biological parents were experiences shared by both religious and secular children in the early Middle Ages, yet alien for many today, it is worth looking farther afield for comparanda. Analogues can familiarize the situation while attention to salient difference can throw into relief the possible role of other associated formative influences.

Bowlby acknowledged that the capacity for attachment, though strongly affected by earliest experiences, could grow and develop; thus the impact of separations endured after the earliest years would be shaped not just by infantile experience, but also by the circumstances of the post-separation environment and the person's later capacity to find meaning in the experience. The experiences of

---

[110] Levison, *England and the Continent*, p. 160; Alcuin, ep. 193; J. Hennig, 'The Feast of All the Saints', *Mediaeval Studies* 10 (1948): 147–61.

[111] A. Angenendt, *Kaiserherrschaft und Königstaufe* (Berlin, 1984); J. Lynch, *Godparents and Kinship in Early Medieval Europe* (Princeton, 1976); B. Jussen, *Spiritual Kinship as Social Practice: Godparenthood and Adoption in the Early Middle Ages*, trans. Pamela Selwyn (Newark, Delaware, 2000).

[112] Garrison, 'The Social World of Alcuin: Nicknames at York and at the Carolingian Court', in Houwen and McDonald (eds), *Alcuin of York*, pp. 64–5; Matthew 12:48–50: who is my mother?

[113] Inga-Britt Krause, *Therapy Across Culture: Psychotherapy and Cultural Diversity, Perspectives on Psychotherapy* (London, 1998), on British culture's literalism about the biological family in all sorts of spheres in contrast to, for example, the African family, where the nieces or nephews count as the aunt's as much as the mother's.

children reared in groups in Israeli kibbutzim may shed some light on the effects of growing up in a group, in the constant presence of a small cohort of other children. Stories of the children of British civil servants working in India in the nineteenth century offer an analogue for education at a distance from parents.[114]

In the case of the children of British civil servants in India, what is most striking is the silence in children's letters to their parents about the anguish and uncertainty they felt when they were sent to England, shuffled between relatives, foster families and boarding schools, or even in some cases, not merely neglected but abused in foster homes.[115] There are scarcely any 'keenly emotional' complaints. While the silence invites comparison with the silence of most oblates about their entrance to the religious life, the reasons are distinct and can be identified. A combination of boarding school supervision of letter writing, epistolary conventions and self-censorship (or repression) accounts for the reticence of the children's letters, while parents, for obvious reasons, did not usually dwell on their pain. Openness about the trauma for the most part had to wait for postcolonial memoirs of old age. Kipling's *Baa Baa Black Sheep* and *Something of Myself* provided a shared point of reference and served as a catalyst and model for later disclosures by others.[116]

The prevailing silence makes letters of a few exceptional children who did dwell on their feelings all the more poignant. The terms 'separation anxiety' and 'anxious attachment' have seemed apposite. For these children, unlike political prisoners, or parents and children whose parental time was limited in a kibbutz, there was no redeeming meaning to their unhappiness. Indeed, in the case of one family's correspondence, the anguish expressed in letters was sharpened by the painful disparity between a nineteenth-century ideal of family domesticity formed before the separation and the actual experience.[117] Ten-year-old

---

[114] Elizabeth Buettner, 'Parent–Child Separations and Colonial Careers: The Talbot Family Correspondence in the 1880s and 1890s', in Stephen Hussey and Anthony Fletcher (eds), *Childhood in Question: Children, Parents and the State* (Manchester, 1999), pp. 115–32; Poul Pederson, 'Anxious Lives and Letters: Family Separation, Communication Networks and Structures of Everyday Life', *Culture and History* 8 (1990): 7–19.

[115] Buettner, 'Parent–Child Separations'.

[116] Buettner, 'Parent–Child Separations', p. 120. Roger Lancelyn Green, *Kipling and the Children* (London, 1965); Rudyard Kipling, *Something of Myself and other Autobiographical Writings* (1937, rpt. Cambridge, 1991).

[117] Buettner, 'Parent–Child Separations', pp. 122–3: Guendolyn Talbot wrote to her parents, 'I feel as if you were kind of locked up toys that one could not have you don't seem to be real out there only a name. You seem like some beautiful thing one caught a glimpse of now and then. I love you very very much you know. I have grown quite used to hardly seeing you now. It seems as ordinary as eating one's dinner. It is almost odd to hear other children talking of their parents as always being with them something too nice for us to enjoy. I seem almost to ache with longing for you. But for your letters and love I should hardly know I

Guendolyn Talbot's letter to her mother echoes some of the themes expressed by Bertgyth: the pain of separation sharpened by comparison with others, the ache of longing, absence experienced as ordinary and inevitable.[118]

As for the kibbutzim: for all the important differences (above all in the earliest years) kibbutz-raised Israeli children of the mid-twentieth century shared with boy-oblates the crucial situation of being raised among a group, rarely alone, not even when sleeping. Many parents found the separation painful and eventually most kibbutzim rescinded some of the most demanding aspects of collective childrearing, but the shared socialist ideals that inspired the experiment meant that it could be meaningful for the parents even when uncomfortable. Kibbutz-raised children later would feel most themselves only in groups and would greatly value harmonious relations in the group. Accounts of schisms in kibbutzim, where a large group seceded, are associated with intense pain, and resonate with similar phenomena in monastic life.[119] The intensity of this concern for group peace parallels those themes in Alcuin's writings, for his images of heaven and of this-worldly joy alike revolve around reunions and harmony. Similarly, Alcuin's distress at quarrels and his retelling of the vision of reunion in heaven at the end of the York poem bespeak the same deep yearning.[120] That account of reunion was no consolatory cliché, but an actual vision vouchsafed to the boy Seneca during Alcuin's youth, decades before Ælberht's death and the composition of the York poem.

In the space available, it is impossible adequately to take account of the diversity of lived experience and scholarly debate associated with either of these two modern comparanda. Together, however, they point to two important variables that need to be set alongside attachment theory. First, there is the role of expectation in sharpening the pangs of separation and loss (already illustrated by Bertgyth and expressed even more explicitly by Guendolyn Talbot); second, there is the profound influence of being raised in a group. So while attachment theory and modern grief studies undoubtedly shed some light on medieval experiences of grief and separation, their insights need to be qualified by attention to differences in family structure, expectations, and social environment. The values associated with institutional life in a group, shared institutional ideals, and a childhood with no time alone all would shape later patterns of attachment, separation and loss.

---

had you dear Mama'. I thank Elizabeth Buettner for discussion, confirming that this letter is utterly exceptional for its direct articulation of the trauma.

[118] See note above.

[119] Bruno Bettelheim, *The Children of the Dream* (New York, 1969). Hrabanus carm. 40, *metrum de transitu monachorum, MGH PLAC II*, pp. 204–5.

[120] Alcuin, *York Poem*, lines 1600–1630, pp. 130–32 and ep. 42, p. 86, line 13.

Gratitude

To evoke heaven as an ideal where the defectiveness of earthly life is made good brings us back to Alcuin's own categories of experience and invites one to question the quality of the light that modern psychology, even when richly contextualized, can bring to *culturally* distinctive patterns as opposed to supposed individual pathologies. Perhaps it is a kind of artificial light, lacking some of the frequencies required for full spectrum colour perception. Private trauma and collective culture meet where people articulate and share meanings in the experiences that have shaped them. When the trauma resists articulation, then the shared silence is also a cultural artifact. It is easy enough to emphasize Alcuin's individuality and originality as a writer or a personality, or concoct possible labels of anxious attachment and melancholia. But he and others found gratitude in their experiences. Indeed, the way that he, Bertgyth, Bede and Orderic Vitalis all linked their experiences of commendation with gratitude points to a shared cultural constant as characteristic of their world as the theme of the great grief at the loss of the religious father. At the same time, as we shall see, their expressions of this gratitude are in each case so individually expressed, and their situations so diverse, that there is no question of mere adherence to convention.

Alongside Alcuin's grief at Ælberht's death and his affection for the whole *familia* at York, an enduring gratitude shines through his writings to the York family. To them he wrote:

> Totum meae deuotionis pectus uestrae caritatis dulcedine impletur, et si quid pleno amoris modio superaddi potest, cotidie crescendo accumulatur; ita ut solius memoriae de uobis suauitas superuenientes saecularis angustiae tribulationes longe a secretis mentis meae cubilibus depellit. Et hoc mihi singulare solacium in spiritu consolationis sanctae dominus Christus perdonare dignatus est.
>
> Uos fragiles infantiae meae annos materno fouistis affectu; et lascivum puericiae tempus pia sustinuistis patientia et paternae castigationis disciplinis ad perfectam uiri edocuistis aetatem et sacrarum eruditione disciplinarum roborastis.
>
> Quid plus dicere habeo? nisi ut aeterna summi regis pietas omnia pietatis in me, famulum suum, per uos benefacta perpetua summae beatitudinis gloria remuneretur? Hoc singulis uigiliarum mearum momentis, hoc cotidiana subplicatione, in hac prece in conspectu altissimi intimas desiderii mei lacrimas .... fundere non cesso ....
>
> O omnium dilectissimii patres et fratres, memores mei estote. Ergo uester ero, siue in uita, siue in morte. Et forte miserebitur mei Deus, ut, cuius infantiam aluistis, eius senectutem sepelietis. Et si alter corpori locus deputabitur, tamen animae, qualemcumque habitura erit – per uestras sanctas, Deo donante, intercessiones, requies uobiscum, credo, donabitur. Quia – sicut puer noster

Seneca se uidisse testatur – nostrae fraternitatis animas in eodem laetitiae loco congregandas esse credimus.[121]

[The whole heart of my devotion is filled by the sweetness of your love and if anything could still be added to a full bushel of love, it would be accumulating with daily increase; so too does the pleasure of your memory drive the tribulations of worldly anxieties far from the inner chambers of my mind. And this is the special consolation that the Lord Christ has deigned to grant me in the spirit of holy consolation.

You tended the fragile years of my infancy with motherly affection and upheld me in the mischievous period of boyhood with kind patience and educated me to the full age of manhood with the discipline of fatherly correction and strengthened me with the erudition of sacred studies.

What more can I say? Except [pray] that that eternal kindness of the highest King may reward you for all your kindness bestowed on me, his servant, with the eternal glory of the greatest blessedness. This I do continually in my vigils and in daily prayer, in that prayer not ceasing to pour out in the sight of the most high the deepest tears of my longing....

O dearest of all fathers and brothers in the world, remember me. I will be yours, whether in life or in death. Perhaps God will pity me, so that you may bury the child you taught when he is old. And if another place is appointed for my body, yet I believe my soul will be granted peace with you by God's grace through your prayers, whatever its place is to be. Since – as our boy Seneca attested he had seen – we believe that the souls of our brotherhood will be gathered together in the same place of rejoicing.][122]

It is revealing to compare Alcuin's experience to the later autobiographical statements by Orderic Vitalis. With Orderic, still more directly, we see possible trauma redeemed, transformed into gratitude. Orderic offers first-hand testimony about how a devout monk could, in retrospect, come to terms with an oblation and accept it as the fulfillment of God's will. Significantly, Orderic utterly refuses to blame the father who gave him away, or to see the gesture as one of abandonment or rejection; instead, he regarded the distant location as a God-given solution to the impediments to religious life of proximity to close kin. When he was ten, Orderic was taken from his home in England to a Norman monastery. He recalled:

---

[121] Alcuin, ep. 42, pp. 85–6.
[122] Alcuin, ep. 42, trans. adapted from Stephen Allott, *Alcuin of York: His Life and Letters* (York, 1974), letter 1, pp. 2–3.

exul in Normanniam ueni, cunctis ignotus, neminem cognoui ....[123]

Iccirco, gloriose Deus, qui Abraham de terra patrisque domo et cognatione egredi iussisti, Odelerium patrem meum aspirasti ut me sibi penitus abdicaret, et tibi omnimodis subiugaret. Rainaldo igitur monacho plorans plorantem me tradidit, et pro amore tuo in exilium destinauit, nec me umquam postea uidit. Paternis nempe uotis tenellus puer obuiare non presumpsi, sed in omnibus illi ultro adquieui, quia ipse michi spopondit ex parte tua si monachus fierem, quod post mortem meam paradisum cum Innocentibus possiderem.[124]

[I came to Normandy as an exile, unknown to all, I knew no one....

On that account, O glorious God, who bade Abraham go out from the house of his father and his kindred, you inspired Odelerius my father to renounce me entirely and submit me to You in all things. And so, as he wept, he handed me over, also weeping, to Rainald the monk, and for the love of You he bound me into exile and never saw me again after that. In tender boyhood, of course I did not dare to oppose these paternal vows, but in all things I assented, since he himself had promised me that if I were to become a monk, after my death I would possess paradise with the Innocents.][125]

Orderic thus came to believe and accept that the oblation was God's will. He states that, at the time, he did not dare oppose his father. Did he even realize that he could have done so, or was it only in later life that the possibility occurred to him? From the secure vantage point of old age, and with steadfast faith in the heavenly reward that had been the goal of his entrance into the monastic life, Orderic could recount the parting without concealing any of its pain, but also with warm gratitude for the kindness and friendliness with which he had been received.

Bede similarly describes his oblation with no trace of regret in the famous autobiographical epilogue to his *Ecclesiastical History*:

Qui natus in territorio eiusdem monasterii, cum essem annorum VII, cura propinquorum datus sum educandus reuerentissimo abbati Benedicto, ac deinde Ceolfrido, cunctumque ex eo tempus uitae in eiusdem monasterii habitatione peragens ... semper aut discere aut docere aut scribere dulce habui.[126]

[I was born in the territory of this monastery. When I was seven years of age I was, by the care of my kinsmen, put into the charge of the reverend Abbot Benedict

---

[123] *The Ecclesiastical History of Orderic Vitalis*, vol. VI, ed. and trans. Marjorie Chibnall (Oxford, 1978), book 13, chapter 45, p. 554.
[124] Orderic, ed. Chibnall, p. 552, my translation.
[125] Orderic, ed. Chibnall, p. 552.
[126] Bede, *Historia Ecclesiastica*, V. 24, p. 566.

and then of Ceolfrid. From then on I have spent all my life in this monastery ... and it has always been my delight to learn or to teach or to write.]127

Perhaps gratitude is implied in the declaration of contentment; certainly Bede felt it intensely at the end of his life.

The deacon Cuthbert wrote a moving and poignant account of Bede's last illness and death; in keeping with its subject, the passage is almost as intensely emotional as some of the writing about Ceolfrith's departure.128 During two weeks when before his death when he was afflicted with 'frequent attacks of breathlessness', Bede continued to give lessons, to chant the psalter, and to give thanks continuously to God. He exhorted his students to penitence and contemplation of their own mortality by quoting sentences from scripture and an Old English poem about the 'dread departure of the soul from the body':129

> Cantabat enim antiphonas ob nostram consoltationem et sui, quarum una est 'O rex gloriose, domine uirtutum, qui triumphator hodie super omnes caelos ascendisti, ne derelinquas nos orphanos, sed mitte promissum Patris in nos Spiritum ueritatis. Alleluia'. Cum uenisset autem ad illum uerbum 'ne derelinquas nos orphanos', prorupit in lacrimas et multum flebat. Et post horam coepit repetere quae inchoauerat, et sic cotidei faciebat. Et nos quidem haec audientes luximus cum illo et fleuimus; altera uice legimus, altera plorauimus, immo cum fletu legimus.130

[He used to sing antiphons, too, for his comfort and ours, of which one is 'O King of Glory, Lord of might, who didst this day ascend in triumph above all t h e heavens, leave us not comfortless, but send to us the promise of the father, even of the Spirit of truth. Alleluia'. But when he came to the words 'ne derelinquas nos orphanos' he broke down and wept.131 It was an hour before he tried to repeat what

---

[127] Bede, *Historia Ecclesiastica*, ed. and trans. Colgrave and Mynors, p. 567. For the significance of *propinqui* and the possibility that Bede may have been an orphan, see Grocock and Wood, *Abbots*, p. lxii.

[128] Cuthbert, *epistola de obitu Bedae*, in *Historia Ecclesiastica*, ed. and trans. Colgrave and Mynors, pp. 579–87.

[129] Cuthbert, p. 580: *Terribili exitu animarum e corpore*.

[130] Cuthbert, p. 582.

[131] '"Leave us not comfortless," he broke down and wept'; 'prorupit in lacrimas et multum flebat, "Ne derelinquas nos orphanos"': Cuthbert, pp. 582–3. Henry Mayr-Harting, *The Venerable Bede, the Rule of St Benedict, and Social Class* (Jarrow Lecture, 1976); Grocock and Wood, *Abbots*, p. lxii. Colgrave and Mynors translate 'orphanos' as 'comfortless' because that is the King James rendering of John 14:18's 'orphanos'; the Douai-Rheims, from the Vulgate, gives, 'do not leave us orphans'.

he had left unfinished, and so it was every day. And when we heard it, we shared his sorrow we read and wept by turns, or rather we wept continually as we read.][132]

Bede and the others passed the time between Easter and Pentecost in this way; Cuthbert emphasizes Bede's joyfulness and his expressions of gratitude to God:[133]

se uidisse alium in tam magna deuotione atque tranquillitate uitam suam finisse dicebant, quia, sicut audisti, quousque anima eius in corpore fuit, 'Gloria Patri' et alia quaedam ad gloriam Dei cecinit, et expansis manibus Deo gratias agree non cessabat.[134]

[All present declared that they had never seen a man end his days in such great holiness and peace, for, as I have said, as long as his soul remained in his body he chanted the 'Gloria Patri' and other songs to the glory of God, and spreading out his hands ceased not to give God thanks.][135]

The account is full of weeping, singing and mourning, of Bede's prayers and thanksgiving, and his praise and rejoicing; Cuthbert indicates that Bede's students wept sometimes in grief and sometimes in compunction. Other tears, after the words in the Antiphon that had moved Bede so deeply, 'ne derelinquas nos orphanos', seem to convey in a more fearful key the same hope expressed in the words of the Benedictine novices' profession: 'Receive me Lord as you have promised, and I shall live; do not disappoint me in my hope' (Ps 118/119:116).[136] They express the deep longing for salvation and God's love, the deep fear of eternal severance from that love, damnation. Although the rule of Benedict was known and followed at Wearmouth-Jarrow, it is not clear whether it was used exclusively; nor is it possible to ascertain whether the ceremony of oblation familiar to Bede included these words; certainly they would have been known to later Benedictine readers of Cuthbert's letter, which circulated extensively on the continent.

---

[132] Bede, *Historia Ecclesiastica* ed. and trans. Colgrave and Mynors, pp. 579–87 authenticity: 'All that I have seen and heard'. The text would be available at Jarrow, so the author could not fabricate. But why would he?

[133] Cuthbert, pp. 582 and 584, line 1.

[134] Cuthbert, pp. 584–6.

[135] Cuthbert, pp. 586–7.

[136] *RB 1980*, cap. 58.21 [Ps 118 [119]:116], p. 268: 'Suscipe me Domine, secundum eloquium tuum et vivam et ne confundas me ab exspectatione mea'.

Conclusion

I have sketched out some possibilities for interpreting Alcuin's experiences of grief and separation according to modern psychoanalytical schemes that are now almost intuitive. The meanings and interpretations available to Alcuin and his contemporaries and Orderic offer a different view. On the one hand, there are the Gospel injunctions to leave behind biological kinship in order to follow Christ, and the Biblical and Augustinian metaphors of life itself as an exile. Then there is the medieval interpretation of oblation as a sacrifice: the oblate was even offered at the Altar with the Gifts at the Mass.[137] Ninth-century eucharistic theology came to interpret Christ's death 'less in the sense of a sacrificial offering made to God than of a joint offering made by [Christ] and his father ... the "price" they together paid – for Christ his human life, God, his only son – for mortals' redemption'.[138] 'The union of the monk's self-offering with the sacrifice of Christ' is assumed in modern Benedictine thought, though nowhere explicitly stated in the Rule of St. Benedict.[139] I have not yet found it spelled out in any early medieval source.[140] Even so, wherever vicarious prayer and vicarious suffering are believed to be redemptive, then the suffering, grief and trauma are not meaningless either to the sufferer or to his society and the pain can be redeemed (as in the case of the white martyrdom of *pergrinatio*, for example). In this perspective, the pangs of separation are redeemed by gratitude and by the sense of a meaningful sacrifice. And so the modern comparanda for the medieval oblate's childhood separation and adult longing for absent friends is not just the child of the kibbutz or the children of British India, but also the Filipino migrant workers who make the sacrifice of leaving their own homes and children to earn money abroad so that the children can eventually have a better life.

Alcuin's statements about absence, separation and grief are easy to associate with modern interpretative categories, yet the apparent reward of the close match comes at the cost of some foreshortening. The concepts of anxious attachment, melancholia and complicated grief bypass eighth-century cultural meanings and responses individual and collective; meaning and gratitude redeem and transform pain. But Alcuin is more than a mouthpiece for collective perceptions of persons, he is a distinct individual; his experiences explored here were characteristic of the culture he grew up in, though not the one he migrated to, and both of those cultures in turn were characterized by significant plurality of norms and practices. Probing his experiences and utterances about grief, loss

---

[137] *RB 1980*, Appendix 5: monastic formation and profession, p. 451; de Jong, *In Samuel's Image*, pp. 170–91.

[138] Celia Chazelle, *The Crucified God in the Carolingian Era: Theology and Art of Christ's Passion* (Cambridge, 2001), p. 12.

[139] *RB 1980*, Appendix 5: monastic formation and profession, pp. 454–5.

[140] *RB 1980*, Appendix 5, p. 455.

and abandonment can bring the elusive aspects of personality and experience into slightly better focus, if not perfect clarity. The exercise can also awaken our empathy. Even with its flaws and the problems of partial knowledge, using the framework of attachment theory nonetheless brings back the profound significance of loss, the reasons it may be uncomfortable to analyse, and its centrality in the lives of those we study.[141]

---

[141] Acknowledgements: My greatest and most recent debt is to Alice Jorgensen and also Frances McCormack and Jon Wilcox for their most generous editorial help and patience. I thank Stephen Jaeger for an invitation to speak on this subject in Illinois in 2004 as well as those who attended that conference for enriching discussion; I thank Alice and all at the Dublin conference for the invitation and intellectual exchange then; Liz Buettner for discussion of material on British India, Stuart Airlie for conversations about Bede and Boniface, Yitzhak and Racheli Hen and other friends in Israel for conversations about kibbutzim and the reception of Bettelheim, and all others I have discussed these topics with over the years, including students in my Medieval Letters special subject.

Bibliography

Reference Works

Baldick, Chris, *The Oxford Dictionary of Literary Terms*, 3rd edn (Oxford: Oxford University Press, 2008).
Bosworth, Joseph and T. Northcote Toller, *An Anglo-Saxon Dictionary* (Oxford: Clarendon Press, 1898), and *Supplement* (Oxford: Clarendon Press, 1921).
British Library, *Catalogue of Illuminated Manuscripts*, at http://www.bl.uk/catalogues/illuminatedmanuscripts
Cameron, Angus, Ashley Crandell Amos, Antonette diPaolo Healey et al., *Dictionary of Old English: A to G online* (Toronto, ON: Dictionary of Old English Project, 2007), at http://www.doe.utoronto.ca
Healey, Antonette diPaolo (ed.) with John Price Wilkin and Xin Xiang, *Dictionary of Old English Web Corpus* (Toronto, ON: Dictionary of Old English Project, 2009), at http://www.doe.utoronto.ca.
Kay, Christian, Jane Roberts, Michael Samuels and Irené Wotherspoon (eds), *Historical Thesaurus of the Oxford English Dictionary*, 2 vols (Oxford: Oxford University Press, 2009).
Ker, N.R., *Catalogue of Manuscripts containing Anglo-Saxon* (Oxford: Clarendon Press, 1957).
Kluge, Friedrich, *Etymological Dictionary of the German Language*, trans. John Francis Davis (London: George Bell and Sons, 1891).
Lanham, Richard A., *A Handlist of Rhetorical Terms*, 2nd edn (Berkeley, CA: University of California Press, 1991).
Lehmann, Winfred, *A Gothic Etymological Dictionary* (Leiden: Brill, 1986).
Lewis, Charlton T. and Charles Short, *A Latin Dictionary. Founded on Andrews' edition of Freund's Latin dictionary.* Revised, enlarged, and in great part rewritten by Charlton T. Lewis, Ph.D. and Charles Short, LL.D. (Oxford: Clarendon Press, 1879).
Niermeyer, J.F., *Mediae Latinitatis Lexicon Minus* (Leiden: Brill, 1976).
Orel, Vladimir, *A Handbook of Germanic Etymology* (Leiden: Brill, 2003).
Oxford English Dictionary Online (Oxford University Press), at www.oed.com
Pfeifer, Wolfgang, *Etymologisches Wörterbuch des Deutschen* (Berlin: Akademie-Verlag, 1993).
Pokorny, Julius, *Indogermanisches etymologisches Wörterbuch*, 3 vols (Bern: Francke, 1959).

Rix, Helmut, Martin Kümmel et al. (eds), *Lexicon Der Indogermanischen Verben. Die Wurzeln und ihre Primärstammbildungen* (Wiesbaden: Dr. Ludwig Reichert Verlag, 2001).

Roberts, Jane and Christian Kay, with Lynne Grundy (eds), *A Thesaurus of Old English*, 2nd edn, 2 vols (Amsterdam: Rodopi, 2000).

Souter, Alexander, *Glossary of Later Latin to 600A.D.* (Oxford: Clarendon Press, 1949).

Toller, T. Northcote, *An Anglo-Saxon Dictionary: Supplement* (Oxford: Clarendon Press, 1921).

Primary Sources

A Feast of Creatures: Anglo-Saxon Riddle-songs, trans. Craig Williamson (Philadelphia, PA: University of Pennsylvania Press, 1982).

Abbots of Wearmouth and Jarrow: Bede's Homily i.13 on Benedict Biscop, Bede's History of the Abbots of Wearmouth and Jarrow, The Anonymous Life of Ceolfrith, Bede's Letter to Ecgberht, Bishop of York, ed. and trans. Christopher Grocock and Ian Wood, Oxford Medieval Texts (Oxford: Clarendon Press, 2013).

Adami Gesta Hammaburgensis ecclesiae pontificum. Ex recensione Lappenbergii, ed. J.M. Lappenberg, 2nd edn by G. Waitz and L.C. Weiland, MGH Scriptores Rerum Germanicarum in usum scholarum seperatim editi (Hanover: Hahn, 1876).

Die Admonitio Generalis Karls des Grossen, ed. Hubert Mordek, Klaus Zechiel-Eckes and Michael Glatthaar, MGH Fontes iuris Germanici antiqui in usum scholarum separatim editi XVI (Hanover: Hahn, 2012)

Ælfric, *Lives of Saints*, ed. Walter W. Skeat, Early English Text Society o.s. 76, 82, 94, 114, 4 parts in 2 vols (Oxford: Oxford University Press, 1881–1900).

Agnellus of Ravenna, *Lectures on Galen's De sectis*, ed. and trans. Leendert G. Westerinck et al. (Buffalo, NY: Department of Classics, State University of N.Y. at Buffalo, 1981).

Alcuin, *Alcuin of York: His Life and Letters*, trans. Stephen Allott (York: William Sessions, 1974).

Alcuin, *The Bishops, Kings and Saints of York*, ed. P. Godman (Oxford: Clarendon Press, 1982).

Alcuin, *Epistolae*, ed. Ernst Dümmler, in MGH Epistolae IV, Epistolae Aevi Karolini II (Berlin: Weidmann, 1895).

Alcuin, *De laude Psalmorum*, ed. Jonathan Black, in Jonathan Black, 'Psalm Uses in Carolingian Prayerbooks: Alcuin and the Preface to *De psalmorum usu*', *Mediaeval Studies* 64 (2002): 1–60, at 45–60.

Alcuin, *Vita Willibrordi*, in W. Wattenbach and E. Dümmler (eds.), *Monumenta Alcuiniana a Philippo Iaffeo praeparata*, Bibliotheica rerum Germanicarum VI (Berlin: Weidmann, 1873).
Alcuin, *Vita Willibrordi archiepiscopi Traiectensis*, in B. Krusch and W. Levison (eds.), *Passiones vitaeque sanctorum aevi Merovingici V*, MGH Scriptores Rerum Merovingicarum 7 (Hanover: Hahn, 1920).
Aldhelm, *De metris et enigmatibus ac pedum regulis*, in Rudolf Ehwald (ed.), *Aldhelmi opera*, MGH AA 15 (Berlin: Hahn, 1919; rpt 1961).
Annales Regni Francorum inde a. 741 usque ad 829, qui dicuntur Annales Laurissenses maiores et Einhardi, ed. G.H. Pertz; rev. edn F. Kurze, MGH Scriptores rerum Germanicarum in usum scholarum separatim editi (Hanover: Hahn, 1895).
Der altenglische Regius-Psalter; eine Interlinearversion in H.S. Royal 2. B. 5 des Brit. Mus., ed. Fritz Roeder, Studien zur englischen Philologie 18 (Halle: Niemeyer, 1904).
Die angelsächsischen Prosabearbeitungen der Benediktinerregel, ed. Arnold Schröer, Bibliothek der angelsächsischen Prosa 2 (Kassel: Georg H. Wigand, 1885–88).
The Anglo-Saxon Chronicle, According to Several Original Authorities, ed. Benjamin Thorpe, 2 vols (London: Longman, Green, Longman and Roberts, 1861).
Anglo-Saxon Manuscripts in Microfiche Facsimile, Volume Two: Psalters, ed. Phillip Pulsiano (Binghampton, NY: Medieval & Renaissance Texts & Studies, 1994).
The Anglo-Saxon Poetic Records: A Collective Edition, ed. George Philip Krapp and Elliott Van Kirk Dobbie, 6 vols (New York: Columbia University Press, 1931–53).
Anglo-Saxon Poetry, trans. S.A.J. Bradley, S.A.J. (London: Dent, 1982).
The Annals of Ulster (to A.D. 1131), eds and trans. Seán Mac Airt and Gearóid Mac Niocall, 2 vols (Dublin: DIAS, 1983).
Aristotle, *The Art of Rhetoric*, trans. H.C. Lawson-Tancred (London: Penguin, 2004).
Asser's Life of King Alfred, ed. William Henry Stevenson (Oxford: Clarendon Press, 1959).
Augustine, *Concerning The City of God Against the Pagans*, trans. Henry Bettenson (Harmondsworth: Penguin, 1972).
Augustine, *On Christian Doctrine*, trans. D.W. Robertson, Jr. (New York: Macmillan, 1958).
Augustine, *Sancti Aurelii Augustini Enarrationes in Psalmos*, ed. E. Dekkers and I. Fraipont, CCSL 38–40, 3 vols (Turnhout: Brepols, 1956).
Augustine, *St Augustine on the Psalms*, trans. Scholastica Hebgin and Felicitas Corrigan, 2 vols (London: Newman Press, 1960–61).

Bald's Leechbook, in Thomas Oswald Cockayne (ed.), *Leechdoms, Wortcunning and Starcraft of Early England*, vol. II, pp. 2–298. Rolls Series 35, 3 vols (London, 1864–66; repr. Millwood, NY: Kraus Reprints, 1965).
Bede, *Commentarius in primam partem Samuelis*, ed. David Hurst, CCSL 119 (Turnhout: Brepols, 1962).
Bede, *Historia Ecclesiastica Gentis Anglorum: Bede's Ecclesiastical History of the English People*, ed. Bertram Colgrave and R.A.B. Mynors, (Oxford: Clarendon Press, 1969).
Bede, *Venerabilis Bedae, Historiam ecclesiasticam gentis Anglorum, Historiam abbatum, Epistolam ad Egcbertum, Historia Abbatum auctore anonymo*, ed. Charles Plummer, 2 vols in 1 (Oxford: Clarendon Press, 1896).
Bede, *In Cantica Canticorum, CCS* 119B (Turnhout: Brepols, 1983).
Beowulf, trans. Kevin Crossley-Holland (Oxford: Oxford University Press, 2008).
Beowulf: A New Verse Translation, trans. Seamus Heaney (London and New York: W.W. Norton & Company, 2000).
Beowulf: A Student Edition, ed. George Jack (Oxford: Oxford University Press, 1997).
Beowulf and the Fight at Finnsburg, ed. Frederick Klaeber (Boston: Heath, rpt. 3rd edn with first and second supplements, 1950).
Biblia Sacra iuxta Vulgatam Versionem, ed. Robertus Weber, Bonifatius Fischer et al., 2 vols, (Stuttgart: Würtembergische Bibelanstalt, 1969; 4th edn, Stuttgart: Deutsche Bibelgesellschaft, 1994).
Bischofs Wærferth von Worcester Übersetzung *der Dialoge Gregors des Grossen*, ed. Hans Hecht, Bibliothek der angelsächsischen Prosa 5 (Leipzig: Wigand, 1900).
Bonifatius, *Epistolae*, ed. Michael Tangl, MGH Epistolae in usum scholarum separatim editi (Berlin: Weidmann, 1916).
Campbell, Martin, dir., *Casino Royale* (MGM-Columbia, 2006).
The Canterbury Biblical Commentaries of Theodore and Hadrian, ed. Bernhard Bischoff and Michael Lapidge (Cambridge: Cambridge University Press, 1994).
Cassiodorus, *Expositio Psalmorum*, ed. M. Adriaen, CCSL 97–98, 2 vols (Turnhout: Brepols, 1958).
Cassiodorus: Explanation of the Psalms, trans. P.G. Walsh, Ancient Christian Writers 51–53, 3 vols (New York: Paulist Press, 1990–92).
Chaucer, *Troilus and Criseyde*, in *The Riverside Chaucer*, ed. Larry D. Benson, 3rd edn (Boston, MA: Houghton Mifflin, 1987).
A Critical Edition of the Old English Gnomic Poems, ed. Carl T. Berkhout, Jr. (Ph.D. thesis, University of Notre Dame, 1975), Xerox University Microfilms, Ann Arbor, Michigan 48106.

Cuthbert, *Epistola de obitu Bedae*, in Bertram Colgrave and R.A.B. Mynors (eds), *Bede's Ecclesiastical History of the English People*, Oxford Medieval Texts (Oxford: Clarendon Press, 1969, rpt. corrected edn, 1991).

Deluxe and Illustrated Manuscripts Containing Literary and Technical Texts, ed. A.N. Doane and Tiffany J. Grade, Anglo-Saxon Manuscripts in Microfiche Facsimile 9 (Tempe, AZ: ACMRS, 2001).

Egil's Saga, trans. Hermann Pálsson and Paul Edwards (Harmondsworth: Penguin, 1976).

An Edition of the Regius Psalter and its Latin Commentary, ed. William Davey, unpublished dissertation (Ph.D. thesis, University of Ottawa, Canada, 1979).

Einhard, *Life of Charlemagne*, trans. Paul Dutton, in *Charlemagne's Courtier: The Complete Einhard* (Toronto: University of Toronto Press, 2nd revised edn, 1998).

Einhard, *Vita Karoli Magni*, ed. G.H. Pertz, G. Waitz and O. Holder-Egger, 6th edn (Hanover: Impensis bibliopolii Hahniani, 1911).

Encomium Emmae Reginae, ed. and trans. Alistair Campbell (Cambridge: Cambridge University Press, 1998).

The Exeter Book, ed. George Phillip Krapp and Elliot Van Kirk Dobbie, ASPR 3 (New York, 1936).

Die Gesetze der Angelsachsen, ed. Felix Liebermann, 3 vols (Halle: Max Niemeyer, 1903–16; rpt. Clark, NJ: Lawbook Exchange, 2007).

Gregory of Tours, *Decem Libri Historiarum*, ed. W. Arndt, MGH SRM 1 (Hanover, 1885).

Gregory the Great, *The Earliest Life of Gregory the Great*, ed. Bertram Colgrave (Cambridge: Cambridge University Press, 1985).

Gregory the Great, *Regula Pastoralis*, ed. Floribert Rommel, Sources Chrétiennes 381–382, 2 vols (Paris: Les Éditions du Cerf, 1992).

Harris, Charlaine, *The Southern Vampire Mysteries* (series) (NY: Ace, 2001–present).

Héliand, ed. J.E. Cathey, Medieval European Studies 12 (Morgantown, WV: West Virginia University Press, 2002).

The Holy Bible, ed. and trans. Bishop Richard Challoner et al. (London: Baronius Press, 2008).

The Holy Bible: Douay Rheims Version (Baltimore, MD, 1899; repr. Rockford, IL: TAN Books, 2000).

The Holy Gospels in Anglo-Saxon, Northumbrian, and Old Mercian Versions, ed. Walter W. Skeat (Cambridge, 1871–87; repr. Darmstadt: Wissenschaftliche Buchgesellschaft, 1970).

Isidore of Seville, *Differentiae uerborum*, ed. María Adelaida Andrés Sanz, *Liber differentiarum* [*II*], CCSL 111A (Turnhout: Brepols, 2006).

Isidore of Seville, *Etymologiarum sive Originum libri XX*, ed. W.M. Lindsay, 2 vols (Oxford: Clarendon Press, 1911).
Isidore of Seville, *The Etymologies of Isidore of Seville*, trans. Stephen A. Barney, W.J. Lewis, J.A. Beach and Oliver Berghof with Muriel Hall (Cambridge: Cambridge University Press, 2006).
King Alfred's Old English Prose Translation of the First Fifty Psalms, ed. Patrick P. O'Neill (Cambridge, MA: Medieval Academy of America, 2001).
King Alfred's West Saxon Version of Gregory's Pastoral Care, ed. Henry Sweet, Early English Text Society 45 and 50, 2 vols (London: Oxford University Press, 1871).
Kipling, Rudyard, *Something of Myself and Other Autobiographical Writings* (Cambridge: Cambridge University Press, 1937; rpt. 1991).
Klaeber's Beowulf and the Fight at Finnsburg, ed. R.D. Fulk, Robert E. Bjork and John D. Niles, 4th edn (Toronto, ON: University of Toronto Press, 2008).
Lacnunga, in Edward Pettit (ed. and comm.), *Anglo-Saxon Remedies, Charms, and Prayers from British Library MS Harley 585: The Lacnunga*, 2 vols (Lewiston, NY: Edwin Mellen Press, 2001).
Der Lambeth-Psalter, ed. Uno Lindelöf, Acta Societatis Scientiarum Fennicae 35.1 and 43.3, 2 vols (Helsinki: Druckerei der Finnischen Litteraturgesellschaft, 1909–14).
Langland, William, *Piers Plowman A-text*, in A.V.C. Schmidt (ed.), *Piers Plowman: A Parallel-text Edition of the A, B, C and Z Versions. Volume I. Text* (London and New York: Longman, 1995).
Leechdoms, Wortcunning and Starcraft of Early England, ed. Thomas Oswald Cockayne, Rolls Series 35, 3 vols (London, 1964–66; repr. Millwood, NY: Kraus Reprints, 1965).
Medieval Latin Lyrics, trans. Helen Waddell (1929; rpt. New York: Constable, 1948).
Middle English Lyrics, ed. Maxwell S. Luria and Richard L. Hoffman (London: Norton, 1974).
Mutti, Angelo, 'Why Does our Mother Cry Tears of Blood', *Echo of Mary, Queen of Peace* 118 (March–April, 1995), 1–2, at http://www.medjugorje.ws/en/echo/echo-118/
The Old English Apollonius of Tyre, ed. Peter Goolden (Oxford: Oxford University Press, 1958).
Old English Glossed Psalters: Psalms 1–50, ed. Phillip Pulsiano (Toronto, ON: University of Toronto Press, 2001).
The Old English Heptateuch and Ælfric's Libellus de Veteri Testamento et Novo, I, *Introduction and Text*, ed. Richard Marsden, Early English Text Society o.s. 330 (Oxford: Oxford University Press, 2008).

The Old English Herbarium and Medicina de Quadrupedibus, ed. Hubert Jan de Vriend, Early English Text Society o.s. 286 (Oxford: Oxford University Press, 1984).

The Old English Orosius, ed. Janet Bately, Early English Text Society s.s. 6 (Oxford: Oxford University Press, 1980).

Orderic Vitalis, *The Ecclesiastical History of Orderic Vitalis*, Vol. VI. trans. and ed. Marjorie Chibnall (Oxford: Oxford University Press, 1978).

Ovid, *Metamorphoses*, with translation by Frank Justus Miller, vol. 1, 2nd edn (London: William Heinemann, 1971; orig. pub. 1921).

The Paris Prose: Edition of the Latin and English of the First Fifty Psalms in the Paris Psalter, MS. Bibliothèque Nationale Fonds Latin 8824, prepared by Richard Stracke, 1999, revised 2002 http://www.aug.edu/augusta/psalms/ (accessed April 2013; link broken at November 2014)

The Paris Psalter: MS Bibliothèque Nationale Fonds Latin 8824, ed. Bertram Colgrave, Early English Manuscripts in Facsimile 8 (Copenhagen: Rosenkilde and Bagger, 1958).

The Paris Psalter and the Meters of Boethius, ed. George Philip Krapp, ASPR 5 (New York: Columbia University Press, 1933).

Peri Didaxeon. Eine Sammlung von Rezepten in Englischer Sprache aus dem 11./12. Jahrhundert, ed. Max Löweneck (Erlangen: Junge, 1896).

Poetae Latini Aevi Carolini II, ed. Ernst Dümmler, MGH Antiquitates (Berlin: Weidmann, 1884).

Practica Alexandri yatros greci cum expositione glose interlinearis Jacobi de partibus et Januensis in margine posite (Lyon, 1504), at http://cisne.sim.ucm.es/record=b1784077*spi

Practica Petrocelli, in S. de Renzi (ed.), *Collectio Salernitana ossia documenti inediti e trattati di medicina appartanenti alla scuola medica salernitana*, 5 vols (Naples: Tipografia del Filiatre-Sebezio, 1852–66), IV.185–291.

The Prose Solomon and Saturn *and* Adrian and Ritheus, ed. James E. Cross and Thomas D. Hill (Toronto, ON: University of Toronto Press, 1982).

Quintilian, *Institutio Oratoria*, in *Institution oratoire de Quintilien*, ed. C.V. Ouizille (Paris: C.L.F. Panckoucke, 1832).

Ragnars Saga Loðbrókar ok Sona Hans, ed. Guðni Jónsson and Bjarni Vilhjálmsson, Perseus Digital Library, at http://nlp.perseus.tufts.edu/hopper/text;jsessionid=2A93873BC88772661AAEE61643DEFA56?doc=Perseus%3Atext%3A2003.02.0029%3Achapter%3D10

RB 1980: The Rule of St Benedict in Latin and English with notes, ed. Timothy Fry OSB (Collegeville, MN: Liturgical Press, 1981).

Regularis concordia anglicae nationis monachorum sanctimonialiumque / The Monastic Agreement of the Monks and Nuns of the English Nation, trans. Thomas Symons (London: Nelson, 1963).

Religious Lyrics of the Fifteenth Century, ed. Carleton Brown (Oxford: Clarendon, 1939).
The Rule of S. Benet: Latin and Anglo-Saxon Interlinear Version, ed. H. Logeman, Early English Text Society o.s. 90 (Oxford: Oxford University Press, 1888).
The Salisbury Psalter, ed. Celia Sisam and Kenneth Sisam, Early English Text Society o.s. 242 (Oxford: Oxford University Press, 1959).
The Seafarer, ed. Ida Gordon (Exeter: University of Exeter Press, 1996).
Shakespeare, William, *Antony and Cleopatra*, ed. J. Wilders (London: Routledge, 1995).
Sidney, Sir Philip, *Astrophil and Stella*, in Katherine Duncan-Jones (ed.), *Sir Philip Sidney* (Oxford: Oxford University Press, 1989).
Sir Gawain and the Green Knight, ed. and trans. James Winny (Peterborough, ON: Broadview, 1992).
Songs and Carols from a Manuscript in the British Museum of the Fifteenth Century, ed. Thomas Wright (London: Richards, 1856).
St Gregory of Nyssa, 'Funeral Oration on the Empress Flacilla', in *Gregorii Nysseni opera* IX, ed. Andreas Spira (Leiden: Brill, 1967).
The Stowe Psalter, ed. Andrew C. Kimmens (Toronto, ON: University of Toronto Press, 1979).
Two of the Saxon Chronicles Parallel, ed. John Earle and Charles Plummer (Oxford: Clarendon, 1898, rpt. 1972).
The Unbound Bible, Biola University 2005–2006, at http://unbound.biola.edu/
Die Vercelli-Homilien: I–VIII Homilie, ed. Max Förster (Hamburg: Wissenschaftliche Buchgesellschaft, 1932).
The Vespasian Psalter, ed. Sherman M. Kuhn (Ann Arbor, MI: University of Michigan Press, 1965).
Vindicianus, *Epitome altera*, in V. Rose (ed.), *Theodori Prisciani Euporiston libri III cum physicorum fragmento et additamentis pseudo-Theodoreis* (Leipzig: Teubner, 1894), pp. 467–83.
Vita Alcuini, ed. Wilhelm Arndt, MGH Scriptores Rerum Germanicarum 15.1 (Hanover: Impensis Bibliopolii Hahniani, 1887).
Wordsworth, William, preface to the second edition of *Lyrical Ballads, with Other Poems*, volume 1 (1800), 14, at http://www.gutenberg.org/ebooks/8905

Secondary Sources

Abu-Lughod, Lila, *Veiled Sentiments: Honor and Poetry in a Bedouin Society* (Berkeley, CA: University of California Press, 1986).
Abu-Lughod, Lila, and Catherine A. Lutz, 'Introduction: Emotion, Discourse, and the Politics of Everyday Life', in Catherine A. Lutz and Lila Abu-Lughod

(eds), *Language and the Politics of Emotion* (Cambridge: Cambridge University Press, 1990).

Acker, Paul, 'Horror and the Maternal in *Beowulf*', *PMLA* 121/3 (2006): 702–16.

Ainsworth, Mary and John Bowlby, *Child Care and the Growth of Love* (London: Pelican, 1965).

Airlie, Stuart, 'The History of Emotions and Emotional History', *Early Medieval Europe* 10 (2001): 229–34.

Althoff, Gerd, 'Empörung, Tränen, Zerknirschung. Emotionen in der Öffentlichen Kommunikation des Mittelalters', *Frühmittelalterliche Studien* 30 (1996): 60–79.

Althoff, Gerd, 'Freiwilligkeit und Konsensfassaden. Emotionale Ausdrucksformen in der Politik des Mittelalters', in K. Herding and B. Stumpfhaus (eds), *Pathos, Affekt, Gefühl. Die Emotionen in den Künsten* (Berlin: Walter de Gruyter, 2004).

Althoff, Gerd, 'Ira Regis: Prolegomena to a History of Royal Anger', in Barbara H. Rosenwein (ed.), *Anger's Past: The Social Uses of an Emotion in the Middle Ages* (Ithaca, NY: Cornell University Press, 1998).

Angenendt, Arnold, *Monachi Peregrini: Studien zu Pirmin und den monastischen Vorstellungen des frühen Mittelalters* (Munich: Wilhelm Fink, 1972).

Angenendt, Arnold, *Kaiserherrschaft und Königstaufe* (Berlin: de Gruyter, 1984).

Arancibia, S., F. Rage, H. Astier and L. Tapia-Arancibia, 'Neuroendocrine and Autonomous Mechanism Underlying Thermoregulation in Cold Environment', *Neuroendocrinology* 64 (1996): 257–67.

Arner, Timothy D. and Paul Dustin Stegner, '"Of þam him aweaxeð wynsum gefea": The Voyeuristic Appeal of *Christ III*', *Journal of English and Germanic Philology* 106 (2007): 428–46.

Auerbach, Erich, *Literary Language and Its Public in Late Antiquity and the Middle Ages*, trans. Ralph Manheim, Bollingen Series 74 (1965; repr. with new foreword by Jan Ziolkowski, Princeton, NJ: Princeton University Press, 1993).

Ayoub, Lois, 'Old English *wæta* and the Medical Theory of the Humours', *Journal of English and Germanic Philology* 94 (1995): 332–46.

Bailey, Richard N., 'Bede's Text of Cassiodorus' Commentary on the Psalms', *Journal of Theological Studies* 34/1 (1983): 189–93.

Bambas, Rudolf C., 'Another View of the Old English *Wife's Lament*', *Journal of English and Germanic Philology* 62 (1963): 303–9.

Banham, Debby, 'England Joins the Medical Mainstream: New Texts in Eleventh-century Manuscripts', in Hans Sauer and Joanna Story (eds) with Gaby Waxenberger, *Anglo-Saxon England and the Continent* (Tempe, AZ: ACMRS, 2011).

Barrow, Julia, 'Demonstrative Behaviour and Political Communication in Anglo-Saxon England', *Anglo-Saxon England* 36 (2007): 127–50.

Bately, Janet, 'Lexical Evidence for the Authorship of the Prose Psalms in the Paris Psalter', *Anglo-Saxon England* 10 (1982): 69–95.
Beaston, Lawrence, 'The Wanderer's Courage', *Neophilologus* 89 (2005): 119–37.
Bednarek, Monika, *Emotion Talk Across Corpora* (Basingstoke: Palgrave Macmillan, 2008).
Belanoff, Pat, '*Ides ... geomrode giddum*: The Old English Female Lament', in Anne L. Klinck and Ann Marie Rasmussen (eds), *Medieval Woman's Song: Cross-cultural Approaches* (Philadelphia, PA: University of Pennsylvania Press, 2002).
Ben-Ze'ev, Aaron, 'The Thing Called Emotion', in Peter Goldie (ed.), *The Oxford Handbook of Philosophy of Emotion* (Oxford: Oxford University Press, 2010).
Bennett, Helen, 'The Female Mourner at Beowulf's Funeral: Filling in the Blanks / Hearing the Spaces', *Exemplaria* 4 (1992): 35–50.
Berger, Peter L. and Thomas Luckmann, *The Social Construction of Reality: A Treatise in the Sociology of Knowledge* (New York: Doubleday, 1966).
Berlin, Brent and Paul Kay, *Basic Color Terms* (Berkeley, CA: University of California Press, 1991).
Bestul, Thomas H. *Texts of the Passion: Latin Devotional Literature and Medieval Society* (Philadelphia, PA: University of Pennsylvania Press, 1996).
Bettelheim, Bruno, *The Children of the Dream* (New York: Macmillan, 1969).
Biggam, Carole, *The Semantics of Colour: A Historical Approach* (Cambridge: Cambridge University Press, 2012).
Bitterauf, Theodor, *Die Traditionen des Hochstifts Fresising: 926–1283* (Aalen: Scientia-Verlag, 1967).
Bjork, Robert, '*Sundor æt rune*: The Voluntary Exile of the Wanderer', *Neophilologus* 73 (1989): 119–29.
Black, Jonathan, 'Psalm Uses in Carolingian Prayerbooks: Alcuin and the Preface to *De psalmorum usu*', *Mediaeval Studies* 64 (2002): 1–60.
Blackburn, Francis A., 'The Husband's Message and the Accompanying Riddles of the Exeter Book', *Journal of English and Germanic Philology* 3 (1901): 1–13.
Blair, Peter Hunter, *The World of Bede* (1970; rpt. Cambridge: Cambridge University Press, 1990).
Blanchfield, Lyn A., 'Prolegomenon: Considerations of Weeping and Sincerity in the Middle Ages', in Elina Gertsman (ed.), *Crying in the Middle Ages: Tears of History* (New York: Routledge, 2011).
Boehm, Christopher, 'The Natural History of Blood Revenge', in Jeppe Büchert Netterstrøm and Bjørn Poulsen (eds), *Feud in Medieval and Early Modern Europe* (Aarhus: Aarhus University Press, 2007).
Bonnano, George, *The Other Side of Sadness: What the New Science of Bereavement Tells Us about Life after Loss* (New York: Basic Books, 2009).

Boswell, John, 'Expositio and Oblatio: The Abandonment of Children and the Ancient and Medieval Family', *American Historical Review* 89 (1984): 10–33.
Boswell, John, *The Kindness of Strangers: The Abandonment of Children in Western Europe from Late Antiquity to the Renaissance* (Chicago, IL: University of Chicago Press, 1988).
Boulter, Jonathan, *Melancholy and the Archive: Trauma, History and Memory in the Contemporary Nove*l (London: Continuum, 2011).
Bourke, Joanna, 'Fear and Anxiety: Writing about Emotion in Modern History', *History Workshop Journal* 55 (2003): 111–33.
Bowlby, John, *Attachment and Loss*, 3 vols (New York: Penguin Books, 1969, 1973, 1980).
Bracher, Frederick, 'Understatement in Old English Poetry', *PMLA* 52 (1937): 915–34.
Breithaupt, Fritz, 'How is it Possible to Have Empathy? Four Models', in Paula Leverage, Howard Mancing, Richard Schweickert and Jennifer Marston William (eds), *Theory of Mind and Literature* (West Lafayette, IN: Purdue University Press, 2011).
Brodeur, Arthur G., *The Art of 'Beowulf'* (Berkeley, CA: University of California Press, 1959).
Brodeur, Arthur G., 'Design for Terror in the Purging of Heorot', *Journal of English and Germanic Philology* 53 (1954): 503–13.
Brown, George Hardin, 'The Psalms as the Foundation of Anglo-Saxon Learning', in Nancy Van Deusen (ed.), *The Place of the Psalms in the Intellectual Culture of the Middle Ages* (Albany, NY: State University of New York Press, 1999).
Brown, Michelle P., *Manuscripts from the Anglo-Saxon Age* (London: British Library, 2007).
Bruce, J. Douglas 'The Anglo-Saxon Version of the Book of Psalms Commonly Known as the Paris Psalter', *PMLA* 9 (1894): 43–164.
Bruce, J. Douglas, 'Immediate and Ultimate Source of the Rubrics and Introductions to the Psalms in the Paris Psalter', *Modern Language Notes* 8 (1893): 36–41.
Buchanan, Tony W. and William R. Lovallo, 'Enhanced Memory for Emotional Material Following Stress-level Cortisol Treatment in Humans', *Psychoneuroendocrinology* 26 (2001): 307–17.
Buettner, Elizabeth, 'Parent–Child Separations and Colonial Careers: The Talbot Family Correspondence in the 1880s and 1890s', in Stephen Hussey and Anthony Fletcher (eds), *Childhood in Question: Children, Parents and the State* (Manchester: Manchester University Press, 1999).
Bullock, Merry and James A. Russell, 'Concepts of Emotion in Developmental Psychology', in Carroll E. Izard and Peter B. Read (eds), *Measuring Emotions in Infants and Children*, 2 vols (Cambridge: Cambridge University Press, 1986).

Bullough, Donald, *Alcuin: Achievement and Reputation* (Leiden: Brill, 2001).
Butts, Richard, 'The Analogical Mere: Landscape and Terror in *Beowulf*', *English Studies* 68 (1987): 113–21.
Byock, Jesse L., *Medieval Iceland: Society, Sagas, and Power* (Los Angeles, CA: University of California Press, 1990).
Cameron, M.L., 'Bald's *Leechbook*: Its Sources and their Use in its Compilation', *Anglo-Saxon England* 12 (1983): 153–82.
Carroll, Noël, 'On Some Affective Relations between Audiences and the Characters in Popular Fictions', in Amy Coplan and Peter Goldie (eds), *Empathy: Philosophical and Psychological Perspectives* (Oxford: Oxford University Press, 2011).
Carroll, Noël, 'On the Ties that Bind: Characters, the Emotions, and Popular Fictions', in William Irwin and Jorge J.E. Gracia (eds), *Philosophy and the Interpretation of Pop Culture* (Lanham, MD: Rowman and Littlefield, 2007).
Cavill, Paul, 'Christianity and Theology in Beowulf', in Paul Cavill (ed.), *The Christian Tradition in Anglo-Saxon England: Approaches to Current Scholarship and Teaching* (Suffolk: D.S. Brewer, 2004).
Cavill, Paul, *Maxims in Old English Poetry* (Cambridge: Brewer, 1999).
Chance, Jane, 'Grendel's Mother as Epic Anti-type of the Virgin and Queen', in Robert D. Fulk (ed.), *Interpretations of* Beowulf (Bloomington, IN: Indiana University Press, 1991).
Chardonnens, László Sándor, *Anglo-Saxon Prognostics, 900–1100: Study and Texts* (Leiden: Brill, 2007).
Chase, Dennis, 'Existential Attitudes of the Old English "Wanderer"', *Language Quarterly* 26 (1987): 17–19.
Chazelle, Celia, *The Crucified God in the Carolingian Era: Theology and Art of Christ's Passion* (Cambridge: Cambridge University Press, 2001).
Chodorow, Nancy, *The Power of Feelings: Personal Meaning in Psychoanalysis, Gender, and Culture* (New Haven, CT: Yale University Press, 1999).
Clark, David, *Between Medieval Men: Male Friendship and Desire in Early Medieval English Literature* (Oxford: Oxford University Press, 2009).
Clemoes, Peter, *Interactions of Thought and Language in Old English Poetry*, Cambridge Studies in Anglo-Saxon England 12 (Cambridge: Cambridge University Press, 1995).
Clemoes, Peter, '*Mens absentia cogitans* in *The Seafarer* and *The Wanderer*', in D. Pearsall and R.A. Waldron (eds), *Mediaeval Literature and Civilisation: Studies in Honour of G.N. Garmonsway* (London: University of London Athlone Press, 1969).
Cole, John R., 'Montaigne's Dead Babies', *Montaigne Studies* 12/1–2 (2000): 167–84.

Cooper, Tracey-Anne, 'The Shedding of Tears in Late Anglo-Saxon England', in Elina Gertsman (ed.), *Crying in the Middle Ages: Tears of History* (New York: Routledge, 2011).

Coplan, Amy, 'Catching Characters' Emotions: Emotional Contagion Responses to Narrative Fiction Film', *Film Studies* 8 (2006): 26–38.

Coplan, Amy, 'Empathetic Engagement with Narrative Fictions', *Journal of Aesthetics and Art Criticism* 62 (2004): 141–52.

Cowen, Alice, '*Byrstas and bysmeras*: The Wounds of Sin in Wulfstan's *Sermo Lupi ad Anglos*', in Matthew Townend (ed.), *Wulfstan, Archbishop of York*, Studies in the Early Middle Ages 10 (Turnhout: Brepols, 2004).

Cross, J.E., 'On the Genre of *The Wanderer*', *Neophilologus* 45 (1961): 63–75.

Crozier, W. Ray, *Blushing and the Social Emotions: The Self Unmasked* (New York: Palgrave, 2006).

Cubitt, Catherine, 'The History of the Emotions: A Debate', *Early Medieval Europe* 10 (2001): 225–7.

Cubitt, Catherine, 'The Politics of Remorse: Penance and Royal Piety in the Reign of Æthelred the Unready', *Historical Research* 85 (2012): 179–92.

Currie, Gregory, 'The Paradox of Caring: Fiction and the Philosophy of Mind', in Mette Hjort and Sue Laver (eds), *Emotion and the Arts* (Oxford: Oxford University Press, 1997).

Damasio, Antonio, *Descartes' Error: Emotion, Reason and the Human Brain* (New York: Putnam, 1994).

Damasio, Antonio, *The Feeling of What Happens: Body and Emotion in the Making of Consciousness* (New York, San Diego and London: Harcourt, 1999; rpt London: Vintage, 2000).

Damasio, Antonio, *Looking for Spinoza: Joy, Sorrow, and the Feeling Brain* (Orlando, FL: Harcourt, 2003; rpt London: Vintage, 2004).

Damasio, Antonio, *Self Comes to Mind: Constructing the Conscious Brain* (New York: Pantheon, 2010).

Darwin, Charles, *The Expression of Emotions in Man and Animals* (London: John Murray, 1872; rpt 1873).

Davey, William, 'The Commentary of the Regius Psalter: Its Main Source and Influence on the Old English Gloss', *Mediaeval Studies* 49 (1987): 335–51.

Dawson, R. McGregor, 'The Structure of the Old English Gnomic Poems', *Journal of English and Germanic Philology* 61 (1962): 14–22.

Day, David, '*Hwanan sio fæhð aras*: Defining the Feud in *Beowulf*', *Philological Quarterly* 78 (1999): 77–96.

Day-Sclater, Shelley, David W. Jones, Heather Price and Candida Yates (eds), *Emotion: New Psychosocial Perspectives* (London: Routledge, 2009).

DeGregorio, Scott, 'Affective Spirituality: Theory and Practice in Bede and Alfred the Great', *Essays in Medieval Studies* 22 (2005): 129–39.

Demos, E.V. (ed.), *Exploring Affect: The Selected Writings of Silvan S. Tomkins* (Cambridge: Cambridge University Press, 1995).

Dendle, Peter, 'Lupines, Manganese, and Devil-sickness: An Anglo-Saxon Medical Response to Epilepsy', *Bulletin of the History of Medicine* 75 (2001): 91–101.

Diller, Hans-Jürgen, '*ANGER* and *TĒNE* in Middle English', in Manfred Markus, Yoko Iyeiri, Reinhard Heuberger and Emil Chamson (eds), *Middle and Modern English Corpus Linguistics: A Multi-dimensional Approach* (Amsterdam: John Benjamins, 2012).

Diller, Hans-Jürgen, 'The Growth of the English Emotion Lexicon: A First Look at the Historical Thesaurus of English', in Katja Lenz and Ruth Möhlig (eds), *Of Dyuersitie & Chaunge of Language: Essays Presented to Manfred Görlach on the Occasion of His 65th Birthday*, Anglistische Forschungen 308 (Winter, Heidelberg: Universitätsverlag, 2002).

Diller, Hans-Jürgen, 'Historical Semantics, Corpora, and the Unity of English Studies', in Monika Fludernik and Benjamin Kohlmann (eds), *Anglistentag 2011 Freiburg Proceedings* (Trier: WVT Wissenschaftlicher Verlag Trier, 2012).

Dixon, Thomas, *From Passions to Emotions: The Creation of a Secular Psychological Category* (Cambridge: Cambridge University Press, 2003).

Doane, A.N., 'Heathen Form and Christian Function in *The Wife's Lament*', *Mediaeval Studies* 28 (1966): 77–91.

Dockray-Miller, Mary, 'Beowulf's Tears of Fatherhood', *Exemplaria* 10 (1998): 1–28.

Dockray-Miller, Mary, 'The Maternal Performance of the Virgin Mary in the Old English "Advent"', *NWSA Journal* 14/2 (2002): 38–55.

Dodwell, C.R., *Anglo-Saxon Gestures and the Roman Stage* (Cambridge: Cambridge University Press, 2000).

Donahue, Charles. '*Beowulf* and Christian Tradition: A Reconsideration from a Celtic Stance', *Traditio* 21 (1965): 55–116.

Douglas, Mary, *Purity and Danger: An Analysis of the Concepts of Pollution and Taboo* (rpt. London: Ark, 1984).

Dronke, Peter, *Women Writers of the Middle Ages: A Critical Study of Texts from Perpetua (†203) to Marguerite Porete (†1310)* (Cambridge: Cambridge University Press, 1984).

Dronke, Peter and Ursula Dronke, *Growth of Literature: The Sea and the God of the Sea*, H.M. Chadwick Memorial Lectures 8 (Cambridge: Department of Anglo-Saxon, Norse, and Celtic, 1998).

Dumville, D.N., 'The Anglian Collection of Royal Genealogies and Regnal Lists', *Anglo-Saxon England* 5 (1976): 23–50.

Durst, Uwe, 'Why Germans Don't Feel "Anger"', in Jean Harkins and Anna Wierzbicka (eds), *Emotions in Cross-linguistic Perspective* (Berlin: Mouton de Gruyter, 2001).

Dyer, Joseph, 'The Psalms in Monastic Prayer', in Nancy Van Deusen (ed.), *The Place of the Psalms in the Intellectual Culture of the Middle Ages* (Albany, NY: State University of New York Press, 1999).
Earl, James W., '*Maxims I*, Part I', *Neophilologus* 67 (1983): 277–83.
Edwards, Thomas Charles, 'Social Structure', in Pauline Stafford (ed.), *A Companion to the Early Middle Ages: Britain and Ireland c.500–1100* (Oxford: Wiley-Blackwell, 2009).
Edwards, Thomas Charles, 'The Social Background to Irish *Peregrinatio*', *Celtica* 11 (1976): 43–59.
Ekman, Paul, 'Basic Emotions', in Tim Dalgleish and Mick Power (eds), *The Handbook of Cognition and Emotion* (Chichester: John Wiley & Sons, 1999).
Ekman, Paul, *Emotions Revealed: Understanding Faces and Feelings* (London: Weidenfeld and Nicolson, 2003).
Ekman, Paul, 'Facial Expression and Emotion', *American Psychologist*, 48 (1993): 384–92.
Emms, Richard, 'The Scribe of the Paris Psalter', *Anglo-Saxon England* 28 (1999): 179–83.
Engberg, Norma J., 'Mod-mægen Balance in Elene, The Battle of Maldon and The Wanderer', *Neuphilologische Mitteilungen* 85 (1985): 212–26.
Fabiszak, Małgorzata, 'A Semantic Analysis of Emotion Terms in Old English', *Studia Anglica Posnaniensia* 34 (1999): 133–46.
Fabiszak, Małgorzata, 'A Semantic Analysis of FEAR, GRIEF and ANGER Words in Old English', in Javier E. Díaz Vera (ed.), *A Changing World of Words: Studies in English Historical Lexicography, Lexicology and Semantics* (Amsterdam: Rodopi, 2002).
Fabiszak, Małgorzata, *The Concept of 'Joy' in Old and Middle English: A Semantic Analysis* (Piła: Wyższa Szkoła Biznesu, 2001).
Fabiszak, Małgorzata and Anna Hebda, 'Emotions of Control in Old English: Shame and Guilt', *Poetica* 66 (2006): 1–35.
Farmer, D.H., 'Lives of the Abbots of Wearmouth and Jarrow', in D.H. Farmer (ed. and trans.), *The Age of Bede* (1965; revised edn, Penguin: Harmondsworth, 1983).
Favez, Charles, *La consolation latine Chrétienne* (Paris: J. Vrin, 1937).
Feagin, Susan L., 'Affects in Appreciation', in Peter Goldie (ed.), *The Oxford Handbook of Philosophy of Emotion* (Oxford: Oxford University Press, 2010).
Ferrari, M.C., 'Alcuin und Hraban. Freundschaft und auctoritas im 9. Jahrhundert', in B. Körkel, T. Licht and J. Wiendlocha (eds), *Mentis amore ligati. Lateinische Freundschaftsdichtung und Dichterfreundschaft in Mittelalter und Neuzeit. Festgabe für Reinhard Düchting zum 65. Geburtstag* (Heidelberg: Mattes, 2001).
Fichtenau, Heinrich, *The Carolingian Empire*, trans. P. Munz (1957; rpt. Toronto, ON: University of Toronto Press, 1978).

Fischer, Bonifatius, 'Bedae de Titulis Psalmorum Liber', in J. Autenrieth and F. Brunhölzl (eds), *Festschrift Bernhard Bischoff zu seinem 65 Geburtstag* (Stuttgart: Anton Hiersemann, 1971).

Frantzen, Allen J., *King Alfred* (Boston: Twayne, 1986).

Frantzen, Allen J., 'Spirituality and Devotion in Anglo-Saxon Penitentials', *Essays in Medieval Studies* 22 (2005): 117–28.

Freud, Sigmund, 'Mourning and Melancholia', in *On Metapsychology: The Theory of Psychoanalysis. The Penguin Freud Library II*, trans. James Strachey, ed. Angela Richards (Harmondsworth: Penguin, 1984).

Frijda, Nico H., 'The Laws of Emotion', *American Psychologist* 43 (1988): 349–58.

Gale, John, 'The Divine Office: Aid and Hindrance to Penthos', *Studia Monastica* 27 (1985): 13–30.

Ganze, Ronald J., 'From *anhaga* to *snottor*: The Wanderer's Kierkegaardian Epiphany', *Neophilologus* 89 (2005): 629–40.

Garrison, Mary, 'Alcuin and Tibullus', in M.C. Díaz y Díaz and J.M. Díaz de Bustamante (eds), *Poesía Latina Medieval (siglos V–XV): Actas del IV congreso del 'Internationales Mittellateinerkomitee', Santiago de Compostela, 12–15 de Septiembre de 2002* (Florence: Sismel, 2005).

Garrison, Mary, 'Alcuin, *carmen ix* and Hrabanus, *Ad Bonosum*: A Teacher and His Pupil Write Consolation', in J. Marenbon (ed.), *Poetry and Philosophy in the Middle Ages: A Festschrift for Peter Dronke* (Leiden: Brill, 2001).

Garrison, Mary, *Alcuin's World through his Letters and Verse* (Ph.D. thesis, Cambridge University, 1996).

Garrison, Mary, 'An Aspect of Alcuin: *Tuus Albinus*: Peevish Egotist? or Parrhesiast?', in Richard Corradini, Matthew Gillis, Rosamond McKitterick and Irene Renswoude (eds), *Ego Trouble: Authors and their Identities in the Early Middle Ages* (Vienna: Austrian Academy of Sciences, 2010).

Garrison, Mary, 'The Bible and Alcuin's Interpretation of Current Events', *Peritia* 16 (2002): 68–84.

Garrison, Mary, 'Les correspondants d'Alcuin', in P. Depreux and B. Judic (eds), *Alcuin de York à Tours: Écriture, pouvoir et réseaux dans l'Europe du haut moyen âge*, Annales de Bretagne et des Pays de l'Ouest 111.3 (Rennes: Presses Universitaires de Rennes, 2004).

Garrison, Mary, 'The Emergence of Carolingian Latin Literature and the Court of Charlemagne, 780–814', in Rosamond McKitterick (ed.), *Carolingian Culture: Emulation and Innovation* (Cambridge: Cambridge University Press, 1994).

Garrison, Mary, '"Praesagum nomen tibi": The Significance of Name-wordplay in Alcuin's Letters to Arn', in M. Niederkorn-Bruck and A. Scharer (eds), *Erzbischof Arn von Salzburg* (Vienna: Oldenbourg Wissenschaftsverlag, 2004).

Garrison, Mary, 'Quid Hinieldus cum Christo', in Katherine O'Brien O'Keeffe and Andy Orchard (eds), *Latin Learning and English Lore: Studies in Anglo-Saxon Literature for Michael Lapidge 1* (Toronto, ON: University of Toronto Press, 2005).

Garrison, Mary, 'The Social World of Alcuin: Nicknames at York and at the Carolingian Court', in L. Houwen and A. MacDonald (eds), *Alcuin of York: Scholar at the Carolingian Court*, Germania Latina vol. 3 (Groningen: University of Groningen, 1998).

Garrison, Mary, 'The Study of Emotions in Early Medieval History: Some Starting Points', *Early Medieval Europe* 10 (2001): 243–40.

Garrison, Mary, 'The Teacher and the King', *BBC History Magazine* 2/7 (July 2001): 22–5.

Geeraerts, Dirk, *Diachronic Prototype Semantics* (Oxford: Oxford University Press, 1997).

Geeraerts, Dirk, *Theories of Lexical Semantics* (Oxford: Oxford University Press, 2010).

Geeraerts, Dirk and Caroline Gevaert, 'Hearts and (Angry) Minds in Old English', in Farzad Sharifian, René Dirven, Ning Yu and Susanne Niemeier (eds), *Culture, Body, and Language: Conceptualizations of Internal Body Organs across Cultures and Languages*, Applications of Cognitive Linguistics 7 (Berlin and New York: Mouton de Gruyter, 2008).

Georgianna, Linda, 'King Hrethel's Sorrow and the Limits of Heroic Action in *Beowulf*', *Speculum* 62 (1987): 829–50.

Gerchow, Jan, *Die Gedenküberlieferung der Angelsachsen* (Berlin: de Gruyter, 1988).

Gerould, Gordon Hall, 'Forerunners, Congeners, and Derivatives of the Eustace Legend', *PMLA* 19 (1904): 335–448.

Gertsman, Elina (ed.), *Crying in the Middle Ages: Tears of History* (New York: Routledge, 2011).

Gevaert, Caroline, 'The Evolution of the Lexical and Conceptual Field of ANGER in Old and Middle English', in Javier E. Díaz Vera (ed.), *A Changing World of Words: Studies in English Historical Lexicography, Lexicology and Semantics* (Amsterdam: Rodopi, 2002).

Gevaert, Caroline, *The History of Anger: The Lexical Field of ANGER from Old to Early Modern English* (Ph.D. thesis, Leuven, 2007).

Gibson, Donald E., 'Emotion Scripts in Organizations: A Multi-level Model', in Neal Ashkanasy and Cary L. Cooper (eds), *Research Companion to Emotion in Organizations* (Cheltenham: Edward Elgar, 2008).

Giora, Rachel, 'On Irony and Negation', *Discourse Processes* 19 (1995): 239–64.

Glaze, Florence Eliza, 'Master–Student Medical Dialogues: The Evidence of London, British Library, Sloane 2839', in Patrizia Lendinara, Loredana Lazzari and Maria Amalia D'Aronco (eds), *Form and Content of Instruction* in *Anglo-Saxon England in the Light of Contemporary Manuscript Evidence* (Turnhout: Brepols, 2007).

Gneuss, Helmut, 'The Origin of Standard Old English and Æthelwold's school at Winchester', *Anglo-Saxon England* 1 (1972): 63–83.

Goddard, Cliff (ed.), *Cross-linguistic Semantics* (Amsterdam: John Benjamins, 2008).

Goddard, Cliff, 'The "Social Emotions" of Malay (Bahasa Malayu)', *Ethos* 24 (1996): 426–64.

Godden, M.R., 'An Old English Penitential Motif', *Anglo-Saxon England* 2 (1973): 221–39.

Godden, Malcolm, 'Anglo-Saxons on the Mind', in Michael Lapidge and Helmut Gneuss (eds), *Learning and Literature in Anglo-Saxon England: Studies Presented to Peter Clemoes on the Occasion of his Sixty-fifth Birthday* (Cambridge: Cambridge University Press, 1985).

Godden, Malcolm, 'Did King Alfred Write Anything?', *Medium Ævum* 76 (2007): 49–61.

Godden, Malcolm, and Susan Irvine (eds), *The Old English Boethius: An Edition of the Old English Versions of Boethius's De Consolatione Philosophiae*, 2 vols (Oxford: Oxford University Press, 2009).

Goffart, Walter, *The Narrators of Barbarian History (A.D. 550–800): Jordanes, Gregory of Tours, Bede, and Paul the Deacon* (Notre Dame, IN: University of Notre Dame Press, 2005).

Goldie, Peter, *The Emotions: A Philosophical Exploration* (Oxford: Oxford University Press, 2000).

Goldie, Peter, *The Mess Inside: Narrative, Emotion, and the Mind* (Oxford: Oxford University Press, 2012).

Gorsuch, Edwin N., 'Emotional Expression in a Manuscript of Bede's *Historia Ecclesiastica*: British Library Cotton Tiberius A XIV', *Semiotic* 83 (1991): 227–49.

Green, Christopher D., 'Where Did the Ventricular Localization of Mental Faculties Come From?' *Journal of the History of the Behavioral Sciences*, 39 (2003): 131–42.

Green, Roger Lancelyn, *Kipling and the Children* (London: Elek, 1965).

Greene, Thomas M., 'The Natural Tears of Epic', in Margaret Beissinger, Jane Tylus and Susanne Wofford (eds), *Epic Traditions in the Contemporary World: The Poetics of Community* (Berkeley, CA: University of California Press, 1999).

Greenfield, Stanley B., 'Grendel's Approach to Heorot: Syntax and Poetry', in Robert P. Creed (ed.), *Old English Poetry: Fifteen Essays* (Providence, RI: Brown University Press, 1967).

Gretsch, Mechthild, *The Intellectual Foundations of the English Benedictine Reform*, Cambridge Studies in Anglo-Saxon England 25 (Cambridge: Cambridge University Press, 1999).

Gruber, Loren C., 'The Agnostic Anglo-Saxon Gnomes: *Maxims I* and *II*, *Germania*, and the Boundaries of Northern Wisdom', *Poetica* 4 (1976): 22–47.

Gunnarsdóttir Champion, Margrét, 'From Plaint to Praise: Language as Cure in "The Wanderer"', *Studia Neophilologica* 69 (1998): 187–202.

Györi, Gabor, 'Cultural Variation in the Conceptualisation of Emotions: A Historical Study', in Angeliki Athanasiadou and Elżbieta Tabakowska (eds), *Speaking of Emotions: Conceptualisation and Expression* (Berlin: Mouton de Gruyter, 1998).

Hale, Dorothy J., 'Aesthetics and the New Ethics: Theorizing the Novel in the Twenty-first Century', *PMLA* 124 (2009): 896–905.

Halsall, Guy, 'Violence and Society in the Early Medieval West: An Introduction', in G. Halsall (ed.), *Violence and Society in the Early Medieval West* (Woodbridge: Boydell, 1998).

Harbus, Antonina, *Cognitive Approaches to Old English Poetry* (Cambridge: D.S. Brewer, 2012).

Harbus, Antonina, 'Exposure to Life-writing as an Impact on Autobiographical Memory', *Memory Studies* 20 (2011): 1–15.

Harbus, Antonina, *The Life of the Mind in Old English Poetry* (Amsterdam and New York: Rodopi, 2002).

Hardie, Philip, *The Cambridge Companion to Ovid* (Cambridge: Cambridge University Press, 2002).

Harding, Jennifer, and E. Deidre Pribram (eds), *Emotions: A Cultural Studies Reader* (London: Routledge, 2009).

Harris, A. Leslie, 'Litotes and Superlative in *Beowulf*', *English Studies* 69 (1988): 1–11.

Harris, Joseph, 'Elegy in Old English and Old Norse: A Problem in Literary History', rpt. in Martin Green (ed.), *The Old English Elegies: New Essays in Criticism and Research* (Rutherford, NJ: Fairleigh Dickinson University Press, 1983).

Harris, Joseph, 'Love and Death in the *Männerbund*: An Essay with Special Reference to the *Bjarkamál* and *The Battle of Maldon*', in Helen Damico and John Leyerle (eds), *Heroic Poetry in the Anglo-Saxon Period*, Studies in Medieval Culture 32 (Kalamazoo, MI: Medieval Institute Publications, 1993).

Harris, Stephen J., 'Happiness and the Psalms', in Michael Fox and Manish Sharma (eds), *Old English Literature and the Old Testament* (Toronto, ON: University of Toronto Press, 2012).

Haybron, Dan, 'Happiness', in Edward N. Zalta (ed.), *The Stanford Encyclopedia of Philosophy* (Fall 2011 Edition), at http://plato.stanford.edu/archives/fall2011/entries/happiness/

Healey, Antonette diPaolo, 'Old English *hēafod* "head": A Lofty Place?', *Poetica* 75 (2011): 29–48.

Heider, Karl G., *The Cultural Context of Emotion: Folk Psychology in West Sumatra* (New York: Palgrave Macmillan, 2011).

Hennequin, M. Wendy, 'We've Created a Monster: The Strange Case of Grendel's Mother', *English Studies* 89 (2008): 503–23.

Hennig, J., 'The Feast of All the Saints', *Mediaeval Studies* 10 (1948): 147–61.

Herman, David (ed.), *Narrative Theory and the Cognitive Sciences* (Stanford, CA: Stanford University Press, 2003).

Hill, John M., *The Narrative Pulse of* Beowulf (Toronto, ON: University of Toronto Press, 2008).

Hill, Joyce, '"Þæt wæs geomuru ides!" A Female Stereotype Examined', in Helen Damico and Alexandra Hennessey Olsen (eds), *New Readings on Women in Old English Literature* (Bloomington, IN: Indiana University Press, 1990).

Hill, Thomas D., '*Beowulf*'s Roman Rites: Roman Ritual and Germanic Tradition', *Journal of English and Germanic Philology* 106 (2007): 325–35.

Hill, Thomas D., 'The Unchanging Hero: A Stoic Maxim in "The Wanderer" and its Contexts', *Studies in Philology* 101 (2004): 233–49.

Hogan, Patrick Colm, *Affective Narratology: The Emotional Structure of Stories* (Lincoln, NE, and London: University of Nebraska Press, 2011).

Hogan, Patrick Colm, 'On Being Moved: Cognition and Emotion in Literature and Film', in Lisa Zunshine (ed.), *Introduction to Cognitive Cultural Studies* (Baltimore, MD: John Hopkins University Press, 2010).

Hogan, Patrick Colm, *What Literature Teaches Us About Emotion* (Cambridge: Cambridge University Press, 2011).

Hollander, Lee M., 'Litotes in Old Norse', *PMLA* 53 (1938): 1–33.

Hollis, Stephanie, 'Scientific and Medical Writings', in Phillip Pulsiano and Elaine Treharne (eds), *A Companion to Anglo-Saxon Literature* (Oxford: Blackwell, 2001).

Holtz, L., 'Alcuin et la renaissance des arts libéraux', in P. Butzer, M. Kerner and W. Oberschelp, (eds), *Charlemagne and His Heritage: 1200 Years of Civilization and Science in Europe* (Turnhout: Brepols, 1997): 45–60.

Howe, Nicholas, *The Old English Catalogue Poems* (Copenhagen: Rosenkilde and Bagger, 1985).

Hrdy, Sarah, *Mother Nature: Maternal Instincts and How They Shape the Human Species* (New York: Ballantine Books, 2000).

Hrdy, Sarah, *Mothers and Others: The Evolutionary Origins of Mutual Understanding* (Cambridge, MA: Harvard University Press, 2009).

Hudson, John G.E., 'Feud, Vengeance and Violence in England from the Tenth to the Twelfth Centuries', in B. Tuten and T. Billado (eds), *Feud, Violence and Practice: Essays in Medieval Studies in Honour of Stephen D. White* (Farnham: Ashgate, 2010).

Hume, Kathryn, 'The Concept of the Hall in Old English Poetry', *Anglo-Saxon England* 3 (1974): 63–74.

Hyams, Paul, 'Was there Really Such a Thing as Feud in the High Middle Ages?' in S. Troop and P. Hyams (eds), *Vengeance in the Middle Ages: Emotion, Religion and Feud* (Farnham: Ashgate, 2010).

Ingham, Patricia Clare, 'From Kinship to Kingship: Mourning, Gender, and Anglo-Saxon Community', in Jennifer C. Vaught with Lynne Dickson Bruckner (eds), *Grief and Gender: 700–1700* (New York: Palgrave Macmillan, 2003).

Irvine, Elizabeth, *The Family in the Kibbutz*, Occasional Paper 4 (London: Study Commission on the Family, 1980).

Irving Jr., Edward B., *Rereading Beowulf* (Philadelphia, PA: University of Pennsylvania Press, 1989).

Jackson, Elizabeth, 'From the Seat of the *þyle*? A Reading of *Maxims I*, Lines 138–40', *Journal of English and Germanic Philology* 99 (2000): 170–87.

Jaeger, C. Stephen and Ingrid Kasten, *Codierungen von Emotionen im Mittelalter* (Berlin: Gruyter, 2003).

Jaeger, Stephen, *Ennobling Love: In Search of a Lost Sensibility* (Philadelphia, PA: University of Philadelphia Press, 1999).

Jager, Eric, 'The Word in the "Breost": Interiority and the Fall in *Genesis B*', *Neophilologus* 75 (1991): 279–90.

James, William, *The Principles of Psychology*, 2 vols (London: Macmillan, 1890).

James, William, 'What is an Emotion?' *Mind* 9 (1884): 188–205.

Jarrett, Jonathan, 'The First Viking raid on England or Francia' (21 September 2011), at http://tenthmedieval.wordpress.com/2011/09/21/the-first-viking-raid-on-england-or-francia/

Jespersen, Otto, *Negation in English and Other Languages* (Copenhagen: Høst, 1917)

Johnson, William C., '*The Wife's Lament* as Death-song', in Martin Green (ed.), *The Old English Elegies: New Essays in Criticism and Research* (Rutherford, NJ: Farleigh Dickenson University Press, 1983).

Jones, Christopher A., *Ælfric's Letter to the Monks of Eynsham*, Cambridge Studies in Anglo-Saxon England 24 (Cambridge: Cambridge University Press, 1998).

de Jong, Mayke, 'From Scholastici to Scioli: Alcuin and the Formation of an Intellectual Elite', in L.A.J.R. Houwen and Alasdair A. McDonald (eds), *Alcuin of York: Scholar at the Carolingian Court*, Germania Latina 3 (Groningen: University of Groningen, 1998): 45–57.

de Jong, Mayke, *In Samuel's Image: Child Oblation in the Early Medieval West* (Leiden: Brill, 1996).
Jorgensen, Alice, 'Historicizing Emotion: The Shame–Rage Spiral in Ælfric's *Life of St Agatha*', *English Studies* 93 (2012): 529–38.
Jorgensen, Alice, '"It Shames Me to Say It": Ælfric and the Concept and Vocabulary of Shame', *Anglo-Saxon England* 41 (2013 for 2012): 249–76.
Jurasinski, Stefan, *Ancestral Privileges:* Beowulf, *Law, and the Making of Germanic Antiquity* (Morgantown, WV: West Virginia University Press, 2006).
Jussen, Bernhard, *Spiritual Kinship as Social Practice: Godparenthood and Adoption in the Early Middle Ages*, trans. Pamela Selwyn (Newark, DE: University of Delaware Press, 2000).
Karl Neff, Paul (ed.), *Die Gedichte des Paulus Diaconus: kritische und erklärende Ausgabe* (Munich: Oskar Beck, 1908).
Kaster, Robert A., *Emotion, Restraint and Community in Ancient Rome* (Oxford: Oxford University Press, 2005).
Keen, Suzanne, 'A Theory of Narrative Empathy', *Narrative* 14 (2006): 207–36.
Kelly, Richard J. (ed.), *The Blickling Homilies: Edition and Translation* (London and New York: Continuum, 2003).
Kieckhefer, Richard. 'Convention and Conversion: Patterns in Late-Medieval Piety', *Church History* 67 (1998): 32–51.
King, Barbara, *How Animals Grieve* (Chicago, IL: University of Chicago Press, 2013).
King, Peter, 'Emotions in Medieval Thought', in Peter Goldie (ed.), *The Oxford Handbook of Philosophy of Emotion* (Oxford: Oxford University Press, 2010).
Klein, M., 'Love, Guilt and Reparation (1939)', in *Love, Guilt and Reparation and Other Works 1921–1945*, with an introduction by R.E. Money-Kyrle (London: Hogarth Press and Institute of Psycho-Analysis, 1981).
Klinck, Anne L., *The Old English Elegies: A Critical Edition and Genre Study* (Montreal: McGill-Queen's University Press, 1992).
Klinck, Anne L., '*Resignation*: Exile's Lament or Penitent's Prayer?' *Neophilologus* 71 (1987): 423–30.
Knuuttila, Simo, *Emotions in Ancient and Medieval Philosophy* (Oxford: Oxford University Press, 2004).
Konstan, David, *The Emotion of the Ancient Greeks Studies in Aristotle and Classical Literature* (Toronto, ON: University of Toronto Press, 2006).
Kövecses, Zoltán, 'Cross-cultural Experience of Anger: A Psycholinguistic Analysis', in Michael Potegal, Gerhard Stemmler and Charles Donald Spielberger (eds), *International Handbook of Anger* (New York: Springer, 2010).

Kövecses, Zoltán, 'Metaphor and Thought', in Raymond W. Gibbs (ed.), *The Cambridge Handbook of Metaphor and Thought* (Cambridge: Cambridge University Press, 2008).

Kövecses, Zoltán, *Metaphors of Anger, Pride, and Love: A Lexical Approach to the Study of Emotion Concepts* (Amsterdam: John Benjamins, 1986).

Kowalik, Jill Anne, *Theology and Dehumanization: Trauma, Grief, and Pathological Mourning in Seventeenth and Eighteenth-century German Thought and Literature*, ed. Gail Hart, Ursula Mahlendorf and Thomas P. Saine, Berliner Beiträge zur Literatur- und Kulturgeschichte (London: Peter Lang, 2009).

Krause, Inga-Britt, *Therapy across Cultures: Psychotherapy and Cultural Diversity, Perspectives on Psychotherapy* (London: SAGE Publications, 1998).

Kringelbach, Morton L., 'Emotions, Feelings, and Hedonics in the Human Brain', in Helena Wulff (ed.), *The Emotions: A Cultural Reader* (Oxford: Oxford University Press, 2007).

Lahaye-Geusen, Maria, *Das Opfer der Kinder: Ein Beitrag zur Liturgie- und Sozialgeschichte des Mönchtums im hohen Mittelalter*, Münsteraner Theologische Abhandlungen 13 (Altenberge: Oros, 1991).

Lakoff, George, *Women, Fire and Dangerous Things: What Categories Reveal about the Mind* (Chicago, IL: University of Chicago Press, 1987).

Lakoff, George and Mark Johnson, *Metaphors We Live By* (Chicago, IL: University of Chicago Press, 1980).

Lambert, T.B., 'Theft, Homicide and Crime in Late Anglo-Saxon Law', *Past and Present* 214 (2012): 3–43.

Lane, Richard D., Lynn Nadel, John J.B. Allen and Alfred W. Kasdzniak, 'The Study of Emotion from the Perspective of Cognitive Neuroscience', in Richard D. Lane and Lynn Nadel (eds), *Cognitive Neuroscience of Emotion* (Oxford: Oxford University Press, 2000).

Lanpher, Ann Park. 'The Problem of Revenge in Medieval Literature: *Beowulf*, *The Canterbury Tales*, and *Ljosvetninga Saga*' (Ph.D. thesis, University of Toronto, 2010).

Lapidge, Michael, *The Anglo-Saxon Library* (Oxford: Oxford University Press, 2006).

Lapidge, Michael, '*Beowulf*, Aldhelm, the *Liber Monstrorum* and Wessex', *Studi medievali* 3rd ser. 23 (1982): 151–91.

Lapidge, Michael, '*Beowulf* and the Psychology of Terror', in Helen Damico and John Leyerle (eds), *Heroic Poetry in the Anglo-Saxon Period*, Studies in Medieval Culture 32 (Kalamazoo, MI: Medieval Institute Publications, 1993).

Larrington, Caroline, 'The Psychology of Emotion and Study of the Medieval Period', *Early Medieval Europe* 10 (2001): 251–6.

LeDoux, Joseph, *The Emotional Brain: The Mysterious Underpinnings of Emotional Life* (London: Phoenix, 1998).
LeDoux, Joseph and Michael Rogan, 'Emotion and the Animal Brain', in R.A. Wilson and F.C. Keil (eds), *MIT Encyclopedia of the Cognitive Sciences* (Cambridge, MA: MIT Press, 1999).
Lehrer, Jonah, *Proust was a Neuroscientist* (Boston, MA: Houghton Mifflin, 2008).
Leick, Nini and Marianne Davidsen-Nielsen, *Healing Pain: Attachment, Loss, and Grief Therapy*, trans. D. Stoner (London: Routledge, 1991).
Lench, Elinor, '*The Wife's Lament*: A Poem of the Living Dead', *Comitatus* 1 (1970): 3–23.
LeVine, Robert A., 'Afterword', in Helena Wulff (ed.), *The Emotions: A Cultural Reader* (Oxford: Oxford University Press, 2007).
Levison, William, *England and the Continent in the Eighth Century: The Ford Lectures* (Oxford: The Clarendon Press, 1946).
Lewis, C.S., *The Allegory of Love: A Study in Medieval Tradition* (Oxford: Oxford University Press, 1936).
Lewis, Michael and Jeannette M. Haviland-Jones (eds), *Handbook of Emotions: Second Edition* (London: Guilford Press, 2000).
Lockett, Leslie, *Anglo-Saxon Psychologies in the Vernacular and Latin Traditions* (Toronto, ON: Toronto University Press, 2011).
Low, Soon Ai, 'The Anglo-Saxon Mind: Metaphor and Common Sense Psychology in Old English Literature' (Ph.D. thesis, University of Toronto, 1998).
Lutz, Catherine, 'The Domain of Emotion Words on Ifaluk', *American Ethnologist* 9 (1982): 113–28.
Lutz, Catherine, *Unnatural Emotions: Everyday Sentiments on a Micronesian Atoll and Their Challenge to Western Theory* (Chicago, IL: University of Chicago Press, 1988).
Lutz, Tom, *Crying: The Natural and Cultural History of Tears* (New York: Norton, 1999).
Lynch, Andrew, '"Now, Fye on Youre Wepynge!": Tears in Medieval English Romance', *Parergon* 9/1 (1991): 43–62.
Lynch, Joseph, *Godparents and Kinship in Early Medieval Europe* (Princeton, NJ: Princeton University Press, 1976).
Mackie, W.S., 'Notes on Old English Poetry', *Modern Language Notes* 40 (1925): 91–3.
MacMullen, Ramsay, *Feelings in History, Ancient and Modern* (Claremont: Regina Books, 2003).
Magennis, Hugh, *Anglo-Saxon Appetites: Food and Drink and Their Consumption in Old English and Related Literature* (Dublin: Four Courts Press, 1999).

Magennis, Hugh, 'Images of Laughter in Old English Poetry, with Particular Reference to the "Hleahtor Wera" of *The Seafarer*', *English Studies* 73 (1992): 193–204.

Magennis, Hugh, 'On the Sources of Non-Ælfrician Lives in the Old English *Lives of Saints*, with Reference to the Cotton-Corpus Legendary', *Notes and Queries* 230 (1985): 292–9.

Maion, Danielle, 'Il Lessico Tecnico *Peri Didaxeon*. Elementi di Datazione', *Il Bianco e il Nero* 6 (2003): 179–86.

Maion, Danielle, 'The Fortune of the So-called *Practica Petrocelli Salernitani* in England: New Evidence and some Considerations', in Patrizia Lendinara, Loredana Lazzari and Maria Amalia D'Aronco (eds), *Form and Content of Instruction in Anglo-Saxon England in the Light of Contemporary Manuscript Evidence* (Turnhout: Brepols, 2007).

Malcolm, Janet, *The Silent Woman: Sylvia Plath and Ted Hughes* (1993; rpt. London: Granta, 1995).

Mandel, Jerome, *Alternative Readings in Old English Poetry* (New York: Peter Lang, 1987).

Manstead, Antony S.R., 'A History of Affect and Emotion Research in Social Psychology', in Arie W. Kruglanski and Wolfgang Stroebe (eds), *Handbook of the History of Social Psychology* (Hove: Psychology Press, 2012).

Marazziti, D., A. Di Muro and P. Castrogiovanni, 'Psychological Stress and Body Temperature Changes in Humans,' *Psychological Behavior* 52 (1992): 393–5.

Marsden, Richard, *The Text of the Old Testament in Anglo-Saxon England*, Cambridge Studies in Anglo-Saxon England 15 (Cambridge: Cambridge University Press, 1995).

Martin, B.K., 'Aspects of Winter in Latin and Old English Poetry', *Journal of English and Germanic Philology* 68 (1969): 375–90.

Matsumoto, David, Seung Hee Yoo and Joanne Chung, 'The Expression of Anger Across Cultures', in Michael Potegal, Gerhard Stemmler and Charles Donald Spielberger (eds), *International Handbook of Anger* (New York: Springer, 2010).

Matto, Michael, 'A War of Containment: The Heroic Image in *The Battle of Maldon*', *Studia Neophilologica* 74 (2002): 60–75.

Matto, Michael, 'True Confessions: *The Seafarer* and Technologies of the *Sylf*', *Journal of English and Germanic Philology* 103 (2004): 156–79.

Mayer, John D., Peter Salovey and David R. Caruso, 'Emotional Intelligence: Theory, Findings, and Implications', *Psychological Inquiry* 15 (2004): 197–215.

Mayr-Harting, Henry, *The Venerable Bede, the Rule of St Benedict, and Social Class*, Jarrow Lecture 1976 (Jarrow: Rector of Jarrow, 1976).

McEntire, Sandra J., *The Doctrine of Compunction in Medieval England: Holy Tears* (Lewiston, NY: Edwin Mellen, 1991).

McFee, Graham, 'Empathy: Interpersonal vs Artistic', in Amy Coplan and Peter Goldie (eds), *Empathy: Philosophical and Psychological Perspectives* (Oxford: Oxford University Press, 2011).
McGillivray, Murray, 'The Exeter Book *Maxims I B*: An Anglo-Saxon Woman's View of Marriage', *English Studies in Canada* 15 (1989): 383–97.
McGowan, Joseph, 'Elves, Elf-shot, and Epilepsy: OE *ælfādl, ælfsiden, ælfsogeþa, bræccoþu*, and *bræcsēoc*', *Studia Neophilologica* 81 (2009): 116–20.
McIlwain, James T., 'Brain and Mind in Anglo-Saxon Medicine', *Viator* 37 (2006): 103–12.
McNamer, Sarah, *Affective Meditation and the Invention of Medieval Compassion* (Philadelphia, PA: University of Pennsylvania Press, 2010).
McNeill, David (ed.), *Language and Gesture* (Cambridge: Cambridge University Press, 2000).
Meritt, Herbert Dean, *Some of the Hardest Glosses in Old English* (Stanford, CA: Stanford University Press, 1968).
Meskin, Aaron, and Jonathan M. Weinberg, 'Emotions, Fiction, and Cognitive Architecture', *British Journal of Aesthetics* 43 (2003): 18–34.
Metcalfe, J. and W.J. Jacobs, 'Emotional Memory: The Effects of Stress on "Cool" and "Hot" Memory Systems', in D.L. Medin (ed.), *The Psychology of Learning and Motivation: Advances in Research and Theory, Vol. 38* (London: Academic Press, 1998).
Metcalfe, J. and W.J. Jacobs, '"Hot" Emotions in Human Recollection: Toward a Model of Traumatic Memory', in E. Tulving (ed.), *Memory, Consciousness, and the Brain: The Tallinn Conference* (Hove: Psychology Press, 2000).
Metcalfe, J. and W.J. Jacobs, 'A "Hot-System/Cool-System" View of Memory under Stress', *PTSD Research Quarterly* 7 (1996): 1–6.
Mikołajczuk, Agnieszka, 'Anger in Polish and English: A Semantic Comparison with Some Historical Content', in Christian J. Kay and Jeremy J. Smith (eds), *Categorization in the History of English*, Current Issues in Linguistic Theory 261 (Amsterdam: John Benjamins, 2004).
Mikołajczuk, Agnieszka, 'The Metonymic and Metaphorical Conceptualisation of *Anger* in Polish', in Angeliki Athanasiadou and Elżbieta Tabakowska (eds), *Speaking of Emotions: Conceptualisation and Expression* (Berlin: Mouton de Gruyter, 1998).
Miller, Alice, *The Drama of the Gifted Child: The Search for the True Self*, trans. Alice Ward (New York: Basic Books, rpt. 1997).
Miller, Rowland S., *Embarrassment: Poise and Peril in Everyday Life* (New York: Guilford Press, 1996).
Miller, William Ian, 'Choosing the Avenger: Some Aspects of the Bloodfeud in Medieval Iceland and England', *Law and History Review* 1 (1983): 159–204.
Miller, William Ian, *The Anatomy of Disgust* (Cambridge, MA: Harvard University Press, 1997).

Miller, William Ian, *Bloodtaking and Peacemaking: Feud, Law, and Society in Saga Iceland* (Chicago, IL: University of Chicago Press, 1990).

Miller, William Ian, *Humiliation and Other Essays on Honor, Social Discomfort, and Violence* (Ithaca, NY: Cornell University Press, 1993).

Mitchell, Bruce, 'Literary Lapses: Six Notes on *Beowulf* and its Critics', *The Review of English Studies* 43 (1992): 1–17.

Mize, Britt 'Manipulations of the Mind-as-container Motif in *Beowulf*, *Homiletic Fragment II*, and Alfred's *Metrical Epilogue to the Pastoral Care*', *Journal of English and Germanic Philology* 107 (2008): 25–56.

Mize, Britt, 'The Mental Container and the Cross of Christ: Revelation and Community in *The Dream of the Rood*', *Studies in Philology* 107 (2010): 131–78.

Mize, Britt, 'The Representation of the Mind as an Enclosure in Old English Poetry', *Anglo-Saxon England* 35 (2006): 57–90.

Mize, Britt, *Traditional Subjectivities: The Old English Poetics of Mentality* (Toronto, ON: University of Toronto Press, 2013).

Moisl, H., 'Anglo-Saxon Royal Genealogies and Germanic Oral Tradition', *Journal of Medieval History* 7 (1981): 215–48.

Morey, James H., 'The Fates of Men in *Beowulf*', in C. Wright, Frederick M. Biggs and Thomas N. Hall (eds), *Source of Wisdom: Old English and Early Medieval Studies in Honour of Thomas D. Hill* (Toronto, ON: University of Toronto Press, 2007).

Mustanoja, Tauno F., 'The Unnamed Woman's Song of Mourning over Beowulf and the Tradition of Ritual Lamentation', *Neuphilologische Mitteilungen* 68 (1967): 1–27.

Nagy, Piroska, *Le Don des Larmes au Moyen Age. Un Instrument Spirituel en Quête d'Institution, Ve–XIIIe siècle* (Paris: Albin Michel, Bibliothèque Histoire, 2000).

Nelson, Janet L., 'Carolingian Contacts', in Carol Ann Farr and Michelle Brown (eds), *Mercia: An Anglo-Saxon Kingdom in Europe* (London: Leicester University Press, 2001).

Nelson, Janet L., 'La mort de Charles le Chauve', *Médiévales* 15/31 (1996): 53–86.

Nelson, Marie, '*Is* and *Ought* in the Exeter Book Maxims', *Southern Folklore Quarterly* (1981): 109–21.

Ní Chonaill, Bronagh, 'Fosterage in Ireland and Wales', in J.T. Koch (ed.), *Celtic Culture: A Historical Encyclopedia* (Oxford: ABC-CLIO, 2006).

Nicholson, Simon, 'The Expression of Emotional Distress in Old English Prose and Verse', *Culture, Medicine and Psychiatry* 19 (1995): 327–38.

Niles, John D., 'Byrhtnoth's Wordplay and the Poetics of Gesture', in Jonathan Wilcox (ed.), *Humour in Anglo-Saxon Literature* (Cambridge: D.S. Brewer, 2000).

Noel, William, *The Harley Psalter* (Cambridge: Cambridge University Press, 1995).
Norris, Robin, 'Deathbed Confessors: Mourning and Genre in Anglo-Saxon Hagiography' (Ph.D. thesis, University of Toronto, 2003).
North, Richard, *The Origins of* Beowulf: *From Vergil to Wiglaf* (Oxford: Oxford University Press, 2006).
Nussbaum, Martha C., *Upheavals of Thought: The Intelligence of Emotions* (Cambridge: Cambridge University Press, 2001).
Ó Néill, Pádraig, 'Irish Transmission of Late Antique Learning: The Case of Theodore of Mopsuestia's Commentary on the Psalms', in Próinséas Ní Catháin and Michael Richter (eds), *Ireland and Europe in the Early Middle Ages: Texts and Transmission / Irland und Europa im früheren Mittelalter: Texte und Überlieferung* (Dublin: Four Courts, 2002).
O'Brien O'Keeffe, Katherine, *Stealing Obedience: Narratives of Agency and Identity in Later Anglo-Saxon England* (Toronto, ON: University of Toronto Press, 2012).
O'Brien O'Keeffe, Katherine, *Stealing Obedience: Narratives of Agency and Identity in Later Anglo-Saxon England*, H.M. Chadwick Memorial Lecture (Cambridge: Cambridge University Press, 2009).
O'Loughlin, Thomas and Helen Conrad-O'Briain, 'The "Baptism of Tears" in Early Anglo-Saxon Sources', *Anglo-Saxon England* 22 (1993): 65–84.
O'Neill, Patrick P., 'The Old English Introductions to the Prose Psalms of the Paris Psalter: Sources, Structure and Composition', *Studies in Philology* 78 (1981): 20–38.
Oatley, Keith, 'Emotions', in R.A. Wilson and F.C. Keil (eds), *MIT Encyclopedia of the Cognitive Sciences* (Cambridge, MA: MIT Press, 1999).
Oatley, Keith, *Emotions: A Brief History* (Malden, MA: Blackwell, 2004).
Oatley, Keith, 'Simulation of Substance and Shadow: Inner Emotions and Outer Behavior in Shakespeare's Psychology of Character', *College English* 33 (2006): 15–33.
Oatley, Keith, 'A Taxonomy of the Emotions of Literary Response and a Theory of Identification in Fictional Narrative', *Poetics* 23 (1994): 53–74.
Oatley, Keith, Dacher Keltner and Jennifer M. Jenkins, *Understanding Emotions*, 2nd edn (Oxford and Malden, MA: Blackwell, 2006).
Ogura, Michiko, 'Old and Middle English Verbs of Emotion', *Poetica* 66 (2006): 53–72.
Ogura, Michiko. 'Verbs of Emotion with Reflexive Constructions', in Christian Kay and Louise Sylvester (eds), *Lexis and Texts in Early English: Studies Presented to Jane Roberts*, Costerus n.s. 133 (Amsterdam: Rodopi, 2001).

Ogura, Michiko. 'Words of EMOTION in Old and Middle English', in Javier E. Díaz Vera (ed.), *A Changing World of Words: Studies in English Historical Lexicography, Lexicology and Semantics*, Costerus n.s. 141 (Amsterdam: Rodopi, 2002).

Ogura, Michiko, 'Words of Emotion in Old and Middle English Psalms and Alliterative Poems', *Chiba University Studies in Humanities* 32 (2003): 393–427.

Ogura, Michiko, 'Words of Emotion in Old and Middle English Translations of Boethius's *De Consolatione Philosophiae*', in Akio Oizumi, Jacek Fisiak and John Scahill (eds), *Text and Language in Medieval English Prose: A Festschrift for Tadao Kubouchi*, Studies in English Medieval Language and Literature 12 (Frankfurt am Main: Peter Lang, 2005).

Orchard, Andy, 'Oral Tradition' in Katherine O'Brien O'Keeffe (ed.), *Reading Old English Texts* (Cambridge: Cambridge University Press, 1997).

Orchard, Andy, *The Poetic Art of Aldhelm* (Cambridge: Cambridge University Press, 1994).

Orton, Peter, 'The Form and Structure of *The Seafarer*', *Studia Neophilologica* 63 (1991): 37–55.

Ortony, Andrew and Terence J. Turner, 'What's Basic About Basic Emotions?', *Psychological Review* 97 (1990): 315–31.

Oswald, Dana, Monsters, *Gender, and Sexuality in Medieval English Literature* (New York: D.S. Brewer, 2010).

Owen-Crocker, Gale, *The Four Funerals of* Beowulf (Manchester: University of Manchester Press, 2000).

Page, R.I., *An Introduction to English Runes* (Woodbridge: Boydell, 1999).

Palmer, James M., '*Compunctio* and the Heart in the Old English Poem *The Wanderer*', *Neophilologus* 88 (2004): 447–60.

Pandit, Lalita, 'Emotion, Perception and Anagnorisis in *The Comedy of Errors*: A Cognitive Perspective', *College Literature* 33 (2006): 94–126.

Pandit, Lalita and Patrick Colm Hogan, 'Introduction: Morsels and Modules: On Embodying Cognition in Shakespeare's Plays', *College English* 33 (2006): 1–13.

Panofsky, Erwin, *Tomb Sculpture: Four Lectures on its Changing Aspects from Ancient Egypt to Bernini* (London: Thames and Hudson, 1964).

Parkes, Colin Murray, 'Traditional Models and Theories of Grief', *Bereavement Care* 17/2 (1998): 21–3.

Parkes, Peter, 'Celtic Fosterage: Adoptive Kinship and Clientage in Northwest Europe', *Comparative Studies in Society and History* 48/2 (2006): 359–95.

Pàroli, Teresa. 'The Tears of the Heroes in Germanic Epic Poetry', in Hermann Reichert and Günter Zimmermann (eds), *Helden und Helden- sage: Otto Gschwantler zum 60. Geburtstag*, Philologica Germanica 11 (Wien: Fassbaender, 1990).

Pasternack, Carol Braun, 'Anonymous Polyphony and *The Wanderer*'s Textuality', *Anglo-Saxon England* 20 (1991): 99–122.
Pavlenko, Aneta, *Emotions and Multilingualism* (Cambridge: Cambridge University Press, 2005).
Payne, Jessica, Lynn Nadel, Willoughby B. Briton and W. Jake Jacobs, 'The Biopsychology of Trauma and Memory', in Daniel Reisberg and Paula Hertel (eds), *Memory and Emotion* (Oxford: Oxford University Press, 2003).
Payne, Richard C., 'Convention and Originality in the Vision Framework of *The Dream of the Rood*', *Modern Philology* 73 (1976): 329–41.
Pederson, Poul, 'Anxious Lives and Letters: Family Separation, Communication Networks and Structures of Everyday Life', *Culture and History* 8 (1990): 7–19.
Philpott, B., *Kindred and Clan in the Middle Ages and After* (Cambridge University Press: Cambridge, 1913)
Plutchik, Robert, *Emotion: A Psychoevolutionary Synthesis* (New York: Harper and Row, 1980).
Plutchik, Robert, 'The Nature of Emotions: Human Emotions Have Deep Evolutionary Roots, a Fact that may Explain Their Complexity and Provide Tools for Clinical Practice', *American Scientist*, 89/4 (2001): 344–50.
Polomé, Edgar C., 'Some Comments on the Vocabulary of Emotion in Germanic', in G.F. Carr, W. Harbert and L. Zhang (eds), *Interdigitations: Essays for Irmengard Rauch* (Bern: Peter Lang, 1998).
Potegal, Michael, Gerhard Stemmler and Charles Donald Spielberger (eds), *International Handbook of Anger: Constituent and Concomitant Biological, Psychological, and Social Processes* (New York: Springer, 2010).
Powell, Raymond A., 'Margery Kempe: An Exemplar of Late Medieval English Piety', *The Catholic Historical Review* 89 (2003): 1–23.
Prinz, Jesse, 'Are Emotions Feeling?', *Journal of Consciousness Studies* 12 (2005): 9–25.
Pulsiano, Phillip, 'Psalters', in Richard W. Pfaff (ed.), *The Liturgical Books of Anglo-Saxon England*, OEN Subsidia 23 (Kalamazoo, MI: Western Michigan University Press, 1995).
Radulescu, Dominica, 'Theorizing Exile', in Dominica Radulescu (ed.), *Realms of Exile: Nomadism, Diasporas, and Eastern European Voices* (Lanham, MD: Lexington Books, 2002).
Rauer, Christine, *Beowulf and the Dragon: Analogies and Parallels* (Cambridge: D.S. Brewer, 2000).
Reddy, William, *The Navigation of Feeling: A Framework for the History of Emotions* (Cambridge: Cambridge University Press, 2001).
Reeves, Christopher, 'Why Attachment? Whither Attachment?: John Bowlby's Legacy, Past and Future', The Online Journal of the American Association

for Psychoanalysis in Clinical Social Work 2 (December 2007), at http://www.beyondthecouch.org/1207/reeves.htm

Remley, Lynn L. 'The Anglo-Saxon Gnomes as Sacred Poetry', *Folklore* 82 (1971): 147–58.

Renoir, Alain, 'Point of View and Design for Terror in *Beowulf*', *Neuphilologische Mitteilungen* 63 (1962): 154–67.

Richardson, Alan, 'Studies in Literature and Cognition: A Field Map', in Alan Richardson and Ellen Spolsky (eds), *The Work of Fiction: Cognition, Culture and Complexity* (Aldershot: Ashgate, 2004).

Richardson, Alan, and Mary Crane (eds), *Annotated Bibliography on Literature, Cognition and the Brain*, at https://www2.bc.edu/~richarad/lcb/home.html#bib

Riché, Pierre, *Education and Culture in the Barbarian West, Sixth through Eighth Centuries*, trans. J. Contreni (Columbia, SC: University of South Carolina Press, 1976).

Riedinger, Anita R., 'The Englishing of Arcestrate: Woman in *Apollonius of Tyre*', in Helen Damico and Alexandra Hennessy Olsen (eds), *New Readings on Women in Old English Literature* (Bloomington, IN: Indiana University Press, 1990).

Rizzolatti, Giacomo, and Corrado Sinigaglia, *Mirrors in the Brain: How Our Minds Share Actions and Emotions*, trans. Frances Anderson (Oxford: Oxford University Press, 2008).

Roach, Levi, 'Public Rites and Public Wrongs: Ritual Aspects of Diplomas in Tenth- and Eleventh-century England', *Early Medieval Europe* 19 (2011): 182–203.

Robinson, Jenefer, *Deeper Than Reason: Emotion and its Role in Literature, Music, and Art* (Oxford: Clarendon Press, 2005).

Rodrigues, Louis, *Anglo-Saxon Verse Charms, Maxims & Heroic Legends* (Middlesex: Anglo-Saxon Books, 1993).

Romano, Manuela, '*Anger* in Old English', *SELIM* 9 (1999): 45–56.

Rosaldo, Michelle, *Knowledge and Passion: Ilongot Notions of Self and Social Life* (Cambridge: Cambridge University Press, 1980).

Rosch, Eleanor, 'Human Categorization', in Neil Warren (ed.), *Studies in Cross-cultural Psychology, Volume One* (London: Academic Press, 1977).

Rosenwein, Barbara (ed.), *Anger's Past: The Social Uses of an Emotion in the Middle Ages* (Ithaca, NY: Cornell University Press, 1998).

Rosenwein, Barbara H., *Emotional Communities in the Early Middle Ages* (Ithaca, NY: Cornell University Press, 2006).

Rosenwein, Barbara H., 'Worrying About Emotions in History', *American Historical Review* 107 (2002): 821–45.

Rosenwein, Barbara H., 'Writing Without Fear About Early Medieval Emotions', *Early Medieval Europe* 10 (2001): 229–34.

Rozin, Paul, Laura Lowery, Sumio Imada and Jonathan Haidt, 'The CAD Triad Hypothesis: A Mapping Between Three Moral Emotions (Contempt, Anger, Disgust) and Three Moral Codes (Community, Autonomy, Divinity)', *Journal of Personality and Social Psychology* 76/4 (1999): 575–86.

Russell, James A., 'A Circumplex Model of Affect', *Journal of Personality and Social Psychology* 39 (1980): 1161–78.

Russell, James A. and Ghyslaine Lemay, 'Emotion Concepts', in Michael Lewis and Jeannette M. Haviland-Jones (eds), *Handbook of Emotions: Second Edition* (London: Guilford Press, 2000).

Salmon, Pierre, *Les 'Tituli Psalmorum' des Manuscrits Latins*, Collectanea Biblica Latina XII (Rome: Abbaye Saint-Jérome, 1959).

Sapir, Edward, *Selected Writings of Edward Sapir in Language, Culture and Personality* (Berkeley, CA: University of California Press, 1949).

Sauer, Hans, 'Ælfric and Emotion', *Poetica* 66 (2006): 37–52.

Schacter, Daniel, *Searching for Memory: The Brain, the Mind, and the Past* (New York: Basic Books, 1996).

Schank, Roger and Robert Abelson, *Scripts, Plans, Goals, and Understanding: An Inquiry Into Human Knowledge Structures* (Hillsdale, NJ: Lawrence Erlbaum Associates, 1977).

Scherer, Klaus, 'The Dynamic Architecture of Emotion: Evidence for the Component Process Model', *Cognition and Emotion* 23 (2009): 1307–51.

Schlauch, Margaret. '"The Dream of the Rood" as Prosopopoeia', in P.W. Long (ed.), *Essays and Studies in Honour of Carleton Brown* (New York: New York University Press, 1940).

Schrader, Richard J., 'Succession and Glory in *Beowulf*', *Journal of English and Germanic Philology* 90 (1991): 491–504.

Schücking, Levin L., 'Das Angelsächsische Gedicht von der *Klage der Frau*', *Zeitschrift für Deutsches Altertum and Deutsche Litertur* 48 (1906): 436–49.

Schweder, Richard A. and Jonathan Haidt, 'The Cultural Psychology of the Emotions', in Michael Lewis and Jeannette M. Haviland-Jones (eds), *Handbook of Emotions: Second Edition* (London: Guilford Press, 2000).

Scragg, Donald, 'Sin and Laughter in Late Anglo-Saxon England: The Case of Old English *(h)leahtor*', in Stuart McWilliams (ed.), *Saints and Scholars: New Perspectives on Anglo-Saxon Literature and Culture* (Cambridge: D.S. Brewer, 2012).

Shay, Jonathan, *Achilles in Vietnam: Combat Trauma and the Undoing of Character* (New York: Macmillan, 1994).

Shippey, T.A., 'Folly and Wisdom in Anglo-Saxon Humor', in Jonathan Wilcox (ed.), *Humour in Anglo-Saxon Literature* (Cambridge: D.S. Brewer, 2000).

Shippey, T.A., *Poems of Wisdom and Learning in Old English* (Cambridge: D.S. Brewer 1976).

'Shock Tactics', *Scotsman*, 25 July 2009, at http://www.scotsman.com/news/shock-tactics-1-1354834

Shoemaker, Stephen J., 'Mary at the Cross, East and West: Maternal Compassion and Affective Piety in the Earliest *Life of the Virgin* and the High Middle Ages', *Journal of Theological Studies* 62 (2011): 570–606.

Shuman, R. Baird and H. Charles Hutchings II, 'The *Un-* Prefix: A Means of Germanic Irony in *Beowulf*', *Modern Philology* 57 (1960): 217–22.

Small, Neal, 'Theories of Grief: A Critical Review', in Jenny Hockey, Jeanne Katz and Neil Small (eds), *Grief, Mourning and Death Ritual* (Buckingham: Open University Press, 2001), 19–48.

Smith, Zadie, *White Teeth* (London: Hamish Hamilton–Penguin, 2000).

Stancliffe, Clare, 'Red, White and Blue Martyrdom', in Dorothy Whitelock, Rosamond McKitterick and D.N. Dumville (eds), *Ireland in Early Mediaeval Europe: Studies in Memory of Kathleen Hughes* (Cambridge: Cambridge University Press, 1982).

Stanley, Eric, 'FEAR chiefly in Old and Middle English', *Poetica* 66 (2006): 73–114.

Stearns, Peter N. and Carol Z. Stearns, 'Emotionology: Clarifying the History of Emotions and Emotional Standards', *American Historical Review* 90 (1985): 813–36.

Steckel, Sita, *Kulturen des Lehrens Im Früh- unde Hochmittelalter: Autorität, Wissenkonzepte und Netzwerke von Gelehrten*, Norm und Struktur: Studien zum Sozialen Wandel In Mittelalter und frühen Neuzeit 39 (Köln: Böhlau, 2010).

Stevens, Martin, 'The Narrator of *The Wife's Lament*', *Neuphilologische Mitteilungen* 69 (1968): 72–90.

Storms, G., 'Grendel the Terrible', *Neuphilologische Mitteilungen* 73 (1972): 427–36.

Storms, G., 'The Subjectivity of the Style of *Beowulf*', in Stanley B. Greenfield (ed.), *Studies in Old English Literature in Honor of Arthur G. Brodeur* (Eugene, OR: University of Oregon Books, 1973).

Szarmach, Paul E., 'Alfred, Alcuin, and the Soul', in Robert Boenig and Kathleen Davis (eds), *Manuscript, Narrative, Lexicon: Essays on Literary and Cultural Transmission in Honor of Whitney F. Bolton* (Lewisburg, PA: Bucknell University Press, 2000).

Talentino, Arnold, 'Riddle 30: The Vehicle of the Cross', *Neophilologus* 65 (1981): 129–36.

Tasioulas, J.A., 'The Mother's Lament: *Wulf and Eadwacer* Reconsidered', *Medium Ævum* 65 (1996): 1–18.

Tatlock, J.S.P., 'Some Mediæval Cases of Blood-rain', *Classical Philology* 9 (1914), 442–7.

Taylor, John R. and Thandi G. Mbense, 'Red Dogs and Rotten Mealies: How Zulus Talk about Anger', in Angeliki Athanasiadou and Elżbieta Tabakowska (eds), *Speaking of Emotions: Conceptualisation and Expression* (Berlin: Mouton de Gruyter, 1998).

Temkin, Owsei, *The Falling Sickness: A History of Epilepsy from the Greeks to the Beginnings of Modern Neurology*, 2nd edn (Baltimore, MD: The Johns Hopkins Press, 1971).

TenHouten, Warren D., *A General Theory of Emotions and Social Life* (Oxford: Routledge, 2007).

Tissari, Heli, Anne Birgitta Pessi and Mikko Salmela (eds), 'Happiness: Cognition, Experience, Language', *Collegium: Studies Across Disciplines in the Humanities and Social Sciences* 3 (2008), at http://www.helsinki.fi/collegium/e-series/volumes/volume_3/index.htm

Tissol, Garth, *The Face of Nature: Wit, Narrative, and Cosmic Origins in Ovid's Metamorphoses* (Princeton, NJ: Princeton University Press, 1997).

Tolkien, J.R.R. '*Beowulf*: The Monsters and the Critics', *Proceedings of the British Academy* 22 (1936): 245–95.

Tolmie, Jane and M.J. Toswell (eds), *Laments for the Lost in Medieval Literature*, Medieval Texts and Cultures of Northern Europe 19 (Turnhout: Brepols, 2010).

Toswell, M.J., 'The Format of Bibliothèque Nationale MS Lat. 8824: The Paris Psalter', *Notes and Queries* 43 (1996): 130–33.

Toswell, M.J., 'Structures of Sorrow: The Lament Psalms in Medieval England', in Jane Tolmie and M.J. Toswell (eds), *Laments for the Lost in Medieval Literature*, Medieval Texts and Cultures of Northern Europe 19 (Turnhout: Brepols, 2010).

Toswell, M. Jane, 'Psalters', in Richard Gameson (ed.), *The Cambridge History of the Book in Britain, Vol. 1, c. 400–1100* (Cambridge: Cambridge University Press, 2012).

Townsend, David, 'The Naked Truth of the King's Affection in the Old English *Apollonius of Tyre*', *Journal of Medieval and Early Modern Studies* 34 (2004): 173–95.

Tribble, Evelyn, *Cognition in the Globe: Memory and Attention in Shakespeare's Theatre* (London: Palgrave Macmillan, 2011).

Tripp, Raymond P., 'The Narrator as Revenant: A Reconsideration of Three Old English Elegies', *Papers on Language and Literature* 8 (1972): 339–61.

Turner, Jonathan H., and Jan E. Stets, *The Sociology of Emotions* (Cambridge: Cambridge University Press, 2005).

Turner, Mark, *Reading Minds: The Study of English in the Age of Cognitive Science* (Princeton, NJ: Princeton University Press, 1991).

Verfaellie, Mieke and Jennifer J. Vasterling, 'Memory in PTSD: A Neurocognitive Approach', in Peter Shiromani, Terrence Keane and Joseph E. LeDoux (eds),

Post-Traumatic Stress Disorder: Basic Science and Clinical Practice (New York: Humana Press, 2009).

Vermeule, Blakey, *Why Do We Care About Literary Characters?* (Baltimore, MD: Johns Hopkins University Press, 2010).

von Moos, Peter, *Consolatio: Studien zur mittelalterlichen Trostliteratur über den Tod und zum Problem der christlichen Trauer*, 4 vols (Munich: Wilhelm Fink, 1971–72).

Wallace-Hadrill, J.M., *The Frankish Church* (Oxford: Clarendon Press, 1983).

Wareham, Andrew, 'The Transformation of Kinship and the Family in Late Anglo-Saxon England', *Early Medieval Europe* 10 (2001): 375–99.

Watkins, Oscar D., *A History of Penance*, 2 vols (London: Longmans, Green and co., 1920).

Weber, Wendolyn, 'Transmitting Fantasies: Sexist Glossing, Scholarly Desires, and Translating the Heroic Woman in Medieval Germanic Literature', *Translation Studies* 5 (2012): 312–26.

Wehlau, Ruth, '"Seeds of Sorrow": Landscapes of Despair in *The Wanderer*, *Beowulf*'s Story of Hrethel and *Sonatorrek*', *Parergon* 15 (1998): 1–17.

Wetherell, Margaret, *Affect and Emotion: A New Social Science Understanding* (London: SAGE, 2012).

Whissell, Cynthia, 'The Flow of Emotion through Beowulf', *Psychological Reports* 99 (2006): 835–50.

White, Geoffrey M., 'Moral Discourse and the Rhetoric of Emotion', in Robert A. LeVine (ed.), *Psychological Anthropology: A Reader on Self in Culture* (Chichester: Wiley-Blackwell, 2010); originally published in Catherine A. Lutz and Lila Abu-Lughod (eds), *Language and the Politics of Emotion* (Cambridge: Cambridge University Press, 1990).

Wierzbicka, Anna, 'Emotion, Language and "Cultural Scripts"', in Shinobu Kitayama and Hazel Rose Markus (eds), *Emotion and Culture: Empirical Studies of Mutual Influence* (Washington, DC: American Psychological Association, 1994).

Wierzbicka, Anna, *Emotions Across Language and Cultures: Diversity and Universals* (Cambridge: Cambridge University Press, 1999).

Wierzbicka, Anna, *Semantics, Culture and Cognition: Universal Human Concepts in Culture-specific Configurations* (Oxford: Oxford University Press, 1992).

Wilcox, Jonathan, 'A Place to Weep: Joseph in the Beer-room and Anglo-Saxon Gestures of Emotion', in Stuart McWilliams (ed.), *Saints and Scholars: New Perspectives on Anglo-Saxon Literature and Culture in Honour of Hugh Magennis* (Cambridge: D.S. Brewer, 2012).

Wilcox, Jonathan, 'Naked in Old English: The Embarrassed and the Shamed', in Benjamin C. Withers and Jonathan Wilcox (eds), *Naked Before God:*

Uncovering the Body in Anglo-Saxon England (Morgantown, WV: West Virginia University Press, 2003).
Wilcox, Jonathan (ed.), *Humour in Anglo-Saxon Literature* (Cambridge: D.S. Brewer, 2000).
Wilmart, André, 'Le manuel de prières de Saint Jean Gualbert', *Revue bénédictine* 48 (1936): 259-99.
Wolfram, Herwig, 'Arn von Salzburg', in Hans Bayr, Peter Kramml and Alfred Weiß (eds), *Lebensbilder Salzbürger Erzbischöfe: aus zwölf Jahrhunderten: 1200 Jahre Erzbistum Salzburg* (Salzburg: Freunde der Salzburger Geschichte, 1998).
Woolf, Rosemary, '*The Wanderer, The Seafarer*, and the Genre of *Planctus*', in Lewis E. Nicholson and Dolores Warwick Frese (eds), *Anglo-Saxon Poetry: Essays in Appreciation for John C. McGalliard* (Notre Dame, IN, and London: University of Notre Dame Press, 1975).
Wormald, Francis, 'The Decoration', in Bertram Colgrave (ed.), *The Paris Psalter: MS Bibliothèque Nationale Fonds Latin 8824*, Early English Manuscripts in Facsimile 8 (Copenhagen: Rosenkilde and Bagger, 1958).
Wouteres, Cas, 'The Civilizing of Emotions: Formalization and Informalization', in Debra Hopkins, Helmut Kuzmics, Helena Flam and Jochen Kleres (eds), *Theorizing Emotions: Sociological Explorations and Applications* (Frankfurt and New York: Campus Verlag, 2009).
Wright, Thomas L., 'Hrothgar's Tears', *Modern Philology* 65 (1967): 39-44.
Würzbach, Natascha and Simone M. Salz, *Motif Index of the Child Corpus: The English and Scottish Popular Ballad* (Berlin: Gruyter, 1995).
Zhou, D. et. al., 'Exposure to Physical and Psychological Stressors Elevates Plasma Interleukin 6: Relationship to the Activation of Hypothalamic-pituitary-adrenal Axis', *Endocrinology* 133 (1993): 2523-2530.
Zunshine, Lisa, *Why We Read Fiction: Theory of Mind and the Novel* (Colombus, OH: Ohio State University Press, 2006).

Index

abandonment 81–2, 133–4, 203–4, 227, 229, 237, 240, 242–3, 246, 256, 261
Adrian and Ritheus 38
Ælberht 238–43, 247, 254–5
Ælfric of Eynsham 11–13, 29, 37n, 100, 113n, 124–5, 131n, 168n, 170n
affect 1, 5, 19–21, 27–8, 30–34, 144, 196, 247
affection 4, 10n, 31, 82, 94, 169, 172–5, 190, 237, 252, 255–6
affective piety 14, 143–4, 146–7, 153–7, 159–61; *see also* faith; prayer
Alcuin 11, 16, 133–4, 227–30, 233–6, 238–45, 247–52, 254–6, 260
  De laude psalmorum 133; *see also* psalms
Aldhelm, Bishop of Sherborne 49, 148, 149n
Alfred, King of the Anglo-Saxons 11, 96n, 101n, 113n, 128–9, 139, 190, 194, 243; *see also The Old English Boethius; Prose Psalms*
Althoff, Gerd 10, 248
Ambrose, St 156
anda 63n; *see also* anger; *belgan*; fury; *gegremian*; *gram*; hate; *hātheort*; madness; *mod*, *wēamod*; rage; *torn*; wrath; *wrāð*; *wōd*; *yrre*
Andreas 66, 79, 202n
angels 101, 123n, 156, 158
anger 3–4, 7–8, 10–13, 22–3, 53–74, 76–7, 91n, 93–4, 96, 133, 153, 166, 179, 182, 184, 188, 191–2, 200, 204, 211, 229, 240, 242, 247–9, 252; *see also anda*; *belgan*; fury; *gegremian*; *gram*; hate; *hātheort*; madness; *mod*, *wēamod*; rage; *torn*; wrath; *wrāð*; *wōd*; *yrre*

Anglo-Saxon Chronicle 157, 190–91, 249n
anguish 30, 135, 159, 199, 234, 237, 244, 253; *see also* grief
anxiety 30, 46n, 84, 136–7, 139, 153, 164, 200, 211, 213, 215, 222–4, 230, 234, 237–8, 241, 243, 253, 255–6, 260; *see also* fear
appraisal 5, 8, 22, 25–6
Apollonius of Tyre 95, 103–5, 107, 113, 171, 173
Aristotle 44, 77, 194
aswarnian 109, 111–12, 116, 118–26; *see also forwandian*; *sceamian*; shame
attachment 230–31, 233, 235, 237–8, 241–3, 246–7, 252–5, 260–61; *see also* loss
Augustine of Hippo, St. 11, 40n, 42, 92–4, 98–9, 105, 107, 129, 135, 138, 140n, 196n, 215, 218, 225, 260
  The City of God 93, 215
  De doctrina Christiana 92, 98
  Enarrationes in Psalmos 140n; *see also* psalms
Auzon Casket inscription 64, 67
awe 16, 100, 112–13, 121, 136; *see also* reverence

The Battle of Brunanburh 84–5, 87–8
The Battle of Maldon 83n, 85n, 141
Bede, the Venerable, St 29n, 43, 111n, 143, 190, 228n, 233, 243–6, 251, 255, 257–9, 261; *see also* Pseudo-Bede
  De tempore rationum 43
  The Ecclesiastical History of the English People 29n, 190n, 243n, 251, 257–9
  Historia abbatum 243–5n
belgan 63n, 67–70, 153, 188; *see also anda*; anger; fury; *gegremian*; *gram*; hate;

hātheort; madness; *mōd, wēamōd*;
    rage; *torn*; wrath; *wrāð*; *wōd*; *yrre*
belief 83, 133, 137–9, 141, 144, 233,
    256–7, 260; *see also* faith
Beowulf 2, 9n, 13n, 16–17, 66–7, 69–71,
    75–9, 81–90, 163–70, 172–5,
    177–92, 202n, 232
Beowulf 16, 66, 68–71, 73–4, 79, 81, 84–5,
    87–8, 163–7, 169, 172–5, 177,
    179–81, 187–9, 192
Bertgyth 227, 229, 236–8, 254–5
blasphemy 67, 71
The Blickling Homilies 157–8
body/bodies 4, 7, 11–13, 15–16, 19, 21–4,
    29–34, 37–9, 42, 44–7, 50n, 55,
    91–5, 99, 101–7, 140, 148, 159,
    161, 166, 172n, 196, 201, 204,
    211–13, 219–21, 226, 230n, 244,
    256, 258–9; *see also* embodiment
Boniface, Archbishop of Mainz and St
    227–9, 247n
    Epistolae 227n, 237n
bravery 163, 186, 192, 201; *see also* courage
breast 35, 38, 47n, 69, 72, 136, 139, 150,
    153, 163, 174–5, 211, 224; *see also*
    breost; heart
breost 12n, 31, 38, 46, 72, 150, 153, 163,
    174–5, 211, 224; *see also* breast, heart
breostcearu 31, 211, 224
breostsefa 72
breostwylm 163, 174–5

cardiocentrism (heart-centred model) 11,
    37, 40, 50–51; *see also* heart
Cassiodorus 97–100, 109–118, 120–23,
    126, 135, 138
    Expositio Psalmorum 109–11, 115n,
    121n
cephalocentrism (head-centred model) 39,
    40, 42–4, 51; *see also* head
Charlemagne 183, 234–5, 241, 248–9, 251
children/childhood 127–8, 136, 171, 173,
    187, 203, 214, 229–31, 233, 237,
    240, 248, 250–54, 256, 260

Christ 6, 16, 66, 71–2, 78, 84n, 143–6, 151,
    156–61
Christ 72, 97–8, 132, 143, 146, 148, 151–2,
    154–6, 158–9, 244, 256, 260
Christ and Satan 66, 78n
Christianity 11, 38, 98, 109–12, 126,
    132–4, 150, 158, 170n, 196n, 225
Christology 98, 132
Ceolfrith, abbot of Wearmouth and Jarrow
    228n, 243–7, 257–8
    Vita Ceolfridi 243–7n
Clemoes, Peter 12, 85, 228n
cognitive science 11, 15, 17, 19–22, 24, 26,
    29n, 30n, 33–4; *see also* neurology;
    neuroscience
comfort 131, 135–6, 156, 158, 207, 237,
    258; *see also* consolation; *frofer*;
    relief
communication 3, 7, 8, 32, 197–206, 208,
    216
community 8, 21, 24, 110, 113, 119, 125–6,
    154, 168–9, 179, 197, 202–5, 208,
    229, 238
complaint 134, 150, 225, 236, 253
compunction 6, 16, 120, 133, 144–7,
    152–3, 155–6, 159–60, 166n, 259;
    see also contrition
confession 117–8, 123, 143
confusion 96–102, 109, 111, 116–19, 124,
    126, 197, 215, 240
consolation 132, 135, 216, 218, 229,
    233–5, 238, 240, 242, 254, 256; *see
    also* comfort; *frofer*; relief
contrition 120, 143; *see also* compunction
conversion 98, 100, 102, 109–22, 126, 223
courage 8, 35, 62, 69, 82, 140–41, 188; *see
    also* bravery
Cross, the 1, 144, 148, 150–51, 155–6, 159,
    160; *see also* crucifixion
crucifixion 1, 98, 143, 146, 148, 158, 161;
    see also Cross, the
Cuthbert, deacon 258–9
Cynewulf and Cyneheard episode 66, 190,
    249

Damasio, Antonio 4, 5n, 23–26, 54n, 212–13
Danes 75–7, 79–81, 86–90, 164–5, 179, 188, 191–2
death 3, 9, 71, 77, 79, 80–81, 83, 86, 88, 90, 93, 133, 146, 151–3, 156, 159, 164, 166–7, 171–3, 175, 178–9, 182, 184–5, 187–8, 190, 203, 205, 207n, 218–20, 222, 228–9, 232, 235, 237, 239, 240–45, 247–9, 254–8, 260; *see also* grief; loss
demons 47–9, 62; *see also* devils
De psalmorum libro exegesis 131; *see also* psalms
De psalmorum usu 133; *see also* Alcuin, *De laude psalmorum*; psalms
The Descent to Hell 79
devils 46, 48–9, 66, 95, 123n, 249; *see also* demons
devotion 1, 16, 95, 110, 128–30, 133, 135, 143–4, 148, 150, 157, 161, 177, 237–9, 241, 246, 256; *see also* affective piety
disgust 8, 23, 54, 77
distress 29, 64n, 179, 181, 211, 221–2, 225, 244, 254; *see also* stress
Dixon, Thomas 4, 5n
Doomsday 141, 146, 158, 161
The Dream of the Rood 1, 84n, 150–51, 156, 159, 160
Dronke, Peter 227n, 236, 237n, 240n

Ealuscerwan 79; *see also meoduscerwan*
Edmund I, King of England 87, 184, 189n
education 16, 128, 193, 200–201, 208, 229, 233, 250, 252–3, 256
Einhard 228, 248, 251n
  Life of Charlemagne 248
Elene 66
embarrassment 23n, 91, 93–5, 97–8, 102–7, 117, 172; *see also* gesture, blushing
embodiment 21, 24, 29–31, 33–4, 55, 149, 212, 221; *see also* body/bodies
emotion
  definitions 3–6, 22, 54, 77
  emotion concepts 6, 15–16, 54, 74, 138, 208
  emotion talk/emotional talk 6–7
  emotion scripts 16, 127–8, 138–9, 141
  emotional community 8, 21n, 113, 119, 126
  emotional contagion 15, 20, 27–8, 32
  emotional expression 3, 5, 7–10, 12, 16, 24, 26–30, 32–3, 54–6, 60, 81n, 91–2, 98, 110, 113, 125, 128n, 131, 134, 136, 141, 145, 151, 164n, 170, 193, 211, 213, 224, 227, 232, 234–5, 238, 249, 252, 255, 259
  emotional landscape 15, 230, 247
  emotional lexicon 53
  emotional memory 217, 220
  emotional opposition 76–81, 83–4, 86–8, 90
  emotional pairs 76–8, 80
  emotives 7
  hydraulic model 11–12, 70, 72, 174
  primary/basic emotions 23, 54–5, 80, 91, 93
  somatic vocabulary 212–13
emotions; *see* abandonment; affection; *anda*; anger; anguish; anxiety; *aswarnian*; attachment; awe; *belgan*; comfort; compunction; confusion; consolation; contrition; devotion; disgust; distress; *ealuscerwan*; embarrassment; fear; *forwandian*; *frofer*; fury; *gegremian*; *geomor*; *gram*; gratitude; grief; happiness; hate; *hātheort*; indignation; joy; lamentation; *langað*; longing; loss; love; madness; melancholy; *meoduscerwan*; misery; pity; rage; relief; reverence; sadness; *sceamian*; shame; *sorg*; sorrow; stress; surprise; thankfulness; *torn*; unhappiness; wrath; *wrāð*, *wyn*; *yrre*
empathy 19, 23, 27–34, 146, 214, 234, 241, 245, 261; *see also* mirror neurons; pity

Encomium Emmae Reginae 16, 171–2
Epistola peri hereseon 42–4
Eustace, St 16, 170–73
    The Life of Saint Eustace 16, 170–73
    Passio Sancti Eustachii 170
The Exeter Book 16, 30, 144
exile 132, 145, 168, 173, 175, 184, 214–16, 218–21, 224, 249, 251, 257, 260
existentialism 179, 215, 222, 224

Fabiszak, Małgorzata 12–13n, 29n, 61
facial expressions 3, 8, 27–9, 54, 91, 136, 145; *see also* gesture
faith 111, 136, 143–4, 203, 207, 215, 225, 257; *see also* belief
fear 4, 8–9, 12, 16, 23, 54, 77, 84–5, 99–100, 109, 112–14, 117–8, 120–21, 124–6, 136, 141n, 147, 150, 160, 173, 175, 187, 191, 195, 197, 204, 222, 229–30, 235, 259; *see also* anxiety
ferhð 36; *see also hyge*; *mod*; *sefa*
feud 177–8, 184, 186, 188–92, 249; *see also* vengeance
forwandian 99, 100, 104, 109, 112–14, 116–21, 123, 125–6; *see also aswarnian*; *sceamian*; shame
Franks Casket; *see* Auzon Casket inscription
frofer 131–2, 135, 139, 141; *see also* comfort; consolation; relief
fury 58, 62–3, 70; *see also anda*; anger; *belgan*; *gegremian*; *gram*; hate; *hātheort*; madness; *mod, wēamod*; rage; *torn*; wrath; *wrāð*; *wōd*; *yrre*

Galen 41–4, 47, 49
Sir Gawain and the Green Knight 91, 94
gegremian 67–8; *see also anda*; anger; *belgan*; fury; *gram*; hate; *hātheort*; madness; *mod, wēamod*; rage; *torn*; wrath; *wrāð*; *wōd*; *yrre*
gender 13–14, 105, 166, 185–6; *see also* women
Genesis 66–8, 74, 82, 84n

geomor 31, 67n, 69, 72, 89, 224; *see also* melancholy; misery; sadness; *sorg*; sorrow
gesture (somatic gestures) 3, 5–8, 14–16, 29, 91–107, 127, 163–70, 172, 175, 211–13, 219–20, 224, 226, 256
blushing (reddening) 15–16, 91–107, 111, 115–17, 121
crying 72, 164n, 246
kissing 91, 163, 165, 167–73, 175, 221, 232, 236n
laughter 14, 91–2, 97, 99–100
sighing 91
smiling 91, 152, 224
sobbing 245–6
tears 16, 65, 67, 72–3, 94, 143–8, 151–7, 159–61, 163–7, 169–70, 172–5, 235–7, 240, 245–7, 256, 259
weeping 3, 6, 14, 16, 30, 67, 72, 91–2, 145–6, 151, 153–6, 159–61, 164–73, 175, 236, 240, 246–8, 257, 259
winking 91, 96–100, 107
gewrecan 68–9; *see also* feud; revenge; vengeance
gifts 84, 86–7, 117, 122, 163, 198, 205, 207, 215, 221, 229, 237, 260
The Gifts of Men 144
glosses 15–16, 42, 48–50, 62, 64, 95, 98–9, 101–2, 106, 109–19, 121–6, 129, 134, 138–9, 141
gnomes 195, 206–7
Godden, Malcolm 11, 37n, 61n, 85n, 123n, 129, 228n
Goldie, Peter 3n, 21–2, 25n, 28–9, 32
Grágás 189–90; *see also* law codes
gram 63n; *see also anda*; anger; *belgan*; fury; *gegremian*; hate; *hātheort*; madness; *mod, wēamod*; rage; *torn*; wrath; *wrāð*; *wōd*; *yrre*
gratitude 133, 145, 165n, 227, 236–7, 250, 255–60; *see also* thankfulness
Gregory the Great, Pope and St 94, 113–14, 145, 201n

Dialogues 94–5
Regula Pastoralis 113–14n, 201
Vita Sancti Gregori 145
Gregory of Tours 191, 248–9n
Grendel 2, 9, 68, 70, 75–7, 79–81, 83, 85–6, 88–90, 163–5, 179, 187–8
Grendel's mother 87, 163, 18, 180, 185–8, 191–2
grief 3, 12–13, 16, 22, 27, 30, 32, 61n, 64, 67, 70–74, 77–8, 91, 148, 151–3, 161 164–7, 175, 177–82, 184–8, 191–2, 211, 222, 227–36, 238–43, 245–50, 252, 254–5, 259, 260; *see also* anguish; death; lamentation; loss; sorrow; *torn*
Guthlac 66–7, 78n, 84n, 144

haemolacria 145–8, 151–7, 159, 160–61; *see also* gesture, tears
happiness 22, 68, 96n, 154, 193–4, 197–9, 201–4, 206–8, 224, 253; *see also* joy; *wyn*
Harbus, Antonina 1, 2 6, 11, 15, 29–30n, 55n, 61n, 85n, 106n, 140n, 195–7n, 199n, 208, 214
Harris, Joseph 9
hate 82–3, 89, 96–7, 37, 139n, 184, 205; *see also anda*; anger; *belgan*; fury; *gegremian*; *gram*; *hātheort*; madness; *mod, wēamod*; rage; *torn*; wrath; *wrāð*; *wōd*; *yrre*
hātheort 63n, 69, 72, 211; *see also anda*; anger; *belgan*; fury; *gegremian*; *gram*; hate; madness; *mod, wēamod*; rage; *torn*; wrath; *wrāð*; *wōd*; *yrre*
head 15, 35–6, 38–40, 44–5, 47, 50–51, 55, 69, 167–8, 180, 192, 221; *see also* cephalocentrism; heart
head-heart opposition 15, 35–6, 40, 51; *see also* cardiocentrism; cephalocentrism; head; heart
heart 5, 7, 15, 31, 35–7, 40, 45–6, 49–51, 55, 68, 72, 82, 98, 128, 133–4, 137, 139–40n, 145, 150, 152–3, 155–6, 160, 167n, 182, 196, 198, 200–201n, 204n, 211–12, 216, 220, 221, 231–2, 235, 23, 256; *see also* cardiocentrism; head
heat/hotness 55, 61–2, 69, 192, 211
heaven 37, 72, 78, 132, 145, 147, 150, 154, 156, 158, 161, 233, 240, 254–5, 257
Hêliand 152–3
hell 37, 78–9, 101, 160
homilies 64, 113, 123n, 157–9n
honour 8, 72, 97, 112, 116–17, 156, 164n, 177–8, 184, 187–9, 191
Hrethel 177–8, 181–5, 87, 191, 232
Hrothgar 16, 66, 70–71, 73–4, 86–9, 163–5, 167–70, 172–5, 178–81, 186–7, 189, 191
The Husband's Message 227
hyge 36, 38, 45, 67, 163, 184, 188, 197–8; *see also ferhð*; *mod*; *sefa*
hygebend 163
hygecræft 197–8
hygemeðe 184, 188
hygesorg 67n

identity 14, 17, 103, 137, 148, 169, 171, 217, 239; *see also* individuality
indignation 58, 65
individuality 6–10, 16, 83, 85, 88, 137, 144–5, 151, 178, 189, 204, 246, 255, 260; *see also* identity; privacy; subjectivity
insults 67, 71–2, 74, 100, 200
irony 76, 79n, 84, 87n; *see also* litotes; negation
Isidore of Seville, St 39–40, 42–3, 48
Differentiae uerborum 40
Etymologiae 39–40, 43, 48

Jager, Eric 12
Jerome, St 96, 111n, 138, 243
Joseph, St 71–3, 145, 156
joy 7, 12, 23, 31–2, 54, 76–9, 83, 88–9, 133–5, 137, 156, 168–9, 173, 175, 181, 194, 197, 202–3, 208–9, 216, 233, 240, 254; *see also* happiness; *wyn*

judgment 4–5, 36, 40n, 77–78n, 96, 109, 111, 115, 120–3, 127, 136, 141n, 144, 147, 160, 185, 192, 248n
Judgement Day I 78n, 144
Judgement Day II 78n
Judith 66–9, 72–4, 84n, 202n
Juliana 62, 84n, 144

Lacnunga 42, 45, 47n, 50–51n
lamentation 9, 30–33, 104, 128n, 131, 135–6, 147, 153, 166–7, 175, 181, 191, 204, 214–17, 222, 224–5, 227–8, 234, 236, 240, 245, 247; *see also geomor*; grief; melancholy; misery; sadness; *sorg*; sorrow
langað 31, 163, 174–5; *see also* longing
law codes 64, 182–5, 189–90, 197; *see also* Grágás
Lemay, Ghyslaine 4, 6, 127n
litotes 15, 75–7, 85–7, 90; *see also* irony
liturgy 95, 130, 141, 159, 241; *see also* prayer; ritual
Lockett, Leslie 2, 7, 11, 15, 37n, 61n, 70, 72, 85n, 106, 139n, 153, 167n, 174, 196
longing 30–31, 144, 163, 217, 223, 225, 227, 234, 236–8, 253–4, 256, 259–60; *see also langað*
loss 16, 71, 103, 146, 164, 166, 175, 178, 192, 203, 218, 220, 222, 229–32, 234–5, 238–40, 242–3, 247, 254–5, 260–61; *see also* attachment; death; grief
love 3, 7–9, 31, 35, 71–2, 74, 82–3, 93n, 103–5, 117, 137, 143, 160, 171–72n, 178, 188, 190, 203, 205, 207, 221, 224, 231–3, 235–7, 241–2, 245, 249, 253n, 256–7, 259; *see also unleof*
Low, Soon Ai 11

McNeill, David 7
madness 45, 47–8, 62, 73, 229; *see also anda*; anger; *belgan*; fury; *gegremian*; *gram*; hate; *hātheort*;

mod, wēamod; rage; *torn*; wrath; *wrāð*; *wōd*; *yrre*
manuscripts
Cambridge, Corpus Christi College MS 140 (Rushworth Gospels) 49n
Cambridge, Corpus Christi College MS 201 169
Cambridge, Trinity College, R.17.1 *see* psalters – *Eadwine Psalter*
Cambridge, University Library, Gg.5.35 43
Durham, Cathedral Library, B.II.30 111n
London, British Library, Cotton Domitian A.VIII (*Chronicle* MS F) 157
London, British Library, Cotton Tiberius B.I (*Chronicle* MS C) 157
London, British Library, Cotton Vespasian A.I *see* psalters - *Vespasian Psalter*
London, British Library, Cotton Vitellius E.XVIII *see* psalters – *Vitellius Psalter*
London, British Library, Harley 603 *see* psalters – *Harley Psalter*
London, British Library, Harley 6258B 44
London, British Library, Royal 2.B.V *see* psalters – *Royal Psalter*
London, British Library, Royal 4.A.XIV 111n
London, British Library, Sloane 475 43
London, British Library, Sloane 2839 43
London, Lambeth Palace 427 *see* psalters – *Lambeth Psalter*
Paris, Bibliothèque Nationale, Fonds Latin 8846 *see* psalters – *Paris Psalter*
Utrecht, University Library, MS 32 *see* psalters – *Utrecht Psalter*
marriage 105, 251
martyrdom 244–5, 251, 260
Mary, Blessed Virgin 71, 145, 154–6

masculinity 93, 164–6, 168, 170, 173; see
    also gender
mass, sacrament of 260
Matto, Michael 12, 85n
Maxims I 16, 38, 67, 193–9, 202, 204–9,
    216n
melancholy 230, 239, 242–3, 255, 260; see
    also *geomor*; grief; misery; sadness;
    sorg; sorrow
memory 16, 23–4, 26, 29–34, 37, 40,
    42–3n, 45n, 92, 127–8, 168, 194,
    211, 214–22, 224–6, 234, 240–41,
    255–6
  autobiographical 32, 215, 218
  emotional 26, 216–18, 220, 222, 226
  encoding 217–20, 222, 224
  episodic 215, 218, 222
  rehearsal 215–17, 224
  remembrance 32–3, 37, 192, 218,
    220–22, 224, 228
  retrieval 215, 217, 222, 224
mentality 2
meoduscerwan 79; see also *ealuscerwan*
Miller, William Ian 10, 91n, 177n, 183,
    185n, 190
mind 1, 2, 7, 9–12, 15–17, 20–21, 23,
    28–33, 36–41, 45–6, 49–51, 55,
    61, 68–70, 72, 140n, 150, 153,
    163, 167–8, 174, 180, 181, 187–8,
    193, 195–9n, 201, 205, 207–8,
    211–15n, 220–22, 224–7, 244,
    256; see also *ferhð*; *mod*; *sefa*
mind-body opposition 12, 37–8, 45, 196, 212
mirror neurons 15, 20, 28, 32; see also
    cognitive science; neurology;
    neuroscience
misery 30, 70, 72, 78, 88, 98, 147, 153, 180,
    187, 192, 225; see also *geomor*; grief;
    lamentation; melancholy; sadness;
    sorg; sorrow
Mize, Britt 2, 12, 214n
mod 12, 15, 36–40, 44–6, 51, 68–9, 76,
    137, 140–41, 147, 153, 167, 193–4,
    196–202, 204–209, 215n, 221; see
    also *ferhð*; *hyge*; mind; *sefa*

    formation/development of 193–9, 201,
        206–8
    ætrenmod 207
    galgmod 187
    geomormod 31, 67n, 72
    hreohmod 67n
    leohtmod 203
    modcearu 30–31, 224–5
    modgeþonc 38
    modig 76, 163
    modsefa 215, 220–21
    stiðmod 201n
    swiðmod 201n
    torhtmod 69
    unmod 46
    wēamod 63n
    werigmod 31, 75, 188
monasticism 8, 14n, 16, 102, 109–10, 119,
    125, 129–30, 145, 229, 233, 244,
    250–51, 254, 256–8; see also oblation

natural semantic metalanguage (NSM)
    57–60, 72
negation 76, 79–81, 83, 86, 88, 90, 203; see
    also irony; litotes
neurology 2, 16, 17, 26, 54, 127, 211,
    213–14, 217, 226; see also cognitive
    science; neuroscience; physiology
neuroscience 3–4, 6, 21–5, 212–13, 217,
    226; see also cognitive science,
    neurology
Nussbaum, Martha 4, 25

Oatley, Keith 5, 19, 22, 25
oblation 16, 127, 227, 229–30, 233,
    236, 241–3, 247, 250–51,
    253–4, 256–7, 259–60; see also
    monasticism
Ogura, Michiko 12, 29n
The Old English Boethius 37n, 129, 194; see
    also Alfred
The Old English Heptateuch 16, 168
The Old English Orosius 66
The Old English Pastoral Care 113, 125; see
    also Gregory the Great

Orderic Vitalis 255–7, 260

paganism 166, 187n, 225
peace 68, 71, 78, 88–90, 96–7, 179, 190, 199, 201, 203, 208, 237, 249, 254, 256, 259; *see also* sibb
penance 110–11, 120; *see also* compunction; contrition; penitence
penitence 120, 123n, 156; *see also* penance
performance 7, 14, 90, 104–5, 109, 128, 133, 138–9, 161, 166, 170, 175, 186, 214
Peri Didaxeon 44, 46–7n
perigrini 228–9, 236, 247, 249, 251; *see also* pilgrimage
Peter, St 152–3
physiology 5, 8, 11, 54–5, 70n, 72–3, 155, 211–13, 218; *see also* neurology
pilgrimage 154n; *see also peregrini*
pity 48, 77, 150, 160, 182, 256; *see also* empathy
Plato 11, 38, 44, 194, 196n
post-traumatic stress disorder (PTSD) 214, 217, 222, 225–6; *see also* trauma
Practica Alexandri 39n, 42
Practica Petrocelli 41–4
praise 78, 93n, 98, 132, 135, 137–8, 150, 202, 259
prayer 49, 123n, 129, 132–3, 136, 138–9, 141, 145, 159, 227, 241, 251, 256, 259–60; *see also* liturgy
Precepts 66
privacy 95, 105, 107, 130, 169, 204, 243, 246–8, 255; *see also* individuality
Prose Psalms 6, 127–30, 132, 134–5, 138–9, 141; *see also* psalms
prosopopoeia 146, 148–9, 159–61
psalms 6, 16–17, 66, 95–8, 101–3, 105–7, 109–13, 117, 121, 123, 125, 127–39, 141; *see also* Alcuin, *De laude psalmorum*; Augustine, *Enarrationes in Psalmos*; Cassiodorus, *Expositio Psalmorum*; *De psalmorum libro exegesis*; *De psalmorum usu*; *Prose Psalms*; psalters

psalters 16, 66–7, 95–6, 99–101, 109–16, 118–19, 121n, 123–32, 134–5, 138, 140, 258; *see also* glosses; psalms
Eadwine Psalter 110
Gallicanum 110n, 115n, 116n, 124, 129
Harley Psalter 101
Lambeth Psalter 99, 110n, 118n, 123–5
Paris Psalter 16, 66–7, 96, 100–101, 110, 113, 127–31, 135, 138, 140
Romanum 110–11, 115n, 124, 129–30, 140
Royal Psalter 100, 109–11, 113–14, 119, 121n, 124–6
Utrecht Psalter 101
Vespasian Psalter 110, 114, 125
Vitellius Psalter 110n, 131
Pseudo-Bede 131–2; *see also* Bede *Argumenta* 131–2, 138
Pseudo-Galen 39; *see also* Galen *Liber tertius* 39, 41–2

Quintilian 149–50
Institutio oratoria 149–50

rage 58, 62–3, 65, 68–70n, 88, 153, 178, 188, 211, 229, 249; *see also anda*; anger; *belgan*; fury; *gegremian*; *gram*; hate; *hātheort*; madness; *mod*, *wēamod*; *torn*; wrath; *wrāð*; *wōd*; *yrre*
rationality/reason 15, 32, 35–8, 40, 42–3n, 49, 51, 149, 193–7, 201, 203, 208, 212; *see also ferhð*; mind; *mod*; *sefa*
Reddy, William 2n, 7
relativism/social constructivism 54–5; *see also* universalism
relief 76–7, 79, 90, 169, 191, 252; *see also* comfort; consolation; *frofer*
revenge *see* vengeance
reverence 16, 99–100, 109, 112–14, 117, 119, 121, 123, 126, 136; *see also* awe
ritual 8, 14, 85n, 116, 137, 141, 167–8, 172, 206, 247, 252; *see also* liturgy

The Riming Poem 67
Robinson, Jenefer 5–6, 21n, 25
Rosenwein, Barbara 2n, 8, 10, 21n, 93n, 113
The Rule of St Benedict 102, 130, 229n, 259–60
The Rune Poem 78
Russell, James 4, 6, 77n, 127n

sadness 7, 16, 23, 54, 60, 67, 69, 72, 77, 82, 92, 133, 152, 160, 181, 186, 202–4, 208, 219–20, 237–8, 245; *see also geomor*; misery; melancholy; *sorg*; sorrow
saints 64, 66, 79, 113, 175, 233, 251
Sapir-Whorf theory 58n
sceamian 84n, 99, 100, 102, 106; *see also aswarnian*; *forwandian*; shame
hleorsceamu 102
Scherer, Klaus 5–6
The Seafarer 9, 200n, 227–8
sefa 32, 36, 72, 147, 167; *see also ferhð*; mind; *mod*
shame 7–8, 12–14, 16, 23, 84–5, 87, 91, 95–107, 109–123, 125–6, 160, 164n, 168, 172, 191, 205, 219, 229; *see also aswarnian*; *forwandian*; *sceamian*
sibb 78–9, 89, 197n; *see also* peace
sin 78, 100, 109, 111, 114, 120–23, 137, 143, 146–7, 156, 159–60, 181
sorg 1, 31, 67n, 69–72, 78–9, 81, 88–9, 147, 153, 177, 179–80, 187, 220–21, 232; *see also geomor*; lamentation; melancholy; misery; sadness; sorrow
sorrow 1, 31, 33, 69, 71, 75–9, 81, 88–9, 128n, 135–7, 139, 143, 145, 147, 152–3, 160, 164, 173, 175, 179, 185, 187, 199, 211, 219, 221–2, 224–5, 229, 232, 236, 238, 246, 259; *see also geomor*; lamentation; melancholy; misery; sadness; *sorg*
soul 11, 35–7, 39–40, 49, 109, 115, 118, 140n, 145, 151, 159–60, 184, 194, 196n, 237, 256, 258–9; *see also ferhð*; mind; *mod*; *sefa*
Soul and Body I 84n
Soul and Body II 78n
stress 215, 217–18, 220–21; *see also* distress
subjectivity 1–2, 17, 34, 80, 151, 182, 214, 226; *see also* individuality
surprise 54, 77, 106

thankfulness 131, 147, 237, 258–9; *see also* gratitude
Theodore of Mopsuestia 131–2, 138, 140
Theodore of Tarsus, Archbishop of Canterbury and St 41, 48, 189–90
torn 15, 53, 55n, 63–74, 89, 179, 204; *see also anda*; anger; *belgan*; fury; *gegremian*; *gram*; hate; *hātheort*; madness; *mod, wēamod*; rage; wrath; *wrāð*; *wōd*; *yrre*
translation 16, 23–4, 29, 41, 44, 49, 54, 58, 66, 68, 70–71, 74, 89, 94–7, 99–103, 109–110, 112–14, 126, 128–31, 134, 137–41, 169–70, 173–4, 185, 194, 199, 202n, 211–12, 224–5
trauma 16, 103, 213–14, 216–18, 220, 222, 224–6, 231, 238, 240–42, 250, 254, 255–6, 260; *see also* post-traumatic stress disorder
Troilus and Criseyde 93, 103

unhappiness 199, 202, 204, 253; *see also* misery; sadness; *sorg*; sorrow
universalism 3, 16, 31, 54–8, 60, 80, 199, 206–7n, 214, 220n; *see also* relativism/social constructivism
unleof 81–3; *see also* love

vengeance 16, 67, 98, 102, 117, 122, 151, 177–92, 232, 247, 249, 252, *see also* feud
Vindicianus 39, 40n, 42
Epitome altera 39, 40n, 42

The Wanderer 9, 30, 32–3, 136, 144, 167–8, 214–15, 217, 222, 224–8
The Wife's Lament 30–33, 136, 214–15, 217, 222, 224–5, 227, 236
wisdom 38, 146, 180, 194, 197–9, 201–4, 208, 215, 232, 238
wrath 58, 63, 65–6, 68, 92, 135n, 249n; *see also anda*; anger; *belgan*; fury; *gegremian*; *gram*; hate; *hātheort*; madness; *mod, wēamod*; rage; *torn*; *wrāð*; *wōd*; *yrre*
wrāð 68, 81; *see also anda*; anger; *belgan*; fury; *gegremian*; *gram*; hate; *hātheort*; madness; *mod, wēamod*; rage; *torn*; wrath; *wōd*; *yrre*

wōd 47, 62–3n, 219; *see also anda*; anger; *belgan*; fury; *gegremian*; *gram*; hate; *hātheort*; madness; *mod, wēamod*; rage; *torn*; wrath; *wrāð*; *yrre*
ellenwōd 62
women 66, 105, 152, 154, 166–7, 186–7n, 195, 236, 251; *see also* gender
Wulf and Eadwacer 196, 214, 227, 236
wyn 31, 78–9, 81n, 88, 216; *see also* happiness; joy

yrre 55, 63n, 67–70, 135, 188; *see also anda*; anger; *belgan*; fury; *gegremian*; *gram*; hate; *hātheort*; madness; *mod, wēamod*; rage; *torn*; wrath; *wrāð*; *wōd*